On Exchange Rates

On Exchange Rates

Jeffrey A. Frankel

The MIT Press
Cambridge, Massachusetts
London, England

This book was set in Palatino by Asco Trade Typesetting Ltd., Hong Kong, and was printed and bound in the United States of America.

Library of Congress Cataloging-in-Publication Data

Frankel, Jeffrey A.
  On exchange rates / Jeffrey A. Frankel.
    p.   cm.
  Includes bibliographical references and index.
  ISBN 0-262-06154-6
  1. Foreign exchange rates. I. Title.
HG3851.F68   1993
332.45′6—dc20   92-40156
                                                                      CIP

A000006103712

To Jessica,
who is more important than these papers

Contents

Introduction   185

8   Tests of Rational Expectations in the Forward Exchange Market   189

9   The Diversifiability of Exchange Risk   205

10 In Search of the Exchange Risk Premium: A Six-Currency Test
    Assuming Mean-Variance Optimization   219

11 Recent Estimates of Time-Variation in the Conditional Variance and
    in the Exchange Risk Premium   235

12 Forward Discount Bias: Is It an Exchange Risk Premium?   245
    (with Kenneth A. Froot)

IV Exchange Rate Expectations
Introduction   263

13 Using Survey Data to Test Standard Propositions Regarding
    Exchange Rate Expectations   267
    (with Kenneth A. Froot)

14 Understanding the U.S. Dollar in the Eighties: The Expectations of
    Chartists and Fundamentalists   295
    (with Kenneth A. Froot)

15 Chartists, Fundamentalists, and Trading in the Foreign Exchange
    Market   317
    (with Kenneth A. Froot)

16 Foreign Exchange Intervention: An Empirical Assessment   327
    (with Kathryn M. Dominguez)

17 The European Monetary System: Credible in 1988–1991?   347
    (with Steven Phillips)

    Notes   361
    References   399
    Index   431

Preface

The field of international monetary economics began a period of revolution in the late 1970s, and the study of exchange rate movements was at the core of it. The field has settled down a bit since then, and the revolutionary spirit has moved on to trade and other fields previously considered stagnant. This perhaps makes it easier to identify, with the benefit of perspective added by time, which of one's papers are more useful and which less. In any case, I have picked seventeen. I have limited this collection to writings on exchange rates, saving other subjects for another volume anticipated in the future.

What differentiates this body of work from most other books in international finance? The answer, I think, lies in the word *empirical*. In principle the demand is very heavy for work that addresses real-world questions. But many students who enter the field wishing to do empirical work are discouraged by the difficulty of doing it well. It is so easy to "shoot down" empirical work. The result is that much econometric work is so technique motivated as to be almost useless for addressing real questions, while much of truly applied work is so unrigorous as to merit contempt from most serious academics. Against this background, the motivation of my collected work is an attempt to demonstrate that it is possible to do empirical work that proceeds in a manner that is interesting from a pure intellectual viewpoint and at the same time genuinely contributes to understanding of key questions in the real world of international finance. That, anyway, is the goal.

This collection is not intended to be a new treatise. Any sense of continuity must come inherently from the logic of the papers themselves, together with the introductions that I have written—one for each of the four parts.

On the other hand, I decided that a little neatening up was in order, to enhance the chances that readers will find this collection useful in the 1990s.

I have routinely made the following changes: adopted a more uniform algebraic notation, updated the references to the most final known form of publication and collected them all at the back of the book, deleted some tables to save space (with a note referring to the relevant table in the original), omitted the word *recently* when describing developments that are no longer recent, corrected typographical errors, and edited lightly to improve the style. Perhaps the greatest sorts of value-added were the splicing together of two related papers to create a new one that I hope is superior to either of its parts, or the substitution of updated empirical results for older ones. (This describes chapters 4, 15, 16, and 17.)

I have made these changes notwithstanding that authors of collected writings often seek in the preface to make a virtue of leaving the articles in their original pristine condition. In my revisions I have tried scrupulously never to abuse hindsight in order to claim undeserved foresight. The exceptionally interested reader who wants to check up on me knows where to find the originals.

I have had the benefit of an outstanding, stimulating, and dispersed set of mentors, colleagues, coauthors, and research assistants. The list of those who have left their mark on my work is long.

I was introduced to economics at Swarthmore College by Bernard Saffran. I first learned international economics there in a course where the textbook was *World Trade and Payments*, by Richard Caves and Ronald Jones; five editions later, I am proud to be a coauthor of it.

At MIT, I learned a lot from Charlie Kindleberger, Stanley Fischer, Franco Modigliani, Bob Hall, Bob Solow, and Jerry Hausman. I was extremely fortunate to begin my thesis research in the brief interval between the time that Rudiger Dornbusch arrived at MIT from Chicago and the time when his rise to superstardom began to attract hoards of students. Here was the key man in the revolution of international monetary economics, and I had the luxury of leisurely afternoons of discussion in his office. I am happy that Rudi is represented in a very direct way in this book as coauthor of the first chapter. The other half of the team, Stan Fischer, was an influence of almost equal importance at MIT.

Intellectual genealogy is closely analogous to the family kind of genealogy, and readers may be interested in hearing a bit more about the family tree. Paul Krugman, Maurice Obstfeld, and Kenneth Rogoff were among my brothers at MIT. (The latter two were my colleagues at Berkeley during the year that I edited this book.) Harry Johnson and Robert Mundell at the

University of Chicago were the origin of the revolution in international finance, which I suppose makes them my intellectual grandparents. Jacob A. Frenkel and Michael Mussa were my uncles, producing many cousins. (Jacob never held against me the endless confusion, among foreign readers and check-in clerks at conference hotels, caused by the similarity in our names.) Their work appears in citations throughout this book.

I soon discovered other families in time spent at the University of Michigan, Yale, the Federal Reserve Board, and the International Monetary Fund. The influence of the portfolio-balance school is clear in parts II and III of this book; it came to me in the personal form of such colleagues as Dale Henderson and James Tobin.

My exposure to the world of policy began with my year on the staff of the Council of Economic Advisers, when Martin Feldstein was chairman, Ronald Reagan was president, and the dollar was king. Feldstein was embroiled in controversy. For me this was pure excitement, and important issues of international finance were at the heart of it. By 1984, international economics had come to be considered of such importance that our chapter on it had worked its way to the front of the *Economic Report of the President*. When the secretary of the treasury told a congressional committee that so far as he was concerned, they could throw the *Report* in the wastebasket, it was this chapter to which he was referring. I was proud as punch.

To those who have not spent time in both realms, it is impossible to convey how absolute are the conflicting demands for loyalty from the goddess of economics and the goddess of politics. I could not have had a better teacher in the art of surviving such conflicts than Feldstein. The answer, for an academic, is that the goddess of economics has priority, even during a stint in Washington, but you can't let people there know that. Writings of mine that were the most directly affected by this experience are for the most part too tied to current events to be suitable for this book. The influence is present to some degree in the later papers; Feldstein's influence is present in chapter 6.

I have been fortunate enough to continue my association with Feldstein and the National Bureau of Economic Research. Also helping to keep me in touch with developments on the East Coast have been recent visits to the Kennedy School of Government at Harvard and the Institute for International Economics in Washington, DC. A good example of the benefits of these visits is my collaboration with Kathryn Dominguez, represented here by the penultimate chapter.

Finally, the next generation has given me some outstanding graduate students at Berkeley, of whom Charles Engel and Ken Froot require special mention. Many appear as coauthors in the credits for the chapters or as research assistants in the acknowledgments. Meriting special credit are Eirik Evenhouse and Siobhán Reilly, who worked as hard on the editing of this collection as I did and did an outstanding job of it. I am very pleased to find that there are still students who know how to write.

Acknowledgments

Revised versions of the following articles are being reprinted here by permission:

Chapter 1: "The Flexible Exchange Rate System: Experience and Alternatives" (with Rudiger Dornbusch). In *International Finance and Trade*, edited by Silvio Borner, International Economics Association, in association with Macmillan Press: London, 1988.

Chapter 2: "Quantifying International Capital Mobility in the 1980's." In *National Saving and Economic Performance*, edited by D. Bernheim and J. Shoven, University of Chicago Press: Chicago, 1991, 227–260. Adapted in *International Finance*, edited by D. Das, Routledge: New York.

Chapter 3: "On The Mark: A Theory of Floating Exchange Rates Based on Real Interest Differentials," *American Economic Review* 69, no. 4 (September 1979), 601–622.

Chapter 4: "Monetary and Portfolio-Balance Models of Exchange Rate Determination." In *Economic Interdependence and Flexible Exchange Rates*, edited by J. Bhandari and B. Putnam, MIT Press: Cambridge, Mass., 1983.

"Tests of Monetary and Portfolio-Balance Models of Exchange Rate Determination." In *Exchange Rate Theory and Practice*, edited by J. Bilson and R. Marston, University of Chicago Press: Chicago, 1984.

"Update to Monetary and Portfolio Balance Models of Exchange Rate Determination." In *International Economic Policies and Their Theoretical Foundations: A Sourcebook*, edited by John Letiche, Academic Press: London, second edition, 1992, 826–832.

Chapter 5:   "Why Interest Rates React to Money Announcements: An Explanation from the Foreign Exchange Market" (with Charles Engel), *Journal of Monetary Economics* 10, no. 1 (January 1984).

Chapter 6:   "Six Possible Meanings of 'Overvaluation': The 1981–85 Dollar," *Essays in International Finance* No. 159, International Finance Section, Princeton University (December 1985).

Chapter 7:   "Zen and the Art of Modern Macroeconomics: The Search for Perfect Nothingness," in *Monetary Policy For a Volatile Global Economy*, William Haraf and Thomas Willett, eds., The American Enterprise Institute for Public Policy Research, Washington, D.C., 1990.

Chapter 8:   "Tests of Rational Expectations in the Forward Exchange Market," *Southern Economic Journal* 46, no. 4 (April 1980).

Chapter 9:   "The Diversifiability of Exchange Risk," *Journal of International Economics* 9 (August 1979).

Chapter 10:   "In Search of the Exchange Risk Premium: A Six-Currency Test Assuming Mean-Variance Optimization" *Journal of International Money and Finance* 1 (December 1982), 255–274.

Chapter 11:   "Recent Estimates of Time-Variation in the Conditional Variance and in the Exchange Risk Premium," *Journal of International Money and Finance* 7 (March 1988), 115–125.

Chapter 12:   "Forward Discount Bias: Is it an Exchange Risk Premium?" (with Ken Froot), *Quarterly Journal of Economics* 104, no. 1 (February 1989), 139–161.

Chapter 13:   "Using Survey Data to Test Standard Propositions Regarding Exchange Rate Expectations" (with Ken Froot), *American Economic Review* 77, no. 1 (March 1987), 133–153.

Chapter 14:   "Understanding the U.S. Dollar in the Eighties: The Expectations of Chartists and Fundamentalists" (with Ken Froot) *Economic Record* (December 1986), 24–38.

Chapter 15:   "Chartists, Fundamentalists, and Trading in the Foreign Exchange Market" (with Ken Froot), *American Economic Review* 80, no. 2 (May 1990), 181–185.

Chapter 17:   "The European Monetary System: Credible At Last?" In *Financial Markets, Institutions and Policy*, edited by Anthony S. Courakis, *Oxford Economic Papers*, vol. 44 (special issue) Oxford University Press: Oxford (April 1992).

I

The Modern International
Monetary System

Introduction to Part I

The structure of the world monetary system changed twenty years ago, in two fundamental ways. The first change was the movement from fixed to floating exchange rates. This fundamental shift dates from 1973, though it is true that the gradual breakdown of the Bretton Woods system had been underway for some years before then and that an experiment with pure floating was to wait until the inauguration of the first Reagan administration in 1981. Chapter 1 is a brief overview of how the floating exchange rate system has operated in practice, particularly in comparison with expectations prior to 1973 about how such a system would operate. The original essay was coauthored with Rudiger Dornbusch, who wrote most of the second half (on current proposals for reform of the system).

The second change was the process of international financial integration that moved the world system from low to high capital mobility. This structural shift is conventionally dated around 1973 or 1974 as well, when Germany and the United States found that, the necessity of shoring up a fixed exchange rate having disappeared, capital controls were no longer needed and could be removed. But the process of international financial integration continued thereafter, and one could argue that the increase in international capital mobility during the period 1979–90 was more rapid and comprehensive than was the case for the early 1970s. Only during the latter period did the United Kingdom, Japan, France, Italy, and a number of smaller countries, all of which had retained extensive capital controls in the 1970s, open up to world financial markets. Chapter 2, "Quantifying International Capital Mobility in the 1980s," applies various statistical approaches to measuring this increase in financial integration. Definitions of capital mobility are made more precise in that chapter, distinguishing particularly between barriers to the movement of capital across national boundaries and barriers associated with the currencies in question.

These two characteristics of the modern international monetary system—floating rates among the major currencies and high capital mobility—are taken as given throughout the rest of the book.

1

The Flexible Exchange Rate System: Experience and Alternatives

with Rudiger Dornbusch

The experience with exchange rates has in many ways differed from what was anticipated in 1973 when the major industrialized countries abandoned the effort to keep the values of their currencies fixed. There is a widespread feeling that exchange rates have turned out to be more volatile than they were expected to be, than they should be, and perhaps than they need be. Many practitioners believe that exchange rates are driven by psychological factors and other irrelevant market dynamics, rather than by economic fundamentals. Support grew in the 1980s for some sort of government action to stabilize currencies—perhaps a reform of the world monetary system.

In this chapter we consider the record with the current flexible exchange rate system and then different alternatives that have been proposed. We will begin in section 1.1 with ten characteristics that economists expected floating exchange rates to have in theory, as of the start of the floating rate era, and then in section 1.2 contrast ten aspects of how they have turned out to work in practice. The chapter concludes in section 1.3 with an analysis of ten proposed alternatives, including (1) proposals for decentralized rules ("new classical" nihilism, gold standard, monetarism, and nominal income targeting), (2) proposals for enhanced coordination of policy-making (setting of "objective indicators" à la G-7, target zones à la John Williamson, "world monetarism" à la Ronald McKinnon, and a supranational fund for foreign exchange intervention à la Takashi Hosomi), and (3) proposals to enhance independence (a "sand in the wheels" tax on foreign exchange transactions, à la James Tobin, and a dual exchange rate à la Dornbusch).

1.1 How the System Was Supposed to Work in Theory

When we recall how economists expected floating exchange rates to operate, we must take care not to draw an over-simplified caricature of the state of the art as of 1973. The large effect that international capital flows would have on exchange rates was recognized in the literature of that time. As we go through the ten attributes that the system was supposed to have, we will note discrepancies with caricature views that may appear in the press and other popular accounts but that have not in fact been widely held by economists for many years.

1. *Exchange rates were supposed to be as stable as macroeconomic fundamentals.* This is not the same thing as saying that exchange rates were supposed to be stable. Milton Friedman (1953) and other early proponents explicitly recognized that if countries followed divergent monetary policies, it would show up in their exchange rates.

2. *Countries would be likely to have divergent policies and divergent inflation rates.* A system of truly fixed exchange rates forces countries to keep their price levels in line, and therefore to keep their macroeconomic policies in line. The penalty of following a more expansionary policy than one's neighbors is a trade deficit. This penalty would be smaller under floating exchange rates, so governments would presumably be more likely to follow different policies. But decentralization of policy-making was considered a virtue, not a drawback, of the system. The logic here is similar to that for a domestic economy: letting each individual actor act independently in his own self-interest is more likely to give the best outcome for the largest number as compared to putting all under the control of a more centralized political process in which the most unreliable actors have as much vote as the reliable (for a statement of this viewpoint, see Corden, 1983).

3. *There would be smaller trade imbalances, and therefore less political pressure for protectionism.* Nobody claimed that trade balances would be zero under floating exchange rates. While it is true that when the central bank follows a policy of refraining from intervening in the foreign exchange market the overall balance of payments is by definition zero, in the presence of international capital flows this is not the same thing as saying that the trade balance is zero. Nevertheless, from the standpoint of the United States in the closing years of the Bretton Woods regime, the deteriorating trade balance seemed to force a clear trade-off between downward flexibility of the value of the dollar on the one hand, versus the imposition of trade restrictions on the other. (In 1971 the U.S. trade balance went into deficit for the first time in the postwar period. In response to the deficit, and to a corresponding loss in international reserves, President Richard Nixon simultaneously placed a tariff surcharge on imports, devalued the dollar in terms of gold and foreign currencies, and ended the U.S. government's commitment to sell gold for dollars to foreign central banks.)

The argument that a move to floating exchange rates would reduce protectionism was made generally, as Dunn (1983, p. 6) reminds us:

In addition to gains for macroeconomic policy, flexible exchange rates also promised to eliminate mercantilism as an argument for tariffs and other protectionist devices, thus producing an era of free or at least more liberal trade. Harry Johnson noted that a tariff merely causes an appreciation of the local currency which taxes export and unprotected import competing industries without improving the trade account or increasing aggregate demand.... The expectation that protectionism can improve the balance of payments and generate an increase in aggregate demand obviously makes no sense if the exchange rate adjusts to maintain payments equilibrium with most of the payments adjustment to the exchange rate occurring in the current account.

4. *There would be less transmission of disturbances internationally.* A corollary is that there would be less need for international coordination of the divergent policies; enhancing independence was considered one of the chief virtues of the system, as mentioned under attribute (2).

Floating exchange rates would not give *complete* insulation from foreign disturbances. At least as far back as Laursen and Metzler (1950), economists had demonstrated a variety of channels of transmission that hold even when the overall balance of payments is set equal to zero by a central bank policy of not intervening in the foreign exchange market. The most important channel is international capital flows, which became even more important in the 1970s and 1980s than in the 1960s. A foreign fiscal expansion, for example, would raise the demand for domestic goods through a foreign trade deficit and domestic trade surplus; the nonzero trade balance is matched by a flow of capital to the country initiating the expansion. But it still seemed that the magnitude of the transmission should be smaller than under fixed exchange rates, at least for monetary policy. A foreign monetary expansion would cause the foreign currency to depreciate, thereby mitigating the deterioration in the foreign trade balance. In fact, in the model of Mundell (1963, 1964a) and Fleming (1962), the currency effect actually reversed the direction of movement of the trade balance and therefore of the international transmission: domestic output would, if anything, fall when the foreign country expanded.

5. *Central banks would have less need to hold foreign exchange reserves, because they would have less need to use them.* In the 1960s, those who pondered reform of the monetary system were concerned about ensuring an adequate supply of reserves for the world economic system as a whole, as much as with adjustment of imbalances among countries. Hence the proposals to raise the price of gold, create Special Drawing Rights, etc. It

was believed that moving to a system of floating exchange rates would be one, at least partial, solution. If the primary reason for holding reserves, to intervene in the foreign exchange market, were removed, then the demand for reserves would fall.

6. *There would be a general tendency for exchange rates in the long run to be determined by relative price levels, that is, by purchasing power parity (PPP).* Not many argued before 1973 that the tendency to return to PPP would be instantaneous and complete. There were still plenty of unreconstructed Keynesians who believed that prices adjusted extremely slowly to conditions of excess supply, if at all. Even Friedman recognized the importance of short-run adjustment costs in prices. And everyone recognized that the long-run real exchange rate could be shifted by real trends, for example, a faster rate of productivity growth in traded goods than in nontraded goods (e.g., Balassa, 1964). But the general consensus was that monetary trends probably dominated supply factors as determinants of the nominal exchange rate. So when economists said that exchange rates would be as stable as fundamentals (point 1 above), they meant observable macroeconomic fundamentals like M1, not unobservable tautologically defined shocks to the equilibrium real exchange rate.

7. *The stickiness of goods prices implies that the return of the real exchange rate to long-run equilibrium would not in fact be rapid.* The slow adjustment of goods prices was of course emphasized in models such as that of Mundell and Fleming, as opposed to the world view of the monetarists. The resulting conflict over exchange rate determination was mirrored in conflicting interpretations of the interest rate. In the Mundell-Fleming view, a high interest rate was a signal of tight monetary policy; as a consequence, there would be increased demand for the country's assets and the currency would appreciate. In the monetarist view, a high nominal interest rate was a signal of inflationary monetary policy; as a consequence, there would be decreased demand for the country's assets and the currency would depreciate. The conflict was reconciled by the overshooting model of Dornbusch (1976c).[1] An increase in the interest rate, to the extent that it is an increase in the *real* interest rate, signifies a tight monetary policy, and thus will appreciate the currency in the short run. But the tight monetary policy and resulting excess supply of goods will then cause the price level to fall gradually over time, eventually restoring the real money supply, the real interest rate, and the real exchange rate, to their original levels. The term "overshooting" is applied to the property that after the initial appreciation, the currency can be expected to depreciate over time. The overshooting

model's synthesis of the Mundell-Fleming and monetarist views had become widely accepted by the late 1970s.

8. *"Speculation" should be stabilizing rather than destabilizing.* The argument originated with Friedman's claim that any class of speculators who added to the variance in the exchange rate must be buying when the price is already high and selling when the price is already low; this is a sure-fire recipe for losing money, and such speculators should disappear from the market over time. (Define speculation as investors' acting on the basis of their expectations of changes in the exchange rate.) Speculation was also stabilizing in the Dornbusch overshooting model, though this was not always recognized by some who focused simplistically on the model's implication of high rate volatility. The high volatility is a result of sticky prices in goods markets combined with instantaneous adjustment in asset markets, not of speculation. When the currency appreciates in the short-run overshooting equilibrium, the investors recognize that it will depreciate in the future toward long-run equilibrium; in response, they reduce their demand for the currency and dampen the original appreciation. The movement in the exchange rate turns out to be smaller than it would have been in the absence of speculation.

9. *Expectations are rational.* Rational expectations imply that (a) exchange rates should not jump except in response to unforecastable information regarding economic fundamentals ("news"), and that (b) any systematic patterns of movement in exchange rates should be incorporated into investors' expectations as reflected, for example, in the forward discount (perhaps adjusted for an exchange risk premium). In the context of the Dornbusch and other monetary models developed in the mid-1970s, this means that (a) exchange rates should not jump discontinuously except in response to news about current money supplies, expected future money growth rates, and real output, and (b) the forward discount or interest differential should be a conditionally unbiased forecast of the future change in the exchange rate. It does *not* mean, as is often asserted, that exchange rate changes should be completely unforecastable, that is, that the exchange rate should follow a random walk. Under rational expectations, we should be able to predict that part of exchange rate changes that is correctly predicted by participants in the foreign exchange market, as reflected in the forward discount. For example, a country that has a record of high money growth and inflation should have a currency that can be predicted to depreciate, at a rate that is appropriately reflected in the expectations of market participants, in the forward discount, and in the interest rate. Another example arises in the overshooting equilibrium; the regressive parameter in inves-

tors' equation of expectations formation should be equal to the *actual* speed of return to long-run equilibrium in the absence of future disturbances.

10. *Markets in forward exchange and other instruments for hedging exchange risk should develop, offering the importer, exporter, or international investor an antidote to the increase in foreign exchange risk that would accompany the move to a floating exchange rate system.* The cost of short-term uncertainty was one of the major concerns of Kindleberger (1969), McKinnon (1976), and the few other original holdouts against floating rates. They thought that the absence of a single international money would retard trade and investment. The standard counter-argument was that one could hedge risk on the forward exchange market. Such markets already existed in major currencies in 1973. But it was predicted that the transactions costs would fall and the trading volume would increase, in response to the increased demand under floating exchange rates.

1.2 How the System Has Apparently Worked in Practice

1. *Exchange rates move inexplicably.* As noted, the fact that exchange rates have turned out to be highly variable, which they have, is not in itself contrary to theory. They were supposed to have been as variable as macroeconomic fundamentals. Nor is it even contrary to theory that the variance of exchange rate changes is greater than the variance of countries' money supply changes. The overshooting theory says that the former should be a multiple of the latter, if the money supply changes are permanent. The multiple can be quite large, if the expected speed of adjustment to long-run equilibrium is slow. The difficulty is, rather, that regression studies of the existing macroeconomic models show poor results by standard statistical criteria (incorrectly signed coefficients, insignificant magnitudes, low R-squared, poor out-of-sample forecasting performance).[2]

Most of these problems could be attributed to small time samples, simultaneity bias, and other problems in the estimation of the parameters. (For example, the positive relationship between the money supply and the exchange rate, which exists in all theories, often does not show up econometrically because the central bank is reacting endogenously to the exchange rate.) But these problems can be addressed. Meese and Rogoff (1983b) tried an entire grid of possible combinations of parameter values, as an alternative to estimating the parameters in-sample. Most important, for present purposes, in no case was the predictive performance impressive compared to the total variation in the exchange rate. The clear conclusion is that exchange rates are moved largely by factors other than the obvious, observable, macroeconomic fundamentals. Econometrically, most of the "action" is in the error term.

This conclusion tends to undermine any defense of exchange rate variability made on the grounds that it is appropriate given changes in monetary policy. If exchange rate changes were in truth explainable by changes in money supplies, either contemporaneous or anticipated, we would have much better results in our regressions than we do. Note that this conclusion holds regardless of sophisticated theories of rational stochastic speculative bubbles, etc., that can be built for the expectations term in the equation.

Saying that there are large unknown factors contributing to movement in the exchange rate is not quite the same thing as saying that these factors make it more variable than it would otherwise be. The error term could in theory be negatively correlated with the macroeconomic fundamentals.

There is an impression that the variance-bounds tests which have been proposed are the way to show excessive volatility. Testing whether exchange rates are more volatile than observable macroeconomic variables has both intuitive appeal and the appearance of being on less restrictive ground econometrically than the traditional regression tests. However, this appearance is illusory. In the context of the foreign exchange market there are two kinds of variance-bounds tests: those that check to see if the variability of expectations is too large given the variability of the future spot rate, and those that check to see if the variability of the spot rate is too large given the variability of macroeconomic determinants (taking account of the rationally expected future spot rate as one of the determinants).[3] The first sort of variance-bounds test, of which Huang (1984) is an example, is analyzed skeptically in the chapter appendix. The second sort of variance-bounds test is crippled by our ignorance as to the correct macroeconomic determinants, let alone the precise parameter values of their coefficients. For example, Diba (1987) points out that the calculation is sensitive to the semi-elasticity of money demand with respect to the interest rate, and that an error made by Huang (1981) and Vander Kraats and Booth (1983) in expressing this parameter is therefore entirely responsible for their finding that the spot rate is more volatile than would be expected from the fundamentals. The conclusion is that, for either sort of variance-bounds test, there exists a more traditional regression equation that tests the identical condition (rational expectations, jointly with other conditions such as the absence of an exchange risk premium). The variance-bounds tests in this context give up the power to reject the null hypothesis gratuitously, with a gain in nothing but complexity. The regression tests in themselves give adequate ground for concluding that exchange rate movements cannot be explained by fundamentals.

2. *The trend in rhetoric is toward greater coordination of policies, rather than the reverse.* Until the mid-1980s, countries wanted to follow independent policies, and floating exchange rates helped achieve some of that independence, as they promised to do. True, the 1974 recession struck across countries, but it was attributable to the common supply shock faced by all oil-importing countries. In the 1970s countries followed increasingly divergent rates of money growth and inflation, as one might expect under a floating-rate system. West Germany and Switzerland were said to be in virtuous cycles of firm monetary policies, low inflation rates, and appreciating currencies. Italy, France, the United Kingdom and—to a lesser extent—the United States were said to be in vicious circles of loose monetary policies, high inflation rates, and depreciating currencies. Subsequently, the United Kingdom in 1979 and the United States in 1980 decided to tighten monetary policy in order to reduce inflation. This represented a sharp change in policy in these countries, with no change in Germany. The consequent appreciation of their currencies helped reduce inflation much faster than would have been possible under fixed exchange rates, though at the cost of lost output in tradable goods sectors. The floating exchange rate system facilitated their independent shifts in policy priorities, just as it was supposed to. But by 1986 the shifts had also brought about a convergence of inflation rates, around the German level, suggesting the possibility of a return to stable exchange rates maintained by convergent policies, if it was desired.

The *mix* of macroeconomic policies, as opposed to the overall degree of expansion, remained widely divergent among the G-5 countries in the 1980s, with the United States having shifted to a massive structural budget deficit unaccommodated by either monetary policy or private saving, and with Japan, Germany, and some other European countries having shifted in the opposite direction. This policy divergence gave us large trade imbalances (the next point to follow) and widespread sentiment for institutional reform to enhance policy coordination (the point after that).

3. *Although variation in national saving rates across countries has on the whole been reflected in variation in current accounts to as great an extent since 1973 as before, the United States financed its increased budget deficit in the 1980s in part by borrowing from abroad on an unprecedented scale.* The resulting record U.S. trade deficit gave rise to new protectionist pressures in the United States, which in turn put the entire world trading system in jeopardy. If it is accepted that the occurrence of large trade imbalances gives

rise to protectionist pressures, then the question is whether this occurrence is more likely under fixed exchange rates or under floating exchange rates. The dollar overvaluation of the early 1970s arose because the exchange rate was not free to move to offset U.S. inflation; the dollar overvaluation of the early 1980s arose precisely because the exchange rate *did* move.

Variation in national saving rates among most countries tended to be reflected in investment rates more than in current accounts to an even greater extent in the years after 1973 than before 1973. This tendency was documented by Feldstein (1983) and Frankel and MacArthur (1988), among many others. (Obstfeld, 1986, and Frankel, 1986d, find that U.S. behavior in the 1980s was an exception in this regard.) Similarly, real interest rates have diverged across countries to a greater extent since 1973. If one thinks of such statistics as tests of the degree of international capital mobility, then the finding appears surprising because many barriers to capital movement have been removed over the latter period. But if one thinks of the greater scope for divergent macroeconomic policies and divergent real interest rates that is possible under a regime of variable nominal and real exchange rates, then this finding is not surprising: even if capital mobility enforces parity among interest rates when expressed in terms of a common currency, a country that suffers a shortfall in national saving can still drive its *real* interest rate above world levels and thus crowd out domestic investment. In other words, the observed tendency for financial policies to have their major real interest rate effects in the country originating them, rather than abroad, is precisely the sort of enhanced independence that floating exchange rates were supposed to give us.

4. *Despite the widespread professed sentiment for increased coordination of monetary policies, there is no agreement on the nature of international transmission.* Therefore there is no agreement on whether coordination means cooperative monetary expansion, or something quite different.

International macroeconomic policy coordination has been the most popular topic for research in the field in recent years.[4] Agreements at the G-7 Summit Meetings in Tokyo in 1986 and Venice in 1987, and at various ministerial meetings in between, purportedly supported an increased degree of coordination. It would appear that there has been a reduction in the desire for increased independence of national policy-making that accompanied the move to floating rates in the 1970s.

But absent is a consensus on precisely what coordinated package of policy changes is called for under current circumstances. In 1986–87, the U.S. Secretary of the Treasury, James Baker, called for lower interest rates in Germany and Japan, under the reasonable-sounding assumption that this would have a positive impact on the U.S. trade balance and on U.S. growth. The Mundell-Fleming model, on the other hand, says that the effect of a depreciated mark and yen would dominate, and that the impact on U.S. trade and growth would be *negative*. Of twelve leading international economic models, half show a positive effect (in the second year after a monetary expansion by the non-U.S. OECD), and half show a negative effect. In part because policy-makers subscribe to different beliefs as to how the economy works, they are likely to be unable to come to an agreement as to the desirable coordinated package of policy changes, even when they find it attractive to agree in principle that coordination is desirable.[5]

5. *Central banks continue to hold and use foreign exchange reserves on a large scale.* Frenkel (1983b) found that there was no downward shift in central banks' demand for reserves in 1973−79 relative to the preceding period, despite the abandonment of the commitment to intervene in the foreign exchange market though others have found evidence of some shift (Heller and Khan, 1978, or Williamson, 1992). The magnitude of intervention, though not sufficiently large to prevent large changes in exchange rates, has from time to time been larger in absolute terms than under the Bretton Woods system. In 1977 and 1978, central banks in Europe and Japan, in an attempt to resist the appreciation of their own currencies, bought up dollars in greater quantities than they had in the final years of defense of fixed exchange rates. Intervention became smaller in the 1980s, particularly because the U.S. government renounced it altogether, but this changed with the Baker initiative to bring down the dollar in 1985. By 1986−87, central banks in Europe, and especially Japan, were once again intervening on a very large scale to dampen the appreciation of their currencies against the dollar.

It is clear why central banks might still intervene in substantial magnitudes, even assuming they are willing to allow a greater degree of flexibility in their exchange rates now than before 1973. A given quantity of intervention, which might have been sufficient to limit exchange rate movement to a certain range in the 1960s, is no longer sufficient to do so. The likely explanations are a higher degree of international capital mobility (investors' asset holdings are highly sensitive to expected rates of return) and a higher "elasticity" of expectations (investors' expectations as to the future level of the spot rate are far more sensitive to the current level of the spot rate than to any notion of fundamental long-run equilibrium).

6. *Not only does purchasing power parity clearly fail in the short run, but it is difficult to disprove the claim that it also fails in the long run.* By the mid-1970s, it had become an academic orthodoxy that PPP was a realistic assumption,

even in the short run, and that this constituted empirical support for the "equilibrium" view of the economy; that prices were flexible enough to equilibrate supply and demand rapidly, not only in the markets for foreign exchange and other assets, but in the markets for goods and labor as well. But under the weight of overwhelming empirical evidence, of which Krugman (1978) and Kravis and Lipsey (1983) were just two examples, the pendulum rapidly began to swing back the other way. It helped that the large nominal appreciation of the dollar in 1981−85 was almost entirely reflected as a real appreciation as well. In the 1980s there was no longer support for the proposition that the speed of adjustment to PPP is infinite, or even that it is high.[6]

Ironically, some proponents of the equilibrium view have swung to the opposite extreme. They claim that the speed of adjustment to PPP is zero. It is true that most statistical studies on post-1973 data fail to reject the proposition that the real exchange rate follows a random walk.[7] What is surprising is that anyone considers this evidence supportive of the equilibrium theory of exchange rate determination or, for that matter, of *any* economic theory.[8]

The argument that a random walk supports the equilibrium theory, which appears often in modern macroeconometrics, is a sort of extrapolation of the rational expectations revolution. In the "bad old days," economists were the omniscient model-builders, who understood the complete model while the actors within the model did not. As a useful correction to this sometimes-arrogant perspective, the theory of rational expectations argued that if there were any empirical regularities that were well established among economists, then rational profit-maximizing individuals would soon take them into account.

The ultimate extrapolation of the argument occurs when the modern macroeconomist derives pride from his failure to explain any movement in the macroeconomic variable in question, in this case the real exchange rate. Theoretical models are derived in which investor behavior is rigorously derived from principles of optimization. Changes in the exchange rate are attributed to shifts in technology and tastes that, though known to all the agents in the economy, are not known to the economist. The theory contains no information that could be used to explain specific changes in the real exchange rate. He then goes on to "test" his theory "empirically" by seeing whether he can statistically reject the hypothesis that the real exchange rate follows a random walk. Rather than being humbled or embarrassed about his statistical failure to explain any movement in the macroeconomic variable that he has been investigating, he proudly proclaims it as confirming his theory, on the grounds that the theory too did not explain any movement in the variable![9]

7. *While the overshooting theory does seem to explain gross movements in the real exchange rate, better at least than competing theories, shorter-term movements remain completely unexplained.* At times it seems that the exchange rate "overshoots the overshooting equilibrium."

In some ways the relationship between the real exchange rate and the real interest differential was clearer in the 1980s than it was in the 1970s, perhaps as a consequence of the movements being larger. By various measures, the long-term real interest differential between the United States and its trading partners increased by about 5 points from 1980 to mid-1984, which would explain a large increase in demand for U.S. assets. The estimate in note 7 suggests that the real exchange rate regresses about 14 percent of the way to long-run equilibrium per year, on average.[10] If this estimate is right, and if the real interest differential is assumed equal to the expected rate of real depreciation (no risk premium), then it follows that between 1980 and 1984 the dollar appreciated by about 35 percent ($= 5/14$) relative to its perceived long-run equilibrium. This matches fairly well the real appreciation of the dollar between 1980 and 1984, as can be seen in figure 15.1. No large shift in the long-run equilibrium real exchange rate need necessarily have taken place. Subsequently, in 1985–87, the real interest differential fell, and the dollar followed suit.[11]

The chief problem with the overshooting theory, and indeed with the more general rational expectations approach, is that it does not explain well the shorter-term dynamics. In the first place, the entire increase in the real interest differential and in the value of the dollar should have occurred in one (or two or three) big jumps, for example, when it was discovered that monetary policy was going to be tighter than previously expected, or fiscal policy looser. Yet the appreciation in fact took place month-by-month, over four years. All the while, investor expectations, as reflected in the forward discount, interest differential, or survey data, forecast a depreciation. It is no good to utter the words "peso problem" and argue that the market was forecasting a correction of macroeconomic policy that happened not to occur in the sample period. If the market systematically mispredicts the direction of policy, that itself is a violation of the rational expectations hypothesis.

In the second place, it is particularly difficult to explain the rapid last 20 percent of the appreciation that took place between July 1984 and February 1985 (see figure 15.1). During this period all measurable fundamentals—not only real interest differentials, but also money growth rates, real growth rates, the current account, and the country risk premium versus the Eurodollar market—were, if anything, moving in the wrong direction. It appears that the dollar overshot the overshooting equilibrium. Some have suggested that this episode may have been an example of a speculative bubble, one that does not conform to rational expectations.[12]

8. *It appears that little of the speculation that takes place is stabilizing.* The arguments come from several directions. In the first place, expectations may not be rational. Studies show that expected exchange rate changes— as reflected in either the forward discount or surveys of market participants—are biased forecasts of actual exchange rate changes. In the case of the forward market, these findings could in theory be attributed to an exchange risk premium, but in the case of the survey data they cannot (see, for example, Frankel and Froot, 1987a, reproduced here as chapter 13).

In the second place, even if speculation is rational, rational speculation may not in fact be stabilizing. All the random-walk, or "near random-walk," results imply that it would be rational for investors to base their expectations as to the future spot rate almost entirely on the current spot rate, and not at all on an estimate of fundamentals equilibrium. If "expected depreciation" is a variable that is always equal to zero, then it cannot have a stabilizing effect on investor behavior. Furthermore, the modern theory of rational stochastic speculative bubbles has all but demolished Friedman's claim that investors who bet on destabilizing expectations will lose money. In a rational speculative bubble, investors lose money if they *don't* go along with the trend.

In the third place, there is direct evidence that most market participants pay scant attention to fundamentals. By 1985, most of the forecasting services that appeared in an annual survey by *Euromoney* were described as using technical analysis: "In the early 1980s, the surveys appeared to have convinced many readers that forecasts could be used profitably and that the most profitable forex forecasters were technical rather than those who focused on economic fundamentals" (August 1987, p. 121). The 1987 survey of services reported that none offered pure fundamentals forecasts, five offered fundamentals forecasts at longer horizons and technical analysis at shorter horizons, three offered forecasts combining the two techniques, thirteen offered only technical analysis, and four did not specify a technique (these last firms show their clients how to hedge risk, rather than trying to outguess the market).[13]

In the model of chapter 14, if technical analysts or "chartists" who rely on time-series extrapolation, make better predictions month after month for four years than "fundamentalists," who forecast a return to macroeconomic equilibrium, then Bayesian portfolio-managers will gradually pay more attention to the chartists and less to the fundamentalists, even though the latter may prove to be correct in the long run. This is only one of a recent group of models with heterogeneous investor expectations. De Long et al. (1987) construct a model in which there exists a class of traders who follow irrelevant noise, and yet who prosper over time,[14] contrary to Friedman's argument that destabilizing speculators would be driven out of the market.

9. *Most short-term variability seems unrelated to news.* To summarize, there are two serious empirical problems with the standard theory. First the proportion of exchange rate changes that are forecastable in any manner—by the forward discount, interest differential, survey data, or models based on macroeconomic fundamentals—appears to be not just low, but almost zero. Second, the proportion of exchange rate changes that we can explain ex post facto—after we have observed the contemporaneous macroeconomic determinants—also appears to be low. Exchange rates must be reacting to something else, either economic variables that are unknown to the economist, as the equilibrium theorists would have it, or to irrelevant noise.

One kind of evidence that prices in financial markets are reacting to noise more than news comes from French and Roll (1986). They looked at days when the New York stock market happened to be closed but business was otherwise conducted normally; they found that stock prices moved much less during such periods compared with periods of equal length when the stock market was open. The implication is that movement in stock market prices comes out of the dynamics of trader interaction within the marketplace, rather than primarily from the processing of new information from the outside. Because foreign exchange markets tend to be open wherever people are awake, it has not been possible to apply the French-Roll test to them.[15] But this is a promising area for future research.

10. *Trading volume in foreign exchange markets has become enormous; most of it seems unrelated to trade in goods, as well as to long-term or medium-term investment.* In March 1986, transactions in the U.S. foreign exchange market (eliminating double-counting) averaged U.S. $50 billion a day among banks (up 92 percent from 1983), and U.S. $34.4 billion a day among brokers and other financial institutions. Most important, only 11.5 percent of the trading reported by banks was with nonbank customers (of which 4.6 percent was with nonfinancial customers), only 14.3 percent of brokers' transactions involved a nonbank, and only 19.2 percent of trading reported by other financial institutions was with customers (of which 7.7 percent

were nonfinancial institutions).[16] In London the total was U.S. $90 billion a day. Only 9 percent of the banks' transactions were directly with customers.[17] Tokyo was counted at U.S. $48 billion. The rest of the Pacific has been estimated at U.S. $29 to $37 billion, and Zurich and Frankfurt together have been estimated as big as New York. These totals are not only many times greater than the volume of international trade in goods and services; they are also many times greater than the volume of international trade in long-term capital.

The prediction that the forward market would become more developed in response to demand for hedging under floating exchange rates has in some ways been borne out (number of currencies traded, number of markets, volume of trading). But the U.S. banks reported that only 4.7 percent of their foreign exchange transactions in March 1986 were in the forward market, as compared to 63.2 percent in the spot market. (Swaps were 29.8 percent and futures and options accounted for the rest.) Though the volume of trade does not appear to have suffered from exposure to exchange risk, only a small proportion of international trade is in fact hedged on the forward market. The evidence is mixed on the prediction that the bid-ask spread in the foreign exchange market would decline. Froot (1989, p. 315) reports that the average bid-ask spread in DM in New York fell from 0.11 percent in 1973 to around 0.05 in the 1980s. But when volatility is high, so that taking an open position, even if only briefly, is risky for a bank, the bid-ask spread widens. The evidence is surveyed in Levich (1985, pp. 997–99).

Clearly, trading among themselves is a major economic activity for banks and other financial institutions. Schulmeister (1987, p. 24) found that in 1985, twelve large U.S. banks earned a foreign exchange trading income of U.S. $1165 million. Every single bank reported a profit from its foreign exchange business in every single year that he examined. Goodhart (1987, p. 25 and Appendix D) surveyed banks that specialize in the London foreign exchange market: "Traders, so it is claimed, consistently make profits from their position-taking (and those who do not, get fired), over and above their return from straight dealing, owing to the bid/ask spread" (p. 59). The banks report that their speculation (that is, taking an open position) does not take place in the forward market (and only 4–5 percent of their large corporate customers were prepared to take open positions in the forward market). Rather the banks take very short-term open positions in the spot market. Apparently they consider the taking of long-term open positions based on fundamentals, or of any sort of position in the forward exchange market, as too "speculative" and risky. But the banks are willing to trust their spot exchange traders to take large open positions, provided they close most of them out by the end of the day,[18] because these operations are profitable in the aggregate. In the description of Goodhart, and others as well, a typical spot trader does not buy and sell on the basis of a model of fundamentals, but rather trades on the basis of knowledge as to which other traders are offering what deals at a given time, and a feel for what their behavior is likely to be later in the day.

The reported profits are not so large that, when divided by the volume of "real" transactions for customers, they need necessarily lie outside the normal (relatively small) band of the bid-ask spread. In other words, the profits represent the transactions cost for the outside customers. One might expect that this large volume of trading therefore cannot be relevant from a larger macroeconomic perspective, that is, for understanding the movement of the exchange rate (except perhaps on an intra-daily basis). But putting together these emerging characteristics of the actual dynamics of trading, it is possible to come up with the loose outlines of an unconventional model of endogenous bubbles in the foreign exchange market.

In the first place, the large volume of trading, which most finance models have absolutely nothing to say about, in itself suggests that market participants are not identical agents who share the same, rational, expectation. Participants are heterogeneous, with respect to both the portfolios they hold and the expectations they hold. (In the expectations survey data, the high-low range of responses averages 15.2 percent).[19] In the second place, most trading is motivated by a very short-term horizon.[20] There were few investors, as of 1984, anxious to buy and hold long-term mark or yen securities merely because the dollar was overvalued according to the fundamentals. This is what McKinnon (1976) refers to as "an absence of stabilizing speculation." In the third place, there is for some reason a breakdown of the economists' rule of rationality that the long run is the sum of a series of expected short runs.[21] The result is that economic fundamentals do not enter into most traders' behavior, even if fundamentals must win out in the long run. Indeed, most traders are so young, and have been at their current job so short a time, that they may not even remember the preceding major upswing or downswing four years earlier! This short-term perspective need not be irrational from the viewpoint of the individual bank. Allowing its traders to take a sequence of many short-term open positions in the spot market may be the bank's only way of learning which traders can make money at it and which cannot.

The high volume of trading arises both when those with pessimistic expectations sell to those with optimistic expectations, and when those who find themselves with too-large open positions in a given currency sell to those without. The high volume of such intra-day trading will in itself create movement—within (the small band of) the bid-ask spread—that is not related to fundamentals. If there existed significant numbers of other investors in the market who were willing to bet on fundamentals, then the intra-day trading could not push the spot rate far from its appropriate value. But if most of the other investors in the market ignore fundamentals, and instead use technical analysis, or form expectations in any other way so that small exchange rate movements become self-confirming, then the rate may drift far away from its appropriate level. As with any other bubble, it does a single investor little good to recognize that the market is incorrectly valuing the currency, if the market is likely to be making the same mistake six months later when he wants to sell. Even though such a model may deviate from the rational expectations norm in that the market is not taking adequate account of the fact that the exchange rate must return to equilibrium eventually, there is no way for an investor to make expected profits from this mistake, unless he has sufficient liquidity, sufficient patience, and sufficiently low risk-aversion, to wait through the high short-term volatility.[22]

1.3   Alternatives

Discussion of reform of the international monetary system is at least 120 years old. In the second part of the nineteenth century international monetary conferences chased one another. The topic of that time was bimetallism and the role of silver. Later, in the early 1920s, silver was largely out and the dollar was in. The Genoa conference moved for a gold exchange standard, with dollars doing the work and gold keeping the system honest, though the pound also lingered on as a reserve currency. By the 1930s the complete breakdown of the international system made international monetary reforms a nonstarter. Roosevelt sank the London Conference in 1933 when he argued: "The sound internal economic system of a nation is a greater factor in its well-being than the price of its currency in changing terms of the currencies of other nations" (Pasvolsky, 1933).

The Bretton Woods reconstruction was built on very pragmatic pillars: capital mobility was not even in the minds of the architects of the new system, widespread exchange control being the rule. Exchange rate policies were narrowly circumscribed to leave room for adjustment only in case of "fundamental disequilibrium"—for any other grief the system provided liquidity.

Gold was still around, but the role of the dollar was even more central. The system lasted until the late 1950s; throughout the 1960s European convertibility for capital account transactions and the growing disparity in current account imbalances raised issues about a system where European currencies were kept undervalued (enhanced by a trade-diverting Common Market) while central banks accumulated ever larger-dollar balances. The background to international monetary reform was the European complaint about a system that gave the United States both seigniorage and an almost exclusive voice in setting the trend of world monetary policy.

The transition to floating rates in the early 1970s was not an amicable divorce. But a post-mortem of the fixed rate system left little doubt that it could not work. The incompatibility of inflation targets put all the burden on surplus countries: they could choose between inflation and appreciation, but they could not force the center deficit country into adjustment.

In the present discussion no easy agreement can be achieved because different parties in the discussion have in mind very different problems. They hold widely differing beliefs about the scope of alternative arrangements and see different aspects of the present exchange rate experience as the chief problem, as we already saw in the preceding part:

• Some argue that one must view exchange rate regimes in the wider context of economic and social arrangements that set an institutional structure for free market forces to play themselves out in the most unimpaired fashion. Foremost among these rules should be a firm circumscription of the role of government, particularly of the arbitrary power of government to interfere with, modify, or dissolve private contracts by changing the value of money.

• Others argue that rates move as much because of the underlying lack of synchronization in policies, a synchronization that might have been more substantial under a regime of more nearly fixed rates. But that leaves the question whether the fixed-rate system merely substitutes more acute crises for extended, massive swings.

• An increasing number of participants in the debate accept that large, persistent exchange rate swings appear almost unrelated to fundamentals (policies and economic trends) and seem more nearly the result of the peculiar operation of speculative, short-horizon markets. Like stock markets, markets for long-term bonds or for precious metals may simply take trips away from fundamentals because they do not have an umbilical cord.

• For some observers economic nationalism, and the independence of monetary and fiscal policies, are the pillars of successful national economic performance. But there are rare opportunities where ad hoc collaboration can enhance each participant's performance. Unwinding of large disequilibria is such an instance because controlled action avoids hard-landing scenarios that might accompany the bursting of a bubble.

• A large number of participants in the debate express concern about the serious risk of trade conflicts induced by large swings in exchange rates. They are therefore concerned to limit exchange rate fluctuations so as to avoid reinforcing protectionist sentiment.

Discussion of monetary reform of the 1980s has each participant holding at least one of these issues to be the central problem of international monetary reform. But since these concerns are very different and vary over a wide field, it is no surprise that proposals pass each other like ships in the fog. In the meantime, policy-makers flirt with the idea of reform and hence keep the debate going.

In the remainder of this part we impose a structure on the discussion by highlighting ten important directions of search for solutions. We organize them under three headings: proposals focusing on decentralized national rules, proposals that make enhanced cooperation their central feature, and, finally, proposals to reduce interdependence.

Group A: Decentralized, National Rules

A return to the gold standard, Friedman-monetarism, or its modern version of nominal income targeting are all in the class of decentralized, national rules. But so is the nihilism of the rational-expectations market-clearing school. We start with the last view.

1. *Rational expectations, market-clearing.* The new classical reconstruction of macroeconomics has not stopped at the borders of the closed economy. Research by Stockman, Helpman and Razin, and others has explored what role the choice of exchange rate regime can play in macroeconomics.[23]

Not surprisingly, the literature concludes that the exchange rate regime plays little role. Monetary policy (other than for unanticipated changes) has no effects on the real equilibrium except when money is used as an instrument of public finance. The welfare economics of exchange rate regimes does not offer much other than prescriptions about monetary policy in a model of optimal taxation.

The literature is important in imposing uncompromising maximizing standards in the discussion, assessing alternative arrangements in terms of welfare criteria. But at the same time the literature is also uncompromisingly uninteresting because its world is without problems. Accordingly the exchange rate regime can make no difference.

2. *The gold standard proposal.* Mundell (1968a, p. 15) once said "Dollars are money, gold is not." No doubt he would find a way of rationalizing the remark. But it is a straining experience to witness the continued advocacy of gold as the center of the international monetary system. Lewis Lehrman, Congressmen Ron Paul, Jack Kemp, and at one time James Baker all share a surprising confidence in what gold could do for macroeconomic stability. Paul and Lehrman conclude their case arguing (1982, p. 200):

Either we must move to a gold standard and monetary freedom, with longrun stability of prices and business, rapid economic growth and prosperity, and the maintenance of a sound currency for every American; or we will continue with irredeemable paper, with accelerating core rates of inflation and unemployment, the punishment of thrift, and eventually the horror of runaway inflation and the total destruction of the dollar. The failure of irredeemable money nostrums is becoming increasingly evident to everyone—even to the economists.

But it would certainly be a mistake to believe that support of the gold standard is a common conservative front. A conservative case against the gold standard was already made in Simons (1948, p. 262) where he writes:

The place of gold in the monetary system is hard to discuss quite seriously. All talk about currencies based on gold is a bit silly.... We may hitch gold to the dollar if and as we choose. To think of hitching the dollar to gold is almost not to think at all; one does not hitch a train to a caboose!

The gold commission, appointed as a result of President Reagan's campaign commitments, came down with a resounding condemnation of gold as a serious part of the world monetary system. Anna Schwartz, who had served as secretary of the gold commission, wrote a particularly forceful survey of the role of gold in monetary history, indicating the absence of magic or sterling performance. She (in Bordo and Schwartz, 1985, p. 20) summarized her findings on the gold standard in the following terms:

The objective factors that served to promote the international gold standard in the past are no longer favorable to such an institution. And, as noted, the psychological factor of reverence for the standard has all but vanished except among a minority of faithful believers. Like Miniver Cheevy, they probably were born too late.

The continued support (not only from cranks, but even from scholarly monetary economists such as Robert Mundell or the late Jacques Rueff) is best explained by Henry Simons's (1948, p. 168) observation:

The worship of gold, among obviously sophisticated people, seems explicable only in terms of our lack of success in formulating specifications for a satisfactory, independent national currency—and certainly not in terms of the need for stable exchange rates for orderly international currency. Indeed, it indicates how little progress liberals have made in showing, by way of answer to revolutionists, what kind of money rules might be adopted to make capitalism a more workable system.

We now turn to such an alternative system, monetary rules.

3. *National monetarism.* Milton Friedman's proposal for a monetary rule was an unusual idea at the time it was proposed.[24] Keynesian economics was in vogue and money had virtually disappeared from academic circulation. But in the aftermath of the inflation shocks of the 1970s, monetary targeting became an integral party of central bank jargon and even of operations. For the strict monetarist a monetary rule, the quantity theory, purchasing power parity, and flexible rates represent the four-leaved clover that grows at the end of the rainbow.

A monetary rule, given the quantity theory, PPP, and flexible rates, would be expected to isolate a country from unwelcome world inflation trends without the need to adjust the domestic wage-price structure. Serious discussion of the costs and benefits of flexible rates, and the possible lack of an anchor, is brushed aside in this discussion by a double argument: the price level (and hence the exchange rate) cannot run off unless authorities accommodate the inflation. Second, speculation is stabilizing. Nurkse (1937) had challenged flexible rates with the argument that expectations and speculation can become self-fulfilling: speculation could set off depreciation, which, via the budget and passive money, leads to inflation and thus becomes self-fulfilling. The argument is turned around, mistakenly, by pointing out that speculators simply anticipate the money creation and inflation, failing to note that without the speculation the inflation would not have occurred in the first place.

Here is an important field of research in the area of multiple equilibria (in policies) that has not even started to be opened up. We owe to simplistic national monetarism the insight into these problems because only the stark assumption of a constant, exogenous growth rate of money (come hell or high water) can highlight that such a thing will not, in practice, be easy to implement. And if money is not exogenous, then expectations and policies have strategic interaction that robs national monetarism of its attractive simplicity and simplistic claims.

4. *National nominal income targeting.* The idea of national income targeting as a decentralized rule for operations under flexible exchange rate system is on the surface not far away from simple monetarism. But the

essence of the proposal, making allowance for velocity shocks, is crucial. This point is altogether obvious when we consider the massive changes in velocity that occurred in the United States, and in other industrialized economies in the early 1980s.

Nominal income targeting, as first proposed by Hicks, Meade, and Tobin, would solve the chief problem of a strict monetary rule, namely, changes in velocity that happen randomly or, in disinflation, systematically. By automatically accommodating velocity changes, the system would avoid, for example, the Mundell problem—high real interest rates during periods of disinflation (see Mundell, 1971).

In the closed economy nominal income targeting takes the simple form of an aggregate demand equation:

$$y + p = x \tag{1}$$

where x denotes the policy determined level of nominal income. Aggregate supply will depend on wages (which may be a proxy for price level expectations in the past) and on supply shocks:

$$y = a(p - w) + u \tag{2}$$

where y, p, and w denote output, the price level and the wage all in logs, and u denotes supply shocks. The behavior of this system can then be contrasted with one where the authorities follow a constant money rule which yields an aggregate demand equation (see, for example, Blanchard et al., 1985):

$$y = g(m - p) + v \tag{1a}$$

where v denotes aggregate demand shocks, for example, shifts in velocity. It is immediately apparent that the constant nominal income rule accommodates aggregate demand shocks (whether stemming from velocity or animal spirits). In the case of aggregate supply shocks it does not necessarily dominate the constant money rule. But even here a case can be made for the nominal income rule, for example, if preferences weigh inflation and output equally.

The open economy version of such a model is considerably more complicated. In the open economy there are some fine points to clarify about nominal income targeting: should the government stabilize nominal spending or nominal income? The difference is important, not only because of the implied shifts in the current account but also because of the difference in reaction to terms-of-trade shocks. Assuming, to keep matters simple, the same aggregate supply equations as in (2), the aggregate demand equation is[25]

$$y = f(e - p) - gi^* + v \qquad (3)$$

where e is the exchange rate and i^* the world rate of interest. Once again the nominal income rule is:

$$x = y + p. \qquad (4)$$

Combining (2) and (4) yields

$$x = (1 + a)p - aw + u \qquad (5)$$

and from (2) and (3) we obtain:

$$p = [f/(a + f)]e + (v - u - gi^*)/(a + f) + [a/(a + f)]w. \qquad (6)$$

It is apparent from the equations that demand shocks or foreign market interest rate shocks (v, i^*) only change the exchange rate, leaving output and prices unchanged. Supply shocks (w, u) affect both output and prices. Specifically, a wage shock increases prices and lowers output. The exchange rate appreciates!

In this simplest case, nominal income targets are unequivocally superior when movements in velocity are the dominant disturbance. When disturbances to aggregate demand and to aggregate supply are also at issue, the nominal income rule may still be preferred, but now that case rests on preferences, parameters, and relative variability. In a closed economy the 1:1 trade-off between output and prices implied by (4) might appear as striking a prudent balance. But in the open economy the variability of the real exchange rate is also an issue. The nominal income rule has a problem in this respect since in the face of a demand shock it immunizes output and prices, shifting the entire burden of adjustment on the exchange rate and the current account.

An entirely different consideration is how decentralized nominal income targeting works out in an interdependent world economy. We noted above that demand shocks translate into real exchange rates and changes in the current account, leaving output and prices unaffected. Such a pattern of adjustment does not have attractive adding-up properties in the world economy unless there is an explicit coordination agreement that renders the targets compatible.[26]

We now turn to a radically different approach, focusing on a cooperative rather than national perspective on the exchange rate system.

Group B: Enhanced Coordination of Policy-Making

There is, of course, a wide variety of proposals for a more integrated world economy. These proposals flourished in the 1960s, when the fixed rate system was breaking down, and they have been springing up once again in response to dissatisfaction with the present flexible rate system. We review here four directions of change: coordination by policymakers, target zones, world monetarism, and an independent intervention fund.

5. *Coordination.* The various summit meetings have, at least in their language, converged on the agreement to consider closer forms of coordination. Coordination presumably already includes the exchange of information, although one is not certain whether the exchange does not consist mostly of disinformation or of explanations why reasonable policy measures cannot be undertaken.

But coordination discussions have also in the more recent past focused on developing a set of "objective indicators" that could trigger policy actions or at least meetings at which pressures for action could be applied. The initial list of indicators designed to prompt cooperation measures included ten items, running from growth and unemployment to budgets, reserves, money growth, exchange rates, inflation, and current account balances. The list was trimmed subsequently and the IMF charged with monitoring the surviving indicators.

The mid-1980s saw a virtual explosion of talk about cooperation. But it was not unlike the talk about world monetary reform in the late 1960s. The cause is the fundamental problem of dollar overvaluation and differences of opinion about who should do what. There is certainly no reason to believe that there is an actual advance in cooperation, except perhaps in the foreign exchange market where intervention has become massive and talking down of the dollar less frequent.

At the academic level, recent research has deprived cooperation of much of its former glamor. The Mundell-Fleming model of the 1960s (as, indeed, the much earlier writings of Modigliani and Neisser) had stressed international interdependence. International macroeconomic models such as Project Link developed the quantitative patterns, and research by Cooper (1986) had built a strong case for cooperation. But that literature took a very different direction when Hamada (1985) and others approached interdependence from a game-theoretic point of view. This approach pointed out the difference between cooperative and Nash equilibria. Work by Oudiz and Sachs (1984, 1985) reached the surprising conclusion that the benefits from cooperation might be quantitatively minor. Rogoff (1985) showed that cooperative monetary policy might be counterproductive.

The case for collaboration has been further weakened by an analysis of various complications in the coordination game. The game runs into obstacles before it has even begun, at the stage where policymakers within each country must decide what they want the other country to do, for example, expand or contract (see Frankel, 1987b).

Policymakers may not diagnose the existing economic situation in the same fashion. (Germans traditionally have thought there is no unemployment in any relevant macroeconomic sense in their country.)

They may have different objective functions in that they differ in the relative weights they assign to such variables as inflation and unemployment.

They may disagree on which is the model of the world economy, and even if they can agree on a model, it may differ from the true model. The combination of all these differences, if they could be considered jointly, makes it doubtful that cooperation could come out ahead.

One starting point of this questioning of cooperation is the recognition that we do not, in fact, know which quantitative model is the correct model for the world economy, or even the one most closely resembling it. Policymakers must therefore pick a model, or a number of models, to pursue their individual policy decisions and their cooperative exercises. Analyzing the predictions of twelve world macroeconometric models, Frankel (1987a) concludes:

There turns out to be relatively little disagreement as to the effects on output, prices and the exchange rate. The greatest disagreement is rather over the question whether a monetary expansion worsens or improves the current account and accordingly whether it is transmitted positively or negatively to the rest of the world.

The model difference is the point of departure for another issue: what if policymakers cooperate, each having in mind a model, but not necessarily the right model. Analyzing the possibilities (with two countries and ten models), Frankel and Rockett (1986) conclude that the United States would be ahead as a result of monetary cooperation only 55 percent of the time; it loses 32 percent of the time, and cooperation makes no difference in 13 percent of the cases. For the rest of the OECD, monetary cooperation results in gains slightly less often.

This kind of finding supports skepticism about the fruits of cooperation. But it is in fact only the tip of an iceberg. The problems go even further because of perceived or actual constraints on policy and because side constraints on policies and preferences over instruments vastly complicate actual bargaining. If that were not enough, there is also an important time dimension coming from the political business cycle and from the differing lead times of policies.

The conclusion then is that grand concerted fine-tuning is unlikely to become reality, but that this may not even be a loss.

6. *Target zones*. Williamson (1985) made the case that countries should agree on target zones for exchange rates, limiting the extraordinary rate swings and fluctuations by adopting suitable exchange rate-oriented monetary policies and by making intervention commitments.

The Williamson proposal has fared well in practice since there is evidence of massive central bank intervention and of implicit target zones in a gradual unwinding of the 1985 dollar overvaluation. Figure 1.1 shows the actual monthly average of the yen since January 1985, as well as a band of plus 5 and minus 10 percent of the average exchange rate over the preceding three months. From late 1985, following the Plaza agreement, the yen lay roughly in these bands for the subsequent seven years. Of course, this

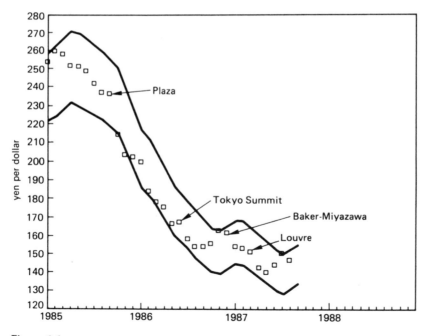

Figure 1.1
The monthly average of the yen since January 1985

is a very weak form of target zones, controlling only the rate at which the dollar overvaluation is undone.

The gradual unwinding of the dollar overvaluation has an interesting aspect, quite independent of the target zone issue. One would have thought that policymakers would be eager to announce publicly a target zone arrangement to enlist the support of stabilizing speculation. But that is not possible when there is an agreement for a gradual (though steep as compared with existing interest differentials) depreciation. The explanation for the secrecy maintained regarding the bands in the Louvre Accord and the other G-7 agreements, assuming they have in fact been serious agreements, is that the authorities were consciously fooling the market. Moreover, looking ahead, if the dollar is to decline another 30 percent, as many observers predict, why does the dollar not collapse in the absence of a compensating differential? The most plausible explanation draws on the absence of long-term stabilizing speculation already discussed in section 1.2.

In the absence of long-term speculation, central banks can reduce the extent of speculation by increasing uncertainty. Moderate changes in interest rates can bring about appreciation as likely as depreciation in the very near term. Speculation is reduced by the elimination of the one-way-only option. Intervention (on a massive scale) becomes a plausible counterweight for the limited amount of long-term speculation. It is of the essence in carrying out this kind of policy that the public should not understand whether authorities truly believe that the dollar is already in the right place or whether they have a firm agreement to bring about another 20 or 30 percent depreciation in a controlled fashion over a year or two. Only if the market is sufficiently uncertain can the depreciation be managed without matching interest differentials.

There is a quite separate question of whether this gradual depreciation is desirable in comparison with a rapid, once-and-for-all drop. The hard-landing discussion, particularly by Marris (1985, 1987), emphasizes the potential inflationary upsurge accompanying a steep dollar decline and the risk that the Federal Reserve may have to stop the spreading of depreciation to wages by extra high interest rates. On the other side of the argument is the real economy. Here an argument can be made the other way: rapid depreciation gives the best chance to reverse the effects of overvaluation on resource allocation. It provides an effective way of exterminating hysteresis effects by depriving foreign companies in the United States of adjustment time to reinforce their beach-heads. It is perhaps not surprising that policymakers favor the controlled descent, since the real resource costs appear small relative to the fear of sharp inflationary pressure, especially in politically sensitive times.

Returning to the Williamson proposal, it is interesting how much it evolved over the four years after its introduction. Initially, exchange rate—oriented monetary policy was the cornerstone of the proposal. In its more recent form (see Williamson and Miller, 1987) the original proposal is barely recognizable. Here are the main policy principles and prescriptions in their current "blueprint":

• The real exchange rate will not deviate more than 10 percent from the agreed "fundamental equilibrium exchange rate."

• The average level of world real interest rates should be set with a view to achieving a target growth of nominal world demand.

• Short-term interest rates in individual countries should supplement intervention in achieving the exchange rate target.

• National fiscal policies should be managed to hold the growth of domestic demand to the target path.

• The rules are implemented subject to the condition that real interest rates stay in their historically normal range and that increasing or excessive ratios of debt to GDP be avoided.

The explicit introduction of real interest rates and fiscal policy takes into account many of the criticisms of the earlier proposal. But in taking these issues into account, it is also clear that the very plausibility of such cooperation is challenged. Few seriously argue that the large exchange rate swings are altogether unrelated to the extravagant monetary or fiscal policies of the past years. Without these policies, exchange rates might not exhibit the same volatility they now show. If this is correct, the "blueprint" has less to do with exchange rates than with imposing limits on the national policy mix. Moreover, since in practice we are talking of currency blocs, the main issue is, as always, the question whether key currency countries can be persuaded to sacrifice some of their national preferences to make the "world" features of this proposal come off.

There is no reason to believe that any change in the unwillingness to sacrifice autonomy has occurred since the 1960s. On the contrary, were it not for the risk of dollar collapse and protection, we might not see the little collaboration that there is. A system that does not have teeth is unlikely to generate collaboration, which is perceived as inconvenient, if not costly.

A major, if not overwhelming, difficulty in the Williamson scheme is the notion of the fundamental equilibrium exchange rate. The need for U.S. budget correction requires acceptance by Europe and Japan of smaller trade surpluses. Much of the adjustment will come from correction of U.S. macropolicies, but there are inevitable repercussions abroad as foreign trade surpluses shrink and dollar depreciation sustains U.S. employment. There are also questions about worldwide real exchange rate adjustments necessitated by the emergence of the NICs that seem to sell in the United States and buy in Japan.

7. *World monetarism.* For over ten years McKinnon has advocated a new monetary system centered on fixed exchange rates between the yen, the deutsche mark, and the U.S. dollar. Already in 1974 he argued for new monetary arrangements based on rigidly fixed rates, but built on stronger foundations—world monetarism rather than national monetary discretion (see McKinnon, 1974). Since then he has refined his plan for monetary integration under rigidly fixed exchange rates—"a gold standard without gold," as he called it (see McKinnon, 1987b).

His proposal has fallen on fertile soil because the dramatic exchange rate volatility makes the financial press and the business community grasp for ready answers. Although the scheme seems to solve the problem of currency instability, there is little theoretical or empirical basis for his standard. McKinnon's analysis has become even more controversial since he added to world monetarism the claim in the late 1980s that the dollar was undervalued and the yen substantially overvalued.

The basic proposition of McKinnon is this: World monetary growth should be targeted to achieve price level stability. Countries should follow an assigned domestic credit target and use symmetric, unsterilized intervention to stabilize exchange rates. The proper level of the dollar is 170–190 yen/U.S. $ and 2.0–2.2 deutsche mark/$ (see McKinnon, 1987c).

The question of PPP has already been discussed in section 1.2, when we discussed short-run deviations and the question of whether the exchange rate has a tendency to revert. We add here the problems posed by trends in the equilibrium real exchange rate due to real changes. Specifically, in a context of cumulative productivity growth, or major shifts in the budget, there is absolutely no presumption that PPP should hold over time, neither absolutely nor even relatively. In the case of the United States and Japan, for example, there is an obvious Ricardo-Kravis-Balassa trend real appreciation due to the much higher productivity growth in Japan.

In earlier work McKinnon has more strongly advocated the view that exchange rate movements are caused predominantly by money demand shifts between different currencies.[27] More recently he recognizes that portfolio disturbances involve, dominantly, shifts between interest-bearing assets. But the basic emphasis on an M1-disturbance view of exchange rates is still lingering. This narrow view of exchange rates determinants leaves out two important explanations for exchange rate movements. Exchange rates can move for any of a number of reasons. But what is the evidence that would support the view that money demand disturbances are the dominant source? If exchange rate movements are not caused primarily by shifts in money demand from one country's M1 to another's, there is no basis for preferring fixed exchange rates over flexible rates. Moreover, there certainly is no presumption for using unsterilized intervention as the rule.

If uncoordinated, large fiscal swings are a possibility there is no presumption that fixed rates with unsterilized intervention are the best kind of monetary policy. A fiscal expansion would now lead to an expansion of home credit and to a contraction abroad. World interest rates would rise and our trading partners risk falling into recession. Neither the fixed rate nor the monetary rule seems in this context a very attractive feature. Of course, that brings out precisely the problems of the 1980s.

If a choice must be made among rules, either so central banks can establish more credible commitments vis-à-vis their domestic constituents not to inflate, or so national governments can establish more credible commitment vis-à-vis each other not to "cheat" on joint bargains (such as coordinated expansions or contractions), then nominal income targeting seems a much sturdier possibility than M1 monetarism. Any rule will turn out to have difficulties for certain disturbances and within a given period would be dominated by discretion. But discretion itself has become suspect because of time consistency problems. With this point in mind, nominal income targets surely dominate commitments to fix the stock of money (not to mention the price of gold).

8. *An independent intervention fund.* The previous directions of change focused on governments' agreeing to more active cooperation. An alternative is to create an institution that, independently, plays the role of achieving the results cooperative policies would otherwise bring about. Such a scheme has been advanced by Hosomi (1985).

The Hosomi plan envisages a fund that is endowed with the main currencies on a sufficient scale to be able to conduct effective intervention policy. This fund would develop criteria for appropriate exchange rates, would announce them and intervene to move markets in the direction of these rates. Decisions would presumably be voted by a board of governors representing the largest central banks, along the lines of the Bank for International Settlements. Individual governments would remain free to pursue their own policies, possibly intervening against the fund, but at least they would be known to be out of line and would have some competition.

The chances of seeing such a fund are, of course, remote. Governments have been extraordinarily slow in giving a major mandate for surveillance to the IMF, for example, and even in the EMS intervention remains a highly politicized issue. On the world level it is doubtful whether Germany or the U.S. Treasury would allow themselves to be outspeculated with their own money. But one can advance a different line of argument. Which is more likely to come about: abandoning monetary sovereignty in a Williamson-Miller coordination agreement, or allowing the emergence of a new institution that competes but not necessarily outcompetes the national authorities? If institution building is the point, a Hosomi fund may be a good route to progress. It is a dimension along which the system realistically could move halfway from the noncooperative solution to the cooperative solution (or however far there is sufficient political support; the less strong the consensus for ceding monetary sovereignty, the smaller would the fund be).

Group C: More Independence for National Policies

In this final section we review a very different strand of proposals emphasizing segmentation of capital markets. This literature takes its respectability from Nurkse, Modigliani, and Tobin, each of whom has noted that excessively mobile capital interferes with policy independence without commensurate gains in terms of resource allocation. The implication for policy is that if hot money flows could be cooled, policy-makers would have more instruments at their disposal to get on with the task of achieving non-inflationary growth.

9. Tax deterrents to hot money. The best-known proposal to interdict hot money flows is Tobin's suggestion to "put some sand in the wheels of international finance." Tobin observes (1978):

I believe the basic problem today is not the exchange rate system, whether fixed or floating. Debate on the regime evades and obscures the essential problem.... The basic problems are these. Prices in goods and labor markets move more sluggishly, in response to excess supply or demand, than the prices of financial assets, including exchange rates.... There are two ways to go. One is toward a common currency, common monetary and fiscal policy, and economic integration. The other is toward greater financial segmentation between nations or currency areas, permitting their central banks and governments greater autonomy.

The Tobin scheme is a moderate, worldwide transactions tax on foreign exchange. The disincentives for trade would be negligible, and so would be the disincentives for long-term capital movements. But the profitability of short-term round trips would be dramatically curtailed. Suppose the rate of return at home is i per year. The required rate of return abroad (including tax evasion and exchange gains) i^* depends on the Tobin tax, t, and on the duration of the investment f (measured as the fraction of years for which a foreign position is held):

$$i^* = (if + t)/f(1 - t). \qquad (6)$$

It is apparent that the Tobin tax penalizes speculative investments more the shorter the horizon. For example, with a home interest rate of 10 percent, a 2 percent tax, and a six-month investment horizon, the foreign yield would have to be 14 percent. If the horizon were only one month, the foreign yield would need to be 34 percent per annum.

There are several objections to such a tax. One is that the taxation of all foreign exchange transactions acts as a disincentive to trade. The counter-argument is that hot money flows by misaligning exchange rates may create macroeconomic costs far in excess of moderate trade taxation and, moreover, may invite protectionism.

The second concern, expressed for example by Marston (1987, p. 53), is that the system would fail to stem the influence of capital flows driven by long-run fundamentals. This is really not an objection but rather a rein-forcement of the Tobin argument. The proposal is specifically designed to strengthen the role of long-term speculation which now is dominated entirely by short-horizon round tripping. It is possible to slip into the mistake of thinking that if a Tobin tax discourages only short-term capital investments, rather than long-term investments, then it can reduce only short-term exchange rate volatility, not long-term misalignment. But we argued in section 1.2 that, in a market where speculators fully adjust their expectations of the future rate to reflect the last fluctuations in the current spot rate, and few investors take positions based on long-term fundamentals, the short-term movements become self-confirming and can cumulate into long-term misalignment.

There are other tax variants that seek the same objective. Specifically Liviatan (1980) and Dornbusch (1986a, 1986b) have argued for a real interest equalization tax. Such a tax, levied cooperatively, would reduce the incentives for short-term money movements and thus remove their dominant influence from exchange rate determination.

A third and common objection to the Tobin tax, or to an interest equalization tax, is that they are impractical because they are difficult or impossible to enforce. There is certainly merit to this objection, particularly when the tax is implemented by an individual country, leaving scope for offshore evasion. When implemented as an international system, the changes are more nearly like those of collecting the corporate income tax from multinationals. No doubt, since the vast majority of gross capital flows have to do with minimizing, avoiding, or outright evading taxes, there won't be massive support for such a policy on the part of financial institutions. But the proposals compete with alternatives that are no more persuasive: a world central bank, coordinated fiscal policy, and so forth. The key point of these proposals, in the end, is to highlight that short-term capital flows may be a major destabilizing factor in the world macroeconomy.

10. *Dual exchange rates.* We conclude with a proposal that (just as the preceding tax proposals) draws its inspiration from the problem of volatile (and often unproductive) short-term capital flows. The proposal envisages instituting a dual exchange rate system. Governments of the main industrialized countries would establish a fixed (or rigid crawling peg with trend) exchange rate for commercial transactions. But for all capital account transactions the exchange rate would be flexible.

A possible macroeconomic advantage of this system is that real exchange rates relevant for trade flows would be more stable, even when fiscal policies get far out of line. Of course, budget deficits that are prevented from showing up as trade deficits will show up elsewhere instead, for example, as crowding out of investment. If elements other than fundamentals are important in asset markets, then goods markets are fully sheltered from their influence.

Dual exchange rates are known from the experience of a number of developing countries, specifically Mexico, but also from Belgium, France, and Italy at various times. Would they work between major currencies? If one takes the view that flexible rates today are dominated by speculation based on considerations other than fundamentals, the shift to another system can be viewed as an advantage. If the speculative influence is only an overlay on real factors, then detaching the asset market rate may make it much more volatile.

1.4 Concluding Remarks

This chapter has taken a broad look at the experience with flexible rates and at alternatives. Where is the bottom line on proposals for change?

The basic question seems to be whether exchange markets are dominated by speculation that drives the price away from fundamentals. If that is not the case, the mere pursuit of more reasonable macroeconomic policies, without much cooperation, will ensure that exchange rates fluctuate much more moderately. Reasonable policies under current circumstances mean first and foremost a correction of the U.S. budget deficit.

But if asset markets are dominated by speculation unrelated to market fundamentals, then there may also be a potential for improvement from basic policy reform. If such speculation dominates, then taxation or decoupling of asset markets theoretically becomes a possible step to enhance microeconomic efficiency. Whether this is best done by a Tobin tax or by dual exchange rates is largely an administrative question. The interesting point of twenty years with flexible rates is the suspicion that speculation might do more harm than good. The possibility is an active part of the research agenda in many areas of finance.[28]

On the other hand, to establish a case for government intervention, it is not sufficient to show that the international financial system as it works in practice is a flawed version of the optimal efficient-markets equilibrium of theory. Nor would it even be sufficient to show theoretically that optimal intervention might improve world economic welfare. It must be recognized that government intervention historically has been every bit as flawed a version of the theoretical optimum as have been the results given by the market.

Appendix 1A: Variance-Bounds Tests

Two different methodologies are in use to test whether expectations are excessively volatile: regression tests and the newer variance-bounds tests.

The traditional regression test of rational expectations uses the equation:

$$\Delta s_{t+1} = a + (b)\Delta s_t^e + u_{t+1},$$

where the left-hand-side variable is the *ex post facto* change in the (log) spot rate and the right-hand-side variable is investors' expected rate of depreciation as measured, for example, by the forward discount (which requires the assumption that no risk premium separates the two). We reject the hypothesis of rational expectations if the estimate of the coefficient is significantly less than 1, which is the usual finding. We could choose to describe a finding that $b < 1$ as a finding that expected depreciation (Δs^e) is excessively volatile (which is how Bilson, 1981a, originally described it: speculators would do better to reduce their expectations toward zero). This would be just another way of saying that expected depreciation is a biased predictor.

Huang (1984, p. 159, eq. 11) applies the variance-bounds test by computing the variance of the prediction error, and arguing that expectations are excessively volatile if it exceeds the variance of the changes in the spot rate. This is a true statement, because

$$\text{Var}(\Delta s_{t+1} - \Delta s_t^e) > \text{Var}(\Delta s_{t+1})$$

implies

$$\text{Var}(\Delta s_{t+1}) + \text{var}(\Delta s_t^e) - 2\text{Covar}(\Delta s_t^e, \Delta s_{t+1}) > \text{Var}(\Delta s_{t+1})$$

$$1/2 > \text{Covar}(\Delta s_t^e, \Delta s_{t+1})/\text{Var}(\Delta s_t^e).$$

This last ratio is simply our regression coefficient b, so it is certainly true that if it is statistically less than 1/2, then it is also statistically less than 1, and we can reject rational expectations. But this would be a foolish way of doing the test, because it needlessly throws away the ability to reject the null hypothesis if b happens to fall into the range between 1/2 and 1. Indeed, Huang is able to reject the null hypothesis for fewer currencies when he applies his variance-bounds test than when he applies the traditional regression test to the same currencies. The variance-bounds test adds absolutely nothing to our understanding in this context. This point is generalized in Frankel and Stock (1987) and Froot (1987a).

Acknowledgment

The authors would like to thank Charles Engel, Kenneth Froot, Charles Goodhart, Alan MacArthur, Stephan Schulmeister, and John Williamson for comments on an earlier draft.

2   Quantifying International Capital Mobility in the 1980s

Feldstein and Horioka upset conventional wisdom in 1980 when they concluded that changes in countries' rates of national saving had very large effects on their rates of investment and interpreted this finding as evidence of low capital mobility. Although their regressions have been subjected to a great variety of criticisms, their basic finding seems to hold up. But is their interpretation of the finding—that it implies imperfect capital mobility—the right one?

Let us begin by asking why we would ever expect a shortfall in one country's national saving *not* to reduce the overall availability of funds and thereby crowd out investment projects that might otherwise be undertaken in that country. After all, national saving and investment are linked through an identity. (The variable that completes the identity is, of course, the current account balance.)

The aggregation of all forms of "capital" has caused more than the usual amount of confusion in the literature on international capital mobility. Nobody ever claimed that international flows of foreign direct investment were large enough that a typical investment project in the domestic country would at no added cost be undertaken directly by a foreign company when there was a shortfall in domestic saving.[1] Rather, the argument was that the typical American corporation could borrow at the going interest rate in order to finance its investment projects, and if the degree of capital mobility were sufficiently high, the going interest rate would be tied down to the world interest rate by international flows of portfolio capital. If portfolio capital were a perfect substitute for physical capital, then the difference would be immaterial; but the two types of capital probably are not in fact perfect substitutes.

This chapter examines a number of alternative ways of quantifying the degree of international capital mobility. One conclusion is that the barriers to cross-border flows are sufficiently low that, by 1992, financial markets could be said to have become virtually completely integrated among the large industrial countries, and among some smaller countries as well. But this is a different proposition from saying that real interest rates are equalized across countries, which is still different from saying that investment projects in a country are unaffected by a shortfall in national saving. We will see that there are several crucial links that can, and probably do, fail to hold.

In many cases, notably the United Kingdom and Japan, and more recently Italy, France, and a number of smaller European countries, the finding of high integration with world financial markets is a relatively new one, attributable to liberalization programs since 1979. Even in the case of financial markets in the United States, integration with the Euromarkets appears to have been incomplete as recently as 1982.[2] An important conclusion of this chapter for the United States is that the current account deficits of the 1980s were large enough, and lasted long enough, to reduce significantly estimates of the correlation between saving and investment. The increased degree of worldwide financial integration in the 1980s is identified as one likely factor that allowed such large capital flows to take place over the past decade. But even if U.S. interest rates are now viewed as tied to world interest rates,[3] there are still other weak links in the chain. The implication is that crowding out of domestic investment can still take place.

2.1 Four Alternative Definitions of International Capital Mobility

By the second half of the 1970s, international economists had come to speak of the world financial system as characterized by perfect capital mobility. In many ways, this was jumping the gun. It is true that financial integration had been greatly enhanced after 1973 by the removal of capital controls on the part of the United States, Germany, Canada, Switzerland, and the Netherlands; by the steady process of technical and institutional innovation, particularly in the Euromarkets; and by the recycling of OPEC surpluses to developing countries. But almost all developing countries retained extensive restrictions on international capital flows, as did a majority of industrialized countries. Even among the five major countries without capital controls, capital was not perfectly mobile by some definitions.

There are at least four distinct definitions of perfect capital mobility that are in widespread use:

1. The *Feldstein-Horioka definition.* Exogenous changes in national saving (i.e., in either private savings or government budgets) can be easily financed

by borrowing from abroad at the going real interest rate and thus need not crowd out investment in the originating country (except perhaps to the extent that the country is large in world financial markets).

2. *Real interest parity.* International capital flows equalize real interest rates across countries.

3. *Uncovered interest parity.* Capital flows equalize expected rates of return on countries' bonds, despite exposure to exchange risk.

4. *Closed interest parity.* Capital flows equalize interest rates across countries when contracted in a common currency.

These four possible definitions are in ascending order of specificity. Only the last condition is an unalloyed criterion for capital mobility in the sense of the degree of financial market integration across national boundaries.[4]

As we will see, each of the first three conditions, if it is to hold, requires an auxiliary assumption in addition to the condition that follows it. Uncovered interest parity requires not only closed (or covered) interest parity but also the condition that the exchange risk premium is zero. Real interest parity requires not only uncovered interest parity but also the condition that expected real depreciation is zero. The Feldstein-Horioka condition requires not only real interest parity but also a certain condition on the determinants of investment. But even though the relevance to the degree of integration of financial markets decreases as auxiliary conditions are added, the relevance to questions regarding the origin of international payments imbalances increases. We begin our consideration of the various criteria of capital mobility with the Feldstein-Horioka definition.

2.2 Feldstein-Horioka Tests

The Feldstein-Horioka definition requires that the country's real interest rate is tied to the world real interest rate by criterion 2. It is, after all, the real interest rate rather than the nominal on which saving and investment in theory depend. But for criterion 1 to hold, it is also necessary that any and all determinants of a country's rate of investment *other* than its real interest rate be uncorrelated with its rate of national saving. Let the investment rate for country i be given by

$$(I/Y)_i = a_i - br_i + u_i, \tag{1}$$

where I_i is the level of capital formation, Y_i is national output, r_i is the domestic real interest rate, and u_i represents all other factors, whether quantifiable or not, that determine the rate of investment. Feldstein and Horioka (1980) regressed the investment rate against the national saving rate,

$$(I/Y)_i = A + B(NS/Y)_i + v_i, \tag{1'}$$

where NS is private saving minus the budget deficit. To get the zero coefficient B that they were looking for requires not only real interest parity,

$$r_i - r^* = 0 \tag{2}$$

(with the world interest rate r^* exogenous or in any other way uncorrelated with $(NS/Y)_i$), but also a zero correlation between u_i and $(NS/Y)_i$.

The Saving-Investment Literature

Feldstein and Horioka's finding that the coefficient B is in fact closer to 1 than to 0 has been reproduced many times. Most authors have not been willing, however, to follow them in drawing the inference that financial markets are not highly integrated. There have been many econometric critiques, falling into two general categories.

More commonly made is the point that national saving is endogenous, or in our terms is correlated with u_i. This will be the case if national saving and investment are both procyclical, as they are in fact known to be, or if they both respond to the population or productivity growth rates.[5] It will also be the case if governments respond endogenously to incipient current account imbalances with policies to change public (or private) saving in such a way as to reduce the imbalances. This "policy reaction" argument has been made by Fieleke (1982), Tobin (1983), Westphal (1983), Caprio and Howard (1984), Summers (1988), Roubini (1988), and Bayoumi (1989). But Feldstein and Horioka made an effort to handle the econometric endogeneity of national saving, more so than have some of their critics. To handle the cyclical endogeneity, they computed averages over a long enough period of time that business cycles could be argued to wash out.[6] To handle other sources of endogeneity, they used demographic variables as instrumental variables for the saving rate.

The other econometric critique is that if the domestic country is large in world financial markets, r^* will not be exogenous with respect to $(NS/Y)_i$, and therefore even if $r = r^*$, r and in turn $(I/Y)_i$ will be correlated with $(NS/Y)_i$. In other words, a shortfall in domestic savings will drive up the world interest rate and thus crowd out investment in the domestic country as well as abroad. This "large-country" argument has been made by Murphy (1984) and Tobin (1983). An insufficiently appreciated point is that the large-country argument does not create a problem in cross-section studies, because all countries share the same world interest rate r^*. Since r^* simply goes into the constant term in a cross-section regression, it cannot be the source of any correlation with the right-hand-side variable. The large-country problem cannot explain why the countries that are high-saving relative to the average tend to coincide with the countries that are high-investing relative to the average.[7]

If the regressions of saving and investment rates were a good test for barriers to financial market integration, one would expect to see the coefficient falling over time. Until now, the evidence has, if anything, showed the coefficient rising over time rather than falling. This finding has emerged both from cross-section studies, which typically report pre-and post-1973 results—Feldstein (1983), Penati and Dooley (1984), and Dooley, Frankel, and Mathieson (1987)—and from pure time-series studies—Obstfeld (1986, 1989)[8] and Frankel (1986d) for the United States. The econometric endogeneity of national saving does not appear to be the explanation for this finding, because it holds equally well when instrumental variables are used.[9]

The easy explanation for the finding is that, econometric problems aside, real interest parity—criterion 2 above—has not held any better in recent years than it did in the past. Mishkin (1984a, p. 1352), for example, found even more significant rejections of real interest parity among major industrialized countries for the floating rate period after 1973/II than he did for his entire 1967/II–1979/II sample period. Caramazza et al. (1986, pp. 43–47) also found that some of the major industrialized countries in the 1980s (1980.1–1985.6) moved further from real interest parity than they had been in the 1970s (1973.7–1979.12).[10] In the early 1980s, the real interest rate in the United States, in particular, rose far above the real interest rate of its major trading partners, by any of a variety of measures.[11] If the domestic real interest rate is not tied to the foreign real interest rate, then there is no reason to expect a zero coefficient in the saving-investment regression. We discuss in a later section the factors underlying real interest differentials.

The U.S. Saving-Investment Regression Updated to the 1980s

In the 1980s the massive fiscal experiment carried out under the Reagan administration rapidly undermined the statistical finding of a high saving-

Table 2.1
The "Feldstein-Horioka coefficient" by decades: 1869–1987

	Constant	Coefficient	Time trend in coefficient	Durbin-Watson statistic	Auto-regressive parameter	R^2
1.	0.411 (1.340)	0.976 (.086)		1.45		0.96
2.	3.324 (1.842)	0.785 (.118)			0.46 (.33)	0.97
3.	3.291 (6.176)	0.854 (.279)	−0.011 (.21)	0.73		0.92
4.	1.061 (1.507)	0.924 (.093)	0.001 (.005)		0.03 (0.08)	0.96

Note: Instrumental variables regression of U.S. investment against national saving (as shares of GNP). Instrumental variables—dependency ratio and military expenditure/GNP.

investment correlation for the case of the United States. The increase in the structural budget deficit, which was neither accommodated by monetary policy nor financed by an increase in private saving, reduced the national saving rate by 3 percent of GNP, relative to the 1970s. The investment rate—which at first, like the saving rate, fell in the 1981–82 recession—in the late 1980s approximately reattained its 1980 level at best.[12] The saving shortfall was made up, necessarily, by a flood of borrowing from abroad equal to more than 3 percent of GNP—hence the current account deficit of $161 billion in 1987. (By contrast, the U.S. current account balance was on average equal to zero in the 1970s.)

By the late 1980s, the divergence between U.S. national saving and investment had been sufficiently large and long-lasting to show up in longer-term regressions of the Feldstein-Horioka type. If one seeks to isolate the degree of capital mobility or crowding out for the United States in particular, and how it has changed over time, then time-series regression is necessary (whereas if one is concerned with such measures worldwide, then cross-section regressions of the sort performed by Feldstein and Horioka are better). Table 2.1 reports, and figure 2.1 illustrates, instrumental variables regressions of investment against national saving for the United States from 1869 to 1987.[13] Decade averages are used for each variable, which removes some of the cyclical variation but gives us only twelve observations. That is one more observation than was available in Frankel (1986d, table 2.2), which went only through the 1970s.

As before, the coefficient is statistically greater than 0 and is not statistically different from 1, suggesting a high degree of crowding out (or a low

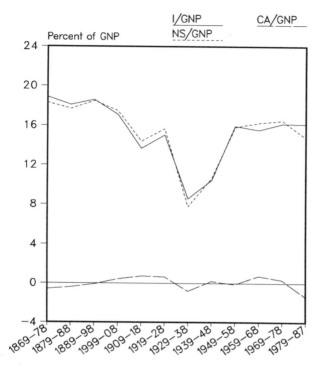

Figure 2.1
U.S. national saving (private saving plus government budget surplus), investment, and current account (ten-year averages)

degree of capital mobility, in Feldstein and Horioka's terms). But the point estimate of the coefficient (when corrected for possible serial correlation) drops from .91 in the earlier study to .79. We can allow for a time trend in the coefficient; it drops from *plus* .01 a year in the earlier study to *minus* .01 a year (or plus .001, when corrected for serial correlation) in the longer sample. Thus the additional years 1980–87 do show up as anticipated: as exhibiting a lower U.S. degree of crowding out, even if the change is small. The trend is not statistically significant, but this is not surprising given the small number of observations.

A data set that begins later would seem more promising than the twelve decade averages. Yearly data are available beginning in 1930.[14] But much of the variation in the yearly data is cyclical, and the preferred method for cyclical adjustment is not possible that early. So table 2.2 reports tests on saving and investment rates that have been cyclically adjusted for a sample

Table 2.2
The "Feldstein-Horioka coefficient" by years: 1955–1987

	Constant	Coefficient	Durbin-Watson statistic	Auto-regressive parameter	R^2
1955–79	−0.68	1.37	1.61		0.73
	(.17)	(.23)			
1956–79	−0.57	1.05		0.35	0.70
	(.18)	(.19)		(.20)	
1980–87	0.39	0.13	2.46		0.30
	(.36)	(.17)			
1981–87	0.58	0.22		−0.13	0.34
	(.37)	(.16)		(.41)	

Note: Instrumental variables regression of U.S. investment against national saving (as shares of GNP and cyclically adjusted).

period that begins in 1955, as illustrated in figure 2.2. The cyclical adjustment of each is accomplished by first regressing it on the GNP gap, defined as the percentage deviation from the Bureau of Economic Analysis's "middle expansion trend" of GNP, and taking the residuals.

In previous work with a sample period of 1956–84, the coefficient in a regression of cyclically adjusted saving and investment rates was estimated at .80, statistically indistinguishable from 1 (Frankel 1986d, pp. 43–44). But now the coefficient has dropped essentially to zero, suggesting a zero degree of crowding out, or a zero degree of "saving-retention" (or, in the Feldstein-Horioka terminology, "perfect capital mobility"). This finding is the result of the addition to the sample of another three years of record current account deficits, 1985–87, a period also in which the cyclically adjusted national saving rate was historically low. When the equation is estimated with an allowance for a time trend in the coefficient, the trend is negative (though statistically insignificant), whereas the earlier sample that stopped in 1984 showed a time trend that was positive (and insignificant).

To verify that the 1980s experience is indeed the source of the precipitous fall in the saving-investment coefficient,[15] the sample period is split at 1980. For the period 1955–79, not only is the coefficient statistically indistinguishable from 1, but the point estimate is slightly *over* 1.[16] It is clearly the unprecedented developments of the 1980s that overturned the previously robust saving-investment relationship for the case of the United States. It is likely that financial liberalization in Japan, the United Kingdom, and other countries and continued innovation in the Euromarkets (and

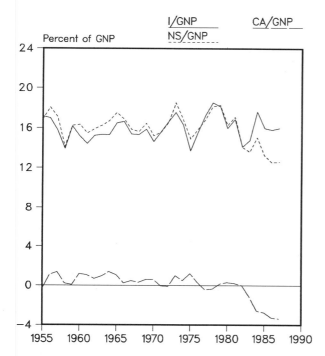

Figure 2.2
U.S. national saving, investment, and current account

perhaps the 1984 repeal of the U.S. withholding tax on borrowing from abroad) resulted in a higher degree of capital mobility, and thereby facilitated the record flow of capital to the United States in the 1980s. But the magnitude of the inflow was in the first instance attributable to the unprecedented magnitude of the decline in national saving.[17]

2.3   Differentials in Expected Rates of Return and Expected Real Depreciation

If the goal is to measure the degree of integration of capital markets rather than the degree to which decreases in national saving have crowded out investment, then it is better to look at differences in rates of return across countries rather than looking at saving-investment correlations.[18] But measuring *real* interest differentials will not do the trick. An international investor, when deciding what country's assets to buy, will not compare the interest rates in different countries, each expressed in terms of expected

purchasing power over that country's goods. When he or she thinks to
evaluate assets in terms of purchasing power, all assets will be evaluated in
terms of the same basket—the one consumed by that particular investor.
The expected inflation rate then drops out of differentials in expected rates
of return among assets.

The differential in expected rates of return on two countries' bonds is the
uncovered interest differential, the nominal interest differential minus the
expected change in the exchange rate: $i - i^* - (\Delta s^e)$. If asset demands are
highly sensitive to expected rates of return, then the differential will be
zero, which gives us uncovered interest parity:

$$i - i^* - (\Delta s^e) = 0. \tag{3}$$

To distinguish this parity condition, which is criterion 3 above, from the
other definitions, it has often been designated "perfect substitutability": not
only is there little in the manner of transactions costs or government-
imposed controls to separate national markets, but also domestic-currency
and foreign-currency bonds are perfect substitutes in investors' portfolios.

Just as criterion 1 is considerably stronger than criterion 2, so is criterion
2 considerably stronger than criterion 3. For real interest parity to hold,
one must have not only uncovered interest parity but an additional condition as well, which is sometimes called ex ante relative purchasing power
parity:

$$\Delta s^e = \Delta p^e - \Delta p^{e*}. \tag{2'}$$

Equations (2') and (3) together imply equation (2). If goods markets are
perfectly integrated, meaning not only that there is little in the manner of
transportation costs or government-imposed barriers to separate national
markets but also that domestic and foreign goods are perfect substitutes in
consumers' utility functions, then purchasing power parity holds. Purchasing power parity (PPP) in turn implies (2'). But as is by now well known,
goods markets are not in fact perfectly integrated. Because of the possibility of expected real depreciation, real interest parity can fail even if criterion 3 holds perfectly. The remainder of this section considers whether ex
ante relative PPP, equation (2'), holds.

The enormous real appreciation of the dollar in the early 1980s and subsequent real depreciation have by now convinced the remaining doubters,
but abundant statistical evidence against PPP was there all along. Krugman
(1978, p. 406), for example, computed for the floating rate period July
1973–December 1976 standard deviations of the (logarithmic) real exchange rate equal to 6.0 percent for the pound/dollar rate and 8.4 percent

for the mark/dollar rate. He also computed serial correlation coefficients for PPP deviations of .897 and .854, respectively, on a monthly basis, equal to .271 and .150 on an annual basis. The serial correlation coefficient is of interest because it is equal to one minus the speed of adjustment to PPP. It may be best not to rely exclusively on the standard deviation of the real exchange rate as a summary statistic for the degree of integration of goods markets, because it in part reflects the magnitude of monetary disturbances during the period.[19]

Consider a longer time span of annual data on the real exchange rate between the United States and Great Britain. (The statistics described here are reported in table 7.1 of this book, and the data are graphed in figure 7.2.) During the floating rate period 1973−87, though there is no significant time trend, there is a large standard error of 15.6 percent. The serial correlation in the deviations from PPP is estimated at .687, with a standard error of .208. This means that the estimated speed of adjustment to PPP is .313 per year and that one can easily reject the hypothesis of instantaneous adjustment.

From the ashes of absolute PPP, a phoenix has risen. In response to findings such as those reported here, some authors have swung from one extreme—the proposition that the tendency of the real exchange rate to return to a constant is complete and instantaneous—to the opposite extreme—that there is no such tendency at all. The hypothesis that the real exchange rate follows a random walk is just as good as the hypothesis of absolute PPP for implying ex ante relative PPP. But there is even less of an a priori case why PPP should hold in rate-of-change form than in the level form.

Although ex ante relative PPP has little basis in theory, it does appear to have some empirical support. Typically, the estimated speeds of adjustment during the floating rate period, .31 in table 7.1 (1973−87), while not so low as to be implausible as point estimates, are nevertheless so low that one statistically cannot reject the hypothesis that they are zero. In other words, one cannot reject the random-walk hypothesis that the autoregression coefficient is 1.0.

A 95 percent confidence interval on the autoregressive coefficient AR covers the range 0.27−1.10. If the null hypothesis is an autoregressive coefficient of 1.0, one cannot legitimately use the standard t-test derived from a regression where the right-hand-side variable is the level of the real exchange rate, because under the null hypothesis, the variance is infinite. There are a number of ways of dealing with this nonstationarity problem. Here one simply applies the corrected Dickey-Fuller 95 percent significance level, 3.00. The .31 estimate for the floating-rate period is insignificantly different from zero.

This failure to reject a random walk in the real exchange rate is the same result found by Roll (1979), Frenkel (1981a, p. 699), Adler and Lehman (1983), Darby (1981), Mishkin (1984a, pp. 1351–53), and Pigott and Sweeney (1985). Most of these studies used monthly data. On the one hand, the greater abundance of data reduces the standard error of the estimate, but, on the other hand, one is no longer testing whether $AR = .69$ is different from 1.0 but rather whether .97 ($= AR^{1/12}$) is different from 1.0, so that it may not be much easier to reject. Another problem is that one does not know that the nature of the true autoregressive process is truly first order on a monthly (or continuous-time) basis. In any case, the tests cited, using monthly data, were generally not powerful enough to reject the random walk.[20]

A more promising alternative is to choose a longer time sample to get a more powerful estimate. Table 7.1 also reports statistics for the entire postwar period 1945–87. PPP held better for the Bretton Woods years than it did after 1973, as measured either by the mean absolute deviation and standard deviation of the real exchange rate or by the ability to reject the hypothesis of zero autocorrelation. But despite the longer time sample, one is only at the borderline of being able to reject the random walk. The 95 percent confidence interval for AR runs from 0.64 to 1.02, and the t-ratio of 1.85 falls short of the Dickey-Fuller 95 percent significance level of 2.93.

The asymptotic standard error of an estimate of AR is approximately the square root of $(1 - AR^2)/N$. So if the true speed of adjustment is on the order of 30 percent a year ($AR = .7$), a simple calculation suggests that we might require at least forty-nine years of data ($2.93^2(1 - .7^2)/(1 - .7)^2 = 48.6$) to be able to reject the null hypothesis of $AR = 1$. It is not very surprising that forty-three years of data are not enough, much less the fifteen years of data used in most studies.[21] (Econometricians consider the asymptotic standard error on which this calculation is based to be a bad approximation in small samples. But the correct power calculation suggests that, if anything, the sample required to reject a random walk would be even larger than 49.[22])

The last column of table 7.1 presents statistics for 119 years of U.S.-U.K. data. With this long a time sample, the standard error is reduced considerably. The rejection of no serial correlation in the real exchange rate is even stronger than in the shorter time samples. More important, one is finally able to detect a statistically significant tendency for the real exchange rate to regress to PPP, at a rate of 16 percent a year. The confidence interval for AR runs from 0.75 to 0.94, safely less than unity, and the t-ratio of 3.12 exceeds the Dickey-Fuller significance level of 2.89.[23]

The motivation for looking at PPP in this section has been to obtain insight into the expected rate of real depreciation, because that is the variable that can give rise to real interest differentials even in the presence of uncovered interest parity.[24] In rejecting the random walk description of the real exchange rate, one has rejected the claim that the rationally expected rate of real depreciation is zero.[25] To take an example, in 1983–84, when the dollar had appreciated some 30 percent above its PPP value, survey data show expected future real depreciation of 4.3 percent per year. It is thus not difficult to explain the existence of the U.S. real interest differential, even without appealing to any sort of risk premium. There is not much support for authors such as Koraczyk (1985, p. 350) and Darby (1986, p. 420) ruling out the possibility of expected real depreciation a priori and thereby concluding that real interest differentials *necessarily* constitute risk premiums.

If the failure of ex ante relative purchasing power parity could, in itself, explain the failure of real interest parity, then it could also, by itself, explain the failure of saving and investment to be uncorrelated. In the 1980s U.S. context, a fall in national saving could cause an increase in the real interest differential and therefore a fall in investment, even if financial markets are perfectly integrated and even if the fall in saving is truly exogenous, provided the real interest differential is associated with expected real depreciation of the dollar.

Demonstrating that the failure of ex ante relative purchasing power parity is *capable* of producing a correlation between saving and investment is, of course, not the same as asserting that this in fact is the explanation for the observed correlation. There are plenty of other competing explanations that have been proposed. But some support for the idea that the existence of expected real depreciation *is* key to the observed correlation comes from Cardia (1988). She simulates saving and investment rates in a sequence of models featuring shocks to fiscal spending, money growth, and productivity, in order to see which models are capable, for empirically relevant magnitudes of the parameters, of producing saving-investment correlations as high as those observed. To get at some of the explanations that have been most prominently proposed, she constructs models both with and without purchasing power parity, both with and without endogenous response of fiscal policy to current account imbalances, and both with and without the small-country assumption. The finding is that the model that

allows for deviations from purchasing power parity is able to explain saving-investment correlations as high as one, while the various models that
impose purchasing power parity are generally unable to do so.[26]

Further empirical support for the idea that the Feldstein-Horioka results
may in fact be due to imperfect integration of goods markets, rather than
imperfect integration of financial markets, is provided by tests of saving
and investment rates across subregions that are known to be more integrated with each other than is the modern world economy. Bayoumi and
Rose (1992) look at correlations of saving and investment rates across
subregions within the United Kingdom. Sinn (1992) looks at correlations
across states within the United States (on 1950s data). Bayoumi and Sterne
(1992) do the same for provinces within Canada (for 1961–90). In every
case, the finding is no positive correlation. These regions are known to
share a common currency and to be highly integrated with respect to their
goods markets, suggesting that exchange rate variability or other sources
of imperfect integration of goods markets may be the source of high saving-investment correlations across countries (although this is not necessarily the authors' interpretations of their own results).

2.4   A Decomposition of Real Interest Differentials for Twenty-five Countries

Because there are so many competing definitions of the degree of international capital mobility, it would be worth knowing if the sort of countries
that register high by one criterion are also the sort that register high by the
others. In this section we look at rates of return in the 1980s across a
sample of twenty-five countries. We begin with the broadest measure of
barriers to international capital mobility, the differential in real interest
rates, defined as:

$$r - r^* = (i - \Delta p^e) - (i^* - \Delta p^{e*}). \tag{4}$$

Subsequently we will decompose the real interest differential into a
component due to "political" or country factors and a component due to
currency factors:

$$r - r^* = (i - i^* - fd) - (fd - \Delta p^e + \Delta p^{e*}), \tag{5}$$

where i is the domestic nominal interest rate, i^* is the foreign nominal
interest rate, and fd is the forward discount on the domestic currency. The
first term $(i - i^* - fd)$ is the covered interest differential. We call it the
political or country premium because it captures all barriers to integration

of financial markets across national boundaries: transactions costs, information costs, capital controls, tax laws that discriminate by country of residence, default risk, and risk of future capital controls. The second term
could be described as the real forward discount. We call it the currency
premium because it captures differences in assets according to the currency
in which they are denominated rather than in terms of the political jurisdiction in which they are issued. As we will see, the currency premium can
in turn be decomposed into two factors, the exchange risk premium and
expected real depreciation.

The decomposition of the real interest differential would not be possible
without the use of data on forward exchange rates. Many previous studies
have used forward rate data to test covered interest parity but only for a
few countries. This study uses forward rate data for a panel of twenty-five
countries, which so far as I know is the largest set ever examined. The set
of twenty-five includes countries both large and small, industrialized and
developing, Atlantic and Pacific. The forward rate data for most of the
countries come from Barclay's Bank in London, via Data Resources, Inc.[27]

Real Interest Differentials

Table 2.3 reports statistics on three-month real interest differentials for the
twenty-five countries, in each case expressed as the local interest rate
measured relative to the Eurodollar interest rate. For local interest rates we
use the interbank market rate or, where no market rate exists, the most
flexibly determined interest rate available.[28] We use, to begin with, the
realized inflation rates during the ex post three-month period. Column (1)
reports the mean real interest differential during the sample period, September 1982 to January 1988. (In this and subsequent tables, because the ex
post data run three months behind the ex ante expectations, they go up to
April 1988.) The numbers are negative for a majority of countries, averaging -1.74 across all twenty-five, which reflects the high level of real
dollar interest rates during this period.

The countries are classified into five groups chosen on a priori grounds.
The group with real interest rates the furthest below the world rate is
Bahrain, Greece, Mexico, Portugal, and South Africa. These five (very di-
verse) countries bear the burden of representing a wide class of LDCs in
our sample. Altogether there are eight countries classified as LDCs that
happen to have forward rate data available and thereby appear in our
sample; three of these are East Asian countries that are thought to have

Table 2.3
Real interest differentials, September 1982 to January 1988

	No. of observ.	Mean	Stan- dard error	Series standard deviation	Root mean squared error	95% band
Open Atlantic DCs						
Canada	63	0.09	0.38	2.09	2.09	3.96
Germany	63	−1.29	0.65	2.77	3.06	5.95
Netherlands	62	−0.71	0.86	3.91	3.97	7.63
Switzerland	62	−2.72	0.81	3.39	4.36	8.43
United Kingdom	63	0.46	0.79	3.45	3.48	5.69
Group	313	−0.83	0.66	3.16	3.46	
Liberalizing Pacific						
Hong Kong	62	−2.89	0.94	4.80	5.62	11.61
Malaysia	62	0.83	1.00	4.61	4.68	8.19
Singapore	61	0.08	0.68	3.33	3.34	6.71
Group	185	−0.67	0.82	4.28	4.62	
Closed LDCs						
Bahrain	60	2.19	1.46	7.10	7.44	12.93
Greece	56	−9.22	1.91	9.36	13.19	21.77
Mexico	62	−20.28	9.43	21.19	29.45	52.13
Portugal	61	−3.90	2.97	11.28	11.95	23.62
South Africa	61	−4.84	1.17	4.85	6.88	11.16
Group	300	−7.25	1.30	12.16	16.06	
Closed European DCs						
Austria	64	−2.20	0.83	3.84	4.43	7.32
Belgium	63	0.53	0.68	2.90	2.95	4.99
Denmark	61	−3.42	0.90	4.34	5.54	9.64
France	64	−0.48	0.72	2.94	2.98	5.54
Ireland	61	1.53	1.03	3.95	4.24	7.13
Italy	61	1.01	0.86	3.62	3.76	5.83
Norway	50	−0.64	0.84	3.23	3.29	6.83
Spain	63	0.53	1.44	5.92	5.95	11.90
Sweden	63	−0.21	1.07	4.52	4.53	8.28
Group	550	−0.37	0.81	4.00	4.29	
Liberalizing Pacific DCs						
Australia	60	1.16	0.90	3.69	3.87	7.43
Japan	63	−0.58	0.62	3.41	3.46	6.03
New Zealand	60	1.04	1.83	7.15	7.23	11.36
Group	183	0.52	0.73	5.00	5.09	
All Countries	1531	−1.74		6.47	8.07	

Note: Interest differential less realized inflation differential (local minus Eurodollar; 3-month rates).

open financial markets in the 1980s (Hong Kong, Singapore, and Malaysia) and so are here classified separately.

One might object that the large negative real interest differentials in the group of five reflect administered local interest rates that are kept artificially low by "financial repression." But countries cannot maintain artificially low interest rates without barriers to capital outflow. These statistics reflect a low degree of capital mobility precisely as we want them to. In this respect, our group of five is typical of LDCs. A number of studies, including much larger LDC samples than available here, have shown the extremes to which real interest rates can go, particularly some very negative levels in the 1970s.

As with the other measures of interest rate differentials that we will be considering below, the mean is not always the most useful statistic. A small mean over a particular sample period may hide fluctuations in both directions. Even if a mean is statistically significant,[29] it is useful to know in addition the variability of the differential. The standard deviation is reported in column (2). We also report the root-mean-squared error in column (3). This would be a superior measure of how closely the rates are tied together if, for example, we are worried about the possibility of a large differential that is fairly constant over time because of government administration of interest rates. Finally we report in column (4) how big a band would be needed to encompass 95 percent of the deviations from real interest parity.

Country-group comparisons of the measures of real interest differential variability in some respects suit a priori expectations: the five closed LDCs constitute the group with the highest variability and the five open Atlantic countries the group with the lowest.[30] But there are some results that are anomalous if the real interest differential is taken as a measure of financial market integration. France, for example, had stringent capital controls in place during our sample period (at least until the latter part) and yet appears to have a *higher* degree of capital mobility by the criterion of real interest differential variability than Japan, which announced liberalization of its capital controls before our sample period (1979–80). One might conceivably argue that the Japanese liberalization must not have been genuine. But the French real interest differential is smaller and less variable even than those of the Netherlands and Switzerland, major countries that are known to be virtually free of capital controls. Only Canada shows a smaller and less variable real interest differential than France.

Because the realized inflation rates could not have been precisely known a priori, it is necessary to project them onto contemporaneously known variables. Three such variables were used: the forward discount, nominal interest differential, and lagged inflation differential.[31] In a majority of cases, a statistically significant amount of the variation in the real interest differential turned out to be forecastable.[32] The standard deviation of the projected differential gives us our final measure of variability. The results for the ex ante real interest differential are mostly similar to those for the ex post. France, for example, still shows a lower degree of variability than the Netherlands.

Covered Interest Differentials: The Country Premium

We now use the Barclay's forward rate data to decompose the real interest differential into one part due to country factors and another due to currency factors, as in equation (5). The first component, the covered interest differential, encompasses all factors related to the political jurisdiction in which the asset is issued. Its size and variability measures barriers to international capital mobility most narrowly and properly defined.

Column (1) of table 2.4 reports the mean of the covered interest differential for each of our twenty-five countries. A good rule of thumb, when the absolute magnitude of the mean or the variability of the differential indicates the existence of significant barriers, is as follows: a negative differential vis-à-vis the Eurocurrency market indicates that, to the extent that barriers exist, they are capital controls or transactions costs currently operating to discourage capital from flowing out of the country. Investors would not settle for a lower return domestically if they were free to earn abroad the higher return covered to eliminate exchange risk. This is the case for all the LDCs in the sample, with the exception of Hong Kong, and for all of the traditionally "closed" European countries, with the exceptions of Austria and Belgium (which should by now probably be classified with the "open" countries). The negative differential that existed for the United Kingdom before Margaret Thatcher removed capital controls in 1979 is now extremely small, as shown in figure 2.3.[33] Similarly, Canada's differential is effectively zero.[34]

Column (4), the size of the band wide enough to encompass 95 percent of deviations from international covered interest parity, can be compared with the approach of Frenkel and Levich (1977). They tested a larger band meant to represent transactions costs between pound and dollar securities. They found, for the case of the United Kingdom, that a smaller percentage of deviations (87.6–89.7 percent, p. 1217) fell within the band. This confirms that capital mobility has increased since the 1970s.

Table 2.4
"Country premia" or covered interest differentials, September 1982 to April 1988

	No. of observ.	Mean	Standard error	Series standard deviation	Root mean squared error	95% band
Open Atlantic DCs						
Canada	68	−0.10	0.03	0.21	0.24	0.44
Germany	68	0.35	0.03	0.24	0.42	0.75
Netherlands	68	0.21	0.02	0.13	0.25	0.45
Switzerland	68	0.42	0.03	0.23	0.48	0.79
United Kingdom	68	−0.14	0.02	0.20	0.25	0.41
Group	340	0.14	0.01	0.21	0.34	
Liberalizing Pacific						
Hong Kong	68	0.13	0.03	0.28	0.31	0.60
Malaysia	63	−1.46	0.16	1.28	1.95	3.73
Singapore	64	−0.30	0.04	0.31	0.43	0.73
Group	195	−0.52	0.05	0.76	1.14	
Closed LDCs						
Bahrain	64	−2.15	0.13	1.06	2.41	4.17
Greece	58	−9.39	0.80	6.08	11.26	20.39
Mexico	43	−16.47	1.83	12.01	20.54	28.86
Portugal	61	−7.93	1.23	9.59	12.49	27.83
South Africa	67	−1.07	1.17	9.55	9.61	2.68
Group	293	−6.64	0.48	8.23	11.82	
Closed European DCs						
Austria	65	0.13	0.05	0.39	0.41	0.39
Belgium	68	0.12	0.03	0.26	0.29	0.59
Denmark	68	−3.53	0.19	1.57	3.89	6.63
France	68	−1.74	0.32	2.68	3.20	7.18
Ireland	66	−0.79	0.51	4.17	4.24	7.80
Italy	68	−0.40	0.23	1.92	1.96	4.11
Norway	50	−1.03	0.11	0.76	1.29	2.10
Spain	67	−2.40	0.45	3.66	4.39	7.95
Sweden	68	−0.23	0.06	0.45	0.51	0.81
Group	588	−1.10	0.09	2.25	2.77	
Liberalizing Pacific DCs						
Australia	68	−0.75	0.23	1.94	2.08	2.59
Japan	68	0.09	0.03	0.21	0.23	0.43
New Zealand	68	−1.63	0.29	2.42	2.92	5.24
Group	204	−0.76	0.12	1.78	2.06	
All Countries	1620	−1.73	0.09	3.81	5.36	

Note: Interest differential less forward discount (local minus Eurodollar; 3-month rates).

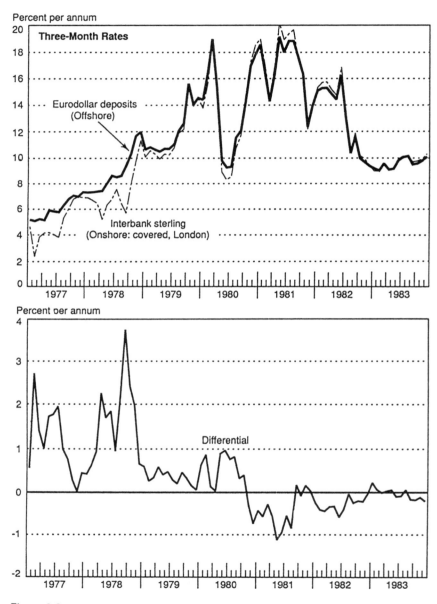

Figure 2.3
Financial liberalization in the United Kingdom: U.K. and Eurodollar interest rates. Note: Data are monthly averages of weekly (Wednesday) observations. Covered interbank sterling rate is calculated using three-month forward premium on sterling-dollar exchange rate. Positive values in lower panel of chart indicate a differential in favor of offshore asset.

Germany and several other neighboring European countries (Switzer-land, the Netherlands, Austria, and Belgium) show higher interest rates locally than offshore, which suggests some barriers discouraging capital *inflow*: investors would not settle for a lower mark return in the Euromarket if they were free to get the higher return in Germany. But the magnitude is quite small, as it has been observed to be ever since Germany removed most of its controls on capital inflow in 1974. Figure 2.4 shows the evidence of the 1974 liberalization (see also Dooley and Isard, 1980; Giavazzi and Pagano, 1985, p. 27).

Japan has a covered differential that by all measures is smaller and less variable than those of Switzerland and Germany, let alone France and most of the other countries. This might come as a surprise to those accustomed to thinking of Japanese financial markets in terms of the large barriers to capital inflow that were in place in the 1970s. The liberalization of Japanese markets, which has been documented elsewhere, continued during our sample period.[35] (See figure 2.5.) Australia and New Zealand, while lagging well behind Japan, also showed signs of liberalization during the course of our sample period.[36]

The covered interest differential for France is much larger and more variable than that for the other major industrialized countries known to be free of capital controls. This is the reverse of the finding from the criterion of real interest differentials in table 2.3. It supports the value of the criterion of covered interest differentials as the proper test of financial market integration. The differential, with its negative sign signifying controls on French capital outflows, has been previously studied, especially its tendency to shoot up shortly before devaluations of the franc.[37] Our data indicate that the last major occurrence of this phenomenon was February 1986; since then, the differential has been close to zero.

Similarly, the same phenomenon for Italy, which has also been previously studied (e.g., Giavazzi and Pagano, 1985), appears to have ended after the February 1986 realignment. France and Italy apparently dismantled their capital controls quickly enough to meet a 1990 deadline for liberalization set by the EEC Twelve.[38] Of four countries that required a later deadline, Spain and Portugal by our measures began liberalizing in the 1980s,[39] but Greece and Ireland did not. Sweden is one non-EC European country that appears to have moved toward liberalization during our sample period, while Norway does not. All of these European countries show up with negative mean differentials, which implies that the remaining controls act to discourage capital outflow rather than inflow. For the EEC coun-

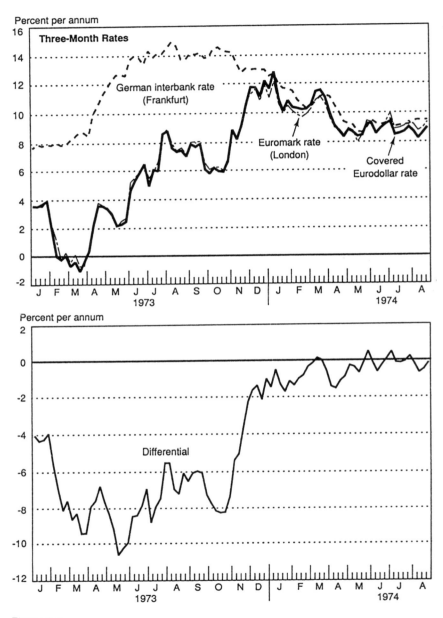

Figure 2.4
Financial liberalization in Germany: German and Eurocurrency interest rates. Note: Data are
Wednesday quotations. Covered Eurodollar rate is calculated using three-month forward
premium for mark–dollar exchange rate. Positive values in lower panel of chart indicate a
differential in favor of offshore asset.

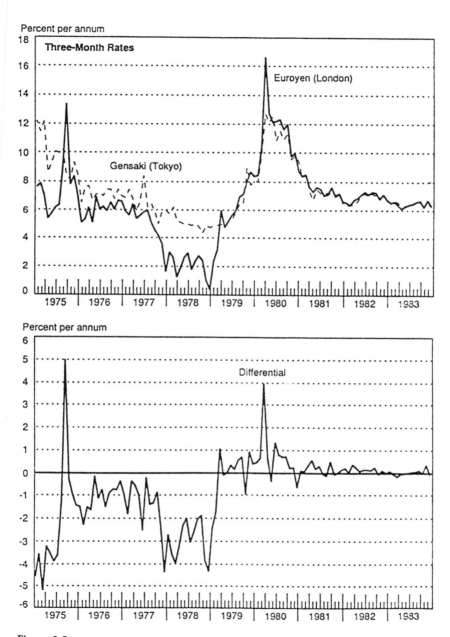

Figure 2.5
Financial liberalization in Japan: Japanese and Euroyen interest rates. Note: Data are month-end figures. Positive values in lower panel of chart indicate a differential in favor of offshore asset.

tries, this finding supports records of the European Commission, which report more freedom for short-term inflows than short-term outflows.[40]

Registering impressively open financial markets are our three East Asian LDCs (which, especially in the case of Singapore, have rapidly outgrown the appellation "less developed"). Hong Kong and Singapore show smaller covered differentials even than some open European countries like Germany. Malaysia's differential has been considerably higher, particularly in 1986, but still compares favorably with some European countries.

Not surprisingly, our remaining LDCs (Mexico, Greece, Portugal, Bahrain, and South Africa) show by far the largest and most variable covered interest differentials.[41] Again, the results are precisely what one would expect if covered interest differentials are the proper criterion for capital mobility but the reverse of what the saving-investment criterion shows.

Why does the covered differential criterion give such different answers from the saving-investment criterion, which shows a high degree of saving-retention among industrialized countries? Feldstein and Horioka (1980, p. 315) argue that financial markets are less well integrated at longer-term maturities, as compared to the three-month maturities used in tests of covered interest parity such as those reported above:

It is clear from the yields on short-term securities in the Eurocurrency market and the forward prices of those currencies that liquid financial capital moves very rapidly to arbitrage such short-term differentials.... There are however reasons to be skeptical about the extent of such long-term arbitrage.

Studies of international interest parity have been restricted by a lack of forward exchange rates at horizons going out much further than one year.[42] But even without the use of forward rate data, there are ways of getting around the problem of exchange risk. Data on currency swap rates can be used in place of forward exchange rates to test the long-term version of interest rate parity. Popper (1990) finds that the swap-covered return differential on five-year U.S. government bonds versus Japanese bonds averaged only 1.7 basis points from October 3, 1985, to July 10, 1986, and that the differential on seven-year bonds averaged only 5.3 basis points. The means mask some variation in the differential. But a band of forty-six basis points is large enough to encompass 95 percent of the observations for the five-year bonds. The band is thirty-four basis points for the seven-year bonds. The means on five-year bonds for some other major countries are as follows: Canada 15.9, Switzerland 18.7, United Kingdom 51.1, and Germany 28.4.

The magnitude of these long-term differentials compares favorably with the magnitude of the short-term differentials. The implication is that Feldstein and Horioka are wrong in their conjecture that there is a term-structure wedge separating national capital markets.[43] The most relevant distinction appears to be not long term versus short term but rather real versus nominal.

"Real Forward Discounts": The Currency Premium

Even for those countries that exhibit no substantial country premium, as reflected in covered interest parity $[fd - (i - i^*) = 0]$, there may still be a substantial currency premium that drives real interest differentials $[(i - \Delta p^e) - (i^* - \Delta p^{e*})]$ away from zero. If real interest differentials are not arbitraged to zero, then there is in turn no reason to expect saving-investment correlations to be zero. Table 2.5 reports the statistics for the currency premium, as measured by the "real forward discount":

$$fd - (\Delta p^e - \Delta p^{e*}).$$

Germany, Switzerland, the Netherlands, Austria, and Japan, for example, all have substantial real forward discounts (or—more precisely—real forward premia), which constitute approximately the entirety of their real interest differentials. These are countries with currencies that have experienced a lot of exchange rate variability, both nominal and real, vis-à-vis the dollar since 1973, and especially since 1980. As a consequence, some combination of exchange risk premiums and expected real depreciation—factors pertaining to the currency, not to the political jurisdiction—produces the gap in real interest rates. For these five financially open industrialized countries, and for Hong Kong as well, the currency factors produce a *negative* real interest differential, while the covered interest differential (though small) is *positive*: the small regulations or frictions that remain in these countries are, if anything, working to resist capital inflow (at least at the short end of the maturity spectrum), not outflow as one would mistakenly conclude from the real interest differential criterion. The other countries all have highly variable currency premiums as well. Indeed the real forward discount (currency premium) is more variable than the covered interest differential (country premium) for all but three of our twenty-five countries (Greece, Mexico, and France). The last rows of tables 2.4 and 2.5 show that the average variability across all countries is higher for the currency premium than for the country premium.

Table 2.5
"Currency premia" or real forward discounts, September 1982 to January 1988

	No. of observ.	Mean	Standard error	Series standard deviation	Root mean squared error	95% band
Open Atlantic DCs						
Canada	63	0.18	0.38	2.08	2.09	4.02
Germany	63	−1.66	0.69	2.89	3.34	6.57
Netherlands	62	−0.92	0.88	3.98	4.09	7.52
Switzerland	62	−3.15	0.84	3.49	4.72	8.79
United Kingdom	63	0.61	0.83	3.56	3.61	5.97
Group	313	−0.98	0.69	3.24	3.65	
Liberalizing Pacific						
Hong Kong	62	−2.99	0.93	4.79	5.66	11.76
Malaysia	62	2.29	1.14	5.06	5.56	10.17
Singapore	62	0.40	0.67	0.32	3.35	6.86
Group	186	−0.10	0.82	4.43	4.95	
Closed LDCs						
Bahrain	60	4.37	1.52	7.27	8.51	16.18
Greece	60	0.83	1.67	9.98	10.01	18.77
Mexico	43	0.03	3.58	15.23	15.23	22.08
Portugal	59	4.94	2.13	11.73	12.74	21.56
South Africa	62	−3.82	1.81	11.36	11.99	14.75
Group	284	1.29	1.37	11.05	11.60	
Closed European DCs						
Austria	62	−2.25	0.88	3.94	4.55	7.68
Belgium	63	0.42	0.69	2.95	2.98	5.05
Denmark	61	0.14	1.01	4.63	4.63	7.13
France	64	1.35	0.54	2.50	2.85	4.82
Ireland	59	2.14	1.40	6.41	6.76	13.85
Italy	61	1.42	0.72	3.15	3.46	5.52
Norway	64	1.07	0.75	3.25	3.43	5.91
Spain	63	3.12	1.26	5.53	6.36	11.08
Sweden	63	0.04	1.07	4.57	4.57	8.29
Group	560	0.83	0.67	4.23	4.54	
Liberalizing Pacific DCs						
Australia	60	1.97	0.88	4.06	4.52	7.85
Japan	63	−0.69	0.64	3.48	3.55	6.32
New Zealand	60	2.82	1.98	7.96	8.46	14.11
Group	183	1.33	0.79	5.48	5.84	
All Countries	1526	0.49		6.11	6.50	

Note: Forward discount less realized inflation differential.

We can project the real forward discount on the same three variables as we did for the real interest differential (the forward discount, nominal interest differential, and lagged inflation differential) to get an ex ante measure.[44] Its standard deviation now shows six countries for which the currency premium is less variable than the country premium (Greece, Mexico, Portugal, France, Italy, and Spain). But the currency premium remains the major obstacle to real interest parity for most countries.

Further Decomposition into Exchange Risk Premium and Expected Real Depreciation

Our decomposition so far has lumped two terms, the exchange risk premium and expected real depreciation, together into the currency premium:

$$fd - \Delta p^e + \Delta p^{e*} = (fd - \Delta s^e) + (\Delta s^e - \Delta p^e + \Delta p^{e*}).$$

In this section we attempt to complete the decomposition by separating these two terms. To do so requires a measure or model of expected depreciation. The usual approach is to use the ex post changes in the spot rate (Δs) as a measure of ex ante expectations (Δs^e) and to argue that under rational expectations the expectational error ($e \equiv \Delta s - \Delta s^e$) should be random (uncorrelated with information currently available contemporaneously).

We can compute the mean value of ($fd - \Delta s$) for each of our countries.[45] Most of the means are positive, showing that the weak-dollar period (1985–88) dominates over the strong-dollar period (1982–85).[46] But only three currencies have mean risk premiums, of either sign, that are statistically significant.[47] Furthermore, in a majority of cases of twenty-five, the sign of the mean return differential is the *opposite* of the sign of the mean real interest differential during the same period (table 2.3, column 1). So this measure of the exchange risk premium does not explain any positive part of the real interest differential.

Measures such as the standard deviation, root-mean-squared-error, and 95 percent band, show very high variability in ($fd - \Delta s$). These are measures of the variability of ex post return differentials, not ex ante. They tell us little about the variability of the exchange risk premium. But the high variability of the exchange rate does tell us two things. First, it provides an obvious explanation—low power—why the first moments might not be statistically significant. On the other hand, the existence of substantial uncertainty regarding the future spot rate suggests, via the theory of optimal portfolio diversification, that a nonzero exchange risk premium may exist, to reward risk-averse investors for holding currencies that are perceived as risky or are in oversupply.

To estimate the ex ante exchange risk premium, we can project ($fd -$ $depr$) onto our same three variables: the forward discount, interest differential, and inflation differential.[48] The regression is statistically significant for a majority of currencies, as many others have found.[49] The standard deviation shows the most variable exchange risk premiums belong to Mexico and New Zealand, but the United Kingdom, Netherlands, Austria, Germany, and Switzerland follow close behind.

The other component of the currency premium is expected real depreciation. As noted earlier, given the widely accepted failure of purchasing power parity on levels, there is no theoretical reason to expect it necessarily to hold in terms of expected rates of change—the hypothesis sometimes known as ex ante relative purchasing power parity. The means of ex post real depreciation are negative, indicating real appreciation of the currency against the dollar, for all European countries and for most others as well. The only five exceptions, countries that experienced real depreciation against the dollar, were our three East Asian developing countries, Australia, and Bahrain. This last was the only one, of either sign, that was statistically significant.[50]

We already know, from the results reported above for the 119 years of U.S.-U.K. data, that we cannot expect to reject ex ante relative PPP on just a few years of data; new disturbances to the real exchange rate are so large that one needs a much longer time sample to find evidence of systematic movement. But the signs of the mean real depreciations are usually the same as the signs of the mean real interest differentials in table 2.3 (twenty of twenty-five), suggesting a high correlation of the real interest differential and expected real depreciation across countries.

To estimate ex ante expected real depreciation, we project ex post real depreciation, again, on the same three contemporaneous variables.[51] The standard deviations for the various currencies are quite similar to those for the projected exchange risk premium.[52] In most cases (eighteen of twenty-five), the projected exchange risk premium is slightly more variable than projected real depreciation.

2.5   Conclusion

We can sum up with four conclusions.

1. Capital controls and other barriers to the movement of capital across national borders remained for such countries as the United Kingdom and

Japan as recently as 1979 and France and Italy as recently as 1986. But a continuing worldwide trend of integration of financial markets in the 1980s had all but eliminated short-term interest differentials for major industrialized countries by 1988.

2. Only the *country premium* has been eliminated; this means that only *covered* interest differentials are small. Real and nominal exchange rate variability remain, and indeed were larger in the 1980s than in the 1970s.[53] The result is that a *currency premium* remains, consisting of an exchange risk premium plus expected real currency depreciation. This means that even with the equalization of covered interest rates, large differentials in *real* interest rates remain.

3. The United States in the 1980s began to borrow on such a massive scale internationally that the traditional "Feldstein-Horioka" finding of a near-unit correlation between national saving and investment has broken down. The process of liberalization in Japan and other major countries was probably one factor behind this massive flow of capital to the United States.

4. In addition to the gaps that distinguish covered interest parity from real interest parity, there is a further gap that separates real interest parity from the proposition that changes in national saving do not crowd out investment because they are readily financed by borrowing from abroad. Bonds are not perfect substitutes for equities, and equities are not perfect substitutes for plant and equipment. Thus, at each stage, there are good reasons to think that it continues to be possible for shortfalls in national saving to crowd out investment, even if to a smaller extent than before 1980.

II

**The Determination
of Exchange Rate
Movements**

Introduction to Part II

The five chapters in part II represent, to my mind, five phases of exchange rate modeling within the celebrated "asset-market approach to exchange rates."

1. In the mid-1970s, economists began excitedly constructing models of exchange rate determination within the new approach and busily trying them out econometrically to see if they fit the post-1973 data. The most popular class of such models at the time, at least from the vantage point of MIT (as well as the University of Chicago), were the monetary models. The Dornbusch overshooting model was certainly the most important single contribution to the field. My "On the Mark" (chapter 3) specified a variety of the Dornbusch model—an attempt to integrate it with the model of those at Chicago focusing on the role of steady-state inflation—and found a relatively good fit with the mark/dollar data of 1974−77. In the years to follow, we were all to discover just how rare such goodness of fit and statistical significance were.

2. During the late 1970s there was an attempt to take stock of the proliferating variety of models. The portfolio-balance models, which had earlier been developed by economists at Yale, Princeton, and the Federal Reserve Board (among others), seemed a promising way of explaining the 1977−78 depreciation of the dollar, which was giving the empirical monetary models trouble. "Monetary and Portfolio-Balance Models of Exchange Rate Determination" surveyed the field. A successor paper, which has here been spliced together with the first to make up chapter 4, tested the various models out on a data set of five exchange rates. None of the models, including a proposed synthesis of the monetary and portfolio-balance models, performed well.

Others were finding similarly poor results. The field entered a period of deep pessimism regarding the performance of models of exchange rate determination, epitomized by the work of Meese and Rogoff. "Findings that the exchange rate follows a random walk," that is, statistical failures to reject the random walk hypothesis, abounded. Econometricians were humbled.

At this point a researcher could go in either of two directions. One could develop new theories that were sufficiently disconnected from the data that they could not be tested empirically, and therefore could not be rejected. Or one could take the random walk as the new appropriately humbling benchmark and try to find something useful that existing theory had to say in at least some circumstances. An epilogue to chapter 4 summarizes my views on this central question of where to go after the random walk results.

3. In the early 1980s, some of the predictions of the overshooting model were borne out. The sharp U.S. monetary contraction of 1980–82 produced a sharp nominal and real appreciation of the dollar (not to mention a recession). Chapter 5, "Why Interest Rates React to Money Announcements: An Explanation from the Foreign Exchange Market" (with Charles Engel), deals with the phenomenon of weekly money supply announcements and the reactions of the financial markets. Such "news studies" or "event studies" are a fertile proving ground for econometric tests. The work finds evidence in favor of the overshooting model, as well as evidence that the Federal Reserve was credibly committed to its announced policy of fixed money supply targets during the period 1980–82. A successor paper confirms that this Federal Reserve credibility did not exist before October 1979.[1]

4. The period 1983–84 saw a continuation of the pattern of a strong dollar together with real interest rates that were higher in the United States than among major trading partners. But unlike 1981–82, this was a period of strong growth, widely attributed to the Reagan fiscal expansion. At the time, I was working for Martin Feldstein at the Council of Economic Advisers, who was sounding early warnings about the dangers of the large federal budget deficit. But while others were becoming increasingly alarmed at the pattern of capital inflow, appreciating dollar, and deteriorating trade balance, Feldstein believed that these were only symptoms of the underlying problem—that the strong dollar was actually a good thing provided one took the existing stance of fiscal and monetary policy as given. This tied in neatly with an idea I had been developing about the desirability of balancing "crowding out" equally between traded and nontraded goods. Section 6.6 of "Six Possible Meanings of 'Overvaluation': The 1981–85 Dollar" (originally written in 1984, chapter 6 here) explains this idea, after having reviewed recent empirical research in exchange rate economics.

5. Meanwhile, "random walkism" was continuing to spread. Particularly devastating for those who still dared hope for explanatory power in the models based on macroeconomic fundamentals was the last phase of dollar appreciation, from mid-1984 to February 1985. (See figure 15.1 for an illustration of how far the behavior of the real exchange rate during this period deviated from what one would expect based on the real interest differential.) Increasingly the choice seemed to come down to two broad alternatives: (1) unspecified and unobservable changes in "tastes and technologies" or (2) speculative bubbles. The former alternative was favored by the random walkers and "equilibrium theorists." My diatribe on this subject

is represented here (chapter 7) by "Zen and the Art of Modern Macro-economics: The Search for Perfect Nothingness" (which continues, from the third section of chapter 2, my views on expected real depreciation). The subject of this critique is Alan Stockman (1990), for no reason other than that he had the misfortune to have me as a conference discussant, when I was looking for an opportunity to vent my views on this school of thought.

The speculative bubble alternative, at the time, was considered synony-mous with the theory of *rational* speculative bubbles. The major problem with this theory is that it has nothing to say about what gets speculative bubbles started, or how they end. In March 1985 (which, ironically, turned out to be the peak of the dollar) I had made an argument against the idea that the appreciation of the dollar that had occurred since 1981 could be a rational speculative bubble.[2] This argument appears here as the appendix to chapter 6. We were not yet ready to consider the possibility of specula-tive bubbles that did *not* fully obey the rules of rational expectations. They are pursued here, however, in chapters 14 and 15.

3

On the Mark: A Theory
of Floating Exchange
Rates Based on Real
Interest Differentials

Much of the recent work on floating exchange rates goes under the name of the "monetary" or "asset" view; the exchange rate is viewed as moving to equilibrate the international demand for stocks of money, rather than the international demand for flows of goods as under the more traditional view. But within the monetary approach there are two very different models. These models have conflicting implications in particular for the relationship between the exchange rate and the interest rate.

The first model might be called the "Chicago" theory because it assumes that prices are perfectly flexible.[1] As a consequence of the flexible-price assumption, changes in the nominal interest rate reflect changes in the expected inflation rate. When the domestic interest rate rises relative to the foreign interest rate, it is because the domestic currency is expected to lose value through inflation and depreciation. Demand for the domestic currency falls relative to the foreign currency, which causes it to depreciate instantly. This is a rise in the exchange rate, defined as the price of foreign currency. Thus we get a positive relationship between the exchange rate and the nominal interest differential.

The second model might be called the "Keynesian" theory because it assumes that prices are sticky, at least in the short run. The most elegant asset-view statement of the Keynesian model is by Rudiger Dornbusch (1976b), to which this chapter owes much.[2] As a consequence of the sticky-price assumption, changes in the nominal interest rate reflect changes in the tightness of monetary policy. When the domestic interest rate rises relative to the foreign rate it is because there has been a contraction in the domestic money supply relative to domestic money demand without a matching fall in prices. The higher interest rate at home than abroad attracts a capital inflow, which causes the domestic currency to appreciate instantly. Thus we get a *negative* relationship between the exchange rate and the nominal interest differential.

The Chicago theory is a realistic description when variation in the inflation differential is large, as in the German hyperinflation of the 1920s to which Frenkel first applied it. The Keynesian theory is a realistic description when variation in the inflation differential is small, as in the Canadian float against the United States in the 1950s to which Mundell first applied it. The problem is to develop a model that is a realistic description when variation in the inflation differential is moderate, as it was among the major industrialized countries in the 1970s.

This chapter develops a model which is a version of the monetary approach to the exchange rate, in that it emphasizes the role of expectations and rapid adjustment in capital markets. The innovation is that it combines the Keynesian assumption of sticky prices with the Chicago assumption that there are secular rates of inflation. It then turns out that the exchange rate is *negatively* related to the nominal interest differential, but *positively* related to the expected long-run inflation differential. The exchange rate differs from, or "overshoots," its equilibrium value by an amount which is proportional to the real interest differential, that is, the nominal interest differential minus the expected inflation differential. If the nominal interest differential is high because money is tight, then the exchange rate lies below its equilibrium value. But if the nominal interest differential is high merely because of a high expected inflation differential, then the exchange rate is equal to its equilibrium value, which over time increases at the rate of the inflation differential.

The theory yields an equation of exchange rate determination in which the spot rate is expressed as a function of the relative money supply, relative income level, the nominal interest differential (with the sign hypothesized negative), and the expected long-run inflation differential (with the sign hypothesized positive). The hypothesis is readily tested, using the mark/dollar rate, against the two alternative hypotheses: the Chicago theory, which implies a positive coefficient on the nominal interest differential, and the Keynesian theory, which implies a zero coefficient on the expected long-run inflation differential.

3.1   The Real Interest Differential Theory of Exchange Rate Determination

The theory starts with two fundamental assumptions. The first, interest rate parity, is associated with efficient markets in which the bonds of different countries are perfect substitutes:

$$d = i - i^*$$
$$(1)$$

when i is defined as the *log* of one plus the domestic rate of interest (which is numerically very close to the actual rate of interest for normal values) and i^* is defined as the *log* of one plus the foreign rate of interest.[3] If d is considered to be the forward discount, defined as the *log* of the forward rate minus the *log* of the current spot rate, then (1) is a statement of covered (or closed) interest parity. Under perfect capital mobility, that is, in the absence of capital controls and transactions costs, covered interest parity must hold exactly, since its failure would imply unexploited opportunities for certain profits.[4] However, d will be defined as the expected rate of depreciation; then (1) represents the stronger condition of uncovered (or open) interest parity. Of course if there is no uncertainty, as in a perfect foresight economy, then the forward discount is equal to the expected rate of depreciation, and (1) follows directly. If there is uncertainty and market participants are risk averse, then the assumption that there is no risk premium, though not precluded, is a strong one.

The second fundamental assumption is that the expected rate of depreciation is a function of the gap between the current spot and an equilibrium rate, and of the expected long-run inflation differential between the domestic and foreign countries:

$$d = -\theta(s - \bar{s}) + \pi - \pi^*$$
$$(2)$$

where s is the *log* of the spot rate; π and π^* are the current rates of expected long-run inflation at home and abroad, respectively. (We can think of them as long-run rates of monetary growth that are known to the public.)[5] The *log* of the equilibrium exchange rate $\bar{s}$ is defined to increase at the rate $\pi - \pi^*$ in the absence of new disturbances; a more precise explanation will be given below. Equation (2) says that in the short run the exchange rate is expected to return to its equilibrium value at a rate which is proportional to the current gap, and that in the long run, when $s = \bar{s}$, it is expected to change at the long-run rate $\pi - \pi^*$. For the present, the justification for equation (2) will be simply that it is a reasonable form for expectations to take in an inflationary world. This claim will be substantiated in appendix 3A, after a price-adjustment equation has been specified by a demonstration that (2), with a specific value implied for θ, follows from the assumptions of perfect foresight (or rational expectations in the stochastic case) and stability.[6] The rational value of θ will be seen to be closely related to the speed of adjustment in the goods market.

Combining equations (1) and (2) gives

$$s - \bar{s} = -\frac{1}{\theta}[(i - \pi) - (i^* - \pi^*)]. \tag{3}$$

We might describe the expression in brackets as the real interest differential.[7] Alternatively, note that in the long run when $s = \bar{s}$, we must have $\bar{i} - \bar{i}^* = \pi - \pi^*$, where $\bar{i}$ and $\bar{i}^*$ denote the long-run, short-term interest rates.[8] Thus the expression in brackets is equal to $[(i - i^*) - (\bar{i} - \bar{i}^*)]$, and the equation can be described intuitively as follows. When a tight domestic monetary policy causes the nominal interest differential to rise above its long-run level, an incipient capital inflow causes the value of the currency to rise proportionately above *its* long-run equilibrium level.

For a complete equation of exchange rate determination, it remains only to explain $\bar{s}$. Assume that in the long run, purchasing power parity holds:

$$\bar{s} = \bar{p} - \bar{p}^*, \tag{4}$$

where $\bar{p}$ and $\bar{p}^*$ are defined as the *logs* of the equilibrium price levels at home and abroad, respectively.[9]

Assume also a conventional money demand equation:

$$m = p + \phi y - \lambda i \tag{5}$$

where m, p, and y are defined as the *logs* of the domestic money supply, price level, and output. A similar equation holds abroad. Let us take the difference between the two equations:

$$m - m^* = p - p^* + \phi(y - y^*) - \lambda(i - i^*). \tag{6}$$

Using bars to denote long-run equilibrium values and remembering that in the long run (when $s = \bar{s}$), $\bar{i} - \bar{i}^* = \pi - \pi^*$, we obtain

$$\bar{s} = \bar{p} - \bar{p}^*$$

$$= \bar{m} - \bar{m}^* - \phi(\bar{y} - \bar{y}^*) + \lambda(\pi - \pi^*). \tag{7}$$

This equation illustrates the monetary theory of the exchange rate, according to which the exchange rate is determined by the relative supply of and demand for the two currencies. It says that in full equilibrium a given increase in the money supply inflates prices and thus raises the exchange rate proportionately, and that an increase in income or a fall in the expected rate of inflation raises the demand for money and thus lowers the exchange rate.

Substituting (7) into (3), and assuming that the current equilibrium money supplies and income levels are given by their current actual levels,[10] we obtain a complete equation of spot rate determination:

$$s = m - m^* - \phi(y - y^*) - \frac{1}{\theta}(i - i^*) + \left(\frac{1}{\theta} + \lambda\right)(\pi - \pi^*). \tag{8}$$

This is the equation that is tested empirically for the deutsche mark in section 3.3.

3.2 Testable Alternative Hypotheses

Equation (8) is reproduced here with an error term:[11]

$$s = m - m^* - \phi(y - y^*) + \alpha(i - i^*) + \beta(\pi - \pi^*) + u \tag{9}$$

where $\alpha \ (= -1/\theta)$ is hypothesized negative and $\beta \ (= 1/\theta + \lambda)$ is hypothesized positive and greater than α in absolute value. Tests of a hypothesis are always more interesting if a plausible alternative hypothesis is specified. One obvious alternative hypothesis is Dornbusch's incarnation of the Keynesian approach, in which secular inflation is not a factor. In fact the model developed in this chapter is the same as the Dornbusch model in the special case where $\pi - \pi^*$ always equals zero.[12] The testable hypothesis is $\beta = 0$.

Another—more conflicting—alternative hypothesis comes from the Chicago theory of the exchange rate attributable to Frenkel and Bilson. The variant presented by Bilson begins with a money demand equation like (5): $m - p = \phi y - \lambda i$. Subtracting the foreign version yields a relative money demand equation like (6): $(m - m^*) - (p - p^*) = \phi(y - y^*) - \lambda(i - i^*)$. Bilson then assumes that purchasing power parity always holds:

$$s = p - p^* = (m - m^*) - \phi(y - y^*) + \lambda(i - i^*) \tag{10}$$

An increase in the domestic interest rate lowers the demand for domestic currency and causes a depreciation. In terms of equation (9), α, the coefficient of the nominal interest differential, is hypothesized to be *positive* rather than negative.

The interest differential $(i - i^*)$ is viewed as representing the relative expected inflation rate $(\pi - \pi^*)$, either because international investment flows equate real rates of interest or because interest rate parity ensures that the interest differential equals expected depreciation, and purchasing power parity ensures that depreciation equals relative inflation. Thus the expected inflation differential (were it directly observable) could be put into

(10) instead of the nominal interest differential:

$$s = (m - m^*) - \phi(y - y^*) + \lambda(\pi - \pi^*) \tag{11}$$

In terms of equation (9), α is hypothesized to be zero and β to be positive, if we use a good proxy for $(\pi - \pi^*)$. Or, more generally, the hypothesis can be represented $\alpha + \beta = \lambda > 0$, $\alpha \geq 0$, $\beta \geq 0$. The relative sizes of α and β would depend on how good a proxy we have for the expected inflation differential.

Indeed Frenkel begins his analysis with the assumption of a Cagan-type money demand function, which uses the expected inflation rate rather than the interest rate:

$$m - p = \phi y - \lambda\pi \tag{12}$$

The assumption of purchasing power parity then gives equation (11) directly. Frenkel uses the expected rate of depreciation as reflected in the forward discount in place of the unobservable expected inflation differential, which, in well-functioning bond markets, would be the same as using the nominal interest differential.

The argument that the nominal interest differential is equal to the expected inflation differential is the same as that given in the derivation of equation (7), and indeed equation (11) is identical to equation (7), except that (7) is hypothesized to hold only in long-run equilibrium while (10) is hypothesized to hold always.[13] The Frenkel-Bilson theory could be viewed as a special case of the real interest differential theory where the adjustment to equilibrium is assumed instantaneous; that is, θ is infinite, which of course is the same as α being zero.

The theory was originally tested by Frenkel on the German 1920–23 hyperinflation during which, it is argued, inflationary factors swamp everything else. In particular, variation in the expected inflation rate dwarfs variation in the real interest rate in the effect on the demand for money and thus the exchange rate. The argument is convincing; it is quite likely that the hypothesis $\alpha < 0$ would be rejected (or the hypothesis $\alpha \geq 0$ could not be rejected) if (9) were estimated on hyperinflation data. This just says that the Frenkel theory is the relevant one in the polar case when the inflation differential is very high and variable, much as the Dornbusch theory is clearly the relevant one in the polar case when the inflation differential is very low and stable.

It is the claim of the real interest differential theory that it is a realistic description in an environment of moderate inflation differentials such as has existed in the years since the beginning of generalized floating in 1973, and that the alternative hypotheses break down in such an environment. Bilson has suggested and tested his theory for this period and has claimed that empirically it works better than any alternative theory proposed.

The various alternative hypotheses are summarized in terms of equation (9):

Keynesian Model, Dornbusch (1976c):	$\alpha < 0$	$\beta = 0$
Chicago Model, Bilson:	$\alpha > 0$	$\beta = 0$
Frenkel:	$\alpha = 0$	$\beta > 0$
Real Interest Differential Model:	$\alpha < 0$	$\beta > 0$

3.3 Econometric Findings

In this section the real interest differential theory is tested on the mark/dollar exchange rate.[14] There are several good reasons for concentrating on this rate. The variation in the German-American inflation differential has been significant, as opposed to, for example, that in the Canadian-American or German-Swiss differentials. The exchange and capital markets were free from extensive government intervention in Germany and the United States, as opposed to, for example, those in the United Kingdom or Japan. In addition, the size of the German and American economies and the fact that there have been unexpectedly large upswings and downswings in the mark/dollar rate make this exchange rate the most important one to explain.

The sample used consisted of monthly observations between July 1974 and February 1978. The results were not greatly affected by the choice of monetary aggregate; only those using M_1 are reported in table 3.1. Industrial production indexes were used in place of national output, since the latter is not available on a monthly basis. Three-month money market rates were used for the nominal interest differential. The results are reported here with interest rates and expected inflation rates expressed on a "percent per annum" basis. Two kinds of proxies for the expected inflation differential were tried: past inflation differentials (averaged over the preceding year) and long-term interest differentials (under the rationale that the long-term real interest rates are equal).[15] The advantage of the long-term interest differential is that it is capable of reflecting instantly the impact of new information such as the announcement of monetary growth targets. Alternative possible measures of expected inflation, such as lagged inflation rates or the forecasts of econometric modelers, have the advantage of

Table 3.1
Test of real interest differential hypothesis (Sample: July 1974–February 1978)

Technique	Constant	$m - m_1^*$	$y - y^*$	$r - r^*$	$\pi - \pi^*$	R^2	D.W.	$\hat{\rho}$	No. of observ.
OLS	1.33 (.10)	.87 (.17)	-.72 (.22)	-.39 (.49)	7.16 (.68)	.80	.76		44
CORC	.80 (.19)	.31 (.25)	-.33 (.20)	-.065 (.49)	1.93 (1.12)	.91		.98	43
INST	1.39 (.08)	.96 (.14)	-.54 (.18)	-1.19 (.42)	6.86 (.57)		1.00		42
FAIR	1.39 (.12)	.97 (.21)	-.52 (.22)	-1.35 (.51)	7.35 (.83)			.46	41

Note: Standard errors are shown in parentheses.

Definitions: Dependent Variable (log of) Mark/Dollar Rate.

CORC = Iterated Cochrane-Orcutt.

INST = Instrumental variables for expected inflation differential are Consumer Price Index (CPI) inflation differential. Wholesale Price Index (WPI) inflation differential (average for past year), and long-term commercial bond rate differential.

FAIR = Instrumental variables are industrial WPI inflation differential and lagged values of the following: exchange rate, relative industrial production, short-term interest differential, and expected inflation differential. The method of including among the instruments lagged values of all endogenous and included exogenous variables, in order to insure consistency while correcting for first-order serial correlation, is attributed to Ray Fair.

$m - m^* = $ log of German M_1/U.S. M_1

$y - y^* = $ log of German production/U.S. production

$r - r^* = $ Short-term German-U.S. interest differential

$(r - r^*)_{-1} = $ Short-term German-U.S. interest differential lagged

$\pi - \pi^* = $ Expected German-U.S. inflation differential, proxied by long-term government bond differential.

being more direct. The long-term government bond rate differential is the proxy used in the regressions reported here, though other proxies are used as instrumental variables. Details on the data are given in appendix 3B.

In each regression the signs of all coefficients are as hypothesized under the real interest differential model. When the single equation estimation techniques are used, the significance levels are weak, especially when iterated Cochrane-Orcutt is used to correct for high first-order autocorrelation.

But when instrumental variables are used to correct for the shortcomings of the expected inflation proxy, the results improve markedly. The coefficient on the nominal interest differential is significantly less than zero. This result is all the more striking when it is kept in mind that the null hypothesis of a zero or positive coefficient is a plausible and seriously maintained hypothesis; the Chicago (Frenkel-Bilson) hypothesis is rejected in this data sample. The coefficient on the expected long-run inflation differential is significantly greater than zero. Thus the unmodified Keynesian (Dornbusch) hypothesis is also rejected. Furthermore, as predicted by the real interest differential model the coefficient on the expected long-run inflation differential is significantly greater than the absolute value of the coefficient on the nominal interest differential.

Several other points are also notably supportive of the theory. (I concentrate on the last regression in table 3.1.) The coefficient of the relative money supply is not only significantly positive but is also insignificantly less than 1.0. The coefficient of relative production is significantly negative, and its point estimate of approximately $-.5$ suits well its interpretation as the elasticity of money demand with respect to income. The sum of the (negative) coefficient on the nominal interest differential and the coefficient on the expected inflation differential is an estimate of the semielasticity of money demand with respect to the interest rate; when expressed on a per annum basis, the estimate is 6.0, which provides another favorable cross-check.[16]

The point estimate of (on a "percent per quarter" basis) α is -5.4. This implies that when a disturbance creates a deviation from purchasing power parity, $(1 - 1/5.4 =)$ 81.5 percent of the deviation is expected to remain after three months, and $(.815^4 =)$ 44.1 percent is expected to remain after one year. The estimate of θ on a per annum basis is $(-log\,.441 =)$ .819. Previous work on the speed of adjustment to purchasing power parity is even less definitive than estimates of money demand elasticities, but the present estimates of the expected speed of adjustment appear reasonable.[17]

As a final indication of the support table 3.1 provides for the real interest differential hypothesis, the R^2s are high. Figure 3.1 shows a plot of the

Figure 3.1
Plot of (log of) mark/dollar rate, OLS regression from table 3.1

equation's predicted values and the actual exchange rate values. The equation tracks the mark's 1974 appreciation, 1975 depreciation, and 1976–77
appreciation.[18]

To apply the estimated equation, let us express it as:

$$s = 1.39 + (m - m^*) - .52(y - y^*) - 1.35(i - i^*) + 7.35(\pi - \pi^*)$$

where the coefficient on the relative money supply has been set to 1.0. The
expression can be decomposed into the equilibrium exchange rate

$$\bar{s} = 1.39 + (m - m^*) - .52(y - y^*) + 6.00(\pi - \pi^*)$$

and the size of the overshooting

$$s - \bar{s} = -1.35[(i - \pi) - (i^* - \pi^*)].$$

As an illustration, let us conduct the hypothetical experiment of an
unexpected 1 percent expansion in the U.S. relative money supply. If the
monetary expansion is considered a once-and-for-all change, then the equilibrium mark/dollar rate decreases by 1.0 percent. But in the short run
the expansion also has liquidity effects; the interest semielasticity of 6.00

implies a fall in the nominal interest rate of (1 percent/6.00 =) 17 basis points.[19] This fall in the real interest differential induces an incipient capital outflow, which in turn causes the currency to depreciate further, until it overshoots its new equilibrium by (1.35 × .17 percent =) .23 percent. The total initial depreciation is 1.23 percent.

This calculation assumes no change in the expected inflation rate. If the monetary expansion signals a new higher target for monetary growth, then the effect could be much greater.[20] Suppose the annualized 12 percent increase raises the expected inflation rate by, say, 1 percent per annum. Then there will be an additional depreciation of 6.00 percent on account of the lower demand for money in long-run equilibrium plus 1.35 percent more overshooting on account of the further reduced real interest differential. Thus the *total* initial depreciation would be 8.58 percent, of which 7.00 percent represents long-run equilibrium and 1.58 percent represents short-run overshooting.

After the initial effects, the system moves toward the new equilibrium as described in appendix 3A, provided capital is perfectly mobile and future money supplies do not deviate from their expected values. American goods are cheaper than German goods; higher demand will gradually drive up American prices faster than the rate of monetary growth, which in turn will drive up U.S. nominal interest rates, reduce the overshooting, and cause the spot rate to rise back toward its new equilibrium. After a year, approximately 44 percent of the initial real interest differential and purchasing power parity deviation will have been closed. In the meantime, there should be an expansionary effect on demand for U.S. output; lower real U.S. prices will stimulate net exports and lower real U.S. interest rates will stimulate investment. However, any effects on output have not been modeled in this chapter.[21]

3.4   Econometric Extensions

It is possible that adjustment in capital markets to changes in the interest differential is not instantaneous and that lagged interest differentials should be included in the regressions. Formally, we could argue that due to transactions costs, the forward discount adjusts fully to the interest differential with a one-month lag:

$$d = h(i - i^*) + (1 - h)(i - i^*)_{-1} \qquad\qquad (13)$$

When (13) is used in place of (1), the spot rate equation (8) is replaced by

$$s = (m - m^*) - \phi(y - y^*) - (h/\theta)(i - i^*) - (1 - h)(1/\theta)(i - i^*)_{-1}$$
$$+ ((1/\theta) + \lambda)(\pi - \pi^*) \qquad\qquad (14)$$

[The results of regressions with a lagged interest differential were reported in a table in the original version, omitted here to save space.] The coefficient on the lagged interest differential is insignificantly less than zero. This evidence supports the idea that capital is perfectly mobile.

There are several reasons why one might wish to constrain the coefficient on the relative money supply to be 1.0 in these regressions, in effect moving the relative money supply variable to the left-hand side of the equation. First, our a priori faith in a unit coefficient is high. It is hard to believe that the system could fail in the long run to be homogeneous of degree zero in the exchange rate and relative money supply. Second, errors in the money demand equation are known to have been large over the last few years. Such errors, since they are correlated with the money stock variable, would bias the coefficient downward; indeed, the coefficient estimate in one regression in table 3.1 appears significantly less than 1.0. By constraining the money supply coefficient to be 1.0, we make sure that any possible errors in the money demand equations will go into the dependent variable, that is, will be uncorrelated with any of the independent variables. Thus they cannot bias the coefficients on the interest and expected inflation differentials, which are our primary objects of concern. A third reason for constraining the coefficient is to remove the simultaneity problem which otherwise occurs if central banks vary their money supplies in response to the exchange rate. The argument even extends to direct exchange market intervention, which has been prevalent under managed floating. The right-

Table 3.2
Constrained coefficient on relative money supplies (sample: July 1974–February 1978)

Technique	Constant	$y - y^*$	$i - i^*$	$\pi - \pi^*$	R^2	D.W.	$\hat{\rho}$
OLS	1.40	−.69	−.44	7.54	.92	.79	
	(.02)	(.21)	(.48)	(.42)			
CORC	1.16	−.41	−.39	2.53	.96		.98
	(.13)	(.22)	(.53)	(1.21)			
INST	1.41	−.52	−1.21	6.93		1.01	
	(.01)	(.18)	(.41)	(.37)			
FAIR	1.43	−.31	−1.40	8.50			69
	(.03)	(.26)	(.68)	(1.06)			

Note: Standard errors are shown in parentheses. Dependent Variable: (log of) Mark/Dollar Rate × German M_1/U.S. M_1. See table 3.1 for definitions.

hand-side variables determine relative money demand; changes in money demand can be reflected in either money supplies (the monetary approach to the balance of payments) or the exchange rate (the monetary approach to the exchange rate), depending on government intervention policy.

Table 3.2 reports the constrained regressions. The results are very similar to those in table 3.1. The R^2s indicate that over 90 percent of the variation in the dependent variable is explained; the remaining 10 percent could be attributed to errors in the two countries' money demand equations.

3.5 Summary

The model developed in this chapter is a version of the asset view of the exchange rate, in that it emphasizes the role of expectations and rapid adjustment in capital markets. It shares with the Frenkel-Bilson (Chicago) model an attention to long-run monetary equilibrium. A monetary expansion causes a long-run depreciation because it is an increase in the supply of the currency, and an increase in expected inflation causes a long-run depreciation because it decreases the demand for the currency.

On the other hand, the model shares with the Dornbusch (Keynesian) model the assumption that sticky prices in goods markets create a difference between the short run and the long run. When the nominal interest rate is low relative to the expected inflation rate, the domestic economy is highly liquid. An incipient capital outflow will cause the currency to depreciate, until there is sufficient expectation of future appreciation to offset the low interest rate. The exchange rate overshoots its equilibrium value by an amount proportional to the real interest differential.

The real interest differential model includes both the Frenkel-Bilson and Dornbusch models as polar special cases. When the spot rate equation (8) is econometrically estimated for the mark/dollar rate from July 1974 to February 1978, the evidence clearly supports the model against the two alternatives.

Appendix 3A: The Price Equation and the Path to Equilibrium

In this appendix we examine the consequences of an additional assumption, a price equation. Unless there is some stickiness in p, it cannot differ from $\bar{p}$, and thus the domestic real interest rate cannot differ from the foreign real interest rate, or the exchange rate from the relative price level. This stickiness can be embodied in the assumption that prices are fixed at a moment in time but move gradually toward equilibrium. In an environment of secular monetary growth, it is necessary that when prices reach their equilibrium, they are increasing at the secular rate. The simplest possible price equation meeting these requirements, using D for the time derivative operator, is

$$Dp = \delta(s - p + p^*) + \pi. \tag{A1}$$

This equation can be rationalized by expressing the rate of change of prices as the sum of a mark-up term π, representing the pass-through of domestic cost inflation and an excess demand adjustment term, where excess demand is assumed a function of the purchasing power parity gap $(s - p + p^*)$.[22] Assuming that the analogous equation holds abroad, the relative price level changes according to

$$D(p - p^*) = \delta(s - p + p^*) + \pi - \pi^* \tag{A2}$$

where δ has been redefined to be the sum of the domestic and foreign adjustment parameters.

The purchasing power parity gap (also called the real exchange rate) can be shown to be proportional to the real interest differential. Substituting (6) into (7) implies

$$\bar{s} = p - p^* - \lambda[(i - \pi) - (i^* - \pi^*)]$$

which with (3) implies

$$s - p + p^* = -\left(\frac{1}{\theta} + \lambda\right)[(i - \pi) - (i^* - \pi^*)]. \tag{A3}$$

Now we use (A2) to solve out $(\pi - \pi^*)$, and collect terms to arrive at the promised result:

$$s - p + p^* = -\frac{1 + \lambda\theta}{\theta - (1 + \lambda\theta)\delta}[(i - Dp) - (i^* - Dp^*)]. \tag{A4}$$

Let us now proceed to derive the path from the initial point after a disturbance (short-run equilibrium) to long-run equilibrium. We already know from equations (3) and (A3) that the gap between s and its equilibrium and the purchasing power parity gap are each proportional to $[(i - \pi) - (i^* - \pi^*)]$, so they must be proportional to each other:

$$(s - p + p^*) = (1 + \lambda\theta)(s - \bar{s}), \tag{A5}$$

Using $\bar{s} - \bar{p} + \bar{p}^* = 0$ and (A5),

$$s - p + p^* = (s - \bar{s}) - (p - \bar{p}) + (p^* - \bar{p}^*)$$

$$= -\frac{1 + \lambda\theta}{\lambda\theta}[(p - p^*) - (\bar{p} - \bar{p}^*)]. \tag{A6}$$

Substituting (A6) into (A2),

$$D(p - p^*) = -\delta(1 + \lambda\theta)/\lambda\theta[(p - p^*) - (\bar{p} - \bar{p}^*)] + \pi - \pi^*. \tag{A7}$$

This differential equation has the solution

$$(p - p^*)_t = (\bar{p} - \bar{p}^*)_t + \exp[-\delta(1 + \lambda\theta/\lambda\theta)t][(p - p^*)_0 - (\bar{p} - \bar{p}^*)_0]. \tag{A8}$$

The relative price level moves toward its equilibrium at a speed that is proportional to the gap. The equilibrium relative price level, it must be remembered, is itself increasing at the rate $\pi - \pi^*$.

An analogous equation holds for s. Equations (A5) and (A6) tell us

$$s - \bar{s} = -\frac{1}{\lambda\theta}[(p - p^*) - (\bar{p} - \bar{p}^*)]. \tag{A9}$$

Taking the time derivative,

$$Ds = -\frac{1}{\lambda\theta}D[(p - p^*) - (\bar{p} - \bar{p}^*)] + D\bar{s}$$

$$= -\frac{\delta(1 + \lambda\theta)}{\lambda\theta}(s - \bar{s}) + \pi - \pi^*. \tag{A10}$$

This differential equation has the solution

$$s_t = \bar{s}_t + \exp[-(\delta(1 + \lambda\theta)/\lambda\theta)t](s - \bar{s})_0. \tag{A11}$$

Comparing (A10), the expression for the rate of change of the spot rate if there are no further disturbances, with (2), the expression for the expected rate of change of the exchange rate, we see that the two are of the same form. Perfect foresight (or rational expectations in the stochastic case) holds if $\theta = \delta(1 + \lambda\theta)/\lambda\theta$, which has the solution

$$\tilde{\theta}_1 = \frac{\delta\lambda + ((\delta\lambda)^2 + 4\delta\lambda)^{1/2}}{2\lambda}$$

$$\tilde{\theta}_2 = \frac{\delta\lambda + ((\delta\lambda)^2 + 4\delta\lambda)^{1/2}}{2\lambda}. \tag{A12}$$

Here we throw out the negative root because θ was assumed positive when

(2) was specified. We can see that $\tilde{\theta}_1$ increases with δ, the speed of adjustment in goods markets. In turn, we know from equation (3) that the sensitivity of the exchange rate to monetary changes decreases with θ. The implication is that the slower is adjustment in the goods market, the more volatile must the exchange rate be in order to compensate.

It is easy to show that we could have derived (2) from the rest of the model and the assumptions of perfect foresight and stability, instead of assuming the form of expectations directly. Substituting the relative money demand equation (6) into the interest parity condition (1),

$$d = (1/\lambda)[(p - p^*) - (m - m^*) + \phi(y - y^*)]$$

$$= (1/\lambda)[(p - p^*) - (\bar{p} - \bar{p}^*)] + \pi - \pi^*. \tag{A13}$$

The perfect foresight assumption is $d = Ds$. Equation (A13) and the price equation (A2) can be represented in matrix form:

$$\begin{bmatrix} Ds \\ D(p - p^*) \end{bmatrix} = \begin{bmatrix} 0 & 1/\lambda \\ \delta & -\delta \end{bmatrix} \begin{bmatrix} s \\ (p - p^*) \end{bmatrix} + \begin{bmatrix} -(1/\lambda)(\bar{p} - \bar{p}^*) + \pi - \pi^* \\ \pi - \pi^* \end{bmatrix}.$$

Let $-\theta_1$ and $-\theta_2$ be the characteristic roots:

$$\begin{vmatrix} \theta & 1/\lambda \\ \delta & -\delta + \theta \end{vmatrix} = -\delta\theta + \theta^2 - \delta/\lambda = 0.$$

The solution is given by (A12). The path of s is given by

$$(s - \bar{s})_t = a_1 \exp(-\theta_1 t) + a_2 \exp(-\theta_2 t)$$

The system is stable if and only if $a_2 = 0$, which, with the initial condition $a_1 = (s - \bar{s})_0$, implies equation (2), and the positive root from (A12).

Appendix 3B

The data are as follows:

Spot rate: Monthly averages of dollars per mark, *Federal Reserve Bulletin (FRB)*.

Money supply: Germany: Position at end of month, seasonally adjusted, in billions of marks, Deutsche Bundesbank (*DB*). United States: Averages of daily figures, seasonally adjusted, in billions of dollars, from the *Economic Report of the President (ERP)*, *FRB*, and *Economic Indicators (EC)*.

Industrial production: Germany: Seasonally adjusted, *DB*. United States: Seasonally adjusted, *ERP* and *Statistical Releases*.

Short-run interest rates: Representative bond equivalent yields on major 3–4-month money market instruments, excluding Treasury Bills, *World Financial Markets (WFM)*.

First expected inflation rate: Long-term government bond yields: at or near end of month, *WFM*. Long-term commercial bond yields: at or near end of month, *WFM*.

Wholesale price index (average logarithmic rate of change over preceding year): Germany: Industrial products, seasonally adjusted, *DB*. United States: Industrial, seasonally adjusted, *ERP, FRB, International Financial Statistics (IFS)*, and *Business Week*.

Consumer price index (average logarithmic rate of change over preceding year): Germany: Cost of living, seasonally adjusted, *DB*. United States: Urban dwellers and clerical workers, *ERP, IFS*, and *EC*.

Acknowledgment

I would like to thank Rudiger Dornbusch, Stanley Fischer, Jerry Hausman, Dale Henderson, Franco Modigliani, and George Borts for comments.

4

Monetary and Portfolio-Balance Models of the Determination of Exchange Rates

4.1 The Asset-Market View of Exchange Rates

The theoretical literature on the "asset-market" view of exchange rates has expanded voluminously. The popularity of this view may be attributed to the compelling realism in today's world of both its distinguishing theoretical assumption and its distinguishing empirical implication. The theoretical assumption that all asset-market models share is the absence of substantial transactions costs, capital controls, or other impediments to the flow of capital between countries, an assumption that will here be referred to as perfect capital mobility. Thus the exchange rate must adjust instantly to equilibrate the international demand for stocks of national assets—as opposed to adjusting to equilibrate the international demand for flows of national goods as in the more traditional view. The empirical implication is that floating exchange rates will exhibit high variability, variability that exceeds what one might regard as that of their underlying determinants.

But beyond this common point, the asset-market models diverge down a bewildering complexity of routes. Synthesis models and comprehensive surveys are notably lacking. Furthermore, the specific empirical implications of the various theories conflict with observed events, as well as with each other. Econometric attempts to relate the theory to data have foundered on dollar depreciation, which, in 1977 and 1978, was too highly correlated with the U.S. current account deficit to be explained readily by the asset-market approach and which rather seemed to fit the more traditional approach.

This chapter proposes a taxonomy of asset-market models of floating exchange rates, as illustrated in figure 4.1. The most important dichotomy is according to whether domestic and foreign bonds are assumed to be perfect substitutes in asset-holders' portfolios. It is important to note the

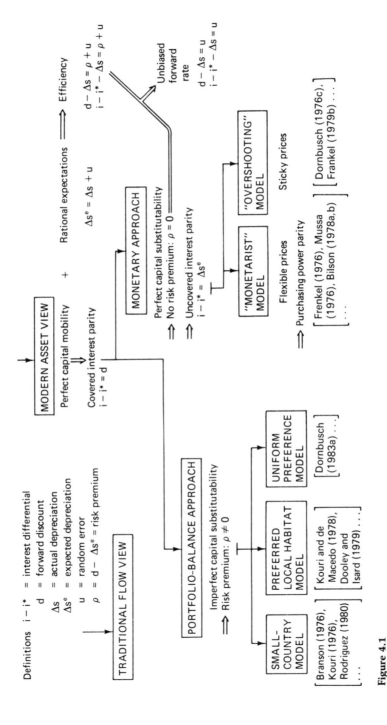

Figure 4.1
Exchange rate models and assumptions

distinction between capital mobility, as the term is used here, and substitutability.[1] Perfect capital mobility between countries means that actual portfolio composition adjusts instantaneously to desired portfolio composition. Assuming no risk of default or future capital controls, perfect capital mobility implies, for example, covered interest parity: The interest rate on a domestic bond is equal to the interest rate on a similar foreign bond plus the forward premium on foreign exchange.[2] Perfect substitutability between domestic and foreign bonds is the much stronger assumption that asset holders are indifferent as to the composition of their bond portfolios as long as the expected rate of return on the two countries' bonds is the same when expressed in any common numeraire. It would imply, for example, uncovered interest parity: The interest rate on a domestic bond is equal to the interest rate on a foreign bond plus the *expected* rate of appreciation of foreign currency.[3]

In one class of asset-market models, domestic and foreign bonds are imperfect substitutes. This is the "portfolio-balance approach" to exchange rates, in which asset holders wish to allocate their portfolios in shares that are well-defined functions of expected rates of return.[4]

In the other class of asset-market models, domestic and foreign bonds are perfect substitutes: Portfolio shares are infinitely sensitive to expected rates of return. Thus uncovered interest parity must hold. But given that it does hold, bond supplies then become irrelevant. The responsibility for determining the exchange rate is shifted onto the money markets. Such models belong to the "monetary approach" to exchange rates,[5] which focuses on the demand for and supply of money.

4.2   The Monetary Approach

The Flexible-Price ("Monetarist") Monetary Model

We have defined the monetary approach by the assumption that not only are there no barriers (such as transaction costs or capital controls) segmenting international capital markets, but domestic and foreign bonds are also perfect substitutes in investor demand functions. In essence, there is only one bond in the world.

As the starting point within the monetary approach we begin with the model that also makes the analogous assumption for goods markets: Not only are there no barriers (such as transportation costs or trade controls) segmenting international goods markets, but domestic and foreign goods are also perfect substitutes in consumer demand functions. In essence, there is only one good in the world.

This assumption, of course, implies purchasing power parity: The domestic price level is equal to the foreign price level times the exchange rate. Large short-run failures of purchasing power parity have been observed empirically.[6] But the assumption can be useful in certain contexts, for example, hyperinflation. And, in any case, the model that assumes one world good as well as one world bond is a powerfully simple prototype that will serve as a point of departure for more sophisticated models.

If perfect price flexibility is considered the crucial characteristic of monetarism, then the best name for the variety of monetary model that assumes purchasing power parity is the "monetarist model."[7] It has been developed by Frenkel (1976, 1977, 1980), Mussa (1976), Girton and Roper (1977), Hodrick (1978), and Bilson (1978a, 1978b).

The fundamental equation in the monetary approach is a conventional money demand function:

$$m = p + \phi y - \lambda i, \tag{1}$$

where

$m \equiv$ log of the domestic money supply,

$p \equiv$ log of the domestic price level,

$y \equiv$ log of domestic real income,

$i \equiv$ the domestic short-term interest rate,

$\phi \equiv$ the money demand elasticity with respect to income,

$\lambda \equiv$ the money demand semielasticity with respect to the interest rate.

We assume a similar money demand function for the foreign country:

$$m^* = p^* + \phi y^* - \lambda i^*$$

where asterisks denote foreign variables and the parameters are assumed the same in both countries. Taking the difference of the two equations gives us a relative money demand function:

$$(m - m^*) = (p - p^*) + \phi(y - y^*) - \lambda(i - i^*). \tag{2}$$

The one-bond assumption gives us uncovered interest parity:

$$i - i^* = \mathscr{E}(\Delta s) \tag{3}$$

where $\mathscr{E}(\Delta s) \equiv$ the expected depreciation of domestic currency. We combine (2) and (3) and solve for the relative price level:

$$(p - p^*) = (m - m^*) - \phi(y - y^*) + \lambda \mathcal{E}(\Delta s). \tag{4}$$

The one-good assumption gives us purchasing power parity:

$$s = p - p^*, \tag{5}$$

where $s \equiv$ log of the spot exchange rate, defined as the price of foreign currency in terms of domestic. A consequence is that expected depreciation is equal to the expected inflation differential:

$$\mathcal{E}(\Delta s) = \mathcal{E}(\Delta p) - \mathcal{E}(\Delta p^*). \tag{6}$$

We combine (5), (4), and (6) to obtain the monetarist equation of exchange rate determination:

$$s = (m - m^*) - \phi(y - y^*) + \lambda(\mathcal{E}\Delta p - \mathcal{E}\Delta p^*). \tag{7}$$

Equation (7) says that the exchange rate, as the relative price of currency, is determined by the supply and demand for money. An increase in the supply of domestic money causes a proportionate depreciation. An increase in domestic income, or a decrease in the expected inflation rate, raises the demand for domestic money and thus causes an appreciation. The equation has been widely estimated econometrically.

Assume that expectations are rational and the system is stable. Assume further that income growth is exogenous (for simplicity equal to zero, so $y - y^* = \bar{y} - \bar{y}^*$), as it usually is in monetarist models. Then the expected inflation rate is equal to the rationally expected monetary growth rate. A benchmark specification of the money supply process is that monetary growth follows a random walk. Then the rationally expected future relative monetary growth rate, and thus the last term in equation (7), is simply the current relative monetary growth rate, which we will represent by $\pi - \pi^*$:

$$s = (m - m^*) - \phi(\bar{y} - \bar{y}^*) + \lambda(\pi - \pi^*). \tag{8}$$

As an alternative to the benchmark specification, a very restrictive special case occurs when we specify the *level* of the money supply, rather than the change in the money supply, to be a random walk. Then the expected relative rate of monetary growth, $\pi - \pi^*$, is zero. The level of the exchange rate is perfectly correlated with the level of the relative money supply. But in today's world the existence of secular inflation and its effect on money demand cannot be ignored.[8]

On the other hand, one could generalize beyond the benchmark case of a random-walk specification for money growth. More sophisticated specifications of the money supply process have appeared in monetarist exchange rate models by Mussa (1976), who distinguishes between transitory and permanent monetary disturbances, and Barro (1978), who distinguishes between anticipated and unanticipated disturbances.

The Sticky-Price ("Overshooting") Monetary Model

As mentioned, purchasing power parity may be a good approximation in the long run, but large deviations appear in the short run empirically. The existence of contracts, imperfect information, and inertia in consumer habits means that prices do not change instantaneously but adjust gradually over time.

We now retain the monetary approach's one-bond representation of financial markets but relax the monetarist model's one-good representation of trade. This gives us a class of models in which changes in the nominal money supply are also changes in the real money supply because prices are sticky, and thus have real effects, especially on the exchange rate.

The sticky-price class of monetary models begins with the well-known analysis of perfect capital mobility by Mundell (1963). Mundell abstracts from expectations, so that uncovered interest parity (3) becomes a simple equality between the domestic and foreign interest rates. In a money demand equation like (1), the combination of a fixed price level and an interest rate tied to the world rate means that a monetary expansion causes a large instant depreciation in the currency: Export demand has to be stimulated sufficiently for the increased income to raise money demand to the level of the new higher money supply *without* lowering the domestic interest rate below the foreign one.

A number of authors have introduced a nonzero expected rate of depreciation into the Mundell model.[9] They argue that as long as the expected future spot rate is less than unit-elastic with respect to the current spot rate, a monetary expansion will not cause as large an increase in the exchange rate and income as in the Mundell model. This is because it is possible for the domestic interest rate to fall below the foreign one without inducing an infinite capital outflow.

At first Argy and Porter (1972) and Dornbusch (1976a) specified expectations adaptively. But then Dornbusch (1976c) offered a model in which expectations are specified rationally. In this model purchasing power parity does hold in the long run, so that a given increase in the money supply raises the exchange rate proportionately as in the monetarist model, but *only* in the long run. In the short run, because prices are sticky, a monetary expansion has the liquidity effects of the Mundell model. The interest rate falls, generating an incipient capital outflow, which causes the currency to depreciate instantaneously *more* than it will in the long run; it depreciates just enough so that the rationally expected rate of future *appreciation* precisely cancels out the interest differential. The phenomenon just described is known as "overshooting" of the spot rate. In its honor, this chapter will use the name "overshooting model" for the sticky-price monetary approach to distinguish it from the monetarist (flexible-price monetary approach) model.[10]

The overshooting model retains the money demand function (1) and uncovered interest parity condition (3) essential to the monetary approach. It replaces the instantaneous purchasing power parity condition (5) with a long-run version:

$$\bar{s} = \bar{p} - \bar{p}^*, \tag{9}$$

where bars over variables signify a relation that holds in the long run. Thus the monetarist exchange rate equation (7) is replaced by a long-run version:

$$\bar{s} = (\bar{m} - \bar{m}^*) - \phi(\bar{y} - \bar{y}^*) + \lambda(\overline{\mathscr{E}(\Delta p)} - \overline{\mathscr{E}(\Delta p^*)}). \tag{10}$$

Precisely as we did in the monetarist model, we assume that expectations are rational and the system is stable; for simplicity, income growth is exogenous (or random with mean zero); and as a benchmark specification, monetary growth follows a random walk. It then follows that the relative money supply, and in the long run the relative price level and exchange rate, are all rationally expected to follow paths along which they increase at the current rate of relative monetary growth $\pi - \pi^*$. Equation (10) becomes

$$\bar{s} = (m - m^*) - \phi(y - y^*) + \lambda(\pi - \pi^*). \tag{11}$$

It remains only to specify expectations. In the short run, when the exchange rate deviates from its equilibrium path, it is expected to close that gap with a speed of adjustment θ. In the long run, when the exchange rate lies on its equilibrium path, it is expected to increase at $\pi - \pi^*$:[11]

$$\mathscr{E}(\Delta s) = -\theta(s - \bar{s}) + \pi - \pi^*. \tag{12}$$

We combine (12) with the uncovered interest parity condition (3),

$$i - i^* = \mathcal{E}(\Delta s) \tag{3}$$

to obtain

$$s - \bar{s} = -(1/\theta)[(i - \pi) - (i^* - \pi^*)]. \tag{13}$$

The gap between the exchange rate and its equilibrium value is proportional to the real interest differential. Intuitively, when a tight domestic monetary policy causes the nominal interest differential to rise above its equilibrium level, an incipient capital inflow causes the value of the currency to rise proportionately above *its* equilibrium level.

Now we combine (11), representing the long-run monetary equilibrium path, with (13), representing the short-run overshooting effect, to obtain a general monetary equation of exchange rate determination:

$$s = (m - m^*) - \phi(y - y^*) + \lambda(\pi - \pi^*) - (1/\theta)[(i - \pi) - (i^* - \pi^*)]. \tag{14}$$

As the basis for econometric estimation, equation (14) is identical to the monetarist equation (8) but for the addition of a fourth explanatory variable, the real interest differential. This variable should show up in a regression with a zero coefficient if the monetarist model is correct; the economic interpretation would be that the speed of adjustment θ is infinite.

As we did in the last section, we can depart from the benchmark specification of the money supply process by considering the simple special case when the *level* of the money supply, rather then the *change* in the money supply, is a random walk. Then the expected long-run inflation differential $\pi - \pi^*$ is zero. This is precisely the context in which this model was originally developed by Dornbusch. Equation (14) becomes

$$s = (m - m^*) - \phi(y - y^*) - (1/\theta)(i - i^*). \tag{15}$$

The Dornbusch equation (15), like the monetarist equation (8), can be viewed as a nested model, which can be tested econometrically by estimating equation (14).

Again as in the last section, one could also depart from the benchmark specification by considering a more general money supply process. More sophisticated specifications of the money supply process have appeared in Dornbusch-type models by Rogoff (1979), who distinguishes between transitory and permanent monetary disturbances, and Wilson (1979) and Gray and Turnovsky [1979], who distinguish between anticipated and unanticipated monetary disturbances.

In the following section we estimate this equation econometrically.

4.3   Estimation for Five Currencies

Prior empirical studies of the monetary model have produced different results depending on the currency used. For example, Bilson (1978a) claimed support for the flexible price version from the pound/dollar data, while I found evidence for the sticky price version in the mark/dollar data in Frankel (1979b, i.e., chapter 3). In this section we test equation (14) for five exchange rates at the same time: the mark, pound, franc, yen, and Canadian dollar, each against the United States dollar.

The sample begins in January 1974 and ends in mid-1981, with the exact limits for each currency depending on data availability. The "equilibrium" money supplies are represented by their current values, though we must recognize that much of the monthly fluctuation in the monetary aggregates is in fact transitory. The equilibrium income levels are represented by industrial production. The equilibrium expected inflation rates are measured by actual CPI inflation over the preceding twelve months. Finally, the nominal interest rates are represented by annualized short-term money market rates.

Estimates for the five exchange rates using the iterative Cochrane-Orcutt technique to correct for high serial correlation are reported in table 7.1 of the original paper. Only in the case of France are all four coefficients of the hypothesized sign. The coefficient on the interest differential is always of the negative sign hypothesized by the sticky price model. In the case of England, this represents a reversal in sign over earlier studies. The reversal is attributable to the unprecedented variation in interest rates of 1980–81, and confirms a finding of Hacche and Townend (1981). But overall, the presence of wrong signs on the other coefficients and the predominance of low significance levels render the results discouraging for the monetary equation.

There are several ways that one can bring more information to bear in order to get more efficient estimates. First, one can impose the constraint of a unit coefficient on the relative money supply.[12] The results indicate no improvement, except for the case of Japan. Second, we can impose the constraint that the coefficients are the same across all five equations. This technique is achieved by "stacking" the regressions. The results, reported in table 4.1, show some improvement. The negative coefficient on the interest differential is now highly significant. But the other three coefficients, though of the correct sign, are still not significantly different from zero. It appears that we must consider theoretical modifications of the monetary model.[13]

Table 4.1
Five monetary equations "stacked" (dependent variable: log of exchange rate per U.S. dollar)

Constant Terms					Coefficients					
Germany	France	U.K.	Japan	Canada	$ml - mlb_{US}$	$y - y_{US}$	$INFL - INFL_{US}$	$i - i_{US}$	ρ	s.e.r.
.77	1.46	−1.08	4.98	.35	.09	−.05	.24	−.36[a]	.97	.028
(.10)	(.09)	(.40)	(.49)	(.25)	(.09)	(.08)	(.19)	(.11)		
1.28	1.10	−4.93	.31	2.66	1.00	−.03	.31	−.39[a]	.96	.031
(.09)	(.09)	(.09)	(.09)	(.09)	(Constrained)	(.08)	(.21)	(.12)		

a. Significant at the 95% level. (Standard errors in parentheses.)
Note: Technique: Cochrane-Orcutt.
Sample: 2/74–7/81 for Germany, 2/74–4/81 for France, 2/74–6/81 for U.K., Japan, and Canada; 444 observations.

4.4   Drift in Velocity and the Real Exchange Rate

Some recent literature on exchange rate determination has proposed modifications in the monetary models, partly in response to poor results like those reported in section 4.3. As a matter of logic, one or more of the assumptions, or building blocks, in sections 4.1 and 4.2 would have to be modified.

First, one could question assumption (9), that purchasing power parity holds, even in the long run.[14] The most commonly cited sources of major shifts in the long-run terms of trade are the oil price rises of the 1970s,[15] though these shifts do not automatically imply changes in the long-run real exchange rate between pairs of industrialized countries, as pointed out by Krugman (1980). Other possible sources include nontraded goods prices that rise more rapidly in countries with more rapid income growth, as argued years ago by Balassa (1964). Whatever the source of shifts in the long-run real exchange rate, they are easily integrated into the monetary equation of exchange rate determination, as in Hooper and Morton (1982). If (9) is replaced by

$$r \equiv \bar{s} - \bar{p} + \bar{p}^*, \tag{9'}$$

then the long-run real exchange rate r simply appears as an additional term in (14).

A second building block that has been called into question is the money demand equation (1). A downward shift in United States money demand in the 1970s has been widely noted. In Frankel (1982a) I argue that there has also been an upward shift in German money demand and that the two shifts explain the fall in the mark/dollar rate of the late 1970s. If we add a shift term to each money demand function,

$$\bar{m} = \bar{p} + \phi\bar{y} + \lambda\bar{\imath} + v$$

$$\bar{m}^* = \bar{p}^* + \phi\bar{y}^* + \lambda\bar{\imath}^* + v^*. \tag{1'}$$

they show up as two more terms in the exchange rate equation:

$$s = (\bar{m} - \bar{m}^*) - \phi(\bar{y} - \bar{y}^*) + \left(\lambda + \frac{1}{\theta}\right)(\pi - \pi^*) - \frac{1}{\theta}(i - i^*)$$

$$+ r - (v - v^*). \tag{14'}$$

The third building block that has been called into question is the uncovered interest parity condition (3). If domestic and foreign bonds are imperfect substitutes, then the interest differential will differ from the expected rate of depreciation by a term that is most naturally thought of as a risk premium. The risk premium can be integrated into the monetary equation as yet another additional term in (14).

The question remains how to represent for empirical work our additional terms arising from shifts in purchasing power parity, money demand, and the risk premium. In each case, authors who have proposed the additional terms have constructed fairly ad hoc measures based largely on the current account. The current account is argued, alternatively, to give signals regarding long-run competitiveness, to constitute an important component of wealth, which in turn belongs in the money demand function, and to be a determinant of the risk premium. Indeed, a major motivation for these modifications has been to "get the current account back into the monetary model." One obvious disadvantage with using these ad hoc measures is that it would be difficult to discriminate among the three alternative rationales.

The aim of this section is the very limited one of identifying which of the possible shifts is responsible for the apparent breakdown in the monetary model, without attempting to model the particular shift in question. This is possible by making use of the one structural variable in the monetary model that does not appear in the "reduced form" (14): the price level. In equation (14') we represent r by a 1-year polynomial distributed lag of the real exchange rate $(s - p + p^*)$, and we represent $v - v^*$ by a 1-year polynomial distributed lag of relative velocity, $(p + y - m) - (p^* + y^* - m^*)$, both in log form. If one variable or the other gets the equation running smoothly again, then at least the source of the malfunction will have been localized.

In table 4.2 the lags on velocity and the real exchange rate are in every case but one highly significant and of the correct sign. Far more interestingly, the coefficients on each of the original four variables are now usually significant and of the correct sign. These results suggest that shifts in the money demand function and the long-run real exchange rate may equally be responsible for the problems of the monetary equation. The results tell us nothing about what is causing these shifts, but they do indicate that these are two promising areas for future research.

It is clearer how to go about modeling the third factor, shifts in the risk premium, than the first two. This leads us to the portfolio-balance approach, the subject of the remainder of the chapter.

Table 4.2
Monetary equation with drift in velocity and the real exchange rate (dependent variable: log of exchange rate per U.S. dollar)

Country	Constant	$m1 - m1B_{US}$	$y - y_{US}$	$INFL - INFL_{US}$	$i - i_{US}$	Velocity	Real Exchange Rate	Sample	ρ	s.e.r.
						Sum of Lag Coefficients				
Germany	−.19	.46[a]	−.26	.81[b]	−.59[a]	.65[a]	1.00[a]	78	.24	.018
	(.15)	(.17)	(.18)	(.45)	(.17)	(.09)	(.11)		(.11)	
France	−.49	.64[a]	−.50[a]	.54	−.54[a]	.38[a]	1.05[a]	86	.51	.019
	(.20)	(.18)	(.12)	(.51)	(.17)	(.17)	(.12)		(.09)	
United Kingdom	.75	.88[a]	−.54[a]	.04[b]	−.14	.52[a]	1.06[a]	88	.49	.021
	(.27)	(.09)	(.13)	(.02)	(.15)	(.12)	(.07)		(.09)	
Japan	1.84	.61[a]	−.81[a]	.51[a]	.06	.77[a]	.81[a]	89	.46	.020
	(.50)	(.13)	(.10)	(.24)	(.14)	(.09)	(.07)		(.09)	
Canada	.27	−.02	.30[a]	.40[b]	−.43[a]	−.38[a]	.98[a]	89	.85	.010
	(.24)	(.10)	(.10)	(.22)	(.13)	(.08)	(.11)		(.06)	

a. Significant at the 95% level and of the correct sign.
b. Significant at the 90% level and of the correct sign.
c. Significant at the 95% level and of the incorrect sign. (Standard errors reported in parentheses.)
Note: Technique: Cochrane-Orcutt.
Samples: 78 = 2/75–7/81, 86 = 3/74–4/81, 88 = 3/74–6/81, 89 = 2/74–6/81.

4.5   The Portfolio-Balance Model and Synthesis

The Portfolio-Balance Equation

The portfolio-balance approach to flexible exchange rates was pioneered in a small country framework by Black (1973), Kouri (1976a), Branson (1977), and Girton and Henderson (1977). In this chapter we will consider a simple model in which only two assets are held in the portfolio: those denominated in domestic currency, and those denominated in foreign currency (dollars). We assume that domestic investors allocate a proportion β_d of their total financial wealth W_d to domestic assets B_d and the remainder to dollars F_d:

$$B_d = \beta_d W_d, \tag{16}$$

where $W_d \equiv B_d + SF_d$. If we could assume that domestic assets were not held by foreign residents, so that all current account imbalances were necessarily financed in dollars, then we could compute F_d as the accumulation of past current account surpluses. With B_d computed as the accumulation of past government budget deficits, and both variables corrected for any foreign exchange intervention, it would be a simple matter to solve (16) for the exchange rate S and estimate the parameter β_d. This is how Porter (1979), for example, proceeds.

However, the "small country" assumption that foreigners hold no domestic bonds is unrealistic for most countries, at least most with floating exchange rates. We must, at a minimum, specify another portfolio balance equation for United States investors:

$$B_{us} = \beta_{us} W_{us}, \tag{17}$$

where $W_{us} \equiv B_{us} + SF_{us}$, and a third equation for residents of the rest of the world:

$$B_r = \beta_r W_r, \tag{18}$$

where $W_r \equiv B_r + SF_r$. Data on B_d, B_{us}, and B_r, or on F_d, F_{us}, and F_r, are not normally available. We can compute only the totals $B \equiv B_d + B_{us} + B_r$ and $F \equiv F_d + F_{us} + F_r$, as the cumulation in each country of the government deficit plus foreign exchange intervention. It is not clear how to express S as a function of B, F, W_d, and W_{us}. But it is clear that the signs in such a relationship would be, respectively, positive, negative, negative, and positive. An increase in the supply of dollar assets F lowers their price S; an increase in B has the opposite effect. An increase in United States wealth W_{us} through a current account surplus, raises the net demand for dollar assets, assuming United States residents choose to allocate a greater share of their portfolio to dollar assets than do residents in the rest of the world, and thus raises their price S; an increase in W_d has the opposite effect. Branson, Haltunnen, and Masson (1977, 1979) and Frankel (1983b) regress the exchange rate against four variables similar to these, for the mark/dollar rate.

The portfolio-balance model is estimated by the Cochrane-Orcutt technique.[16] Though the own asset and wealth variables are significant for some of the countries, the results in general are as poor as those for the monetary equation that we've described first. Particularly dismal is the equation for Germany: the coefficients on mark and dollar assets have the wrong signs. The supply of mark bonds, like the German money supply, has increased during precisely those periods in which the mark has *appreciated* rather than depreciated, due largely to the Bundesbank's habit of resisting such appreciation through foreign exchange intervention.

4.6 The Risk Premium and Synthesis with the Monetary Equation

The portfolio-balance model has always specified that the shares β_d and β_f depend on rates of return: the domestic and foreign interest rates i and i^*, and the expected rate of depreciation Δs^e. But recent applications of finance theory by Kouri (1976b), Kouri and de Macedo (1978), de Macedo (1980), Krugman (1981), and Dornbusch (1983) have shown the precise nature of this dependence, on the assumption that investors determine the parameters in their asset demand functions by mean-variance optimization rather than arbitrarily. The asset demand functions are

$$B_d = [a_d + b(i - i^* - \Delta s^e)]W_d, \tag{16'}$$

$$B_{us} = [a_{us} + b(i - i^* - \Delta s^e)]W_{us}, \tag{17'}$$

$$B_r = [a_r + b(i - i^* - \Delta s^e)]W_r, \tag{18'}$$

The coefficient b is related inversely to the coefficient of relative risk aversion, assumed to be the same in both countries, and to the variance of the exchange rate; it multiplies the risk premium to give the "speculative portfolio." The constant terms a_d, a_{us}, and a_r are related positively to the shares of consumption that resident of the three countries allocate to domestic goods; they constitute the "minimum variance" portfolio.

To use aggregate world data, we must add the three equations, which gives us

$$B = a_d W_d + a_{us} W_{us} + a_r W_r + b(i - i^* - \Delta s^e) W,$$

where we have defined world wealth $W \equiv W_d + W_{us} + W_r$. We solve for the risk premium:

$$i - i^* - \Delta s^e = \frac{1}{b}\left(\frac{B}{W}\right) - \frac{a_d - a_r}{b}\frac{W_d}{W} + \frac{a_r - a_{us}}{b}\frac{W_{us}}{W} - \frac{a_r}{b}. \tag{19}$$

Notice first that an increase in the relative supply of domestic assets that must be held in investor portfolios requires a higher relative return on domestic assets. Now assume that domestic residents have the greatest preference for domestic asset and United States residents for dollar assets. (Krugman [1981] has shown that this requires not only that residents of each country consume relatively more of their own goods but also that the constant of relative risk aversion be greater than one.) Then equation (19) implies also that a redistribution of wealth from the rest of the world toward domestic residents will raise the net world demand for domestic assets, and thus lower the relative returns that must be paid on them. A redistribution of wealth toward United States residents will have the opposite effect.

One might wish to make the risk premium equation (19) into a complete model of exchange rate determination like that estimated in the previous section. It would be necessary to specify the determination of the interest rates (e.g., by the proportions of money and bonds within the asset variables) and of expected depreciation (e.g., by a rationally expected future path of the asset supplies and a saddle-point stability assumption).

Here, instead, we integrate the portfolio-balance model with the monetary model of the first part of the chapter. We simply allow for deviations from the uncovered interest parity condition (3), substituting instead our new risk premium equation (19), much as we earlier allowed for deviations from the long-run purchasing power parity condition and the money demand equations. The risk premium is added to the monetary equation of exchange rate determination (14), in the form of the relative asset supply and the distribution of wealth variables:

$$s = (\overline{m} - \overline{m}_{us}) - \phi(\overline{y} - \overline{y}_{us}) + \left(\lambda + \frac{1}{\theta}\right)(\overline{\pi} - \overline{\pi}_{us}) - \frac{1}{\theta}(i - i_{us})$$

$$+ \frac{1}{\theta b}\left(\frac{B}{W}\right) - \frac{a_d - a_r}{\theta b}\left(\frac{W_d}{W}\right) + \frac{a_r - a_{us}}{\theta b}\left(\frac{W_{us}}{W}\right) - \frac{a_r}{\theta b}. \tag{20}$$

We have special cases (a) uniform asset demand preferences ($a_d - a_r = a_r - a_{us} = 0$) and (b) perfect substitutability ($b = \infty$) in addition to the usual special case within the monetary model of (c) perfect price flexibility ($\theta = \infty$).

When the synthesis equation is estimated, the results are surprising.[17] Contrary to what one might expect from the earlier poor portfolio-balance results, each of the three risk premium variables has a coefficient that appears significant and of the correct sign for most of the countries. But one cannot claim that the synthesis works better than the sum of the parts, because the coefficients on the variables from the monetary model are almost invariably insignificant.

To sum up the empirical findings of this chapter, only those in table 4.2 could be described as at all favorable.[18] The implication is that further research into shifts in money demand and in the long-run real exchange rate, within the framework of the monetary model, appears justified.

Epilogue

Much has happened in the years since the exchange rate models of the 1970s were developed and tested.

The early 1980s saw a wave of pessimism among international economists as to the empirical performance of the existing models, or indeed as to the possibility of ever constructing a model that would perform well. Hacche and Townend (1981), Dornbusch (1980b), Frankel (1984b), and Backus (1984) were typical of the mounting pile of studies showing poor results by standard statistical criteria (incorrectly signed coefficients, insignificant magnitudes, low R^2, etc.). Surveys of the empirical models include Levich (1985) and Isard (1988).

Rendering the devastation seemingly complete was a series of papers by Meese and Rogoff (1983a, 1983b, 1988). Meese and Rogoff (1983a) showed that the popular models of Frenkel (1976), Bilson (1978a, 1978b), Dornbusch (1976c), Frankel (1979b), and Hooper and Morton (1982), were of no use whatsoever in predicting exchange rates outside the sample in which the models had been estimated; in every case, a simple random walk predicted better than the structural models. In one sense, this finding should not have been at all surprising. A typical in-sample regression shows unsensible coefficient estimates (for example, near-zero or negative coefficients on the money supply variables, as in the results observed above, attributed to simultaneity bias). Thus, it should not have been surprising that the estimated equations made bad predictions out-of-sample.

But Meese and Rogoff (1983b) then tried an alternative to estimating the equations in-sample. They tried out an entire grid of possible combinations of parameter values, for example, a range of possible values of the semi-elasticity of money demand from -3 to -10. This way, any failure to predict could not be blamed on bad estimates arising from small samples or from simultaneity bias. The results were again discouraging. While many plausible combinations of parameter estimates gave predictions that beat a random walk, many other combinations did not, and in no case was the predictive performance very impressive compared to the total variation in exchange rates. What made these findings particularly humiliating is that from the beginning the authors had given the structural models the benefit of the doubt by using ex post realized values of the explanatory variables (money supply, income, interest rates, etc.) rather than making the models forecast them ex ante before forecasting the exchange rate.

Some economists tried to convert this finding—the inability of the structural models to predict—from a liability to an asset. Their argument, in its least sophisticated form, was essentially a misunderstanding of the point by Dornbusch (1980) and Frenkel (1981a) regarding the importance of "news" in determining exchange rates. The argument was that under the asumptions of high capital mobility and rational expectations, which almost all of the standard theoretical models share, new information regarding the money supply or other macroeconomic variables should have a big effect on the contemporaneous exchange rate, and this effect should not have been predictable before the information is known. While this statement is true so far as it goes, it does not follow that the poor empirical performance of structural models is anything other than a major strike against the standard theory.

There are two respects in which the empirical results are disturbing from the viewpoint of standard theory. First, the proportion of exchange rate changes that we are able to predict over the short term seems to be not just low but close to zero. According to rational expectations theory, we should be able to predict that proportion of exchange rate changes that is correctly predicted by participants in the foreign exchange market. For example, a country that has a record of high money growth and inflation should have a currency that can be predicted to depreciate, at a rate that is appropriately reflected in the expectations of market participants, in the forward discount, and in the interest rate. Yet the Meese-Rogoff papers found that a random walk beats not only all the structural models but also the forward exchange rate, as well as standard time-series techniques (ARIMA and VAR).[19] The finding that the forward exchange rate is of zero benefit in predicting which way the spot rate will move is confirmed in the very large literature testing unbiasedness in the forward exchange market. These studies typically regress the ex post change in the spot rate against the forward discount at the beginning of the period. Rather than getting a coefficient of 1.0, as would be implied by the hypothesis of unbiasedness, they usually get a coefficient much closer to zero, confirming the random walk. (For surveys of this literature, see Levich, 1985; Boothe and Long-worth, 1986; or Hodrick, 1988.) A new measure of the expectations of market participants, survey data, shows results similar to those for the forward rate. Expectations as reflected in surveys are worse predictors than the contemporaneous spot rate; investors could improve their forecasts by putting more weight on the contemporaneous spot rate, perhaps even 100 percent weight (chapters 12 and 13 of this book, written with Froot). The "random walk" results seem remarkably robust.

The second respect in which existing empirical results are disturbing is that even if we accept that we are able to predict only a very small part—or no part—of exchange rate changes ex ante, for example because the predictable component is statistically dwarfed by the "news," we would still hope to be able to explain a large part of exchange rate changes ex post, after we are able to observe the realized values of the macroeconomic variables. This we seem unable to do, at least on a monthly basis, without in-sample overfitting.

The response of international finance economists to their inability to predict or explain exchange rate movements was to redefine the problem. Many were predisposed in any case to move away from the money-demand or portfolio-balance functions that were assumed in the models above, considering them too ad hoc, and instead to derive investor behavior more rigorously from principles of optimization. This is the way the theory proceeded in the 1980s. A demand for money enters the utility function directly, or by assuming a "cash-in-advance" constraint for trans-actions. (Examples include Stockman, 1980; Lucas, 1982; and Svensson, 1985. For a survey, see the last section of Obstfeld and Stockman, 1985).

Whatever their motivation, these models have the distinct advantage, from the viewpoint of their evolutionary survival, that they are generally too abstract to be subjected to genuine empirical testing at all. In fact, proponents of these models, in the economists' public relations coup of the decade, managed to claim as econometric verification their *inability* to explain changes in the exchange rate. Examples typical of modern macro-economic logic are Roll (1979) and Stockman (1987), who argue that the very slow tendency of the exchange rate to return to purchasing power parity supports the optimizing ("equilibrium") models against the over-shooting ("disequilibrium") models. It is ironic that the earlier incarna-tion or equilibrium models, those called "flexible-price monetary" above, claimed support from the alleged empirical observation that the speed of adjustment to purchasing power parity was near-infinite, while the current generation of equilibrium models claims support from the alleged empiri-cal observation that the speed of adjustment of purchasing power parity is near-zero. Meanwhile, proponents of overshooting have consistently claimed a slow but positive rate of adjustment.

The argument goes essentially as follows. According to the optimization models, exchange rate changes are due to shifts in technology and tastes that, though known to all agents in the economy, are not known to the economist. In fact, the economist does not even care to commit on ques-tions such as whether the trend in domestic productivity is greater or less than in foreign productivity. Thus, as far as he or she is concerned, the exchange rate could as easily move up as down. The theory, which is admitted to be in its infancy, as yet contains no information that could be used to explain specific changes in the real exchange rate. The economist then goes to "test" the theory "empirically" by seeing whether he or she can statistically reject the hypothesis that the real exchange rate follows a random walk. Rather than being humbled or embarrassed about the statisti-cal failure to explain any movement in the macroeconomic variable that he or she is investigating, the economist proudly proclaims it as confirming the theory, on the grounds that the theory too did not explain any move-ment in the variable![20]

If the goal is considered to be to explain exchange rate changes rather than not to explain them, then the empirical developments of the 1980s, ironically, are in many respects more supportive of some of the structural models of the 1970s than were the empirical developments of the 1970s. In particular, the broad outlines of the 1981–84 appreciation of the dol-lar—roughly 50 percent in either nominal or real terms—and its 1985–87 reversal are consistent with the theory of exchange rates based on differ-entials in real interest rates (what is above called the "sticky-price monetary model"). Long-term real interest differentials now seem to explain the real exchange rate better than the short-term real interest differentials that were used in earlier specifications (e.g., chapter 3), and there are some theoretical reasons for preferring them as well.[21] By a variety of alternative measures, the long-term real interest differential between the United States and its major trading partners rose by about five points between 1980 and late 1984.[22] Thus, a ready account is provided by the overshooting theory:

the increase in U.S. real interest rates—due, presumably, to a shift in the mix between monetary and fiscal policy—attracted capital into the country, causing the dollar to appreciate, until it had become sufficiently "overvalued" that expectations of future depreciation back toward equilibrium were sufficient in investors' minds to offset the interest differential. After 1984, the real interest differential declined, and the dollar followed.

A theory that claims only to explain exchange rate movements on the basis of two or three observations per decade is not very testable when only fifteen years of data are available. A lot more work would be needed before we could claim to have explained exchange rates well. A number of recent studies on monthly or quarterly data have claimed a degree of success with long-term real interest differentials: Shafer and Loopesko (1983), Hooper (1984), Sachs (1985), Hutchison and Throop (1985), Golub et al. (1985), and Feldstein (1986). Given how often in the past a model that appeared to work well for one sample period is observed to go awry subsequently, it would be foolhardy to claim too much for these or any other regression studies. But neither is it necessary for economists to abjure any ability to explain exchange rate movements at all.

Acknowledgment

This material was based on work supported by the National Science Foundation under grant no. SES-8007162 and further supported by a research grant from the Institute of Business and Economic Research at the University of California, Berkeley. Thanks are due to Allen Berger, Eric Fisher, Brian Newton, and, especially, Charles Engel for research assistance, and Peter Kenen and Hali Edison for very useful comments and suggestions.

5

Why Interest Rates React to Money Announcements: An Explanation from the Foreign Exchange Market

with Charles Engel

5.1 Why Does the Interest Rate Rise after Announcements of Money Growth?

One striking empirical regularity has been the tendency for interest rates to rise whenever the Federal Reserve Board announces an increase in the money supply greater than had previously been expected. This relationship appears almost every week in credit market developments as reported in the financial press.[1] At first glance, the phenomenon might seem puzzling to a student of textbook IS-LM models, which predict that liquidity effects should make interest rates fall when the authorities expand the money supply. At second glance, however, the student should realize that there is not necessarily an inconsistency. Interest rates may indeed fall during a week in which the Fed *actually* increases the money supply. But when the *announcement* occurs ten days later, interest rates will change purely because the announcement alters the market's expectations of future monetary policy.

There is, in fact, an explanation of this weekly occurrence that is consistent with the Keynesian (IS-LM) view that tighter money causes the real interest rate to rise. Money growth that is faster than expected by the market is typically faster than what was expected by the Fed as well. Weekly blips in the money supply are unintended errors—due to fluctuations in private money demand or in the banking system—beyond the monetary authorities' control. The Fed subsequently corrects the errors to bring the money supply back in line with its target growth rates. Thus the announcement of a large money supply increase generates the expectation of future contraction in credit and higher interest rates. In anticipation, interest rates jump on bonds with terms that include the period in which money markets will be tighter. The fact that rates on even very short-term bonds increase indicates a belief that the Fed wastes no time in beginning to correct errors.[2]

This explanation of the announcement effect on interest rates is commonly given by staff writers of the *Wall Street Journal*:

The Federal Reserve System may be forced to boost the discount rate from 12% in its battle to halt the soaring growth of the nation's money supply.... Fears of Fed credit tightening sent the markets reeling Friday after release of the latest money supply statistics. Prices of long-term U.S. government bonds tumbled by more than a point, or $10 for each $1,000 face amount of securities. Interest rate increases of 1/2 percentage point were common on short-term securities. (January 25, 1982)

However, there is a second, very different, explanation of the phenomenon that, ironically, is propounded in the same newspaper, but in the editorial column. The announcement of rapid money growth causes the market to raise its estimate of the Fed's target money growth rate, the expected inflation rate rises, and it is reflected in a higher nominal interest rate:

A reduction in money growth will constrict the supply of credit, but it will also lower inflationary expectations. If the markets are convinced the Fed is really serious about slowing money growth, the drop in the inflationary premium will swamp the impact on the real rate of interest, and nominal rates will fall. This is precisely what seems to be happening this week in the wake of the latest money supply figures. (January 7, 1981)

One might think of other ways of describing the positive correlation between money announcements and interest rate changes. But they can be seen to fall into the category of one or the other of these two competing explanations, if one groups them by reference to the decomposition of the nominal interest rate into the real interest rate and the expected inflation rate. According to the first explanation, a large money announcement raises the nominal interest rate because it raises the real interest rate. We will refer to this as the liquidity effect. According to the second explanation, the announcement raises the nominal interest rate because it raises expected inflation. We will refer to this as the inflation-premium effect.

It would be useful to be able to distinguish between the two hypotheses, since they might give an indication of how the market views the Fed's policies. The liquidity effect requires that the market expect the Fed to stick to its preannounced money growth target and to correct any aberration. The inflation premium explanation implies that the Fed is not trusted to keep a steady course; the market, like the *Wall Street Journal* editors, is ready to interpret any deviation in money growth as a signal that the Fed is changing its targets.

Fortunately, there is a quite simple way to choose between the two hypotheses. If expected inflation increases, then the value of the dollar should fall (the exchange rate should rise) as demand for the currency declines. On the other hand, if tight monetary policy causes the real interest rate to rise, then a capital inflow should cause an appreciation of the dollar. Thus, if the inflation premium view is correct, the exchange rate should have the same positive correlation with money announcements that the interest rate has. If the liquidity view is correct, the exchange rate should have the opposite correlation with the other variables.[3]

Section 5.2 formalizes the intuitive argument that the exchange rate depends on the expected future path of the money supply. The model is a discrete-time generalization of a synthesis of Jacob Frenkel's (1976) monetarist version of the monetary approach to exchange rate determination and Rudiger Dornbusch's (1976c) Keynesian version of the approach, (the synthesis of chapter 3). The reader familiar with this literature, or willing to accept the intuitive argument, is encouraged to skip directly to the empirical results in section 5.3. There, it is discovered that the evidence strongly favors the liquidity effect.

5.2   A Model of the Exchange Rate's Dependence on Monetary Tightness

In this section we illustrate in a particular model how the exchange rate jumps in response to changes in the perceived general future path of monetary policy. Thus in the case where announcements of unexpectedly large money supplies are interpreted as increases in the Fed's target money growth rate, the exchange rate increases. In the case where such announcements are interpreted as transitory deviations bringing future contraction, the exchange rate falls.

We begin with a conventional money demand equation

$$m_t - p_t = -\lambda i_t + a_t. \tag{1}$$

Here m_t and p_t are the logs of the money supply and price level, i_t is the very short-term interest rate, and a_t represents the influence of real income and other exogenous shifts in money demand.

In a flexible-price monetarist world, the combination of purchasing power parity in rate-of-change form and interest rate parity (equation (6) below) would tie the domestic interest rate to the foreign interest rate, with an allowance for expected inflation. Then the domestic price level p_t would be determined by the money demand equation (1) and a money supply process.

We are going to allow prices to be sticky, to be prevented from jumping at a moment in time. Thus purchasing power parity does not hold in the short run. But prices adjust to excess demand over time, so purchasing power parity does hold in long-run equilibrium:

$$\bar{s}_t = \bar{p}_t, \tag{2}$$

where $\bar{s}$ is the log of the equilibrium spot exchange rate, $\bar{p}$ is the log of the domestic equilibrium price level, and the log of the foreign equilibrium price level is taken as exogenous and is here normalized at zero. The domestic equilibrium price level is in turn defined by the stable ("no bubble") rational expectations solution to

$$\bar{m}_t - \bar{p}_t = -\lambda[E_t\bar{p}_{t+1} - \bar{p}_t + i^*] + a_t, \tag{3}$$

where $E_t p_{t+1} - p_t$ is the equilibrium inflation rate expected at time t and i^* is the foreign interest rate, also taken to be exogenous, which is equal to i in long-run equilibrium. This is a logical way to determine $\bar{p}$, because it is the way we would determine p in a flexible-price world.

We find the rational expectations solution as follows. Solve equation (3) for p_t in terms of $E_t\bar{p}_{t+1}$. Then substitute the solution for $E_t\bar{p}_{t+1}$ in terms of $E_t\bar{p}_{t+2}$. Continuing to substitute recursively, we obtain

$$\bar{p}_t = \frac{1}{1+\lambda} \sum_{\tau=0}^{\infty} \left(\frac{\lambda}{1+\lambda}\right)^{\tau} E_t(m_{t+\tau} - a_{t+\tau}) + \lambda i^*. \tag{4}$$

We see that $\bar{p}_t$ is an indicator of how expansionary the entire future path of money supply is expected to be relative to money demand. As an example, if money supply and demand are expected to be constant at m_t and a_t, respectively, then $\bar{p}_t$ is simply $m_t - a_t + \lambda i^*_t$. Below we will consider two alternative specific money supply processes to narrow the range of possibilities under (4).

Now we are going to see how changes in the unobservable $\bar{p}_t$ are reflected as changes in the observable s_t. We assume a form of regressive expectations for the exchange rate:

$$E_t s_{t+1} - s_t = \theta(\bar{s}_t - s_t) + E_t\bar{s}_{t+1} - \bar{s}_t. \tag{5}$$

In the long-run equilibrium, when $\bar{s} - s = 0$, the spot rate s is, of course, expected to increase at the rate of the equilibrium spot rate $\bar{s}$, which will be the same as the rates of increase of the equilibrium price level (by purchasing power parity) and money supply (by money demand homogeneity). But in the short run, if the spot rate exceeds what the market considers its equilibrium path ($s - \bar{s} > 0$), then the currency is thought to be "undervalued" and is expected in the future to appreciate ($E_t s_{t+1} - s_t < 0$) relative to the equilibrium path, at a rate that is proportional to the gap. Equation (5) is of the general form that expectations are assumed to take in chapter 3 and Mussa (1977). In appendix 5A, we show (5) to be precisely the rational form for expectations to take when the system contains an equation specifying the price level to adjust gradually according to an excess demand function plus a term for the equilibrium inflation path.

Our final assumption is uncovered interest parity:

$$i_t - i^* = E_t s_{t+1} - s_t. \tag{6}$$

Return to the money demand function (1). An announcement of monetary growth at time t, as opposed to the event itself over the preceding period, does not change the money supply, or the price level or real money demand, and thus does not change the short-term interest rate i_t.[4] Thus, by (6) it does not change expected depreciation $E_t s_{t+1} - s_t$, which in turn is the left-hand side of (5):

$$0 = \theta((\bar{s}_t - \bar{s}_{t'}) - (s_t - s_{t'})) + (E_t \bar{s}_{t+1} - E_{t'} \bar{s}_{t+1}) - (\bar{s}_t - \bar{s}_{t'}), \tag{5'}$$

where we are using t' to denote the value of a variable the instant before the announcement.[5]

We are interested in the change in the current spot rate induced by the announcement:

$$s_t - s_{t'} = \bar{s}_t - \bar{s}_{t'} + \frac{1}{\theta}[(E_t \bar{s}_{t+1} - E_{t'} \bar{s}_{t+1}) - (\bar{s}_t - \bar{s}_{t'})]. \tag{6}$$

We use (2):

$$s_t - s_{t'} = \bar{p}_t - \bar{p}_{t'} + \frac{1}{\theta}[(E_t \bar{p}_{t+1} - \bar{p}_t) - (E_{t'} \bar{p}_{t+1} - \bar{p}_{t'})]. \tag{7}$$

The expression in brackets is the revision in the market's expected equilibrium inflation rate. The equilibrium money demand equation (3) tells us, with m_t, i_t^*, and a_t tied down, that the effect of the announcement on the market's expected equilibrium inflation rate is related to the effect on the equilibrium price level:

$$\bar{p}_t - \bar{p}_{t'} = \lambda[(E_t \bar{p}_{t+1} - \bar{p}_t) - (E_{t'} \bar{p}_{t+1} - \bar{p}_{t'})]. \tag{3'}$$

We combine (3') and (7):

$$s_t - s_{t'} = (1 + 1/\lambda\theta)(\bar{p}_t - \bar{p}_{t'}). \tag{8}$$

Equation (8) is the promised result that revisions in $\bar{p}$, the indicator of expected future credit conditions, cause proportional jumps in the spot exchange rate. The equation is a generalization of Dornbusch's celebrated overshooting result that an unanticipated increase in the money supply causes an equilibrium increase in the exchange rate of the same percentage and in addition causes the current exchange rate to overshoot its equilibrium by $1/\lambda\theta$.

We could stop here. Equation (4) establishes $\bar{p}_t$ as an indicator of the entire expected future path of monetary policy and, equation (8) establishes that s_t jumps with $\bar{p}_t$. If the announcement of an unexpectedly high money supply induces the public to raise its expectation of future money supplies relative to money demand, a sudden increase in s_t will tell us so. On the other hand, if the announcement induces expectation of monetary contraction in the near future, a sudden fall in s_t will tell us so.

To make these two cases more concrete, we now consider two particular alternative money supply processes. Both involve a target path for the money supply with growth rate μ_t:

$$\bar{m}_t = \bar{m}_{t-1} + \mu_t. \tag{9}$$

In both cases we also assume here that real money demand a_t follows a random walk; to get our results (qualitatively) it is sufficient that a_t be autocorrelated. (Recall that a_t includes real income.)

Under money supply process A, the Fed succeeds in hitting its money supply target even on a weekly basis, but it keeps changing the target growth rate according to a random walk:

$$m_t = \bar{m}_t \tag{10a}$$

$$\mu_t = \mu_{t+1} + v_t. \tag{11a}$$

This implies $E_t m_{t+\tau} = m_t + \tau\mu_t$. If we use this money supply process in equation (4), we find that the announcement of a money supply 1 percent greater than expected raises $\bar{p}_t$ by $\lambda\%$:[6]

$$\bar{p}_t - \bar{p}_{t'} = \lambda(m_t - E_{t'} m_t). \tag{12a}$$

Intuitively, under money supply process A, the announcement of m_t is interpreted as a one-for-one increase in the steady-state inflation rate, which reduces steady-state real money demand—or raises the equilibrium price level—by that amount times the semielasticity of money demand. From (8):

$$s_t - s_{t'} = \left(\frac{1 + \lambda\theta}{\theta}\right)(m_t - E_{t'}m_t). \tag{13a}$$

The announcement of an unexpectedly high money supply in this case causes an immediate depreciation of the dollar.

Under the alternative of money supply process B, the Fed sticks to its preset target growth rate, but the actual money supply deviates from the target due to unintended weekly fluctuations:

$$m_t = \bar{m}_t + u_t \tag{10b}$$

$$\mu_t = \mu. \tag{11b}$$

If we use this money supply process in equation (4), we find that the announcement of a money supply 1 percent greater than expected reduces $\bar{p}_t$ by $\lambda/(1 + \lambda)$:

$$\bar{p}_t - \bar{p}_{t'} = -\frac{\lambda}{1 + \lambda}(m_t - E_{t'}m_t). \tag{12b}$$

Intuitively, under money supply process B, the announcement is interpreted as requiring a one-for-one contraction in the following period. It is true that the public has discovered the money supply in the most recent period to be higher than it had estimated. But it necessarily discovers at the same time that money demand a_t is higher than it had thought. Under our assumption that a_t is autocorrelated, the upward shift in money demand is expected to remain next period. But under our assumption of money supply process B, the money supply is anticipated to shift back next period. In expression (4), representing the expected present discounted sum of present and future credit market conditions, expected money supply has fallen relative to expected money demand. This tightening in expectations of monetary policy is reflected in a sudden fall in $\bar{p}_t$. From (8),

$$s_t - s_{t'} = -\frac{1 + \lambda\theta}{\theta(1 + \lambda)}(m_t - E_{t'}m_t). \tag{13b}$$

In this case, the dollar appreciates with the announcement of an unexpectedly high money supply—the opposite from case A.

With either money supply process A or B, the nominal rate of interest would increase with a higher-than-anticipated money supply announcement. However, with process A, it would be the inflation premium that

Table 5.1
(Dependent variable: MFE_t = logarithmic monetary forecast error at t)

c	MFE_{-1}	MFE_{-2}		R^2	D.W.
−.00042			$F(1,203) = 1.42$	0	2.05
(.00035)					
−.00042	−.028		$F(2,201) = 0.76$	.0008	2.00
(.00036)	(.071)				
−.00041	−.028	.014	$F(3,199) = 0.49$	.0010	1.99
(.00036)	(.071)	(.072)			

Note: Sample period: Sept. 1977–Aug. 1981, weekly data. (Standard errors reported in parentheses.)

would rise, while in case B the real rate would jump. (This is demonstrated formally in appendix 5A.) The two processes are distinguishable by their differing implications for exchange rate movements.

5.3 Empirical Tests of Announcement Effects

The market's anticipation of the next money growth announcement is determined not only by the most recent money supply figures but by many other factors as well. Any attempt to measure expected money growth by, for example, an ARIMA model of the money supply time series is unlikely to be accurate. It turns out that there is a very convenient measure of the market's opinion of what the Fed is going to announce. Money Market Services, Inc., each week surveys sixty individuals who predict what the announcement will be. It is these survey numbers that we use as our measure of expected money growth.

It would add to the credibility of the survey numbers if we could show that they are unbiased predictors of the actual money supply announcements. Grossman (1981) has shown that the Money Market Services forecasts are unbiased for the period September 1977–September 1979. Table 5.1 shows some simple tests performed on an updated time sample. The first regression is a test of whether the mean forecast error from September 1977 to August 1981 was different from zero. The next two equations test for information in lagged forecast errors.[7] In no case is any coefficient significantly different from zero. This finding supports the unbiasedness of the forecasts.

The money forecasts are actually made on Tuesdays, while money supply figures were released usually on Thursdays until February 1980 and usually on Fridays after then. Ideally, we would like to know the market's guess at the money supply immediately before the announcement. Money Market Services, Inc., believes that little new information comes in between Tuesday and Friday to change market opinions. The previous week's money supply figures have already been released and digested, and most other relevant information, such as observed interest rate changes, should have come in the week that the change in the money supply actually occurred. To test this claim, it is possible to check whether the exchange rate or the interest rate on the morning of the announcement contains any information that would improve the prediction. Table 5.2 reports regressions of the forecast error on various combinations of the exchange rate and the interest rates and lagged values of those two variables and the forecast error. F-statistics indicate an inability to reject the null hypothesis that all coefficients, including the constant, are zero. Thus, these guesses at the soon-to-be-revealed money stock numbers are efficient with respect to some obvious potential sources of information.[8]

Before we examine the effect of larger-than-expected monetary announcements on interest rate and exchange rate changes, we should pause to consider why we are treating the monetary forecast errors as the independent variable. If our observations of the financial variables are taken close enough in time to the announcement, before and after, then we can hope that the changes are explained largely by the announcement effect. However, we will certainly not get a perfect fit; other factors will contribute to the changes. The question is whether the errors that do intervene in the relationship are independent of the monetary forecast errors. There is an excellent reason to believe that they are: both the announced money supply figures and their forecasts as measured by Money Market Services are predetermined, by several days, at the time that the announcement is made. A claim of econometric exogeneity on the part of the monetary forecast error can be supported by a Granger causality test. A necessary condition for monetary forecast errors to be exogenous with respect to a particular variable is that, after taking account of the information in the lagged forecast errors, the variable in question does not help predict the forecast error. Table 5.3 shows that neither the interest rate nor the exchange rate Granger causes the monetary forecast error.

Having confirmed the desirable properties of the monetary forecasts, we now proceed to the main results. Table 5.4 attempts to confirm the empirical regularity on which the chapter is predicated: the positive dependence of interest rate changes on monetary announcements. The interest rate is the one-month Eurodollar rate. We look at the change from 10:00 A.M. on

Table 5.2
(Dependent variable: MFE_t = logarithmic forecast error at t)

c	MFE_{-1}	MIN	MIN_{-1}	MEX	MEX_{-1}		R^2	D.W.
-.00058 (.001)		.0014 (.0092)				$F(2,202) = 0.72$	.0001	2.05
-.00048 (.0011)		.035 (.048)	-.035 (.048)			$F(3,200) = 0.63$	.0027	2.07
-.00057 (.0011)	-.028 (.071)	.0013 (.0093)				$F(3,200) = 0.50$	.0009	2.00
.00070 (.0025)				.0017 (.0037)		$F(2,202) = 0.81$	.0010	2.05
.00069 (.0026)				-.0019 (.024)	.0035 (.024)	$F(3,200) = 0.52$	.0010	2.05
.00066 (.0025)	-.029 (.071)			.0016 (.0037)		$F(3,200) = 0.56$	.0017	1.99
.00054 (.0026)		.0020 (.0093)		.0018 (.0037)		$F(3,201) = 0.55$	.0012	2.05

Note: Sample period: Sept. 1977–Aug. 1981, weekly data
MIN = one-month Eurodollar rate on announcement morning
MEX = log New York market bid exchange rate, announcement morning

Table 5.3
Causality test (Dependent variable: MFE_t = logarithmic monetary forecast error at t)

c	MFE_{-1}	MFE_{-2}	MFE_{-3}	MFE_{-4}	MIN_{-1}	MIN_{-2}	R^2	D.W.
.0073	−.154	−.024	−.038	−.089	−.023	−.041	—	—
(.0033)	(.108)	(.115)	(.116)	(.112)	(.059)	(.083)		
	MIN_{-3}	MIN_{-4}	MIN_{-5}	MIN_{-6}	$F(6, 86) = 1.50$		.115	1.99
	−.064	−.022	.086	−.030				

c	MFE_{-1}	MFE_{-2}	MFE_{-3}	MFE_{-4}	MEX_{-1}	MEX_{-2}	R^2	D.W.
.0017	−.069	.065	.0071	.083	.0042	−.084		
(.0038)	(.107)	(.109)	(.109)	(.106)	(.037)	(.053)		
	MEX_{-3}	MEX_{-4}	MEX_{-5}	MEX_{-6}	$F(6, 86) = 1.44$		.121	2.02
	−.140	−.0060	−.054	.0019				
	(.053)	(.055)	(.054)	(.058)				

Note: Sample Period: October 1979–August 1981

Table 5.4
(Dependent variable: one-day change in Eurodollar rate)

Regression technique	MFE	D.W.	$\hat{\rho}$	R^2
OLS	.236	1.099		.007
	(.138)			
CORC	.162		.456	.206
	(.110)		(.091)	

Note: Sample period: October 1979–August 1981

Table 5.5
(Dependent variable: one-day change in log exchange rate)

Regression technique	MFE	D.W.	R^2
OLS	−.393	1.729	.069
	(.145)		

Note: Sample Period: October 1979–August 1981

the day of the announcement (which is made at 4:00 P.M.) to 10:00 A.M. the following day. The sample period is restricted to October 1979 to August 1981.[9] The coefficient in the regressions is positive and, when estimated by Cochrane-Orcutt, is significant at the 90 percent level. Somewhat stronger results were obtained by Grossman using Treasury bill rates that were recorded at 3:30 P.M. and 5:00 P.M. on announcement days.

Table 5.5 presents the regression of the change in (the log of) the dollar/mark exchange rate between noon the day of the announcement and noon the following day, against the monetary announcement forecast error. The coefficient turns out to be negative and highly significant. So on days when the money supply figures turn out to be greater than expected, the currency appreciates. This indicates that the real interest rate rises: the nominal interest rate rises because of liquidity effects, not because of the expected inflation premium.

5.4   Conclusion

The announcement phenomenon is a valuable tool for cutting through the web of simultaneous causality that plagues much of empirical macro-economics. The negative effect that the announcements had on the exchange rate indicates that the market believed that the Fed was following a steady money growth policy in the period beginning October 1979.

When the money supply grows more rapidly than had been expected, the market assumes that the Fed will reverse the error in the future, not that it has raised its money growth target. The expectation of future tightening causes the interest rate to rise and the exchange rate to fall.

The results of this chapter also shed light on a second issue. It is sometimes claimed that goods prices are flexible and that fluctuations in the interest rate mostly consist of fluctuations in the expected inflation rate, rather than the fluctuations in the real interest rate that characterize a Keynesian model.[10] In terms of the model developed in section 5.2, the speed of adjustment θ is thought to be close to infinite. Changes in the nominal money supply or expected inflation rate are reflected immediately in the price level and real money supply and thus have no effect on the real interest rate. One way people have tested this view of the world is to run a regression of the exchange rate against money supplies, real income levels, interest rates, and inflation rates. A significant negative coefficient on the interest rate indicates a rejection of perfectly flexible prices (e.g., chapter 3). One difficulty with this approach is that there are serious simultaneity problems with considering the interest rate and expected inflation rate as independent variables. And instrumental variable techniques are only partial solutions because it is hard to find exogenous variables. (A second difficulty is that the results have proved to be sensitive to the particular currency and sample period chosen.)

The results in Tables 5.4 and 5.5, when taken together, provide evidence against the flexible-price view in a context free from simultaneity problems, as diagrammed in table 5.6. Given just the positive correlation of monetary announcements and interest rate changes, one could rationalize the flexible-price model by arguing that unanticipated money growth raises expected future money growth and thus raises expected inflation. That is, we could be in the first column of row A in the table. Given just the negative correlation of monetary announcements and exchange rate changes, one could rationalize the flexible-price model by arguing instead that unanticipated money growth generates the expectation of future contraction, thus reducing the expected inflation. That is, we could be in the first column of row B. But the two results taken together can be explained only by granting a role to sticky prices and to fluctuations in the real interest rate.[11] We can only be in the second column of row B. Once again: the money growth announcement causes the real interest rate to rise, which explains *both* the rise in the nominal interest rate and the fall in the exchange rate.

Table 5.6
Reactions to money announcements

		If goods prices are flexible,	If goods prices are sticky,
A	and expected future money rises,	the rise in expected inflation implies { AN INCREASE IN i and A FALL IN THE DOLLAR	the real interest rate falls, implying { AN DECREASE IN i and A FALL IN THE DOLLAR
B	and expected future money falls,	the rise in expected inflation implies { AN DECREASE IN i and A RISE IN THE DOLLAR	the real interest rate rises, implying { AN INCREASE IN i and A RISE IN THE DOLLAR

Appendix 5A

In this appendix we show that expectations of the form of (5) are consistent with a Mussa (1981a) price-adjustment equation.[12] We also derive the change in the real and nominal interest rates for money supply processes A and B of section 5.2.

Substitute the uncovered interest parity relation (6) into the money demand function (1), and subtract (1) from (3):

$$0 = p_t - \bar{p}_t - \lambda(E_t s_{t+1} - s_t) + \lambda(E_t \bar{p}_{t+1} - \bar{p}_t).$$

Using long-run PPP (2):

$$E_t s_{t+1} - s_t - (E_t \bar{s}_{t+1} - \bar{s}_t) = 1/\lambda(p_t - \bar{p}_t). \tag{A1}$$

From the expectations relation (5), and (A1), we have:

$$-\frac{1}{\lambda\theta}(p_t - \bar{p}_t) = s_t - \bar{s}_t. \tag{A2}$$

Leading (A2) one period, and taking expectations:

$$-\frac{1}{\lambda\theta}E_t(p_{t+1} - \bar{p}_{t+1}) = E_t(s_{t+1} - \bar{s}_{t+1}). \tag{A3}$$

Subtracting (A2) from (A3) yields:

$$E_t s_{t+1} - s_t - (E_t \bar{s}_{t+1} - \bar{s}_t) = -\frac{1}{\lambda\theta}[E_t(p_{t+1} - \bar{p}_{t+1}) - (p_t - \bar{p}_t)]. \tag{A4}$$

Using (A1) and (A4) and rearranging we have:

$$E_t p_{t+1} = p_t + (E_t \bar{p}_{t+1} - \bar{p}_t) - \theta(p_t - \bar{p}_t). \tag{A5}$$

(A5) is consistent with a Mussa-type price-adjustment equation:

$$p_{t+1} = p_t + (E_t \bar{p}_{t+1} - \bar{p}_t) - \theta(p_t - \bar{p}_t). \tag{A6}$$

Furthermore, substituting long-run PPP (2) and the expectations equation (5),

$$p_{t+1} = p_t - \theta(p_t - \bar{p}_t) + E_t s_{t+1} - s_t + \theta(s_t - \bar{s}_t).$$

Again, using long-run PPP (2):

$$p_{t+1} = p_t + E_t s_{t+1} - s_t + \theta(s_t - p_t). \tag{A7}$$

This form of the price-adjustment equation is helpful in deriving the interest-rate relations.

We assume that the n-period ahead interest rate, $_ni_t$, is simply the average of the expected one-period rates for the next n periods.

$$_ni_t = \frac{1}{n}[E_t s_{t+n} - s_t] + _ni_t^*. \tag{A8}$$

From (A7):

$$E_t s_{t+n} = E_t p_{t+n} + (1 - \theta)E_t(s_{t+n-1} - p_{t+n-1}) = E_t p_{t+n} + (1 - \theta)^n(s_t - p_t). \tag{A9}$$

Then, from (A2):

$$E_t s_{t+n} = E_t \bar{s}_{t+n} - \frac{1}{\lambda\theta}(E_t p_{t+n} - E_t \bar{p}_{t+n}) = -\frac{1}{\lambda\theta}E_t p_{t+n} + \left(1 + \frac{1}{\lambda\theta}\right)E_t \bar{p}_{t+n}. \tag{A10}$$

Substituting from (A9) and rearranging:

$$E_t s_{t+n} = -\frac{(1 - \theta)^n}{1 + \lambda\theta}(p_t - s_t) + E_t \bar{p}_{t+n}.$$

Taking expectations at t' and subtracting (and using the fact that $p_t = p_{t'}$):

$$E_t s_{t+n} - E_{t'} s_{t+n} = \frac{(1 - \theta)^n}{1 + \lambda\theta}(s_t - s_{t'}) + E_t \bar{p}_{t+n} - E_{t'} \bar{p}_{t+n}.$$

Using (A8)

$$_ni_t - _ni_{t'} = \frac{1}{n}\left[\frac{(1 - \theta)^n}{1 + \lambda\theta} - 1\right](s_t - s_{t'}) + \frac{1}{n}[E_t \bar{p}_{t+n} - E_{t'} \bar{p}_{t+n}]. \tag{A11}$$

Let the n-period real interest rate be $_nr_t$:

$$_nr_t = _ni_t - \frac{1}{n}[E_t p_{t+n} - p_t]. \tag{A12}$$

From (A8) and (A9)

$$_ni_t - _ni_{t'} = \frac{1}{n}[(E_t s_{t+n} - E_{t'} s_{t+n}) - (s_t - s_{t'})]$$

$$= \frac{1}{n}(E_t p_{t+n} - E_{t'} p_{t+n}) + \frac{1}{n}((1 - \theta)^n - 1)(s_t - s_{t'}).$$

So we get

$$_n r_t - _n r_{t'} = \frac{(1 - \theta)^n - 1}{n}(s_t - s_{t'}).\tag{A13}$$

Since $(1 - \theta)^n - 1 < 0$, the exchange rate always moves in the opposite direction of the real rate of interest when new money stock figures are revealed.

Let $_n \pi_t$ be the inflation premium on n-period bonds:

$$_n \pi_t = \frac{1}{n}(E_t p_{t+n} - p_t).$$

Subtracting (A13) from (A11), it follows from (A12):

$$_n \pi_t - _n \pi_{t'} = \frac{1}{n}\left[\frac{-\lambda\theta(1 - \theta)^n}{1 + \lambda\theta}\right](s_t - s_{t'}) + \frac{1}{n}[E_t \bar{p}_{t+n} - E_{t'} \bar{p}_{t+n}].\tag{A14}$$

For money supply process A, it can be shown from (4):

$$E_t \bar{p}_{t+n} - E_{t'} \bar{p}_{t+n} = (n + \lambda)(m_t - E_{t'} m_t).\tag{A15a}$$

Substituting (A15a) and (13a) into (A11), we get:

$$_n i_t - _n i_{t'} = \frac{(1 - \theta)^n + n\theta - 1}{n\theta}(m_t - E_{t'} m_t).\tag{A16a}$$

Since

$$(1 - \theta)^n > 1 - n\theta,$$

the interest rate will move in the same direction as the unexpected change in the money supply. In this case, the rise is entirely attributable to an increase in the inflation premium since:

$$_n r_t - _n r_{t^*} = \alpha_1 (m_t - E_{t'} m_t); \quad \alpha_1 = \frac{((1 - \theta)^n - 1)(1 + \lambda\theta)}{n\theta} < 0,\tag{A17a}$$

$$_n \pi_t - _n \pi_{t'} = \beta_1 (m_t - E_{t'} m_t); \quad \beta_1 = \frac{n + \lambda(1 - (1 - \theta)^n)}{n} > 0.\tag{A18a}$$

For money supply process B,

$$E_t \bar{p}_{t+n} - E_{t'} \bar{p}_{t+n} = -(m_t - E_t m_t).\tag{A15b}$$

So, from (13b) and (A11):

$$_n\dot{\imath}_t - {}_n\dot{\imath}_{t'} = \frac{(1 - \theta) - (1 - \theta)^n}{n\theta(1 + \lambda)}(m_t - E_{t'}m_t). \tag{A16b}$$

Since

$$(1 - \theta) > (1 - \theta)^n$$

this model is also adequate to explain the observed movements of interest rates on days of monetary announcements. In this case, though, the nominal rate rises because of an increase in the real rate:

$$_nr_t - {}_nr_{t'} = \alpha_2(m_t - E_{t'}m_t); \quad \alpha_2 = \frac{(1 - (1 - \theta)^n)(1 + \lambda\theta)}{n(1 + \lambda)} > 0 \tag{A17b}$$

$$_n\pi_t - {}_n\pi_{t'} > \beta_2(m_t - E_{t'}m_t); \quad \beta_2 = \frac{-(1 + \lambda(1 - (1 - \theta)^n))}{n(1 + \lambda)} < 0. \tag{A18b}$$

Acknowledgment

This is a slightly revised version of NBER Working Paper no. 1049. The idea for the paper originated in a comment made by Ronald McKinnon to one of the authors in 1978. We are also indebted to Robert Flood, James Hamilton, Dale Henderson, Peter Isard, and Maurice Obstfeld for their valuable insights; to Richard Meese for comments on an earlier draft; to Money Market Services, Inc., for their survey data on money supply expectations; and to the National Science Foundation for research support under grant number SES-8007162, administered through the Institute of Business and Economic Research, University of California, Berkeley.

An abridged version of this chapter appeared in the *Journal of Monetary Economics*, January 1984.

6

Six Possible Meanings of "Overvaluation": The 1981–85 Dollar

6.1 Introduction

There is near-unanimity that the dollar was greatly overvalued in the early 1980s. As soon as 1982, Bergsten et al. (p. 1) warned:

The dollar is overvalued by at least 20 percent.... These imbalances are as great as those in the final, breakdown stage of the Bretton Woods system of fixed exchange rates. They add significantly to national growth problems, both in countries with overvalued currencies (which suffer competitive losses) and countries with undervalued currencies (which are driven to adopt restrictive monetary policies).

According to later calculations of Williamson (1985, pp. 85–86),

The peak overvaluation of the dollar in late February and early March 1985 was more than 40 percent,... about double the estimated overvaluation of the dollar which brought the collapse of the Bretton Woods system of fixed parities in the early 1970s.

What does this word "overvalued" mean? Economists have an instinctive aversion to it. But it is clear that the value of the dollar during the first half of the 1980s was indeed very high, not only relative to its past history but relative to such long-term fundamentals as relative price levels or money supplies and income levels. This fact is documented in section 6.2 below.

This essay proposes six possible and very distinct definitions of the words "overvaluation" and "undervaluation," or the equivalently ambiguous term "disequilibrium," and uses them as an organizing principle to discuss theoretical and empirical research in the economics of exchange rates.

First, these words could refer to *nonclearing of financial markets*, where, because of barriers to capital movements, the exchange rate is at a level at which the supply of foreign exchange does not equal the demand.

Second, "overvaluation" could mean that a currency's private supply exceeds its private demand and that *foreign-exchange intervention* by one or more central banks is supporting the value of the currency at a level higher than it would be in a completely free market. These two definitions are discussed in section 6.2.

Third, "overvaluation" could describe a currency with a value that is higher than dictated by long-term fundamentals because it is determined by short-term macroeconomic fundamentals such as the real interest rate. This is the phenomenon of *overshooting* discussed in section 6.3.

Fourth, "overvaluation" could mean that speculators can expect to make money by selling the currency forward. This is the possibility *of irrational expectations* discussed in section 6.4.

Fifth, "overvaluation" could mean that, even if expectations are rational, the exchange rate nevertheless diverges from the equilibrium determined by fundamentals, short run as well as long run. This is the possibility of *speculative bubbles* discussed in section 6.5.

Sixth, "overvaluation" could pertain to the real effects of the exchange rate rather than to its determinants. Under this interpretation, the loss in competitiveness by domestic industries that export or that compete with imports is undesirable. Or the reverse effects in foreign countries are undesirable for them. The possibility of overvaluation in a *normative* sense is addressed in section 6.6.

A distinction that proves to be necessary throughout is between long-term swings and short-term volatility in exchange rates. Both have been large. To anticipate the conclusions regarding long-term swings, the 1980–85 real appreciation of the dollar is attributed primarily to an increase in the U.S. real interest rate relative to foreign real interest rates, as in the overshooting model of exchange rates. The increase in the U.S. real interest rate is in turn attributed to two causes, corresponding to the two halves of the period: first, the sharp tightening of U.S. monetary policy that was first signaled in October 1979 and that ended in mid-1982, and, second, the emergence of record federal budget deficits that were a source of growing concern from 1982 to 1985. Two other possibilities, irrational expectations and rational speculative bubbles, are rejected as major explanations for the dollar overvaluation. This still leaves to each a possible role in causing short-term exchange-rate volatility.

As to welfare effects, discussed in section 6.6, high short-term exchange-rate volatility which generates uncertainty must have a resource cost, but there is no evidence that it is large. The welfare effects of longer-term swings are more controversial. An argument is presented that a large real appreciation can affect the terms of the aggregate trade-off between output and inflation, by reallocating output among sectors, each of which is characterized by its own concave supply curve. When a country adopts contractionary monetary policies to fight inflation, as the United States did in 1980–82, the tendency of its currency to appreciate has a favorable effect on the trade-off. It serves to balance the contraction between the sectors producing traded and nontraded goods, mitigating the loss in total output for any given level of reduction in inflation. But when a real appreciation is the result of an expansionary fiscal policy, as has been the case for the United States in recent years, the resulting squeeze on the traded-goods sector produces a "lopsided recovery," with a lower level of total output for any given level of inflation.

6.2 Long-Term Monetary Fundamentals

The monetarist model is a useful starting point for considering the determination of exchange rates on the basis of fundamental variables (see, e.g., Frenkel, 1976). One component of this model views the bonds of different countries as essentially perfect substitutes in investors' portfolios and views barriers to instantaneous adjustment of portfolios as low. As a consequence, uncovered interest-rate parity holds: international arbitrage equates the nominal interest-rate differential to the expected rate of depreciation. The second component of the model views the *goods* of different countries as essentially perfect substitutes and views barriers to instantaneous adjustment in goods markets as low. As a consequence, purchasing-power parity holds: the exchange rate is given by the ratio of domestic to foreign price levels. The price levels are in turn given by nominal money supplies relative to real money demands, the latter usually modeled as functions of real income levels and rates of return.

The empirical evidence is all against the assumption of purchasing-power parity, and in turn against the monetarist model, even as an approximate description of short-run or medium-run reality. Two episodes in the history of the dollar stand out.

In 1977–78, the dollar depreciated sharply against the yen, the mark, and other European currencies. Contrary to the purchasing-power-parity doctrine, the change in the exchange rate was not at all matched by a change in relative price levels. That is, the dollar depreciated in real terms. Nor did the change in the exchange rate correspond to a change in relative money supplies. Indeed, central banks in Europe and Japan were allowing their money supplies to grow at a substantially *faster* rate than in the

Table 6.1
Changes in the value of the dollar and its monetary determinants, 1976–84
(percentage rate of change in the annual average)

	1976–78	1978–80	1980–82	1982–84
Effective exchange value of the dollar[a]				
Nominal	−6.5	−2.7	+15.5	+9.0
Real	−6.9	−0.3	+14.8	+7.4
Consumer price index				
U.S.	7.1	12.4	8.2	3.8
Average of trading partners	7.4	9.4	8.8	5.4
Difference	−0.3	+3.0	−0.6	−1.7
Money supply				
U.S.[b]	7.9	6.9	6.8	9.0
Average of trading partners	13.8	5.8	9.1	8.8
Difference	−5.9	−1.1	−2.3	−0.2
GNP				
U.S.	5.3	1.3	0.2	5.3
Average	3.6	3.1	1.1	2.7
Difference	+1.7	−1.8	−0.9	+2.6

a. Federal Reserve Board's multilateral exchange rate.
b. M1 (from *International Economic Conditions*, Federal Reserve Bank of St. Louis).
Note: Numbers for trading partners are an average of six countries (Canada, France, Italy, Japan, United Kingdom, and West Germany) using 1980 GDP weights (from OECD *Economic Outlook*).
Sources for other statistics: IMF *International Finance Statistics* and International DRI FACS financial data base.

United States. While one could always explain the fall in the dollar's value tautologically as a fall in relative U.S. money demand, real income (the most important conventional determinant of money demand) was actually increasing faster in the United States than abroad. The first column of table 6.1 shows the relevant numbers.

From 1980 to 1985, the entire process was reversed. The dollar appreciated sharply against the yen, the mark, and other European currencies. The change in the exchange rate was again not matched by a change in relative price levels. The dollar appreciated enormously in real terms. Nor did the change in the exchange rate correspond closely to a change in relative money supplies. While U.S. money growth in the 1980–82 period did drop below the growth rate for an average of its trading partners, the difference was only a small fraction of the size of the dollar appreciation, as shown in the third column of table 6.1. And from mid-1982 until March 1985, the dollar continued to appreciate even though money growth was as rapid in the United States as abroad. Dornbusch (1982, p. 6) put the nail in the coffin: "By now there are, I believe, no more serious claims for the empirical relevance [of the simple monetarist model]."

The large swings that exchange rates have experienced in the absence of corresponding movements in the fundamentals have led some economists to conclude that exchange rates are not determined by fundamentals. The very high real value of the dollar in 1984 or 1985 was/is considered to have been unjustified.

The numbers clearly support the claim that the dollar was overvalued in some sense. It is no good giving the noninterventionist's automatic reaction that whatever rate the market comes up with must by definition be the correct rate. But when we use the term "overvalued," we must be prepared to explain what we mean by it. Let us consider further the first two meanings of that term or of the similar term "disequilibrium."

First, "disequilibrium" is often used in economics to mean that the price does not equate current supply and demand. But given the very low levels of transactions costs, capital controls, and other barriers to capital movements among the United States, Canada, Germany, the United Kingdom, and Japan,[1] such a disequilibrium can be ruled out. Individuals are holding the portfolios they desire. (Exceptions should be made for France and other countries with effective capital controls in the early 1980s.) If there is any sense in which the rate can be said to be out of equilibrium, it must be in the alternative mathematical sense of equilibrium in which the exchange rate is not changing over time or at most is changing at a long-run steady-state rate.

According to the second possible meaning of currency overvaluation, the central bank is intervening in the foreign-exchange market, adding to the market demand for the currency in order to keep its price at a higher level than it would otherwise be. Under a system of fixed exchange rates, the central bank is committed to maintain the price by buying up as much of the currency as is necessary, which is the excess supply left over from the private components of the balance of payments. A balance-of-payments deficit is often referred to as a disequilibrium, and it is one in the sense that the situation cannot persist indefinitely, because the central bank will eventually run out of foreign-exchange reserves.

Under floating exchange rates, the overall balance-of-payments deficit is a much less useful concept. It was usually U.S. policy in the early 1980s not to intervene in the foreign-exchange market (except to calm disorderly markets), which implies an overall balance of payments equal to zero. While many foreign central banks continued to intervene in the market, it is no more accurate to say that they were accommodating or financing an imbalance exogeneously determined by the private sector than to say that their exogeneous intervention is what allowed the private sector to run an imbalance. In any case, intervention, when it took place, was generally "leaning against the wind." Central banks fought the 1980–85 appreciation of the dollar by selling dollar reserves in exchange for foreign currencies, rather than the reverse. (This includes Japan; it is ironic that the Japanese government was sometimes accused of manipulating the yen downward.) It follows that the United States technically ran a *surplus* on the overall balance of payments, defined as the sum of the current-account balance and private capital-account balance—not a deficit, as popularly supposed.[2] Foreign countries were the ones running overall balance-of-payments deficits, financed by central banks' purchases of their currencies. If the dollar is considered to have been overvalued, then the intervention definition cannot be the one that is meant.

Having thus dismissed the first two possible meanings of overvaluation, the remainder of this chapter will consider the other four in more detail, beginning with overshooting and finishing with the normative question. Along the way, we will have the opportunity to visit many of the sites where recent theoretical and empirical research on the economics of exchange rates has been taking place.

6.3 Overshooting: Overvaluation Due to Short-Term Fundamentals

The third possible meaning of overvaluation is that one can predict on the basis of economic fundamentals that the currency will in the future decline toward some long-run equilibrium. In other words, the exchange rate is subject to dynamics that reflect the influence of short-run fundamentals. This is the phenomenon of overshooting.

Our third definition of overvaluation corresponds to Williamson's (1985, pp. 13–17) definition of misalignment: "a deviation of the market rate from fundamental equilibrium." Williamson intends the definition to connote the criterion for a devaluation under the Bretton Woods system:

Although the term was never formally defined, the IMF's (1970) report on the exchange-rate system implied that fundamental disequilibrium was a situation in which a country could not expect to generate a current account balance to match its underlying capital flow over the cycle without, on the one hand, depressing its income below "internal balance" or imposing trade controls for payments purposes or, on the other hand, importing inflation.... [This concept] is also what people usually have in mind when they describe rates as "overvalued" or "undervalued." (pp. 13–14)

The deviation from fundamental equilibrium is seen to hold even though the exchange rate is in "market equilibrium" (there is no intervention, that is, no overvaluation under our second definition). It is also seen to hold even though the exchange rate is very possibly in what Williamson calls "current equilibrium," in that it is properly valued given such temporary factors as interest rates and net foreign-asset positions (the short-run fundamentals that drive the exchange rate away from its fundamental equilibrium, that is, make it overvalued under our third definition).

Overshooting is associated with volatility of the exchange rate. But it is consistent with market efficiency, at least in the sense that one cannot expect to make excess (risk-adjusted) profits out of the dynamics. This will be the case when the expected future depreciation is fully reflected in a positive forward discount and interest-rate differential (with or without a risk premium), which is usually true in the overshooting models. It is another question whether overshooting is consistent with efficiency in the sense that the market rate signals a desirable allocation of real resources in the economy, given macroeconomic policy.

There are two major directions in which the simple monetarist model discussed above can be altered to make it more realistic and give it dynamics that arise from fundamentals, so as to produce overshooting. In each case, the dynamics must come from a variable that is not free to jump at a moment in time—so that all the impact of, say, a decrease in the money supply is reflected in the exchange rate instead—but that does adjust gradually over time, thus reversing the initial change in the exchange rate. We consider, first, a sticky price level, and then the country's international asset position.

Sticky Prices and the Degree of Overshooting

The first direction is to relax the assumption of purchasing-power parity. The variable that is not free to jump is the price level. With sticky prices, a decrease in the nominal money supply is in the first instance a decrease in the real money supply. It raises the real interest rate, inducing an incipient capital inflow and an appreciation of the currency. Both the high real interest rate and the loss in competitiveness reduce the demand for goods and labor. If the market is foresighted, it realizes that the slack economy will reduce prices below their previously expected path, eventually undoing the contraction in the real money supply and with it the overvaluation of the currency. Under the rational-expectations hypothesis, this expectation of future depreciation must be sufficient to offset the interest-rate differential, so that investors cannot expect to make excess profits by holding the assets of one country or the other. The fact that the currency initially appreciates to a level in excess of what is expected in the long run is referred to as exchange-rate overshooting.

This is exactly what happened in the U.S. economy, beginning in 1980. As a result of a reduced rate of growth of the money supply, interest rates rose. The U.S. long-term government bond rate, for example, averaged 13.3 percent over the 1981–82 period, a two-point increase relative to 1980.

It is often difficult to measure the real interest rate, because the expected inflation rate is not directly observable. For this reason, real interest rates are calculated in table 6.2 under a wide variety of alternative assumptions. By all four available measures of expected inflation, the expected U.S. inflation rate fell sharply during the 1981–82 period of monetary stringency, so that the real interest rate rose even more than the nominal rate. Nominal and real interest rates also rose among U.S. trading partners, but not by as much. The *differential* between the U.S. real interest rate and a weighted average of those of trading partners (the United Kingdom, France, West Germany, and Japan) rose by 2 to 3 percent in 1981–82, as we can see by various measures in the lower third of table 6.2. Furthermore, the differential between the rate of return on equity capital in the United States and abroad also rose sharply, measured by either the dividend/price ratio or the earnings/price ratio in table 6.2. In response to the shift in real rates of return, foreigners' demand for U.S. assets increased and the dollar began its steep ascent. Because U.S. producers lost competitiveness on world markets as the dollar rose, the burden of the monetary contraction was not borne exclusively by residential construction, business investment, and other interest-sensitive sectors but was transmitted to the tradable-goods sector as well. Partly as a result, the 1981–82 recession was the deepest of the postwar period.

The overshooting story (Dornbusch, 1976c, and chapter 3) is by now a very familiar one. It can be used to explain not only large medium-term swings but also high short-term volatility, as new information about interest rates and other variables comes in every day. However, one point that is occasionally missed is that the instability implied by overshooting is *not* a consequence of "speculation" per se, that is, of the introduction of expectations into the model. Rather, it is solely a consequence of slowly adjusting goods markets.

Table 6.2

Interest-rate differentials between U.S. and foreign assets, and other measures of the expected rate of dollar depreciation, 1976–85 (percent per annum)

	1976–78	1979–80	1981–82	1983–84	1985
Expected nominal rate of depreciation					
1.1 One-year interest-rate differential[a]	−0.48	2.29	3.00	1.73	1.15
1.2 One-year forward discount	0.18	2.57	3.34	1.85	1.32
1.3 Ten-year interest-rate differential	−0.50	0.56	1.91	2.47	2.92
1.4 *Economist* survey[b]	na	na	8.57	8.60	7.12
1.5 American Express survey[c]	0.64	na	6.67	6.99	na
Expected inflation-rate differential					
2.1 One-year lag	−1.01	3.54	0.88	−0.35	0.06
2.2 Three-year distributed lag	−1.96	2.70	1.89	−0.18	−0.16
2.3 DRI three-year forecast[d]	na	2.20	0.96	0.23	0.15
2.4 OECD two-year forecast[e]	1.42	2.24	0.62	0.61	−0.20
2.5 American Express survey[f]	−0.75	na	4.11	2.68	na
Expected real rate of depreciation					
1.1–2.1 One-year interest-rate differential	0.53	−1.24	2.12	2.09	1.08
1.3–2.2 Ten-year with distributed lag	1.47	−2.15	0.02	2.64	3.08
1.3–2.3 Ten-year with DRI forecast	na	−1.64	0.95	2.24	2.77
1.3–2.3 Ten-year with OECD forecast	−1.92	−1.68	1.29	1.86	3.12
1.5–2.5 American Express survey	1.39	na	2.56	4.31	na
Dividend/price ratio[g]	na	1.10	1.79	1.65	1.80
Earnings/price ratio[g]	na	1.60	3.99	2.60	3.09

a. Calculated as $\log(1 + i)$. 1985 contains data through June. Rates for Japan are not available for 1976–77.

b. Available at twenty-four survey dates (see table A-1 in Frankel and Froot, 1985). From *Economist Finacial Report*.

c. Available at eleven survey dates (see table A-2 in Frankel and Froot, 1985). From *American Express Bank Review*.

d. Averages of same twenty-four dates as in footnote b, from DRI forecasts.

e. 1976–78 is only December 1978. 1985 is June 1985, from OECD *Economic Outlook*.

f. Available at same eleven survey dates as footnote c, for the United States, United Kingdom, and West Germany. Available at only four survey dates (1976–78) for France.

g. End-of-quarter averages. 1979–80 include data only for 1980. 1985 is end of quarter I, 1985. Foreign ratios represent the aggregate of Europe, Australia, and the Far East, from *Capital International Perspective*, Geneva.

Note: The foreign variables are GNP-weighted averages of France, Japan, United Kingdom, and West Germany, unless otherwise specified.

Sources for other statistics: IMF *International Financial Statistics* and Data Resources, Inc., International DRI FACS financial data base.

Let us consider the volatility issue, first by going back to the old elasticity-pessimism view according to which export and import elasticities are so low that the Marshall-Lerner condition fails. If a floating exchange rate were called upon to equilibrate the trade balance by itself, the system would be unstable. A depreciation would raise the cost of imports and cause an initial trade deficit, which is an excess demand for foreign exchange, causing further depreciation, and so on. The empirical evidence is that trade elasticities are in fact high enough to imply technical stability, once some time has been allowed to elapse. But one still needs to introduce capital movements to get the country through the short run, say the first year. Foreigners will lend to the country to finance its transitory trade deficit. In this sense, capital mobility stabilizes the foreign-exchange market.

What about *speculative* capital flows, considered to be destabilizing by Nurkse (1944) and others since? Speculation presumably refers to investors' acting in response to expectations of future changes in the exchange rate. But, given slow adjustment in goods markets and rapid adjustment in asset markets, the introduction of expectations turns out to *reduce* exchange-rate volatility. A decrease in the money supply must be met, one way or another, by a decrease in the demand for money. The Mundell-Fleming model of perfect capital mobility had no role for expectations. The domestic interest rate was completely tied to the foreign interest rate. In that model, a decrease in the money supply had to produce an appreciation large enough to induce a fall in output sufficient to lower money demand. As Niehans (1975) pointed out, the fact that trade elasticities are low in the short run means that the requisite change in the exchange rate would have had to be enormous. Introducing the possibility of expected future depreciation allows the domestic interest rate to rise above the foreign interest rate, thus producing some of the necessary fall in money demand—it need not all come from reduced output. If output need not fall as much, then the currency need not appreciate as much. Thus rational speculation is stabilizing.

As the upper third of table 6.2 shows, U.S. interest rates, both long term and short term, rose relative to foreign interest rates in 1981–82. The differential between long-term nominal interest rates (row 1.3) continued a relatively steady upward trend in 1983–85. The short-term differential (row 1.1) came back down a bit, but it too remained positive throughout the 1981–85 strong-dollar period. Equivalently, reflecting covered interest-rate parity, the dollar consistently sold at a discount on the forward market, as is also reported in table 6.2 (row 1.2). This implies that investors consistently held expectations of future depreciation. If investors were acting on the basis of these expectations, then speculation subtracted from the demand for the dollar and thus reduced the extent of contemporaneous overvaluation.

Portfolio Balance and the Effect of the Current Account

Besides relaxing the assumption of purchasing-power parity that follows from perfect substitutability of domestic and foreign goods in consumption, we can alter the simple monetarist model in a second major direction. We relax the assumption of uncovered interest-rate parity that follows from perfect substitutability of domestic and foreign bonds in investors' portfolios. This immediately invalidates the use in table 6.2 of nominal interest-rate differentials to measure expected depreciation. There is a gap between the two variables, which is usually identified as a risk premium. However, there are other ways to measure exchange-rate expectations. The *Economist Financial Report* has surveyed thirteen leading international banks six times a year since 1981, and American Express has conducted a survey of 250 to 300 central and private bankers, corporate treasurers, and economists more irregularly since 1976. Table 6.2 reports the weighted average of one-year expected depreciation of the dollar against the four major foreign currencies in rows 1.4 and 1.5. (Both surveys also cover the Swiss franc, but it is excluded from the calculations for purposes of comparability with the other lines in table 6.2.) These numbers show an even greater increase in expected depreciation than do the interest-rate differentials. The American Express data show that the rate of expected depreciation of the dollar was close to zero in the period 1976–78[3] but turned sharply positive in the 1980s. Both measures show an expected rate of depreciation in excess of 6 percent between 1982 and 1985. Thus we need not rely on the interest-rate differential or forward discount to make the argument that in the 1980s speculation worked to reduce the value of the dollar relative to what it would otherwise have been, rather than to increase it as was widely believed.

When we relax the assumption of perfect substitutability, investors are seen to balance their portfolios among all sorts of assets, including different countries' bonds, on the basis of expected returns. In the portfolio-balance approach, the variable that is not free to jump at a moment in time is not the price level but the level of domestic claims on foreigners or, more generally, the worldwide distribution of wealth. A decrease in the money supply in this case leads to a fall in domestic demand for foreign assets, both because it constitutes a fall in the overall supply of domestic assets and because it increases the domestic interest rate. With the supply of foreign assets fixed at a moment in time, the fall in demand must induce a fall in their price, the exchange rate. The loss in competitiveness from the change in the exchange rate will mean a fall in exports and an increase in imports. A current-account deficit means that the level of domestic claims on foreigners declines over time, eventually undoing the initial excess supply of foreign assets and with it the appreciation of the domestic currency. Once again, the initial response of the exchange rate turns out to have been an overshooting of its long-run equilibrium. And once again, to the extent that the market foresees the future depreciation, speculation will reduce the current demand for domestic assets and thus mitigate rather than exaggerate the initial appreciation.[4]

One virtue of the portfolio-balance approach may be the important role it gives the trade balance. The neglect of trade flows by the early monetary models was a by-product of the excitement accompanying the dethroning of the old flow approach to international monetary theory, and it is appropriate that the pendulum swung back after that. The approach was less useful for explaining why the dollar appreciated from 1980 to 1985, a period when the U.S. trade and current-account deficits reached enormous levels, than for thinking about why the dollar might have been expected to come down in the future. The theory suggests that foreign (and domestic) residents would reach a point where they were unwilling to allocate ever-larger shares of their portfolios to dollar assets. As the demand for dollars begins to fall and the supply continues to rise, the price of dollars would begin to decline.

It is worth noting that the portfolio-balance model is neither sufficient nor necessary to imply a role for the current account. It is not sufficient because, if exchange risk is the reason why investors view domestic and foreign bonds differently, then it is the "supply of foreign bonds" that matters, and this is given by the cumulated foreign-government deficit (corrected for foreign-exchange intervention, if any), not by the cumulated domestic current-account surplus. On the other hand, the cumulated current account *will* determine the worldwide distribution of wealth. It will thus still affect the exchange rate, via the *demand* for foreign assets rather than the supply, provided domestic residents have a lower propensity to hold foreign assets than do foreign residents.

Dooley and Isard (1980, 1985) argue that the primary reason for imperfect substitutability may be political and country risk rather than exchange risk. Bonds are identified by country of issuer rather than currency of denomination, with the implication that the current account again plays a key role. To the extent that political risk matters, the relevant "supply of foreign bonds" is the sum of positive and negative claims on foreigners. But the exchange rate can no longer be determined by the valuation effect, because foreign assets may not be denominated in foreign currency. Instead, the exchange rate is determined so as to give rise to a current-account deficit equal to the rate at which foreigners wish to acquire claims on the domestic country. Dooley and Isard (1985) argue that a significant part of the 1981–85 appreciation of the dollar can be explained by an increase in foreigners' desired claims on the United States, where the claims are perceived to be less likely to be confiscated either formally or informally. This is the famous "safe haven" explanation. Dooley and Isard (1985), Marris (1985), and Krugman (1985) each estimated the future U.S. current-account deficits implied by the path of the overvalued dollar under the assumption that it would depreciate no faster than 3 percent, in line with the forward discount. Krugman and Marris considered the increase in U.S. indebtedness implied by that assumption too large to be sustainable; they predicted a more rapid fall, or even crash, of the dollar. Dooley and Isard, on the other hand, were not willing to conclude that the implied increase in U.S. indebtedness was too large to be inconsistent with a safe-haven shift of foreigners' portfolio preferences into claims on the United States. In their view, the political or country-risk framework was consistent with rational overshooting of the dollar.

The portfolio-balance model is not necessary to imply a role for the current account because it is not difficult to find other ways of getting the current account into the monetary model. Even if perfect bond substitutability is assumed, the current account can be viewed as an indicator of changing factors, such as productivity, that determine the long-run real exchange rate. Or the cumulated current account acting as a component of domestic wealth will still affect the exchange rate if wealth is a determinant of the demand for money. There is one aspect of these models that may or may not be attractive: while like the portfolio-balance model they imply a role for the current account, unlike the portfolio-balance model they rule out any effect of sterilized foreign-exchange intervention. Sterilized foreign-exchange intervention changes the supplies of domestic-denominated versus foreign-denominated bonds, but not the supplies of money. Yet there was little empirical evidence that such intervention in fact affected the exchange rate in the early 1980s. For example, an intervention study by a working group formed after the Versailles Summit of 1982 reported "broad agreement" that sterilized intervention did not generally have a lasting effect (*Report of the Working Group on Exchange Market Intervention*, 1982, p. 72).

Econometric Troubles

To try to discover whether exchange-rate movements are caused by the sorts of fundamentals discussed here, we naturally turn to the econometric models. Certain basic empirical regularities, such as the high degree of volatility of nominal and real exchange rates, are very much in line with the theoretical models. Indeed, the models were originally developed to fit these properties.

When it comes to prediction, we must be careful. From the beginning, it has been an implication of the asset-market models that most changes in the exchange rate cannot be predicted. The argument is that if a change could have been foreseen, it would already have been incorporated in the previous exchange rate. (This is the point about the "news" emphasized by Dornbusch, 1980, and Frenkel, 1981a.) But there is danger of a "cop-out" here. We do not want to say that it would be consistent with the models if we could not explain *any* exchange-rate movement empirically. In the first place, we might hope to be able to predict, based on past information, the component of an exchange-rate change that is rationally reflected in the forward discount or interest-rate differential (perhaps corrected for a risk premium). In the second place, we would certainly hope to be able to explain ex post, using *contemporaneous* information, a good part—ideally all—of an exchange-rate movement.

In some empirical studies of the first five years of floating, it seemed possible to track exchange-rate movements closely using contemporaneous values of the variables that appear in the models, such as money supplies, real income levels, nominal interest rates, and inflation rates. But there were always errors, and they tended to have a high degree of serial correlation that was never adequately explained. More important, the models began subsequently to veer seriously off track. It is disquieting to have to make alterations in the model to fit each new episode. Econometricians' worst fears were confirmed by Meese and Rogoff (1983a), who found that the monetary models are not as good as the lagged spot rate at predicting the current spot rate out of sample, a state of affairs they attribute to chronic structural change. All in all, the record with such regression equations must be pronounced discouraging.

The most damaging aspect of the regression studies is that parameter estimates appear statistically insignificant, or even significant and incorrect in sign. The problem is common with the coefficients on asset supplies: money supplies in the monetary models and net government-debt supplies in the portfolio-balance models. (See chapter 4 for dismal econometric results of this sort, and for a general survey of asset-market models of exchange-rate determination.) The reason for such results is not hard to see: simultaneity problems are endemic. For example, in the 1977–78 episode of dollar depreciation, foreign central banks leaned strongly against the wind, that is, they fought against the appreciation of their currencies by intervening in the foreign-exchange market to buy up large quantities of dollars. To the extent that this intervention was not sterilized, it swelled foreign money supplies. This explains the perverse movement in the exchange rate and relative money supplies that we already noted in table 6.1. To the extent that the intervention was sterilized, and much of it was, it swelled foreign debt supplies, yielding an empirical relationship opposite from that predicted by the portfolio-balance model. The 1980 turnaround in the dollar constituted the reversal of the process. Foreign central banks fought depreciation of their currencies by selling dollar reserves. To the extent that the intervention was not sterilized, foreign money supplies fell relative to the U.S. money supply, again giving us a perverse movement at times from the viewpoint of the monetary model. To the extent that the intervention was sterilized, it reduced relative foreign debt supplies, yielding a perverse relationship from the viewpoint of the portfolio-balance model as well.

Monetary/Fiscal Mix as the Explanation for the Dollar

If leaning against the wind accounts for the perverse movement of the aggregate asset supplies, what accounts for the wind? The Federal Reserve was following a fairly expansionary monetary policy in the late 1970s. The consequences predicted by mainstream macroeconomic theory in fact occurred: real interest rates were low, output and employment were relatively high, and inflation was rising. All the exchange-rate theories mentioned above, and probably any other serious exchange-rate theory that one could imagine, predict a currency depreciation resulting from a monetary expansion.

The second episode was more dramatic. As we have seen, the Federal Reserve tightened policy sharply. This policy switch was formalized by a change in operating procedures in October 1979 and began to take hold seriously in the second quarter of 1980. Real interest rates rose sharply, output and employment fell, and inflation began to decline.[5] Again, all exchange-rate theories predict the result that occurred—the sharp appreciation of the dollar.

Beginning in mid-1982, the Federal Reserve eased up on money growth, as reflected in table 6.1. Yet the differential between real interest rates did not fall. Indeed, it continued to rise in 1983–84 by most of the measures in table 6.2. As of March 1985, the U.S. long-term real interest rate stood about 3 percent above the weighted average of the four trading partners. Why were real-rate-of-return differentials higher throughout the 1981–85 period than in 1980, not only during the first two years of tight monetary policy and recession but also during the following three years of recovery? The question is a subject of some controversy, and two explanations are often given. Think of investment as depending negatively and national saving as depending positively on the real interest rate. National saving is defined as private saving plus (usually negative) public saving, that is, it is the amount of saving left over after financing the government budget deficit. The first hypothesis is that there was a backward shift of the national saving function in the form of an increase in the federal budget deficit that, for whatever reason, was not offset by an increase in private saving. The second hypothesis is that there was an outward shift in the investment function, attributed to more favorable tax treatment of capital beginning in 1981 (accelerated depreciation allowances and the investment tax credit) and, more generally, to an improved business climate. Either shift would drive up the real interest rate. If we are to choose between them, we must look at the saving and investment levels: a fall would support the first explanation; a rise would support the second.

National saving and investment both fell sharply as a share of GNP in the period 1980 to 1982. But this is the usual pattern in recessions. National saving and investment both rose rapidly during the subsequent recovery. It is more relevant to look at the average levels of saving and investment over one complete business cycle. From 1981 to 1984, gross national saving averaged 14.5 percent of GNP, down from 16.1 percent in the period 1973 to 1980. Gross investment was also down to 15.4 percent of GNP (from the same 16.1 percent in the preceding period). On balance, the period is better described as low national saving dragging investment down with it via the higher interest rates than as high investment pulling saving up with it via the higher interest rates.

We can use the phrase "monetary/fiscal mix" to embrace the tight-money explanation for high real interest rates and a high dollar during the

1980–82 period, as well as the loose-budget explanation during the 1983–85 period. It is true that the statistical relationships among these variables are far from perfect. But the 1980–85 period represents the clearest test ever of the theory of exchange rates under conditions of high capital mobility that was developed thirty years ago by Mundell and Fleming and enshrined in textbooks. In the past, monetary policy has tended to be at least partly accommodating of fiscal policy in the United States, and even more so in other countries, preventing clear tests of the theory. The 1980–85 period was the first in which monetary and fiscal policies ran strongly in opposite directions, with the predicted effects on real interest rates and the dollar. Simultaneity bias and other econometric problems should not blind us to consistency of our theories with the gross facts.

If the theories have some merit on this sort of gross long-term level, one would expect some predictive power on a long-term basis. To do meaningful long-term out-of-sample testing when the total data set spans only ten years, it is necessary to specify parameter estimates a priori rather than use up most of the data to estimate them. In the light of the simultaneity problems and perverse regression estimates discussed above, this is just as well. Meese and Rogoff (1983b) pursue this strategy and find that the predictive performance of some structural models does improve slightly for horizons longer than a year. At the three-year horizon, the sticky-price monetary model does about 50 percent better than the random walk in terms of root-mean-square-error and mean absolute error for plausible parameter values (although the structural models still do worse than the random walk for some other possible parameter values). In a subsequent paper, Meese and Rogoff (1988) show that adding the 1981–84 strong-dollar period to the sample improves the out-of-sample performance of the monetary models relative to the random walk. For example, the models have some ability to predict direction of change, especially at longer horizons.

The possibility of this sort of long-term explanatory power is of little comfort to the econometrician (not to mention the speculator or businessman!). It leaves out large quarterly and monthly, or even daily and hourly, fluctuations that he or she ideally would like to be able to explain ex post, if not predict ex ante. One would like more empirical evidence before accepting the mainstream macroeconomist's world view on faith. For example, how do we know that the high nominal interest rates of 1980–82 in fact represented tight monetary policy and high real interest rates, as opposed to loose monetary policy and high expected inflation rates?

One useful piece of empirical evidence comes from a specific selection of those short-term fluctuations that are normally so troublesome. Every week, the Federal Reserve announces what the money stock was in the preceding week. In 1981 and 1982, the announcements were made at 4:10 P.M. on Friday afternoons and referred to the money stock nine days earlier. When the figure was higher than the market had anticipated, the interest rate would jump up.

Does this mean that the market had no confidence in the ability of the Federal Reserve to stick to its money-growth targets—that the market interpreted the news as indicating higher future rates of money growth and inflation, which were then built into a higher nominal interest rate? Or, to the contrary, does it mean that the market trusted the Federal Reserve to stick to its targets, recognized that the monetary aggregates could fluctuate as a result of disturbances in the banking system or in the private economy, and expected the Federal Reserve to correct the deviation in the future, in anticipation of which the contemporaneous real (and nominal) interest rate rose? The foreign-exchange market contained the information that enables us to choose between these two competing hypotheses. If the cause was an expectation of looser monetary policy, the exchange-rate models predict that the dollar would fall on the news. If the cause was an expectation of tighter monetary policy, the models predict that the dollar would rise on the news. Empirically, the answer is the latter, and to a statistically significant degree. This finding supports both the sticky-price model and the view that the high interest rates were high real rates, if any further evidence was needed (see chapter 5). Similarly, statistically significant positive reactions of the dollar to Federal Reserve announcements of industrial production and many other indicators of cyclical activity (see Hardouvelis, 1988) support the monetary model, in all forms, against the old flow approach in which the higher imports caused by higher income were believed to depreciate the currency.

The announcement example is nice because it is one case where the econometrics are free from simultaneity bias. The factors that go into the Friday-to-Monday change in the exchange rate are likely to be independent of the error in the market's earlier prediction of the money supply. But the systematic reaction to an announcement does not last long, and it is only one of many fluctuations that occur throughout the week. What causes the others? More important, what causes the monthly fluctuations that our "reduced form" exchange-rate equations are utterly unable to track? Surely they are not all related to fundamentals. We turn now to two other possible meanings of disequilibrium: irrational expectations and speculative bubbles.

6.4   Overvaluation Due to Irrational Expectations

The Theoretical Argument against Destabilizing Speculation

We have already seen that speculation, defined as capital flows in response to expected exchange-rate changes, is normally stabilizing, not destabilizing, if the expectations are rational. This is the powerful argument against the existence of destabilizing speculation originally made by Friedman (1953). Assume some natural oscillation in the exchange rate due only to fundamentals such as seasonal agricultural fluctuations or the fluctuations in the money supply considered above. If speculation were destabilizing, it would have to add to the demand for foreign currency when its price was high anyway, in order to make its price higher, and add to the supply of foreign currency when its price was low anyway, in order to make its price lower. But then the speculators would be buying high and selling low, hardly a good prescription for making money! Friedman's argument was that such speculators would soon go out of business.

But let us now consider the possibility that irrational speculators do exist, even if they are on average losing money. Perhaps there *is* a sucker born every minute. Certainly there is by now a large literature devoted to testing this possibility econometrically.

Testing Forward-Market Efficiency

There are many technical pitfalls in testing the hypothesis of market efficiency—the joint hypothesis that the market's expectation is rational given available information and that no barriers prevent the forward rate from reflecting the market's expectation.[6] Even when the econometric problems have been dealt with, however, the forward rate often still deviates systematically from the future spot rate (see, e.g., Hansen and Hodrick, 1980). The final, and hitherto most daunting, pitfall has been that this finding could be due to a risk premium that separates the forward rate from the market's expected future spot rate rather than to irrational expectations that separate the market's expectation from the rational one. Some, like Cumby and Obstfeld (1981), assume that it is due to a risk premium; others, like Bilson (1981b), assume that it is due to a failure of rational expectations.

If the finding is due to a risk premium, one might expect deviations to be systematically related to variables on which the risk premium theoretically depends—asset supplies and asset demands, the latter being functions of the worldwide distribution of wealth and the variances and covariances of returns. However, the econometric evidence seems to be that there is no such systematic relationship. More telling still, even assuming that the risk premium in fact exists, the hypothesis that investors optimize their portfolios with respect to the mean and variance of their wealth implies that fluctuations in the risk premium must be extremely small. Using plausible values for the coefficient of risk aversion and other relevant parameters, it is possible to show that an increase in the supply of dollar securities equal to 1 percent of world wealth cannot drive up the risk premium by much more than 0.02 percent (2 basis points). Any incipient change in expected rates of return larger than that would induce investors to shift their desired portfolios so as to eliminate it; risk would not be sufficient to discourage investors from doing so. If the fluctuations in the risk premium are indeed this small, systematic differences between the forward rate and future spot rate can be attributed only to a failure of rational expectations.[7]

On the other hand, it is possible that investors do not maximize a simple function of the mean and variance of their wealth, or even a more general expected-utility function. Some statistical tests are able to reject the constraints imposed by these optimization hypotheses.[8] If the survey data reported in table 6.2 are to be believed, the rate of dollar depreciation expected by the market differs significantly from the rate embodied in the forward discount or interest-rate differential. This would imply that risk premiums are substantial, the theory of expected-utility maximization notwithstanding.

The Implications of Irrational Expectations for Exchange-Rate Volatility

It might seem that as soon as we admit the possibility of irrational expectations, the Friedman argument about stabilizing speculation is untenable. Could "irrational expectations" account for fluctuations in exchange rates, and in particular the overvaluation of the dollar?

In tests of rational expectations, not enough attention has been paid to the alternative hypothesis. One common test is to regress actual realized changes in the exchange rate against the forward discount. With market efficiency and risk neutrality, we would expect a unit coefficient. Instead, the coefficient often turns out to be significantly less than 1.[9] Similar results are found in regressions against the expected rate of depreciation as measured by the *Economist* and American Express survey data (Frankel and Froot, 1985). Bilson (1981a) urged us to consider the alternative hypothesis seriously. It says that investors' expectations tend to put too much weight on factors other than the contemporaneous spot rate, such as the long-term fundamentals, a situation he called "excessive speculation." In the context of the overshooting model, however, it turns out that such speculation will move the spot rate closer to the equilibrium path determined by long-run fundamentals, and thus *reduce* exchange-rate volatility. When the value of the currency lies above its long-run equilibrium path and investors overestimate the speed at which it will depreciate toward that path, because they are concentrating on the fundamentals, they will reduce their demand for the currency, and thus reduce its price, by more than if their expectations were rational. If the 1981–85 expectation of future dollar depreciation was too great, as suggested by the measures in the top third of table 6.2, then the dollar must have been overvalued less than it would otherwise have been.[10]

There are other ways in which expectations might fail to be rational. But those that have been detected empirically do not necessarily imply greater volatility for the exchange rate. Perhaps some sort of failure of rational expectations does explain those short-term fluctuations in the spot rate that our models are incapable of explaining. But it seems less likely that irrational expectations can explain large swings like the 1980–85 appreciation of the dollar. If one accepts the positive interest-rate differential or forward discount as reflecting a market expectation of future dollar depreciation (that is, one accepts the absence or small size of the risk premium), the conclusion seems inescapable that speculators are damping the dollar overvaluation, relative to a situation in which they do not expect the exchange rate to change. If one believes that the interest-rate differential misstates the rate of expected depreciation (because of a risk premium) in the direction indicated by the expectations survey data, the argument follows even more strongly.

6.5 Overvaluation Due to Speculative Bubbles

The Theory of Bubbles with Crashes

Our consideration of whether the market overestimates the speed with which the spot rate moves toward long-run equilibrium left aside the possibility that the market might expect the spot rate to move in the *opposite* direction from long-run equilibrium. Such expectations could even be rational if they are self-validating. This is the possibility of the speculative bubble.

Theorists have long been nettled by the saddle-path stability problem, a mathematical property of solutions to perfect-foresight models. Because of self-confirming expectations, there are an infinite number of paths that satisfy the condition that expectations are correct, only one of which constitutes a stable path toward the equilibrium that is based on fundamentals alone. The typical strategy has been to rule out the explosive solutions by assumption.[11] This strategy has seemed justified by the observation that there have in fact been relatively few episodes in history that one wants to nominate as "speculative bubbles," and none that did not eventually come to an end. As soon as one admits that any bubble must eventually burst, rational expectations would seem to prevent it from ever getting started in the first place.

But there has been an interesting theoretical development in this area— a recognition that one can easily build in at each point in time a probability of the collapse of the bubble and the return to fundamentals equilibrium (see Blanchard, 1979). As the probability of collapse during any given month is small, there will be some rate of appreciation in the event of noncollapse that, together with the interest-rate differential, is sufficient to persuade speculators to continue to hold the currency despite the possibility of collapse. When a bubble actually collapses, the market price can in theory jump to any of an infinite number of other rational-expectations paths. But if each speculator is always guessing which path all the *other* speculators are expecting, it seems likely that only two paths have finite probabilities at each point in time: whatever path the asset price has previously been following (a continuation of the bubble path, in the event of noncollapse) and the stable path (to which the price returns in the event of collapse).

What is exciting about this development is that it allows us to think about speculative bubbles regularly getting started and bursting in the real world. Even if the probability of collapse is taken as exogenous and constant, it is a fact that every Blanchard bubble will come to an end eventually. Furthermore, one might attempt to model the probability of collapse endogenously, and to model the actual collapse as the outcome that occurs when speculators (rationally) see the probability of collapse rise above some arbitrarily specified critical level. (The stochastic element would have to come in through asset supplies or through nonspeculative components of asset demands.) If one introduced risk aversion into the model, one might even be able to get the appealing result that the current probability of collapse is greater the longer the bubble has gone on, because the risk of holding the currency is greater the further from fundamental equilibrium the currency has diverged.

These considerations suggest the possibility that small-scale speculative bubbles are going on all the time. These may be the "runs" that market participants report on an hourly or daily basis. Speculative bubbles would seem to be the ultimate counterexample to Friedman's proof that destabilizing speculation cannot exist: the variance of the exchange rate is higher in a bubble world, and yet speculators are on average neither earning nor losing money. Bubbles may even be the large and continuing deviations that are not explained by fundamentals in econometric models using monthly data.

Long-Term Overvaluation or Short-Term Volatility?

Could a speculative bubble explain the high 1981–85 value of the dollar? For an asset price to be subject to a single prolonged bubble, it is not normally enough that it be overvalued; it must be increasingly overvalued over time. Furthermore, the overvaluation must *accelerate* over time if there is a perceived probability of collapse, in order to counterbalance the increasingly large distance that the price might fall. However, it may be difficult to spot such a trend with the naked eye. In the first place, even if there is an obvious trend in the value of the currency, it could be due to fundamentals. One would have to perform a test like the bubbles test of Flood and Garber (1980).[12] In the second place, and more relevant, a positive interest-rate differential could take the place of a trend, as Dornbusch (1983c, pp. 15–16) ingeniously points out. This could be the case if the interest-rate differential is as large as the expected depreciation of the currency (the probability that the bubble will burst times the distance the currency will fall if the bubble does burst). In appendix 6A, I show that we can reject this possibility with some confidence, given the actual sizes of the appreciation and the interest-rate differential in the 1981–85 period. The appreciation went on far too long to represent a single rational bubble.

There is another objection to the hypothesis that the long appreciation of the dollar could be a single speculative bubble. A single bubble is in theory a smooth path, whereas exchange rates are observed to undergo wild short-term fluctuations. Of course, a stable path based on a single set of fundamentals is also in theory smooth, but it is easy to posit a perpetual

inflow of bits of information, pertaining to monetary policy or other fundamentals, that displace that path. In the case of a single speculative bubble,
it would seem that any event that jolted the asset price off its previous
smooth path would send it crashing all the way to the stable fundamentals
path.[13] This does not mean that bubbles do not occur, perhaps frequently.
It just means that they may be more promising as an explanation of short-
term movements in the neighborhood of the fundamentals path than as an
explanation of prolonged overvaluation.

Thus we are led to the same conclusion regarding rational speculative
bubbles that we reached regarding irrational expectations. They may exist,
and they may account for some of the short-term fluctuations that have
characterized floating rates and that introduce large monthly error terms
into exchange-rate equations, but they do not account for prolonged
swings. For that we are left with models based on the real interest rate and
other fundamentals. For the remainder of this chapter, I will adopt the view
that the strength of the dollar from 1981 to 1985 was due to an unusual
monetary/fiscal policy mix, as in the models of section 6.3.

6.6   The Welfare Effects of Overvaluation

Each of the possible interpretations of overvaluation considered so far has
dealt with the *determination* of exchange-rate movements. None addressed
the question of the *effects* of exchange-rate movements. Indeed, the literature has lavished attention on the former question to the relative neglect of
the latter. We now turn to the "value judgment" implicit in the term
"overvaluation," that is, to the welfare effects of exchange-rate variability.

If we rule out the first and fourth definitions of overvaluation, barriers to
portfolio adjustment and irrational expectations, we have the property of
market efficiency. But the proposition that financial markets are efficient in
this technical sense tells us nothing about whether resources are efficiently
allocated in the economy. Even if we were also to rule out speculative
bubbles, which would leave us with dynamics based only on Dornbusch
overshooting or other short-run fundamentals, there would still be no
guarantee that these exchange-rate movements are desirable. Whenever we
admit macroeconomic considerations like sticky goods prices, all optimality
theorems derived from the theory of competitive markets are void. Given
inefficiencies in goods markets, we cannot even argue that welfare is necessarily higher with "efficient" capital markets than without them. Dornbusch
(1983c, p. 26) writes:

[Such an argument] mistakes the short-term money market rate for the social productivity of capital. Suppose a country reduces money growth and this leads (as it will) to an increase in the interest rate on financial assets. Incipient capital flows will lead to currency appreciation and a current account deterioration financed by borrowing abroad. It is hard to argue that the current account deficit is a reflection of enhanced investment opportunities or increased time preference that, in an efficient and integrated capital market, would call for a redirection of lending toward the home country. On the contrary, the decline in demand will have reduced the profitability of domestic real capital. It therefore would not be optimal for capital to flow toward the country with a tightened monetary policy. Policy intervention, in these circumstances, could well enhance the efficiency of capital allocation in the world.

Thus the desirability of market-produced exchange-rate changes must be evaluated; there is no automatic appeal to optimality.

The Effects of Short-Term Uncertainty

A distinction is generally made between the effects of short-run exchange-rate variability and the effects of longer-run swings of overvaluation or undervaluation. We consider first short-term variability. Before floating exchange rates became a reality, the major argument against them was that they would make international trade and investment riskier. For example, the importer with an obligation to pay a certain amount of foreign currency in ninety days would not know immediately how much it was going to cost in domestic currency. This chapter has devoted much attention to exchange-rate volatility because of this risk argument. One counterargument is that the importer could buy the foreign currency on the forward-exchange market if he wished to protect himself against exchange risk. Friedman (1953) correctly predicted that under floating rates an active forward-exchange market would develop in response to the need. The volume handled by the forward-exchange market and the number of currencies covered have indeed increased. But transactions costs, as represented by the bid-ask spread, have also increased according to some, because of the increased risk faced by any bank that takes an open forward position even for a few hours (see, e.g., Young, 1984).

The other component of the cost of forward exchange—the risk premium that separates the forward rate from the expected future spot rate—has probably also gone up. But, as we have seen, the risk premium may be too small to matter empirically. Note that if importers in the United States must pay a forward price for pounds greater than the expected future spot price as the cost of hedging their future pound payments, importers in

Great Britain will be paying a forward price for dollars *less* than the expected future spot price as the cost of hedging their future dollar payments.[14] If the risk premium is a negative factor for U.S. imports, it is a
positive factor for British imports, so the net effect on trade may not be
negative.[15] But the risk premium is determined in a market equilibrium in
which somebody must be compensated for taking an open position. The
forward price for dollars will be less than the expected future spot price
only if some participants in the market are prepared to take and hold
positive open dollar positions. Under the old trade-flow approach, this
must be the cast if Britain runs a positive trade surplus.[16] But if Britain runs
a surplus, the U.S. imports for which the risk premium is a negative factor
are larger than the British imports for which the risk premium is a positive
factor. In this sense, exchange risk discourages trade, which is the result we
would expect.

Hooper and Kohlhagen (1978) conclude that increased short-term exchange-rate uncertainty has not had a significant negative effect on the
volume of world trade. More recent studies by Akhtar and Hilton (1984),
Young (1984), and Kenen and Rodrik (1986) do find something of a negative effect on trade, holding other variables constant. The subject deserves
further study. But current detractors of floating rates seem to be less
concerned with short-term exchange-rate uncertainty than with the large
medium-term swings that exchange rates have experienced, such as the
dollar overvaluation. Kenen believes that "there has been too much emphasis on short-term instability.... The medium-term swings in exchange
rates, nominal and real, have done more damage" (in Bergsten et al., 1982,
p. 38). Dornbusch (1983c, p. 29) sees "no very good case why small noise
in the market should be smoothed" in contrast to a "massive disturbance
such as the dollar appreciation."

The Effects of Long-Term Overvaluation

Even if we consider only the welfare effects of long-term fluctuations, there
is an enormous amount to be said. I will focus on one particular aspect:
effects on the allocation of resources among sectors and their implication
for the aggregate output/inflation trade-off.

Let us begin with the 1980–82 dollar appreciation and take as given that
its cause was a contractionary monetary policy initiated in the United
States at the end of 1979 in order to fight inflation. (I do not here pass
judgment on whether the contraction was worth the cost.) The price of
bringing down inflation will be lost output and high unemployment.

Clearly, the appreciation of the dollar hurt output and employment in U.S. export and import-competing industries. The question is whether the appreciation made the terms of the aggregate U.S. trade-off between output and inflation better or worse than it would otherwise have been.

The appreciation of the dollar also meant higher import prices for U.S. trading partners. To avoid losing ground in their own fight against inflation, foreign governments felt it necessary to match the U.S. contraction part way with a monetary contraction of their own, as measured, for example, by real interest rates. They complained that the dollar appreciation made them worse off. Thus a second question is whether the dollar appreciation made the terms of the foreign trade-off between aggregate output and inflation better or worse.

It has been suggested that the rise of the dollar after 1980 is an example of undesirable competitive appreciation: countries would do better to expand cooperatively, but each holds back in an effort to keep its currency strong (see, for example, Oudiz and Sachs, 1984). According to such arguments, currency appreciation is a "negative externality" internationally because it is a means of exporting inflation to trading partners. It should be pointed out that in other times, such as the 1930s and to a lesser extent the 1970s, the argument has gone in the opposite direction: competitive *depreciation* is considered the negative externality because it is a means of exporting unemployment. In any case, it is not clear that the dollar appreciation was a deliberate consequence of a U.S. slow-growth policy or that U.S. policy-makers refrained from expanding for fear of a depreciation.

Dornbusch (1982, pp. 595–596) has made the claim, "There is no sensible argument that tightening of money should involve as a desirable side effect a loss of exports [and] an increase in imports.... Because these side effects are undesirable, both here and abroad, we should attempt to the maximum possible extent to immunize the world economy against these spillovers." But a sensible argument *can* be made that, given the U.S. monetary contraction, *welfare was higher, both in the United States and in foreign countries, with an appreciation of the dollar than it would have been if the exchange rate had not changed, in the sense that in each country the terms of the output-inflation trade-off were more favorable.* The argument is formalized in Frankel (1983d), but an intuitive account is easily made.

The key assumption needed to derive the conclusion is that within each of two domestic sectors, an exportable sector and a nontradable sector, the trade-off between inflation and output is nonlinear: at high levels of unemployment and excess capacity, demand expansion goes relatively more into output and less into the rate of price increase; at lower levels of unemployment, demand expansion goes relatively more into the rate of price increase and less into output. If we are interested in maximizing aggregate output and minimizing average inflation throughout the economy, it follows that a change in the level of demand is best shared equally by the two sectors. If we decide to contract to fight inflation, we should contract the two sectors equally. If we contract the nontradable sector more, an imbalance will develop in which the marginal benefit to contraction in exportables, in terms of the reduction in inflation per unit of lost output, will be greater than the marginal benefit to contraction in the nontradable sector.

This imbalance is precisely what would have occurred if the United States had contracted in 1980–82 without allowing the dollar to appreciate. High real interest rates would have cut demand for housing and other nontraded goods and services even more than they actually did, but manufacturing, agriculture, and other exportable sectors would have been relatively buoyed by foreign demand. Allowing the dollar to appreciate meant that the exportable sector shared equally in the misery.

Now for the effect on other countries. It is not enough merely to observe, as many have done, that floating rates will not fully insulate them from a U.S. contraction, or to identify the impact on them when their policies are passive.[17] Foreign governments will react to the disturbance by resetting their policies so as to return as closely as possible to their chosen combination of output and inflation. If the exchange rate had somehow been kept fixed when the United States contracted, foreigners would have suffered a loss in export demand and found themselves at lower levels of output and inflation than desired (assuming that they were previously at their optimum). They would have responded with policies to increase expenditure.

The other countries' expansion would necessarily be concentrated relatively more in the nontradable sector. To achieve a better balance between the two sectors, foreign currencies would have to depreciate against the dollar to make the exportable sector more competitive. Fortunately, as we have seen, this is exactly what is best for the U.S. trade-off as well, and it is what in fact happens anyway when the foreign-exchange market operates undisturbed![18]

Of course, there is no guarantee that the actual dollar appreciation will be optimal. It could be too big or too small. To compare the actual and optimal changes in the exchange rate, it would be necessary to specify a complete model of exchange-rate determination, to make assumptions about foreign-exchange intervention practices and the monetary/fiscal policy mix, and to come up with estimates for the parameters of the model and of the elasticities of demand for tradables and nontradables. The relatively model-free argument made here has the more modest objective of establishing that at least *some* degree of appreciation is desirable. Economic analysis must go beyond lamenting the cost of the strong dollar to export and import-competing industries. It must evaluate the desirability of our current exchange-rate system, not the desirability of current macroeconomic policy. To do so, it must use as its hypothetical standard of comparison a situation in which we suffer from the same macroeconomic policy *without* the strong dollar, not a utopia where we suffer from neither.

We now consider the continued—indeed increasing—appreciation of the dollar during the period 1983–1984, the years after the tight U.S. monetary policy and accompanying recessions ended. I have argued that the high real interest rates and strong dollar of this period are more readily explained by the high budget deficit than by the leading alternative proposed, an increase in investment: it seems more accurate to say that national saving pulled national investment down than to say that national investment pulled national saving up.

Either way, the gap between national saving and national investment has grown, with a capital inflow from abroad making up the difference. The capital inflow is, of course, the counterpart to the trade or current-account deficit; the rest of the world lends to the United States to finance the gap. The U.S. trade deficit reached a then-record level of $108 billion in 1984 ($123 billion if imports are counted on a c.i.f. basis). Of the roughly $50 billion deterioration in the U.S. trade deficit between 1983 and 1984, over 60 percent can be attributed to the continued real appreciation of the dollar (at an annual rate of 13 percent over the preceding several years) and the resulting loss of competitiveness of U.S. producers on world markets. The remaining 40 percent can be attributed to the recovery: because the growth of real income in the United States exceeded that among trading partners (by 6.8 percent versus 3.5 percent for the rest of the OECD), U.S. imports from the rest of the world increased much faster than the rest of the world's imports from the United States.

Standard models forecast that the lagged effects of the appreciation of the dollar were the only remaining factors widening the trade deficit.[19] There was also a large loss in U.S. net exports to Latin America after 1981 as a result of the international debt problem, but the worst of this shift ($20 billion) was completed in 1983. Thus the cause of the increasing trade deficit can be traced primarily to the high levels of the real interest rate and the dollar.

The U.S. current-account deficit and associated capital inflow attained a record $102 billion in 1984. Like the trade deficits, the current-account deficits represented a loss of output and employment in industries that export or compete with imports. But, at the same time, the capital inflow kept U.S. real interest rates below what they would have been in its absence. Thus it allowed investment and the other interest-sensitive sectors to grow faster, given the level of saving, than they otherwise would have. Foreigners in effect financed over half the U.S. federal budget deficit in the mid-1980s, making that much more saving available for investment. This was the safety valve that prevented the federal budget deficit from crowding out investment one-for-one.

What are the implications of such a continued imbalance for the terms of the overall trade-off between output and inflation? The model described above is not directly applicable because it disaggregates into only two sectors: a traded-goods sector that is relatively more responsive to the exchange rate and a nontraded-goods sector that is relatively more responsive to other factors like the interest rate. We need a more complex model that has at least a third sector that is relatively more responsive to fiscal policy. One possible disaggregation is into four sectors corresponding roughly to the $C + I + G + X - M$ model of standard Keynesian textbooks. The four sectors are those facing demand that is especially sensitive to (1) tax cuts (consumption goods, C), (2) interest rates (investment goods, I), (3) government expenditure (military equipment, health, education, etc., G), and (4) the exchange rate (exports, X). Taking as given high levels of production in sectors C and G as the result of expansionary fiscal policy, the question would then be: What is the optimal way to distribute the remaining demand between sectors I and X so as to obtain the lowest possible aggregate inflation rate for a given level of aggregate output (or the highest possible level of aggregate output for a given aggregate inflation rate)? In the spirit of the previous model, convexity in each sector would imply that the answer is to balance demand as equally as possible between the remaining two sectors.

We are taking as given that the C and G sectors crowd out spending in the rest of the economy, presumably via the increase in the real interest rate. Imagine that we are somehow able to keep the dollar from appreciating, for example, by using capital controls to limit the inflow of capital that would otherwise be attracted by high U.S. real interest rates. A lower value for the dollar will stimulate output in the X sector. But the capital inflow is currently helping to keep the U.S. real interest rate lower than it would otherwise be. The cost of shutting off the increased demand for U.S.

assets will be a higher real interest rate than we are currently experiencing. Thus the interest-sensitive sector I will suffer a loss in demand.

Indeed, the loss in output in the I sector would have to be sufficient to offset the gain in output in the X sector if aggregate output is constrained to prevent "overheating" of the economy. (For example, some observers suggest that the Federal Reserve is, or should be, targeting aggregate GNP.) Because the I sector is producing at a point far down its concave inflation/output curve, the overall inflation rate will be higher than if the same level of aggregate output were distributed more evenly among the sectors. This argument was a rationale underlying warnings from Martin Feldstein, chairman of the Council of Economic Advisers in 1983 and 1984, that the recovery, though strong, was nevertheless alarmingly "lopsided" (see, e.g., the 1984 *Economic Report of the President*, p. 57).

The "lopsided" effects of interest-rate and exchange-rate crowding out are inherently "second order." How important are they quantitatively for the terms of the aggregate trade-off between output and inflation? The answer depends on two factors: (1) the extent to which the increase in the real interest rate or real value of the dollar redistributes demand from some sectors to others, and (2) the concavity of the price-output supply relationship within each sector (that is, the extent to which the slope at high demand levels exceeds the slope at low demand levels). One can get an idea of the first factor by comparing actual growth rates in different sectors since 1980. Industries do not in fact neatly sort themselves into internationally traded sectors that are highly sensitive to the exchange rate and nontraded sectors that are not. But manufacturing and mining are generally taken to be primarily traded, and construction and services to be primarily nontraded.

It would be interesting to perform such an analysis separately for the 1980–82 period of monetary contraction and the 1983–85 period of fiscal expansion in order to test two separate propositions: (1) that the appreciation of the dollar in the first period allowed a more even balance among sectors of the economy than would otherwise have occurred, given the increase in real interest rates; and (2) that the appreciation in the second period exacerbated the imbalance. The problem is that those sectors of the economy that tend to be most sensitive to real interest rates and the exchange rate—manufacturing and agriculture as opposed to services—tend also to be most sensitive to the aggregate level of economic activity. Manufacturing contracted more sharply than services in 1980–82 and expanded more rapidly in 1983–84 simply because it is more procyclical.

Table 6.3
U.S. employment in nontraded vs. traded sectors, 1980−85 (in millions)

	1980	August 1985[a]	Percentage change
Construction	4,346	4,678	+7.6
Government	16,241	16,338	+0.6
Private services-producing	48,507	56,641	+16.8
Total "nontraded"	69,094	77,657	+12.9
Manufacturing and mining			
(total "traded")	21,312	20,353	−4.5
Total nonfarm employment	90,406	98,010	+8.4

a. Preliminary.
Source: *Employment and Earnings*, U.S. Department of Labor, Bureau of Labor Statistics, September 1985, Table B.1, p. 43.

To avoid cyclical complications, table 6.3 shows changes over the entire period of dollar appreciation, from 1980 to August 1985. We see that employment in construction, government, and services increased by 12.9 percent, but employment in manufacturing and mining actually *shrank* by 4.5 percent. It has been argued that the shift of employment away from manufacturing toward the private service-producing sector can be explained entirely by long-term structural trends in productivity and demand patterns and that no special overvalued-dollar effect is present (Kling, 1985, and Solomon, 1985, p. 10). If this argument is correct, it simply means that the manufacturing and services sectors cannot properly be identified with traded and nontraded goods. Given a trade deficit equal to 3 percent of GNP, it is necessarily true that firms that are sensitive to foreign demand have on average been hurt, whatever sector they may be in. Nor should we be surprised that some of those adversely affected are producers of services. Internationally traded services that are of importance to the United States include transportation, banking, insurance, engineering, higher education, and medical services. Furthermore, even producers of nontraded services will be hurt if their usual customers earn *their* incomes on international markets; think of a restaurant in Peoria, Illinois.

The effect of the traded/nontraded imbalance on the overall level of output and inflation depends on the concavity of the supply relationships in the individual industries. But even if that concavity is no larger than is implied by a constant elasticity of supply with respect to price (call it $1/\varepsilon$), for a given level of overall inflation it can be shown that if a proportion b of output is allocated to nontraded goods instead of the optimal proportion β, aggregate output will be equal to a fraction $\{\beta(b/\beta)^{1/\varepsilon} + (1 - \beta)[(1 - b)/(1 - \beta)]^{1/\varepsilon}\}^{\varepsilon}$ of what it would otherwise be. (The fraction is less than 1 if $1/\varepsilon > 1$.) If the elasticity of supply is high, particularly if it becomes higher at low levels of demand, there could be a nonnegligible output loss from the current U.S. allocation of demand away from traded goods.

6.7 Conclusion

Of the six possible meanings of overvaluation, two are immediately and clearly not applicable to the 1980–85 dollar: the nonclearing of financial markets and foreign-exchange intervention. Two more—irrational expectations and rational speculative bubbles—though interesting concepts, particularly as possible explanations for shorter-term exchange-rate movements, have been argued here to be unpromising ways of explaining the dollar overvaluation. Even if we allow for expectations that are not rational, speculation since 1980 must have been a force acting to reduce the value of the dollar below what it would otherwise have been. This follows from the investors' expectation of future dollar depreciation that shows up in the nominal-interest-rate differentials, the forward discounts, and the survey data. And for all or part of the dollar appreciation to have been attributable to a single rational speculative bubble, the implicit probability each month of the bubble's bursting would have had to be high enough to make it improbable that the bubble could have lasted for more than fifty months without actually bursting.

The meaning of overvaluation that appears to be most relevant is overshooting. The exchange rate in 1984 was in "market equilibrium": there were no barriers to portfolio adjustment and there was no intervention in the foreign-exchange market. Nevertheless, the value of the dollar was far above the level dictated by long-term fundamentals such as purchasing-power parity. It had been driven up by short-term fundamentals such as the real-interest-rate differential. The increase in the real-interest-rate differential could in turn be attributed to the macroeconomic policy mix, specifically the tighter monetary policy of 1981–82 and the growing structural federal budget deficit of 1983–85.

The last meaning of overvaluation, and the one of ultimate concern to policy-makers, is the normative one that no matter which factor explains the value of the currency, that value is higher than optimal from the standpoint of its effect on the economy. The welfare effects of a distorted allocation of resources between traded and nontraded goods may be unde-

sirable. It can be argued that, given a monetary contraction to fight inflation, an appreciation of the currency reduces this distortion: it allocates the
loss of output and employment equally among sectors relative to what
would happen if the exchange rate were somehow held fixed. But by 1985
the dollar appreciation had long since passed the point where it was helping to balance growth among sectors. Instead, the U.S. economy had become split into a strong nontraded-goods sector and a weak traded-goods
sector, with unfavorable implications for the health of the aggregate national economy.

Appendix 6A   Was the Dollar Appreciation 1981–85 a Rational Speculative Bubble?

Assume that at any time, t, there is a probability p_t that in the coming
month the bubble will burst and the spot exchange rate S_t will return to its
long-run equilibrium level $\bar{S}_t$ that is determined by fundamentals, Then a
short-term interest-rate differential $(i - i^*)_t$ is sufficient to support a large
continuing overvaluation, measured by $(\bar{s} - s)_t$ in log form, if the bubble
path, on which the spot rate will remain for one more period with probability $1 - p_t$, involves continued appreciation at a rate a_t, such that

$$(i - i^*)_t = p_t(\bar{s} - s_t) + (1 - p_t)(-a_t). \tag{A1}$$

In other words, the interest-rate differential, which must equal the expected
depreciation, is a weighted average of what will happen if the bubble bursts
and what will happen if it does not. Even if $a_t = 0$, as in the Dornbusch
(1983c) example, an interest-rate differential of 3 percent per year, or
0.25 percent per month, is sufficient to sustain a continuing overvaluation
$(\bar{s} - s)$ of 25 percent with a probability of collapse of 0.01 per month.

  The dollar in fact experienced, not a constant overvaluation relative to
PPP, but rather continuing appreciation a_t, at a rate of 7.80 percent per year
(0.65 percent a month) against the mark between January 1981 and March
1985. One can solve equation (A1) for the implicit market-perceived probability of collapse at any given time:

$$p_t = \frac{(i - i^*)_t + a_t}{(\bar{s} - s_t) + a_t}. \tag{A2}$$

As of March 1985, the interest-rate differential between the United States
and Germany was 3.07 percent a year, or 0.26 percent a month, and the
real mark/dollar rate had increased 64 percent relative to 1980. If all the

real appreciation of the dollar is attributed to a bubble, implying that the appreciation will all be instantaneously reversed in the event that the bubble bursts, it follows that the perceived probability of collapse in the month of March was $(0.0025 + 0.0065)/(0.6400 + 0.0069) = 1.4$ percent.

We can repeat this calculation for every month during the four years of dollar appreciation, solving for the implicit probability of the bubble bursting during the month in question as a function of the interest-rate differential and how much real appreciation has already taken place. Table 6A.1 reports these calculations under the extreme form of the bubble hypothesis, namely that all the real appreciation of the dollar against the mark is attributable to a bubble. It is also assumed that the rate of appreciation in the event of noncollapse (a_t) is constant at 7.80 percent a year. (The calculations are not very sensitive to how a_t is estimated.)

To find the probability that the bubble could have lasted T periods, we simply take the product of $(1 - p_t)$ for t running from 1 to T. No assumption of a normal probability distribution is needed; we overcome the "peso problem" by brute force. Nor is any special assumption of independence needed in order to multiply the probabilities; each p_t is the market's evaluation of the probability of collapse during the coming period conditional on the bubble having lasted to period t. The cumulative probability of noncollapse is reported in the fifth column of table 6A.1. The probability that a bubble could have lasted to March 1985 without bursting is only 16 percent. This is evidence against the hypothesis that a single rational bubble in fact explains the whole appreciation of the dollar, though it is not as low a probability as would be required to reject a hypothesis in a formal statistical test.

It might seem that assigning all of the 64 percent increase in the real mark/dollar rate to a speculative bubble is an unnecessarily extreme form of the hypothesis. Let us consider the alternative hypothesis, which appears more plausible, that part of the appreciation is attributable to a bubble and part to fundamentals. It turns out that this alternative hypothesis is *less* likely to be true, given the observed data. This counterintuitive result follows from the property of equations (A1) and (A2) that to get the same expected depreciation, p_t must be larger the nearer the exchange rate is to equilibrium. For example, suppose that at each point in time, half the real appreciation has been due to a bubble. Then, to satisfy equation (A2), p_t would have to be almost twice as high. The last two columns of table 6A.1 present the implicit probabilities under this scenario. As of March 1985, the probability of collapse would be 2.8 percent. The cumulative probability of noncollapse from January 1981 through March 1985 would be only 3

Table 6A.1
Probability of collapse in mark/dollar rate under bubble hypothesis (trend logarithmic appreciation $a_t = 7.80$ percent per year)

Month	Nominal appreciation of dollar $(-\ln S_t)$ $1973-79 = 0$	Real "overvaluation" of dollar $[-\ln(S_t/\bar{S}_t)]$ $1973-79 = 0$	Forward discount (FD_t)	All real appreciation due to bubble		Half real appreciation due to bubble	
				Probability of collapse (p_t)	Cumulated probability of noncollapse $\left[\prod_{t=1}^{T}(1-p_t)\right]$	Probability of collapse (p_t)	Cumulated probability of noncollapse $\left[\prod_{t=1}^{T}(1-p_t)\right]$
Jan 81	−13.09%	8.61%	10.88%	0.168	0.83	0.314	0.69
Feb 81	−6.80	15.17	5.75	0.071	0.77	0.137	0.59
Mar 81	−8.26	13.69	2.68	0.061	0.73	0.117	0.52
Apr 81	−5.69	16.24	3.85	0.057	0.68	0.110	0.46
May 81	0.13	22.51	7.04	0.053	0.65	0.104	0.42
June 81	3.78	26.61	5.85	0.042	0.62	0.082	0.38
Jul 81	6.52	29.87	7.14	0.041	0.59	0.080	0.35
Aug 81	8.90	32.68	6.79	0.036	0.57	0.072	0.33
Sep 81	2.75	27.04	5.12	0.039	0.55	0.076	0.30
Oct 81	−1.67	22.43	4.69	0.045	0.55	0.088	0.28
Nov 81	−2.81	21.09	2.78	0.041	0.50	0.079	0.25
Dec 81	−1.32	22.56	2.33	0.036	0.49	0.071	0.24
Jan 82	0.14	23.64	3.79	0.040	0.47	0.077	0.22
Feb 82	3.38	26.87	5.32	0.040	0.45	0.078	0.20
Mar 82	3.92	27.32	5.83	0.041	0.43	0.079	0.18
Apr 82	4.71	28.27	6.34	0.041	0.41	0.080	0.17
May 82	0.97	24.77	6.57	0.047	0.39	0.092	0.15
June 82	5.96	29.88	6.38	0.039	0.38	0.076	0.14
Jul 82	7.43	31.76	5.28	0.034	0.37	0.066	0.13
Aug 82	8.02	32.61	2.61	0.026	0.36	0.051	0.13

Table 6A.1 (continued)

Sep 82	9.02	33.43	3.81	0.028	0.35	0.056	0.12
Oct 82	10.06	34.35	3.58	0.027	0.34	0.053	0.11
Nov 82	11.14	35.00	2.89	0.025	0.33	0.049	0.11
Dec 82	5.59	28.77	3.32	0.032	0.32	0.062	0.10
Jan 83	4.32	27.40	3.78	0.034	0.31	0.067	0.09
Feb 83	6.00	28.99	3.36	0.031	0.30	0.061	0.09
Mar 83	5.16	28.33	4.49	0.035	0.29	0.069	0.08
Apr 83	6.44	30.01	4.61	0.034	0.28	0.066	0.08
May 83	7.51	31.41	3.99	0.031	0.27	0.060	0.07
June 83	10.81	34.69	4.61	0.029	0.26	0.057	0.07
Jul 83	12.42	36.37	5.31	0.030	0.25	0.058	0.06
Aug 83	15.64	39.57	5.10	0.027	0.25	0.053	0.06
Sep 83	15.37	39.56	4.27	0.025	0.24	0.049	0.06
Oct 83	12.91	37.32	4.24	0.026	0.23	0.052	0.05
Nov 83	15.94	40.35	3.92	0.024	0.23	0.047	0.05
Dec 83	18.35	42.66	4.06	0.023	0.22	0.045	0.05
Jan 84	20.60	45.05	4.10	0.022	0.22	0.043	0.05
Feb 84	16.64	41.24	4.09	0.024	0.21	0.047	0.05
Mar 84	12.68	37.44	4.93	0.028	0.21	0.055	0.04
Apr 84	14.51	39.58	5.32	0.027	0.20	0.054	0.04
May 84	18.38	43.69	5.63	0.025	0.20	0.050	0.04
June 84	18.03	43.31	5.95	0.026	0.19	0.051	0.04
Jul 84	21.92	47.68	6.44	0.025	0.19	0.048	0.04
Aug 84	23.23	49.56	6.59	0.024	0.18	0.047	0.03
Sep 84	28.03	54.75	6.28	0.021	0.18	0.042	0.03
Oct 84	29.40	55.84	5.15	0.019	0.17	0.038	0.03
Nov 84	26.87	53.14	3.94	0.018	0.17	0.036	0.03
Dec 84	30.53	56.72	3.22	0.016	0.17	0.032	0.03
Jan 85	32.63	58.42	2.67	0.015	0.17	0.029	0.03
Feb 85	36.61	62.40	2.62	0.014	0.16	0.027	0.03
Mar 85	38.60	64.39	3.07	0.014	0.16	0.028	0.03

percent. Thus we can reject at the 95 percent confidence level the hypothesis that half the real appreciation is attributable to a rational bubble. We can reject at even higher confidence levels the hypothesis that one-quarter or any smaller (but finite) fraction of the appreciation is attributable to a rational bubble.

It should be noted that the emphasis in the rejected hypothesis is on the word "rational" rather than the word "bubble." For example, the same low probability would attach to the hypothesis that investors for four years rationally expected a collapse of the dollar attributable to a sudden change in the monetary/fiscal policy mix or other fundamentals, in place of a collapse attributable to a bubble bursting. But the finding still leaves the possibility of an *irrational* bubble. There is no reason a bubble could not have continued for four years if the true probability of bursting was less than the probability in speculators' expectations. The proposition that speculators made the same prediction error repeatedly is not an attractive one from the standpoint of rational-expectations theory, but it nevertheless seems to follow inescapably from a continuous four-year history of expected dollar depreciation—as reflected in either the forward discount or the expectations survey data—with no *ex post* depreciation materializing (see Marris, 1985, or Frankel and Froot, 1985).

Acknowledgment

I thank Kenneth Froot for extremely efficient research assistance; Charles Engel and Steven Kohlhagen, in addition to the participants at a General Accounting Office seminar on exchange rates in Washington on February 18, 1983, for useful comments and suggestions; the National Science Foundation (under grant number SES-8218300) and the Institute for Business and Economic Research at the University of California, Berkeley, for research support; and Laura Knoy of the Institute for International Economics for data.

7

Zen and the Art of Modern Macroeconomics: The Search for Perfect Nothingness

Alan Stockman (1990) addresses one of the most difficult and interesting questions that international economists have to consider: what to say of use to monetary policymakers rather than to fellow economists only. He first evaluates two competing theories, namely, the equilibrium model—short for "dynamic stochastic general equilibrium models based on individual optimization"—and the sluggish-price or disequilibrium models. Stockman's discussion is reasonable and modest. He does not bang on the table and say, "I know the right answer." He does the opposite. His answer to the question "What does the theory have to say about what policymakers should do?" is, in essence, "Nothing."

But there is a danger that the answer, "I have nothing to recommend to policy makers" becomes "I recommend that policy makers do nothing." The word "nothing" will play a key role in my comments. The word does not often appear explicitly in the writings of equilibrium theorists. The popular phrase in the econometric writings is "random walk." (The usual conclusion is stated as "I have found that such and such a variable follows a random walk" or, at best, "I cannot reject the hypothesis that this variable follows a random walk." You seldom hear someone say, "After studying this variable for six months, I have absolutely nothing to say that would help to predict its movements." But the statements mean the same thing.) In Stockman's discussion, the telling phrase is "in the current state of knowledge," as in "In the current state of knowledge ... exchange rates and the current account should play little role [in the conduct of monetary policy]."

I should make clear that my remarks do apply not just to Stockman but equally to other "equilibrium" writings, and indeed to much of modern macroeconomics. I shall refer to the disease as the "Zen" of modern macroeconometrics, that is, the search for perfect nothingness.[1] Let me explain.

The goal in econometric work was once to get results that were statistically significant, to reject the null hypothesis. In order to stand in front of a conference proudly or to expect to publish a paper in a journal, the author first sought significant results.[2] Significant results are difficult to obtain in macroeconomics. The world is a complicated place; it is unlikely that the few key variables that emerge from the particular theory that one has developed will actually go far toward explaining a real-world time series. So what we have done—quite cleverly—is to redefine the rules. Now the goal is to fail to reject the null hypothesis—that is, we now try to get results that are statistically insignificant, or, in essence, to find *nothing*. It is far easier to find nothing than to find something. Typically one fails to reject many hypotheses every day, even in the shower or on the way to work.

Examples abound of the goal of finding nothing, from tests of Euler conditions to Ricardian equivalence.[3] But I shall pick an example that is central to Stockman's evaluation of the two competing theories of exchange rates: the question of whether the real exchange rate follows a random walk.[4]

Not long ago, it was argued that (1) purchasing power parity held fairly well, even in the short run—that is, that there was a near-infinite speed of adjustment of the real exchange rate toward a long-run equilibrium constant (or slow-moving trend)—and that (2) this was evidence in favor of the equilibrium view of goods markets. Subsequently, clear statistical rejections established the fact that purchasing power parity does not hold in the short run, and the question became whether it holds in the long run. Many of the equilibrium theorists now claim that (1) the speed of adjustment of the real exchange rate toward purchasing power parity is zero, or close to it, and (2) this is evidence in favor of the equilibrium view of goods markets.

It is true that it is difficult to reject the hypothesis that the real exchange rate follows a random walk, or comes close to it. A typical estimate is that the speed of adjustment of the real exchange rate to long-run equilibrium is 3 percent a month (an autoregressive coefficient of .97), or 30 percent a year (an autoregression coefficient of .70) and that this speed is not significantly greater than zero. But (even waiving the change in position) one might wonder why anyone would consider the finding of a zero speed of adjustment as evidence in favor of the equilibrium view.

The logic goes as follows. When one has finished running through some mathematics of the dynamically optimizing equilibrium, one comes out with nothing to say about movements in the real exchange rate. The rate can move up as easily as down. (The problem is that the equilibrium theorists have not identified the "fundamental disturbances"; this is the "gap in the evidence" to which Stockman refers. As Stockman says, in his 1987 study, the theory is still in its infancy.)[5] In other words, as far as the theorist knows, the real exchange rate follows a random walk.

The sticky-price model of Rudiger Dornbusch (1976c), on the other hand, *does* have something to say of use in predicting movements in the real exchange rate. It says that when the real exchange rate has overshot its long-run equilibrium (in response, for example, to a shift in the monetary-fiscal policy mix), as the dollar clearly had by 1984, the best expectation is for it to return gradually toward that equilibrium. So a failure to reject the hypothesis that the real exchange rate follows a random walk is (understandably) interpreted as evidence against the sticky-price theory. But it is also interpreted as evidence in favor of the equilibrium theory, even though the latter has no more testable implications for the real exchange rate than does the proposition that nine is a prime number.

Stockman has offered a second kind of evidence. In addition to arguing that some of the things predicted by the sticky-price model seem not to be true (the adjustment of the real exchange rate toward a long-run equilibrium), he argues that some of the things that the model does successfully predict can also be explained by varieties of the equilibrium theory.[6] Two examples stand out.

One piece of evidence that is traditionally considered to support the sticky-price model is the observation that fluctuations in the real exchange rate are very highly correlated with fluctuations in the nominal exchange rate. Figure 7.1 shows changes in the nominal and real mark/dollar rate. But Stockman has an explanation of how such behavior can also come out of an equilibrium model. To begin with, there are always real shocks to productivity, technology, tastes, trade policy, and taxes that would move the real exchange rate no matter what the regime. Why do these movements in the real exchange rate happen to show up almost entirely as movements in the nominal exchange rate instead of the price level? He says that it is because the monetary authority tries to stabilize the price level.

The second piece of evidence that is traditionally considered the exclusive preserve of the sticky-price model is the observation that the fluctuations in the real exchange rate are much greater for countries and time periods in which there is a floating exchange rate than when there is a fixed exchange rate. Surely this clinches the case? No. Stockman (1988) has shown how to coax out of the equilibrium theory an explanation for this fact, too. This story begins with the proposition that under fixed exchange rates, governments are likely to put on (and take off) trade controls more often, in order to protect their foreign exchange reserves. Then Stockman

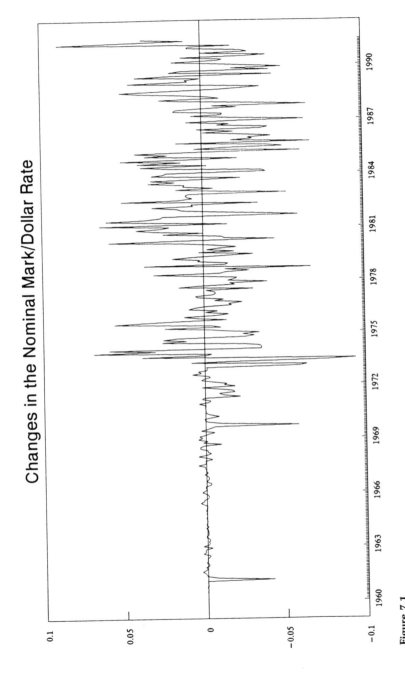

Figure 7.1
Fluctuations in the nominal and real mark/dollar exchange rates

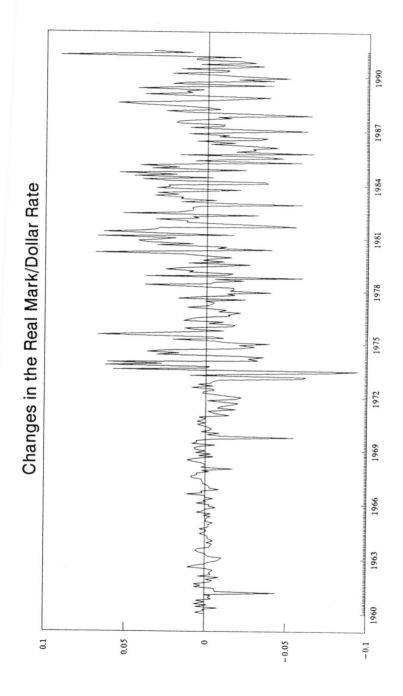

turns loose his dynamically optimizing agents, who manage to adjust to this behavior on the part of the government in such a way as to smooth out fluctuations in the real exchange rate. Voilà! An equilibrium model that is "consistent" with the facts. Such explanations are clever and make for good journal articles that are popular among academic economists. But that does not make them true.

Speaking of agents, spy novels are a good analogy for stories that are clever and make entertaining reading but that may not necessarily represent the truth. Datum: At the conference at which Alan Stockman's discussion and the present commentary were originally presented, I got up from my chair next to Alan Stockman on the stage and walked over to take my place at the lectern. At the least, the following three hypotheses could have emerged:

• I was a spy for a foreign power, Alan was a CIA counterspy who was about to assassinate me, and so I had gotten up to move out of range. This hypothesis is "consistent with the facts" in the sense that, if true, it would explain them. But it is convoluted and not very plausible.

• John Le Carré was in British intelligence before he began his second career as a novelist. This hypothesis is an interesting subject for speculation. I have no idea whether it is true. It is also "consistent with the facts" in the weak sense that it does not contradict the datum. But it seems no more relevant than the statement that nine is a prime number, the proposition that economic agents dynamically optimize, or the hundreds of other hypotheses that I "fail to reject" every morning in the shower.

• I went to the lectern for the simple reason that the American Enterprise Institute invited me to comment on Alan's study. While not as clever as the other propositions, this hypothesis is simple, plausible, and consistent with the facts in the strong sense that it would explain them while most other hypotheses would not.

I will leave it to the reader to decide which hypothesis is the correct one.

Thus far I have addressed two kinds of empirical claims in favor of the equilibrium theory—namely, that it is "consistent" with the statistical failure to reject a random walk on the real exchange rate (an empty statement) and that it can be made consistent with the observed variability of the real exchange rate in a regime of floating exchange rates (too convoluted). But what about the claim that if the alternative sticky-price model were correct, one should be able statistically to reject the random walk hypothesis? What about the disturbing reality that most studies have in fact failed to reject it?

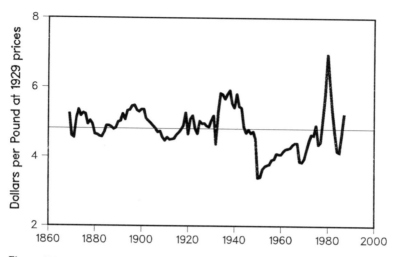

Figure 7.2
Dollar/pound real exchange rate, 1869–1987

My answer is that one should not even *expect* to be able to reject a random walk on the basis of the mere fifteen or twenty years of post-1973 data that almost all of the tests use. Imagine that the truth is that the speed of adjustment to purchasing power parity is .03 per month or approximately .30 per year. A simple calculation suggests that one should then not expect to be able to reject statistically the hypothesis that the coefficient is zero unless one has at least forty-nine years of data.[7]

A long time series for the real exchange rate is available for the dollar-pound sterling rate (see figure 7.2). Tests of the speed of adjustment toward purchasing power parity give the following results (see Table 7.1). On post-1973 data, the speed is not statistically greater than zero. On post-1945 data, it still does not quite appear statistically greater than zero.[8] As I have noted, however, this is precisely what one would expect from forty-three years of data if the true speed were .30 per year or less. On the complete data set of 1869–1987, the speed of adjustment *is* clearly statistically greater than zero.[9] In my view this not only tends to vindicate the sticky-price view but also provides a neat illustration of the irrelevance of tests that "find nothing" or "fail to reject the null hypothesis" merely because they have not looked in the right places.

Where does all this leave monetary policy? Stockman's list of proposed reasons why monetary policy might want to pay attention to the exchange rate and the current account is very good. As should be clear by now, I

Table 7.1
Purchasing power parity between the United States and the United Kingdom, 1869–1987

	1973–1987	1945–1972	1945–1987	1869–1987
Statistics on percentage deviation from mean				
Mean absolute deviation	.120	.074	.110	.093
Standard deviation	.156	.091	.156	.121
Time trend	.001	−.001	.006[b]	−.001[b]
	(.010)	(.002)	(.002)	(.000)
Autoregression of real exchange rate				
Deviation from mean	.687[b]	.722[b]	.830[b]	.844[b]
	(.208)	(.130)	(.092)	(.050)
Deviation from trend	.688[b]	.730[b]	.741[b]	.838[b]
	(.208)	(.131)	(.101)	(.052)
Regression against nominal exchange rate				
Coefficient[a]	2.516[b]	1.220[b]	1.687[b]	.916[b]
	(.417)	(.103)	(.186)	(.093)
Autocorrelation coefficient	.959[b]	.989[b]	.992	.988[b]
	(.054)	(.015)	(.011)	(.014)

Note: Standard errors are reported in parentheses.
a. With constant term and correction for autocorrelation.
b. Significant at the 95 percent level.

reject the notion that the state of our ignorance (great as it is) is in itself a reason for policymakers to pay no attention to these two important economic variables. I do agree with the conclusion that the monetary authorities should focus primarily on the price level and real output as goals, rather than the international variables. But this is because I see many advantages to targeting nominal gross national product for monetary policy.

I do not subscribe to the view that the U.S. current account deficits of recent years should not be a subject of concern. It is important, of course, for economists to keep explaining to the general public, as Stockman does, that not all deficits are bad deficits and that a country may choose to go into current account deficit and to borrow from abroad to finance a high level of investment arising from productive opportunities or to finance a high level of consumption arising from the knowledge that income will be higher in the future. Korea's current account deficits of the 1970s are a good example. Nevertheless, the recent U.S. deficits are not of the Korean type. Their origin lies instead in the large federal budget deficits that we began to run in the 1980s, which in turn originated in faulty economic reasoning and political gridlock, not in intertemporal optimization. I would add something to Stockman's list of proposed reasons to pay attention to the international variables—namely, that the current account deficit implies that we are going further and further into debt to the rest of the world. The only reason that I agree that monetary policy should not focus primarily on the current account deficits is that the job belongs to fiscal policy.

To say that one can construct models in which a current account deficit is "nothing" to worry about because it is the outcome of dynamic optimization is not the same thing as to say that the U.S. deficit of the 1980s is in fact nothing to worry about in the real world. It is true that we remain largely in ignorance of precisely how the economy works. But at some stage, economists have to come down from their towers of fantasy and decide what they really think. The alternative is to leave the decision making to those who may be still more ignorant.

III

Is There an Exchange Risk Premium?

Introduction to Part III

Part III is devoted to testing the systematic prediction errors that separate the forward exchange rate from the expected future spot exchange rate and to the question of whether this observed gap is attributable to an exchange risk premium. It should be evident from part II that this question is key to the choice between monetary and portfolio-balance models of exchange rates. It is key to other questions as well, such as whether a market participant can do better than accept the forward rate as the optimal predictor, whether agents can make apparently systematic mistakes, and whether sterilized intervention in the foreign exchange market offers central banks an effective tool for controlling the exchange rate.

Chapter 8, "Tests of Rational Expectations in the Forward Exchange Market," belongs to what is now a very large literature. These papers test, and usually reject, the proposition of unbiasedness in the forward rate.[1] This chapter can serve as an introduction to this literature, as many of the methodological points that appear here have become subjects of sub-literatures of their own. The famous *Siegal paradox* and its resolution are mentioned here as the "third methodological point."[2] The more famous *peso problem* appears in note 9 and the last three paragraphs.[3] The *overlapping observations* problem appears as the "final methodological point" in section 8.4.[4] One important innovation missing from the formal tests reported here but standard in later work is to express both the forward rate and future spot rate as premiums over the current spot rate (to eliminate "unit roots").[5] It has become routine for such tests to find that the forward discount is a biased predictor of changes in the exchange rate, though it is more common to interpret such findings as evidence of an exchange risk premium than of biasedness in expectations.

"The Diversifiability of Exchange Risk" (chapter 9) is the exception in this book: a purely theoretical piece. It adduces special conditions under which the exchange risk premium could be zero, even if investors are risk averse. This same point can be made with investors who are assumed to optimize a general intertemporal utility function, which has become the standard approach.[6] I made the choice to apply the simpler framework of one-period mean-variance optimization in this and the subsequent chapters. For me, the ultimate goal is to match the theoretical propositions with the data. This means that some specific functional restrictions will have to imposed at some stage. My personal preference is to impose any such restrictions in a clear and explicit way early on. This eliminates the need at the empirical stage for a large leap from theory to econometrics (such as proposing proxies for "state variables" that the theory has not explicitly identified).

Because the conditions under which the exchange risk premium is literally zero are very stringent, in my view the primary lesson to take away from chapter 9 and other papers like it is only that more of exchange risk is diversifiable than was previously thought. Assuming that economic actors (investors, borrowers, importers, and exporters) take full advantage of the scope for diversifying or hedging, it follows that the risk premium is smaller than would otherwise be thought.

The remainder of the chapters in part III examine the specific question of whether the observed bias in the forward market, which shows up in chapter 8 and in so many other papers, should be attributed to the exchange risk premium. I have approached this question in two different ways.

I began by following the logic that if the systematic component of prediction errors is indeed attributable to a risk premium, then it should be empirically related to those observable determinants of the risk premium given to us by theory. The theory in chapter 9 suggests that the determinants of the risk premium are asset supplies and variances/covariances. (Among other contributors to the theory of the risk premium, Dornbusch, 1983a, produced the same two determinants in a more elegant and convenient specification.) At the simplest level, one could regress prediction errors against a suitable measure of asset supplies. Such tests are typically unable to reject the null hypothesis of a zero coefficient.[7]

"In Search of the Exchange Risk Premium," the third chapter on this subject, offers a more powerful test by bringing to bear all the constraints of the theory. The specification for the determination of the risk premium includes the variance-covariance matrix as well as asset supplies (the latter expressed as portfolio shares, and entered multiplicatively with the former). The distribution of wealth across nationalities is allowed to enter as well.[8] The empirical finding is, once again, a failure to find any evidence of a risk premium. A related paper considers the case where goods prices are stochastic and also shows how to test explicitly the assumption that investors choose their portfolios so as to diversify optimally.[9]

A failure to reject a null hypothesis does not, of course, entitle the author to assert that he or she has found evidence establishing the null hypothesis. It appeared easy to attribute the persistent failures to find evidence of a risk premium in work such as "In Search of the Exchange Risk Premium" to insufficient power in the test. But subsequent developments suggest that this may in fact not be the problem. If one accepts a priori the framework of mean-variance optimization, conventional estimates of risk aversion (in the range from 1 to 4), and a definition of total wealth that is at all comprehensive,[10] then it turns out to follow that the risk premium must be quite small. Relatively small shifts in expected returns should be sufficient to induce investors to make large shifts in asset supplies.[11] This proposition was implicit in the earlier continuous-time stochastic formulation of Krugman (1981) (another classic paper that was never published). The conclusion—that optimal diversification implies a risk premium much smaller than previously realized—applies also to the equity market, where the standard reference is Mehra and Prescott (1985).[12]

A major research development in this area in the late 1980s was allowing for variation over time in the variances and covariances. It had long been noted that variances themselves varied. Early on, the major relevance of heteroscedasticity seemed to be the need to correct standard errors in tests such as those in chapter 8. This application became increasingly common as the White correction became increasingly standard in econometrics software. But such corrections usually made little difference for the results. (Modeling the time-series properties of the variance of the exchange rate also became increasingly popular because both theory and empirical findings seemed to close off the possibility of predicting changes in the *level* of the exchange rate.)[13]

To my mind, the most interesting application of time-varying variances is to questions where economic behavior is thought to depend on them, as in determination of the risk premium. Changes in the variance cause changes in the risk premium. Chapter 11, "Recent Estimates of Time-Variation in the Conditional Variance and in the Exchange Risk Premium," reviews the evidence on the magnitudes. It turns out to remain true that the theory implies (1) the risk premium is on average relatively small, for example, too small to explain the observed bias in the forward exchange market, and (2) changes in asset supplies, such as are the result of foreign exchange intervention, should on average have small effects. This conclusion, like the earlier papers described, depends on the a priori acceptance of the idea that most assets in the world portfolio are held by investors who diversify optimally, with the conventional magnitude of risk aversion given to us from applications outside finance theory.

As noted above, I have approached the question whether the observed bias in the forward market should be attributed to the exchange risk premium in two different ways. The first was to see if the systematic component of forward rate prediction errors was empirically related to the theoretical determinants of the risk premium. The second, which I have pursued in a line of research with Ken Froot, is to adopt an entirely different measure of investors' expectations: data from surveys of participants in international financial markets. We applied these data to the question at hand in "Forward Discount Bias: Is it an Exchange Risk Premium?" (chapter 12). Even if one follows the economist's standard skepticism regarding survey data and allows for the likelihood that they reflect investors' true expectations only subject to a measurement error, the results are quite striking. Measuring the risk premium directly as the difference between the forward rate and the expected future spot rate as reflected in the survey data, there is some evidence of its existence, but it behaves nothing like the systematic component of the forward rate prediction errors.

If one wishes to reconcile all the different findings reproduced in part III of this book, one is led to the conclusion that investors do not in fact make their portfolio decisions based on foreknowledge of the mean and variance of the return distribution, or else that those who do hold a relatively small share of world wealth.

8

Tests of Rational Expectations in the Forward Exchange Market

This chapter presents tests of the hypothesis that the forward rate is equal to the expected future spot rate. These are tests of rational expectations if there are no transactions costs or risk premia. Progressively broader definitions of the information set (upon which expectations are conditional) are taken. To summarize the findings, the null hypothesis is rejected in a majority of cases. A statistical rationale, involving the possibility of discontinuously large errors, is suggested.

8.1 Inaccuracy of the Forward Rate as a Predictor

We begin by examining some figures on how well one-month forward rates have done at predicting spot rates, for seven currencies against the U.S. dollar, between 1973 and 1978.[1] Column (1) of table 8.1 shows the root mean squared prediction error in the forward rate. The figures are quite high; since the data are in logs, a figure like .0321 for Germany means that it takes a band of ± 6.41 percent to encompass 95 percent of the prediction errors, assuming a lognormal distribution. For most of the countries the prediction errors are even higher during the first year and a half, a period of adjustment in international exchange markers, than in the subsequent period. Column (4) compares the squared prediction errors to the total variation in the spot rate. It has the interpretation of an R^2.[2] For example, it indicates that 83 percent of the total variation in the deutsche mark spot rate during the period was predicted by the forward rate; if the first year and a half is excluded, the figure goes up to 89 percent.

The percentage of variation predicted by the forward rate is higher for currencies with a long-run trend, like pound sterling, than for those with no trend, like the Canadian dollar. Predicting the spot rate is, of course, an easier task when there is an obvious trend. Column (6) shows how well the

Table 8.1
Size of percentage prediction errors of the four-week forward rate

Currency	Sample	(1) Root mean square prediction error $\sqrt{\dfrac{\sum(s_{t+4}-f)^2}{T}}$	(2) Mean square prediction error $\dfrac{\sum(s_{t+4}-f)^2}{T}$	(3) Variance of spot rate $\dfrac{\sum(s_{t+4}-\bar{s})^2}{T}$	(4) Proportion of spot rate variation predicted by forward rate $1-\dfrac{(2)}{(3)}$	(5) Mean square four-week change in spot rate $\dfrac{\sum(s_{t+4}-s)^2}{T}$	(6) Proportion of spot rate changes predicted by forward rate $1-\dfrac{(2)}{(5)}$
Deutsche	271	.0321	.00103	.00609	.831	.00105	.019
mark	78	.0500	.00250	.00092	.639	.00257	.027
	193	.0210	.00044	.00385	.886	.00045	.022
French	271	.0303	.00092	.00411	.776	.00086	-.070
franc	78	.0446	.00194	.00480	.585	.00192	-.036
	193	.0221	.00049	.00377	.870	.00044	-.114
Pound	271	.0224	.00050	.02115	.976	.00050	.000
sterling	78	.0245	.00060	.00144	.585	.00053	-.132
	193	.0218	.00047	.01670	.972	.00050	.060
Italian	271	.0283	.00080	.02714	.971	.00071	.127
lire	78	.0303	.00092	.00275	.665	.00091	-.011
	193	.0276	.00076	.01954	.961	.00064	-.188
Swiss	271	.0333	.00111	.01755	.937	.00114	.026
franc	78	.0481	.00231	.00438	.437	.00231	.000
	193	.0251	.00063	.00852	.926	.00068	.074
Dutch	271	.0303	.00092	.00483	.810	.00090	-.022
guilder	78	.0462	.00213	.00422	.496	.00216	.014
	193	.0210	.00044	.00291	.849	.00040	-.100
Japanese yen	193	.0184	.00034	.00484	.930	.00034	.000

Sample periods: 271 = January 5, 1973 to April 4, 1978; 78 = January 5, 1973 to June 28, 1974; 193 = July 5, 1974 to April 4, 1978

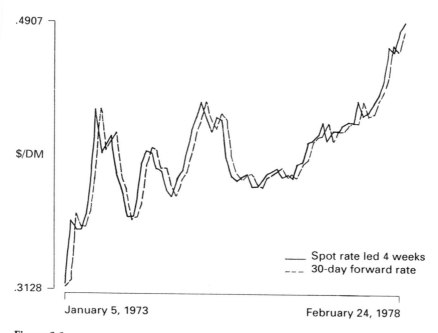

Figure 8.1
The forward rate is closer to the contemporaneous spot rate than to the future realized spot rate

forward market has done at predicting *changes* in the spot rate. The figures are very low; for example, only 2 percent of the mark rate changes were predicted by the forward rate. In a few cases, the number is less than zero, suggesting that the forward rate was actually a worse predictor than the contemporaneous spot rate.

Figure 8.1 plots the future spot dollar/mark rate and the corresponding forward rate that is an attempt to predict it. It is evident that the forward rate follows the contemporaneous spot rate far more closely than the future spot rate. This is still more evidence that the forward rate is a poor predictor, and explains why the percentage of variation in changes predicted by the forward rate is so much lower than the percentage of variation in levels.

The large size of the prediction errors in the forward rate says nothing regarding market efficiency. A failure of market efficiency would require the discovery of alternative predictors that had consistently lower prediction errors, or, equivalently, of a consistent *bias* in forward rate prediction errors, as opposed to a high absolute magnitude. But it is important to make note of the high variability in the spot rate, and the high risk to which *any* predictor is likely to be subject, before we examine the evidence on the question of bias in the forward rate.

8.2 Methodology of Testing Rational Expectations

There are a number of methodological points to be made, each of them occasionally confused in the growing literature testing the proposition that the forward rate is equal to the expected future spot rate.[3]

The first point is that the hypothesis being tested consists of the two joint hypotheses that people form expectations of the spot rate rationally, given the information available to them, and that the mean of their expectational distribution is reflected in the market's forward rate. It is very difficult to evaluate empirically the first proposition alone, because expectations are not directly observable.[4] The second proposition could very well fail because a risk premium could separate the forward rate from the expected future rate. The joint hypothesis of rational expectations and perfect markets (i.e., competitive markets with low information and transactions costs) constitutes the hypothesis of market efficiency. But even market efficiency is not sufficient to imply that the forward rate equals the expected future spot rate. As has been pointed out, the latter condition could fail because of the existence of an exchange risk premium, without market efficiency failing.[5] On the other hand, the fact that people are risk averse does not in itself imply that a substantial risk premium must separate the forward rate from the expected future spot rate. Rather, it is possible that exchange risk is largely or completely diversifiable.[6]

The second important methodological point is that whether the rational expectations hypothesis is true or false depends on the definition of the information set that market participants are assumed to have when they form their expectations. Expectations are strongly or weakly rational, depending on whether the information set is defined broadly or narrowly. For example, we would not expect rational expectations to hold if "inside information" is included. This chapter begins with the narrowest definition of the information set and then progresses to broader definitions, though never moving beyond obviously relevant and publicly available variables.

The hypothesis to be tested is that the expected value of the future spot rate, given the current information set, is equal to the current forward rate:

$$E(SR_{t+1}|I_t) = FR_t.$$

Bilson (1981b) calls this hypothesis "speculative efficiency" to differentiate it from the weaker hypothesis of market efficiency. It will be loosely referred to hereafter as the "rational expectations hypothesis," though the rationality of expectations itself is a still weaker condition. A more precise term for the hypothesis tested here would be "unbiasedness in the forward market."

Equivalently, the prediction error (the future spot rate minus the current forward rate) is equal to an error term that is independent of the current information set.

$$(SR_{t+1} - FR_t) = \varepsilon_t, \qquad E(\varepsilon_t I_t) = E\varepsilon_t EI_t = 0.$$

Thus, when we regress the prediction error against variables in the information set, we should get zero coefficients. It is this set of variables that is progressively broadened in the tests that follow.

One point that was not appreciated in early work and is still frequently misunderstood is that rational expectations imply that prediction errors are white noise, not that first differences in the spot rate are white noise (Dooley and Shafer, 1976; Logue et al., 1977; Poole, 1967). Rational expectations do *not* require that the spot rate follow a random walk, in the proper definition of the term.[7]

The third methodological point is that the expected future spot rate should be defined in real terms rather than in nominal terms; the real value (purchasing power) of profits made in the exchange market is not independent of the exchange rate itself. This is the economic explanation behind the fact that if the forward rate and the expected future spot rate are precisely equal when defined in units of domestic currency per unit of foreign currency (i.e., because the real value of domestic currency is constant), then they *cannot* be precisely equal when defined in units of foreign currency per unit of domestic currency. This fact is sometimes called the Siegal paradox; its mathematical explanation is simply Jensen's inequality and the convexity of the inverse function (Siegal, 1972). The next chapter shows that in a one-good world, the market-clearing forward rate, assuming no risk premium, is:

$$FR = E(1/P^*_{+1})/E(1/P_{+1}),$$

where P^*_{+1} is the future price of the good in foreign currency, and P_{+1} is the future price of the good in domestic currency. (We now drop the "t" sub-scripts, for notational ease.) The forward rate is equal to the ratio of the expected purchasing power of the foreign currency to the expected purchasing power of the domestic currency. The future exchange rate, by purchasing power parity, will be $SR_{+1} = P_{+1}/P^*_{+1}$. FR, in general, lies between $E(SR_{+1})$ and $1/E(1/SR_{+1})$.

One special case in which the convexity problem has a clear solution is a hyperinflation. Because the variation takes place overwhelmingly in the real value of *domestic* rather than foreign currency, the tests should be run with the exchange rate defined as the price of domestic currency in terms of foreign (not the other way around as is sometimes done (Frenkel, 1977)).

Two approaches have been taken to the convexity problem. One is first to run all tests of rational expectations using SR and FR and then to run them again using 1/SR and 1/FR. The argument is that, since "the truth lies in between," if one gets similar answers each way, then there is no problem. This approach is not a solution, however. In both cases, the discrepancy between the expected spot rate and the ratio of the expected currency values can be regarded as an errors-in-variables problem. The slope coefficient in a regression like $SR_{+1} = \alpha + \beta FR + \varepsilon$ will be biased downward either way. The second approach, and the one followed here, is to run the tests using the logs of SR and FR, which we will represent by s and f, respectively. Unbiasedness is then: $E(s_{+1}|I) = f$. Then it makes no difference whether the exchange rates are defined from the point of view of the domestic country or the foreign country.[8]

8.3   Only a Constant Term in the Information Set

The weakest possible test of rational expectations defines the information set to contain nothing other than a constant; the criterion is simply $E(s_{+4} - f) = 0$, or, in other words, the mean prediction error is zero. It would be quite surprising if the market failed this easy test.[9] Indeed, the mean prediction errors computed in table 8.2 are uniformly low; the highest is a 1 percent overprediction of the value of the Swiss franc during the first year and a half. The means are generally lower during the second part of the sample and, in any case, are always much smaller than their standard errors.

Let us turn for a moment from emphasizing the "efficient markets" interpretation of the joint null hypothesis to the "zero risk premium" interpretation. The insignificance of the means in table 8.2 suggests that there has been no systematic risk premium, where "systematic" is defined as persisting over the length of the sample period. Of course, there could be a risk premium that fluctuates frequently between positive and negative. But if the risk premium is systematically related to variables like the expected variability of the currency value and the stock of assets denominated in the

Table 8.2
Mean prediction error $(s_{+4} - f)$

Currency	January 5, 1973– April 4, 1978 271 observations	January 5, 1973– June 28, 1974 78 observations	July 5, 1974– April 4, 1978 193 observations
Deutsche mark	.0050 (.0316)	.0093 (.0491)	.0033 (.0207)
French franc	.0053 (.0298)	.0055 (.0443)	.0052 (.0215)
Pound sterling	.0007 (.0224)	.0047 (.0240)	−.0009 (.0216)
Italian lire	.0038 (.0280)	.0010 (.0303)	.0049 (.0271)
Swiss franc	.0078 (.0324)	.0101 (.0470)	.0069 (.0242)
Dutch guilder	.0053 (.0299)	.0091 (.0452)	.0038 (.0207)
Japanese yen			.0056 (.0174)

Note: Standard deviations are given in parentheses.

currency, one might expect these variables and, therefore, the risk premium, to change slowly.[10]

Even so, we could interpret the point estimates as risk premia. The generally positive sign indicates a smaller return on dollar assets than on assets denominated in the other currencies. This is consistent with the idea that the dollar is a safe currency, and holders of other currencies must be compensated for greater riskiness. On the other hand, the only negative risk premium appears for the United Kingdom (July 1974–April 1978); this is inconsistent with one's a priori expectations that the pound sterling was the *riskiest* of the currencies. On the whole, the evidence does not favor the existence of systematic risk premia.

8.4   The Forward Rate Added to the information Set

A stronger test of rational expectations is to include the forward rate itself in the information set. The criterion is then $E(s_{+4} - f \mid f) = 0$. If we run the regression

$$s_{+4} = \alpha + \beta f + \varepsilon,$$

we should obtain $\alpha = 0$ and $\beta = 1$ under the null hypothesis.

Before proceeding with the tests, we must consider a final methodological point. Because the observations are more frequent than the contract length, that is, contracts overlap, the error term will not be independent of past errors but will follow a moving-average process.[11] In this case, when four consecutive contracts overlap, the error process will be a third-order moving average. This proposition is proved in appendix 8A. On an intuitive level, it is clear that new information bearing on s_{t+4} becomes available between periods t and $t + 3$ that is correlated with information bearing on s_{t+5} that becomes available between periods $t + 1$ and $t + 4$.

Ignoring the moving average error process biases the estimated standard errors downward, making rejection of the null hypothesis spuriously easy. There are several possible strategies. One is simply to include in the sample only every fourth observation.[12] Since the contracts no longer overlap, the errors are then independent under the null hypothesis. The obvious drawback is that throwing away data reduces the power of the test. An alternative strategy is to use all observations, estimate the error process from the residuals of the first-stage OLS regression, and then attempt to transform the data appropriately, with the aim of attaining efficient estimators.[13] However, it has been pointed out that correlation between the transformed forward rate and the error term will render these two-step procedures inconsistent unless the forward rate is not only contemporaneously uncorrelated with the error term (as it is under the null hypothesis of rational expectations), but is also strictly exogenous (an unrealistic assumption).[14] The strategy adopted here is to perform separate tests on four subsamples, each formed by taking every fourth observation. Since the tests are not independent, there is no way of knowing how to combine optimally the results of the four separate tests into one efficient test, but using all the data must add to our knowledge.

The regressions of the future spot rate against the current forward rate are reported in table 8.3. Of the six currencies tested, only two (the pound sterling and the Swiss franc) pass this test of rational expectations. The others (the deutsche mark, the French franc, the Italian lire, and the Dutch guilder) have estimated constant terms that are significantly different from zero and slope coefficients that are significantly less than one, whether the hypotheses are tested separately with t-tests or jointly with F-tests.[15] The results suggest a tendency for the spot rate to return toward its mean to an extent not recognized by the forward market.[16]

It has been suggested that if failure of tests like these is due to discrepancies between the forward rate and the expected future spot rate (i.e., is due to the existence of risk premia) rather than to a failure of market

Table 8.3
Forward rate in information set, $s_{+4} = \alpha + \beta f + \eta$, Ordinary Least Squares
(sample period: January 5, 1973–April 4, 1978)

Currency	Sample	$\hat{\alpha}$	Standard error	$\hat{\beta}$	Standard error	F
Deutsche mark	1	−.096	(.045)*	.889	(.049)*	3.95*
	2	−.082	(.043)	.905	(.047)*	3.31*
	3	−.099	(.046)*	.885	(.050)*	3.50*
	4	−.099	(.043)*	.886	(.047)*	4.50*
French franc	1	−.201	(.078)*	.866	(.051)*	5.13*
	2	−.197	(.081)*	.869	(.053)*	4.85*
	3	−.208	(.083)*	.861	(.054)*	5.20*
	4	−.231	(.087)*	.847	(.056)*	5.20*
Pound sterling	1	.013	(.014)	.983	(.018)	1.02
	2	.012	(.013)	.984	(.018)	0.94
	3	.015	(.014)	.981	(.018)	1.05
	4	.017	(.015)	.978	(.020)	1.19
Italian lire	1	−.280	(.135)*	.957	(.021)*	3.32*
	2	−.258	(.122)*	.960	(.019)*	3.51*
	3	−.261	(.124)*	.960	(.019)*	3.62*
	4	−.293	(.139)*	.955	(.021)*	3.34*
Swiss franc	1	−.030	(.030)	.962	(.030)	3.08
	2	−.013	(.028)	.979	(.028)	3.16*
	3	−.036	(.030)	.955	(.031)	3.64*
	4	−.023	(.030)	.969	(.030)	2.89
Dutch guilder	1	−.106	(.049)*	.884	(.051)*	4.16*
	2	−.090	(.048)	.900	(.050)	3.37*
	3	−.101	(.049)*	.888	(.051)*	4.07*
	4	−.112	(.050)*	.877	(.053)*	4.38*

* Significantly different from the hypothesized value ($\alpha = 0$) or ($\beta = 1$), at the 95 percent level. The reported F-statistic tests the joint hypothesis ($\alpha = 0$, $\beta = 1$), and is calculated by:

$$\frac{(\text{Constrained SS} - \text{Unconstrained SS})/2}{\text{Unconstrained SS}/t - 2}.$$

The 95 percent critical value is $F(2, 65) = 3.14$.
Sample sizes: $1 = 68$, $2 = 68$, $3 = 68$, $4 = 67$.

efficiency, then the difficulty can be treated as an errors-in-variables problem, biasing the estimate of β downward (Obstfeld, 1978). The proposal is to use Durbin's instrument, which consists of a rank ordering for the forward rate, under the argument that if the discrepancies are small enough, the instrumental variable estimator will be consistent. But a comparison of instrumental variable estimations to the OLS estimations shows that the differences are negligible.[17] It appears that if the failure of these tests is due to discrepancies between the forward rate and the true expected future spot rate, rather than to a failure of market efficiency, these discrepancies are too large to be eliminated by Durbin's instrument. We are stuck with testing market efficiency and the absence of a risk premium jointly.

8.5   The Last Prediction Error Added to the Information Set

We are now ready to add another variable to the set of information that market participants are assumed to take into account when we define rational expectations: the most recent prediction error. In other words, rational expectations require that prediction errors made in (nonoverlapping) forward contracts be serially uncorrelated:

$$E(s_{+4} - f \mid s - f_{-4}) = 0.$$

We first consider the information set to consist of the constant term and the most recent prediction error. Table 8.4 presents regressions of the following equation:

$$(s_{+4} - f) = \gamma(1 - \rho) + \rho(s - f_{-4}) + \eta.$$

The null hypothesis that $\gamma = 0$ is never rejected.[18] The null hypothesis that $\rho = 0$ is sometimes rejected for Germany, the United Kingdom, and Italy. It is puzzling that in each of these cases the results are quite different, depending on which subsample one looks at—for example, whether one looks at the subsample $4n$ ($n = 1,67$) or the subsample $1 + 4n$ ($n = 1,67$).

The last test performed here includes the constant term, the forward rate, and the last prediction error, in the information set simultaneously. The equation estimated in Table 8.5 is:

$$s_{+4} = \gamma(1 - \rho) + \beta f + \rho(s - f_{-4}) + \eta.$$

In the case of Germany, the joint hypothesis that all three rational expectations conditions are met is uniformly rejected. The results for the other countries are more varied but show rejections about half the time.

Table 8.4
Constant and last prediction error in information set,
$(s_{+4} - f) = \gamma(1 - \rho) + \rho(s - f_{-4}) + \eta$, Ordinary Least Squares
(sample period: January 5, 1973–April 4, 1978)

Currency	Sample	$\gamma(\hat{1} - \rho)$	Standard error	$\hat{\rho}$	Standard error	F
Deutsche	1	.004	(.004)	.113	(.123)	1.66
mark	2	.004	(.004)	.189	(.121)	2.57
	3	.003	(.004)	.199	(.117)	2.50
	4	.002	(.003)	.261	(.108)*	4.03*
French	1	.004	(.004)	.132	(.125)	2.14
franc	2	.004	(.003)	.160	(.120)	2.05
	3	.004	(.003)	.160	(.120)	2.28
	4	.003	(.004)	.007	(.114)	0.92
Pound	1	.000	(.002)	.448	(.113)*	8.40*
sterling	2	−.000	(.002)	.445	(.114)*	8.13*
	3	−.000	(.003)	.158	(.120)	1.33
	4	−.000	(.003)	.213	(.118)	2.16
Italian	1	.003	(.004)	.109	(.123)	1.34
lire	2	.002	(.003)	.322	(.117)*	4.96*
	3	.003	(.003)	.253	(.119)*	3.47*
	4	.003	(.004)	.168	(.122)	1.86
Swiss	1	.006	(.004)	.069	(.124)	2.12
franc	2	.006	(.004)	.211	(.119)	4.14*
	3	.005	(.004)	.138	(.111)	2.74
	4	.005	(.004)	.104	(.113)	2.25
Dutch	1	.005	(.004)	.064	(.124)	1.57
guilder	2	.005	(.004)	.123	(.123)	3.52*
	3	.004	(.004)	.131	(.117)	1.88
	4	.003	(.003)	.110	(.110)	1.58

* Significantly different from the hypothesized value ($\gamma = 0$) or ($\rho = 0$), at the 95 percent level. The reported F-statistic tests the joint hypothesis ($\gamma = 0$, $\rho = 0$), and is calculated by:

$$\frac{\text{(Constrained SS} - \text{Unconstrained SS)}/2}{\text{Unconstrained SS}/t - 2}.$$

The 95 percent critical value is $F(2, 65) = 3.14$.
Sample sizes: $1 = 67$, $2 = 67$, $3 = 67$, $4 = 66$.

Table 8.5
Constant, forward rate, and last prediction error in information set
$s_{+4} = \gamma(1 - \rho) + \beta f + \rho(s - f_{-4}) + \eta$, Ordinary Least Squares
(sample period: January 5, 1973–April 4, 1978)

Currency	Sample	$\gamma(\hat{1} - \rho)$	Standard error	$\hat{\beta}$	Standard error	$\hat{\rho}$	Standard error	F
Deutsche	1	−.120	(.049)*	.864	(.053)*	.160	(.120)	3.37*
mark	2	−.105	(.047)*	.880	(.051)*	.235	(.119)	3.67*
	3	−.086	(.049)	.901	(.054)	.233	(.116)*	2.87*
	4	−.059	(.043)	.933	(.047)	.280	(.108)*	3.44*
French	1	−.217	(.080)*	.856	(.052)*	.192	(.119)	4.14*
franc	2	−.215	(.083)*	.858	(.054)*	.180	(.121)	3.81*
	3	−.196	(.080)*	.871	(.052)*	.204	(.117)	3.66*
	4	−.194	(.082)*	.872	(.054)*	.053	(.111)	2.62
Pound	1	.014	(.012)	.981	(.017)	.450	(.113)*	6.06*
sterling	2	.014	(.012)	.981	(.016)	.447	(.114)*	5.91*
	3	.017	(.014)	.976	(.019)	.164	(.120)	1.42
	4	.020	(.014)	.973	(.019)	.216	(.117)	2.17
Italian	1	−.285	(.138)*	.956	(.021)*	.088	(.121)	2.39
lire	2	−.240	(.119)*	.963	(.018)*	.297	(.115)	4.80*
	3	−.264	(.122)*	.959	(.019)*	.228	(.117)	3.98*
	4	−.310	(.140)*	.953	(.021)*	.146	(.119)	2.97*
Swiss	1	−.208	(.032)	.965	(.032)	.087	(.125)	1.82
franc	2	−.010	(.286)	.984	(.029)	.220	(.121)	2.83*
	3	−.006	(.029)	.988	(.030)	.140	(.112)	1.87
	4	.003	(.029)	.998	(.029)	.105	(.115)	1.49
Dutch	1	−.126	(.054)*	.863	(.056)*	.115	(.121)	3.11*
guilder	2	−.110	(.053)*	.880	(.055)*	.173	(.122)	3.03*
	3	−.075	(.052)	.918	(.055)	.159	(.117)	2.01
	4	−.055	(.051)	.939	(.053)	.130	(.111)	1.53

* Significantly different from the hypothesized value ($\gamma = 0$), ($\beta = 1$), or ($\rho = 0$), at the 95 percent level. The reported F-statistic tests the joint hypothesis ($\gamma = 0$, $\beta = 1$, $\rho = 0$), and is calculated by:

$$\frac{\text{(Constrained SS} - \text{Unconstrained SS)}/3}{\text{Unconstrained SS}/t - 3}.$$

The 95 percent critical value is $F(3, 64) = 2.75$.
Sample sizes: $1 = 67$, $2 = 67$, $3 = 67$, $4 = 66$.

Table 8.6
Rejections of rational expectations (95 percent F-statistic in OLS Regressions)
Out of Four Samples

Currency	Variables in information set			
	Constant 8.2[a]	Constant, f 8.3	Constant, $(s - f_{-4})$ 8.4	Constant, f, $(s - f_{-4})$ 8.5
Deutsche mark	0	4	1	4
French franc	0	4	0	3
Pound sterling	0	0	2	2
Italian lire	0	4	2	3
Swiss franc	0	2	1	1
Dutch guilder	0	4	1	2

a. Roman numerals indicate table sources.

8.6 Conclusion

We could carry the tests of rational expectations further. Additional variables could be included in the information set, such as the contemporaneous spot rate (Bilson, 1981b; Tryon, 1979), a time trend, various macroeconomic variables, or the predictions of a specific exchange rate model (Levich, 1979b). To distinguish between the market efficiency and risk premium components of the joint hypothesis, we could include in the list of regressors variables to which the risk premium is supposed to be systematically related, such as some measure of exchange rate variability, the correlation of the exchange rate with the value of a portfolio of real assets (Cornell and Dietrich, 1978), or the sizes of the outstanding stocks of nominal assets denominated in the two currencies (Frankel, 1979c). In another vein, multivariate least squares (Zellner's "Seemingly Unrelated Regressions") could be used to estimate the equations simultaneously for all six countries, taking advantage of the joint distribution of the error terms to obtain more efficient estimates.[19]

However, it is time to sum up our findings. Table 8.6 summarizes the results of Tables 8.2 to 8.5 by counting the frequency with which the F-test rejected the null hypothesis. The most powerful test appears to be the one that conditions on the contemporaneous forward rate. It rejects unbiasedness for all subsamples in the case of the mark, franc, lire, and guilder and for two of the four samples in the case of the franc. This test does not reject unbiasedness in the case of the pound, perhaps because of a predictable underlying trend in the level. But the serial correlation test does find bias for two of the pound subsamples.

To focus on this last particular example, judging only from the first or second subsamples one would conclude that the forward market's prediction errors for the pound/dollar rate are highly autocorrelated. This suggests a way of making profits on the forward exchange market. The estimated autocorrelation coefficient is about .45. If one had bought pounds forward whenever the current value of the pound had been underpredicted by the last forward rate by an amount at least equal to transactions costs divided by .45, and sold pounds forward whenever the current value had been overpredicted by the last forward rate by the same amount, one would have made money on the average. Frenkel and Levich (1975) have estimated transactions costs at roughly .15 percent. Table 8.1 indicates that the standard prediction error was 2.24 percent ($\sqrt{.0005}$). This indicates that sufficiently large prediction errors were quite common: assuming a (log-) normal distribution, 90 percent of the prediction errors were greater than .15 standard errors, which is .33 (transactions cost divided by .45). An alternative strategy to reduce the risk from such profit-making activities (for example, because one has limited access to capital) would be to wait for the unusually large prediction errors before entering the market.

There are a number of important qualifications to the apparent rejection of market efficiency. First, in the particular case of the pound/dollar rate, these results do not apply to the third or fourth subsamples. Of course, one could pursue the profit-making strategy only every fourth week. But it is highly implausible that rational expectations would hold, in effect, only on alternate Fridays. The variation of results among subsamples must be a matter of chance. We cannot combine the results of the different subsamples without knowing the covariances of the estimates, but the high significance levels of the first two subsamples make it seem likely that an overall test would reject the null hypothesis.

The second qualification is that just because one could have made money with a particular strategy in the past does not necessarily mean that one could do so in the future. However, this caveat is more important when the strategy is a complicated one based on an elaborate model (e.g., a high-order ARIMA process) fit to a particular sample period, in which case the model should be tested on postsample data. The caveat is less relevant when the strategy is based on a model as obvious as the first-order auto-correlation of prediction errors. If prediction errors are indeed autocorrelated, the forward market should have caught on long before the end of the sample period.

The final and perhaps most important qualification is related to what has come to be called the "peso problem." If the random error term includes the possibility of a discontinuously large event, such as a sudden withdrawal by the central bank of its support for its currency, then the statistical results are heavily dependent on whether that event actually occurred in the sample period. Of course, under the best of circumstances, there is a 5 percent chance, depending on the random errors, that we will mistakenly reject a true hypothesis. But this confidence level requires the assumption that the estimator either is normally distributed or else converges quickly to a normal distribution. In a case where the error term includes the possibility of a discontinuously large event, the sample size needed for convergence to normality may be much larger than we are generally accustomed to accepting. In finite samples, the actual distribution may be quite different from the normal distribution, making t-tests and F-tests invalid (Krasker, 1980).

A related and perhaps more important point is that a drastic event, such as the withdrawal of support for a currency, may not be an independent event. It may be that if there has not been a devaluation so far this year, the probability of one occurring next week is reduced. (On the other hand, it may be that if there has not been a devaluation so far, the probability is *increased*.) The technical problem is autocorrelation of the errors, but it is not a simple kind of first-order autocorrelation or ARMA process that can be easily corrected. It biases the estimated standard error downward and makes rejection spuriously easy. This problem may be relevant to the pound, which was subject to precipitous falls in value during parts of 1975 and 1976; a key role was played by speculation as to whether the Bank of England would withdraw support or whether OPEC investors would withdraw their deposits.

If discontinuously large and temporarily dependent events are a real problem, there is little we can do to repair the damage to tests of rational expectations, short of using new estimation techniques (like nonparametric tests) or explicitly modeling the events (as with a probit model). But this argument should not lead us to discard the rational expectations tests for those countries and sample periods in which there is no reason to suspect unusual discontinuities in the error distribution.

Appendix 8A: The Moving-Average Error Process

We can prove formally that if the term maturity is longer than the interval between observations, the error term follows a moving-average error process even under the null hypothesis of rational expectations.

Assume that the "true" model of the spot rate is a linear combination of all information: $s = I'\beta$. Information is obviously correlated over time; it will not affect the conclusion if we assume, for simplicity, that the nature of the autocorrelation is first-order: $I'_{+1} = I'\rho + \eta'$, where ρ is the matrix of autocorrelation coefficients and η represents all information that becomes known between time t and time $t + 1$.

First, we consider the case where the term maturity coincides with the interval between observations: $s_{+1} = I'_{+1}\beta = [I'\rho + \eta']\beta$. Under the strongest form of rational expectations we have $f = E(s_{+1}|I) = EI'\rho\beta + E\eta'\beta = I'\rho\beta$. Now, if we run the regression $s_{+1} = \beta_0 + \beta_1 f + \varepsilon_{+1}$, under the null hypothesis we have $s_{+1} = \beta_0 + \beta_1(I'\rho\beta) + \varepsilon_{+1}$. The test of rational expectations will have been passed if $\beta_0 = 0$, $\beta_1 = 1$, implying $\varepsilon_{+1} = \eta'\beta$. There is no autocorrelation of the disturbances.

Now, assume that the term maturity of the forward rate is two periods: $s_{+2} = I'_{+2}\beta = (I'_{+1}\rho + \eta'_{+2})\beta = (I'\rho^2 + \eta'_{+1}\rho + \eta'_{+2})\beta$. Under rational expectations we have $f = E(s_{+2}|I) = I'\rho^2\beta$. If we run the regression $s_{+2} = \beta_0 + \beta_1 f + \varepsilon'_{+2}$ under the null hypothesis we have $s_{+2} = \beta_0 + \beta_1(I'\rho^2\beta) + \varepsilon_{+2}$. The test will have been passed if $\beta_0 = 0$, $\beta_1 = 1$, implying $\varepsilon_{+2} = (\eta'_{+1}\rho + \eta'_{+2})$. We thus have a moving-average error process that dies out before maturity is reached. The result extends to four-period maturities.

9   The Diversifiability of
       Exchange Risk

9.1   Introduction

It is often argued that if the future spot exchange rate is uncertain and if market participants are risk averse, then the forward rate will differ from the expected future spot rate by a risk premium. Market participants will be prepared to buy forward exchange only up to the point where the expected return is cancelled out by the marginal risk of their open position. Because of the existence of exchange risk, the demand for foreign exchange will be less than perfectly elastic with respect to the forward rate, and there will be no reason for the clearing of the forward market necessarily to take place at the point where the forward rate is equal to the expected future spot rate.

Furthermore, it is conventionally presumed that an increase in domestic holdings of foreign debt will increase exposure to risk and cause a downward shift in the demand schedule for forward exchange and thus a fall in the forward exchange rate. And it is conventionally presumed that if the domestic country is a net creditor, an increase in the variability of the future value of the foreign currency, with no change in its expectation, will also increase exposure to risk and cause a fall in the forward exchange rate. (If the domestic country is a net debtor, the presumption is reversed.)

The risk premium argument has important implications in two areas: (1) tests of efficiency in the forward exchange market and (2) models of spot rate determination. (1) The implication for tests of efficiency is that the expected future spot rate can differ from the forward rate, even though the market is efficient, if the domestic country is a net creditor or net debtor. Levich (1979a) surveys tests of efficiency in the forward exchange market and concludes that they are not valid since they test efficiency jointly with the hypothesis of a zero risk premium. (2) The conclusions regarding the forward rate carry through to the spot rate (by covered interest parity), given the interest differential and expected future spot rate. The effect of an increase in the quantity of foreign debt is to cause the exchange rate to fall. This effect is appealing because it says that the price of foreign assets (the exchange rate) falls when their supply increases, just as with any good that faces less-than-perfectly-elastic demand. The effect of an increase in variability is described by Schadler (1977, p. 286): "If the domestic country is a net debtor (creditor), the increase in uncertainty will force the exchange rate to depreciate by more (less) or appreciate by less (more) than if the degree of uncertainty had not changed".

It is the contention of this chapter that much of the literature on exchange risk has ignored the fact that when domestic residents hold claims on foreign residents, such as bonds or forward exchange contracts, *variability in the exchange rate creates risk not only for domestic residents, but also for foreign residents.*[1] The two risks are offsetting: an unexpected rise in the exchange rate raises the value of domestic residents' assets *and* the cost of foreign residents' liabilities. Residents of the two countries can trade these risks with each other, either by agreeing to denominate debt in a weighted average of the two currencies or (if institutional factors dictate that foreign debt be denominated in foreign currency) by the domestic creditors selling foreign exchange to foreign debtors on the forward market, allowing both sides to hedge their exchange risks. In the resulting market equilibrium, *all exchange risk can be diversified away*, under certain conditions. Then the risk premium will be equal to zero despite the presence of uncertainty and risk aversion. Under more general conditions, a nonzero risk premium does indeed separate the forward rate from the expected future spot rate; but the risk premium is still not necessarily related to foreign indebtedness and variability of the exchange rate in the way conventionally presumed.

The chapter demonstrates the following three propositions in a one-good model with no transactions costs:

1. There is no risk premium if two conditions are met. (i) All assets are nominal assets (money and bonds) whose returns are fixed in terms of existing currencies, or else—if there are other assets (goods and human and nonhuman capital)—their real returns are independent of currency values. The latter condition obtains, for example, in exchange rate models in which real output is assumed exogenously determined in the short run.[2] (ii) All nominal assets are "inside" assets, that is, either they are privately issued debt or else—if they include assets issued by the government— they are viewed by the residents of the country as entailing offsetting liabilities such as future taxation.

2. If there are "outside" assets that are assumed denominated in the currency of the country that issues them, then there is a risk premium. The risk premium is positively (negatively) related to the stock of foreign (domestic) assets, holding total wealth constant. The risk premium is also positively (negatively) related to the variability of the value of the foreign (domestic) currency to the extent that the outside assets are issued by the domestic (foreign) government. This conclusion is similar to the common presumption, except that what matters is the government's domestically denominated indebtedness, whether to its own citizens or to foreigners, not the net indebtedness of residents of one country to residents of the other.

3. If the value of a country's currency is correlated with the value of real assets, then there is again a risk premium. But the presumption that the risk premium is positively related to the variability in the value of the foreign currency holds only if real disturbances come from the supply side (for example, variations in the weather or the terms of trade) so that the country's price level is negatively correlated with its real output. If real disturbances come from the demand side (for example, variations in fiscal or monetary policy) so that the country's price level is positively correlated with its real output, then the presumption is reversed.

9.2 The Model

The model used here is the simplest one possible that is capable of answering the relevant questions. In each period, individuals allocate their financial wealth between B units of domestically denominated assets, in terms of their known value in domestic currency next period, and B^* units of foreign-denominated assets, in terms of their known value in foreign currency next period. S_{+1} is defined as next period's spot exchange rate (the price of foreign currency in terms of domestic currency), which is uncertain this period. F is defined as the *current* price of foreign assets, payable next period, in terms of domestic assets.[3] We are going to find the value of F that clears the market for assets, and see how it is affected by variability in currency values and by net domestic or foreign indebtedness, relative to the expected future spot rate.

The natural interpretation of F is that it is the forward exchange rate.[4] Without changing anything in the analysis that follows, we could give a simpler interpretation to the model by assuming that non-interest-bearing money is the only asset. F would be identical to the current spot rate. Expected future appreciation or depreciation would then in itself constitute a risk premium. Though all the insights of the model could be obtained under this simpler interpretation, we will maintain the more realistic interpretation that B and B^* include interest-paying bonds and that F is the forward exchange rate.

The next-period value of all real assets (human and nonhuman capital) is represented by X_{+1} in real terms. V_{+1} and V^*_{+1} are defined as the inverse of the price level (the real value of the currency) next period, at home and abroad, respectively. There is only one good in the model (or, equivalently, one basket of goods), so purchasing power parity always holds: $V_{+1}S = V^*_{+1} \cdot X$, V_{+1}, V^*_{+1} and S_{+1} are all uncertain this period. No presumption is made as to direction of causality among them.

The final assumption is that individuals allocate their financial wealth so as to maximize the expected value of a utility function that is quadratic in the real value of next period's wealth. Intertemporal allocations play no role. Some people may be borrowers and some lenders, for whatever reasons; all that matters is how they allocate their (positive or negative) financial wealth.

Individual i's next period wealth is

$$W_{i_{+1}} = B_i + S_{+1} B_i^* + \frac{1}{V_{+1}} X_i$$

in domestic nominal terms, or $V_{+1} W_{i_{+1}} = V_{+1}(B_i + S_{+1} B_i^*) + X_{i_{+1}}$ in real terms. He or she acts to maximize the expected value of

$$U_{i_{+1}} \equiv V_{+1} W_{i_{+1}} - b_i(V_{+1} W_{i_{+1}})^2$$
$$= V_{+1}(B_i + S_{+1} B_i^*) + X_{i_{+1}} - b_i[V_{+1}(B_i + S_{+1} B_i^*) + X_{i_{+1}}]^2,$$

where b_i is a measure of risk aversion.[5] Letting E represent the expectation operator, the quantity to be maximized is $EU_{i_{+1}}$. Since the current price of foreign assets in terms of domestic assets is F, the condition for maximization is that F equal the marginal rate of substitution between foreign and domestic assets:

$$F = \frac{\partial EU_{i_{+1}}/\partial B_i^*}{\partial EU_{i_{+1}}/\partial B_i} = \frac{E(V_{+1}S_{+1}) - 2b_i EV_{+1}S_{+1}[V_{+1}(B_i + S_{+1}B_i^*) + X_{i_{+1}}]}{E(V_{+1}) - 2b_i EV_{+1}[V_{+1}(B_i + S_{+1}B_i^*) + X_{i_{+1}}]},$$

$$(1)$$

where the derivative operator has been passed through the expectation operator. We multiply through by the denominator of the last expression and remember that B_i and B_i^* are not random variables:

$$F\left[\frac{1}{2b_i}EV_{+1} - (B_i EV_{+1}^2 + B_i^* EV_{+1}^2 S_{+1} + EV_{+1}X_{i_{+1}})\right]$$
$$= \frac{1}{2b_i}EV_{+1}S_{+1} - (B_i EV_{+1}^2 S_{+1} + B_i^* EV_{+1}^2 S_{+1}^2 + EV_{+1}X_{i_{+1}}S_{+1}).$$

Now we sum the equation over all individuals i:

$$F\left[\frac{1}{b}EV_{+1} - (\bar{B}EV_{+1}^2 + \bar{B}^* EV_{+1}^2 S_{+1} + EV_{+1}X_{+1})\right]$$
$$= \frac{1}{b}EV_{+1}S_{+1} - (\bar{B}EV_{+1}^2 S_{+1} + \bar{B}_i^* EV_{+1}^2 S_{+1} + EV_{+1}X_{+1}S_{+1}).$$

where we have made the following definitions:

$\dfrac{1}{b} \equiv \sum_i \dfrac{1}{2b_i}$ (a measure of aggregate risk aversion),

$\bar{B} \equiv \sum_i B_i$ (the stock of domestically denominated outside assets, since all inside assets cancel out),

$\bar{B}^* \equiv \sum_i B_i^*$ (the stock of foreign-denominated outside assets), and

$X \equiv \sum_i X_i$ (the aggregate value of real assets).

We solve for the current exchange rate F:

$$F = \frac{EV_{+1}S_{+1} - b(EV_{+1}X_{+1}S_{+1} + \bar{B}EV_{+1}^2 S_{+1} + \bar{B}^* EV_{+1}^2 S_{+1}^2)}{EV_{+1} - b(EV_{+1}X_{+1} + \bar{B}EV_{+1}^2 + \bar{B}^* EV_{+1}^2 S_{+1})}.$$

Finally, we use the purchasing power parity condition $V_{+1}S_{+1} = V_{+1}^*$:

$$F = \frac{EV^* - b(EV^*X + \bar{B}EVV^* - \bar{B}^* EV^{*2})}{EV - b(EVX + \bar{B}EV^2 + \bar{B}^* EVV^*)}. \tag{2}$$

(Henceforth the time subscript $(+1)$ is omitted.) This is the basic equation for the current forward exchange rate which is used throughout the remainder of this chapter. Notice that the formula does not depend on any characteristics of individuals. In particular it does not matter if domestic residents are indebted to foreign residents or if they are more risk averse than foreign residents. Only aggregate variables matter: in particular the stock of domestically denominated outside assets, the stock of foreign-denominated outside assets, the aggregate value of real assets, and aggregate risk aversion.

This derivation can be made somewhat more intuitive by observing that the marginal expected utility of an additional asset unit is given by its marginal expected real value (the inverse of the price level) minus marginal exposure to real risk (the covariance of the real value of the asset with the real value of wealth). Thus expression (1), representing the ratio of the marginal expected utilities, can be interpreted as:

$$F = \frac{\text{Expected}\begin{bmatrix}\text{future value} \\ \text{of foreign} \\ \text{currency}\end{bmatrix} - \begin{bmatrix}\text{a measure} \\ \text{of } i\text{'s risk-} \\ \text{aversion}\end{bmatrix}\text{Expected}\begin{bmatrix}\begin{pmatrix}\text{future value} \\ \text{of foreign} \\ \text{currency}\end{pmatrix}\begin{pmatrix}\text{future} \\ \text{value of} \\ i\text{'s wealth}\end{pmatrix}\end{bmatrix}}{\text{Expected}\begin{bmatrix}\text{future value} \\ \text{of domestic} \\ \text{currency}\end{bmatrix} - \begin{bmatrix}\text{a measure} \\ \text{of } i\text{'s risk-} \\ \text{aversion}\end{bmatrix}\text{Expected}\begin{bmatrix}\begin{pmatrix}\text{future value} \\ \text{of domestic} \\ \text{currency}\end{pmatrix}\begin{pmatrix}\text{future} \\ \text{value of} \\ i\text{'s wealth}\end{pmatrix}\end{bmatrix}}$$

where the future value of i's wealth depends on the asset holdings he chooses this period and the future value of the two currencies. The manipulations after expression (1) show that the equation can be aggregated over all individuals. Equation (2) looks similar to equation (1) and has essentially the same intuitive explanation, except that individual i's measure of risk aversion and future wealth are replaced by a measure of *aggregate* risk aversion and future *aggregate* wealth, respectively.

9.3   When There Is No Risk Premium

First, consider the case of risk neutrality, where $b = 0$. (It is sufficient that $b_i = 0$ for any single individual—assuming, of course, unlimited access to capital.)

$F = EV^*/EV.$

The current exchange rate is given by the ratio of the expected values of the purchasing powers of the two currencies. In the special case in which the value of domestic currency V is a constant, $F = EVS/V = ES$. In the special case in which the value of foreign currency V^* is a constant,

$$F = \frac{V^*}{EV^*/S} = \frac{1}{E1/S}.$$

Even under risk neutrality the current forward rate is not in general precisely equal to the expected future spot rate. Indeed, under the special conditions under which they are equal from the domestic viewpoint ($F = ES$), they cannot be equal from the foreign viewpoint ($1/F \neq E1/S$). This consequence of the convexity of the inverse function and Jensen's inequality is sometimes called the Siegal paradox (Siegal, 1972). The intuitive explanation is that people seek to maximize expected wealth in real terms rather than in terms of domestic currency, and the real value of domestic currency varies with the exchange rate (except in the special case in which the domestic price level is constant). The usual view is that the phenomenon is a mathematical inconvenience but not a matter of economic or empirical significance.

Now we assume that people are risk averse, that is, $b > 0$. We consider first the case where there are no outside assets, which means that net assets in each currency, $\bar{B}$ and $\bar{B}^*$, are zero, and where future total real income X is independent of the value of either the domestic or foreign currency: $EV^*X = EV^*EX$ and $EVX = EVEX$. From (2) we have

$$F = \frac{EV^*(1 - bEX)}{EV(1 - bEX)} = \frac{EV^*}{EV}.$$

This is precisely the same expression we got in the risk-neutral case. There is no risk premium. An increase in the net indebtedness of one country and net assets of the other has no effect on the current rate, not even if we assume that such debt must be denominated in the currency of the debtor country. Nor does an increase in the variability of the values of the currencies have any effect.

The reason there is no risk premium can be seen intuitively. Since the exchange rate is uncorrelated with real wealth, exchange risk is completely diversifiable. The holder of risky foreign assets will sell foreign exchange forward; there is a corresponding holder of the risky foreign liability who will be glad to buy the foreign exchange forward. In market equilibrium, no one will be subject to risk associated with variability of the exchange rate. This completes the demonstration of proposition (1) above.

9.4   When There Are Outside Assets

Now we consider the case where there are outside assets $\bar{B} > 0$ denominated in the domestic currency and outside assets $\bar{B}^* > 0$ denominated in the foreign currency. From (2):

$$F = \frac{EV^* - b\bar{B}EVV^* - b\bar{B}^*EV^{*2}}{EV - b\bar{B}EV^2 - b\bar{B}^*EVV^*}.^6 \tag{3}$$

To see the effect of an increase in $\bar{B}$, we differentiate. For simplicity, we assume that we are starting from a position of zero outside assets:

$$\frac{\partial F}{\partial \bar{B}} = b\frac{-EVV^*EV + EV^2EV^*}{[EV]^2}. \tag{4}$$

This quantity is positive iff

$$\frac{EV^2}{EV} > \frac{EVV^*}{EV^*}.$$

To obtain an alternative version of this condition we use the facts

$$\text{var } V = EV^2 - (EV)^2,$$

$$\text{cov}(V, V^*) = EVV^* - EVEV^*, \quad \text{and}$$

$$\text{corr}(V, V^*) = \text{cov}(V, V^*)/\sqrt{(\text{var } V)}\sqrt{(\text{var } V^*)}:$$

$$\frac{\sqrt{(\text{var } V)}}{EV} > \text{corr}(V, V^*)\frac{\sqrt{(\text{var } V^*)}}{EV^*}. \tag{5}$$

The ratios on each side of the inequality represent the variability of V and V^*, respectively, normalized by their means. A sufficient condition is that the variability of V is greater than the variability of V^*. Another sufficient condition is that V and V^* are not positively correlated. When either of these conditions is met, an increase in the stock of outside assets denominated in domestic currency causes the risk premium on foreign currency to fall and the current exchange rate to rise. The effect is the same as in the conventional presumption.

On the other hand, when these conditions are not met, that is, when the value of foreign currency is highly variable and is highly correlated with the value of domestic currency, we get the surprising result that an increase in the supply of domestically denominated assets *lowers F*, the relative price of foreign-denominated assets. The explanation for this result lies in the characteristic of the quadratic utility function that it implies increasing absolute risk-aversion.[7] An increase in $\bar{B}$ is an increase in wealth, which causes an increase in risk aversion and thus a shift in demand to the less risky asset.

To see the effect of an increase in foreign-denominated outside assets, we look at the derivative with respect to $\bar{B}^*$, again evaluated at zero for simplicity:

$$\frac{\partial F}{\partial \bar{B}^*} = b\frac{-EV^{*2}EV + EVV^*EV^*}{[EV]^2}. \tag{6}$$

This quantity is negative iff

$$\frac{\text{var } V^*}{EV^*} > \text{corr}(V, V^*)\frac{\text{var } V}{EV}. \tag{7}$$

An increase in foreign outside assets causes the risk premium to rise and the current exchange rate to fall, provided the variability of the domestic currency value is large relative to the variability of the foreign currency value, or else provided the currency values are not highly correlated. Again, if these conditions fail, we get the surprising result that an increase in the supply of foreign-denominated assets *raises F*, the relative price of foreign-denominated assets. Again, the explanation is that the increase in wealth causes an increase in risk aversion and thus a shift in demand to the less risky asset.

To avoid the problem of increasing absolute risk aversion, we can ask what happens if the asset supplies are varied with total wealth held constant. In other words, what happens if the central bank (of either country) increases $\bar{B}$ and decreases $\bar{B}^*$ subject to $d\bar{B} + F\,d\bar{B}^* = 0$? Such a policy has precisely the interpretation of intervention on the forward exchange market: if a central bank buys foreign exchange forward, it is giving the private sector foreign-denominated liabilities (the obligation to supply foreign exchange in the future) in return for domestically denominated assets (future payment in domestic exchange) at the going market rate (F).

Of course, if the obligations of the central bank are regarded by the public as implying future tax liabilities, then they are inside assets and we are back to section 9.3. But if they are regarded as outside assets, then we can apply the results of this section, with $d\bar{B}^* = -(1/F)\,d\bar{B}$:

$$dF = \left(\frac{\partial F}{\partial \bar{B}} - \frac{1}{F}\frac{\partial F}{\partial \bar{B}^*}\right) d\bar{B}.$$

Again, we start from a position of zero outside assets, allowing us to use equation (4) for $\partial F/\partial \bar{B}$, equation (6) for $\partial F/\partial \bar{B}^*$, and EV^*/EV for F.

$$dF = \frac{b}{EV}\left[EV^2\frac{EV^*}{EV} + EV^{*2}\frac{EV}{EV^*} - 2EVV^* \right] d\bar{B}.$$

$dF/d\bar{B} > 0$ if the expression in brackets is positive. Since the expression in brackets is equal to

$$\mathrm{var}[V\sqrt{(EV^*/EV)} - V^*\sqrt{(EV/EV^*)}],$$

it is always positive. In other words, forward market purchases of foreign exchange always raise its price, as one would expect.

Now we consider the effect of a change in the variance, at a given level of outside debt. We express equation (3) in terms of correlations and variances rather than just expected values:

$$F = \frac{EV^* - b\bar{B}[\text{corr}(V, V^*)\sqrt{(\text{var } V)}\sqrt{(\text{var } V^*)} + EVEV^*] - b\bar{B}^* \text{var } V^* + (EV^*)^2}{EV - b\bar{B}[\text{var } V + (EV)^2] - b\bar{B}^* \text{corr}(V, V^*)\sqrt{(\text{var } V)}\sqrt{(\text{var } V^*)} + EVEV^*}.$$

First we consider the case where all outside assets are domestically denominated: $\bar{B}^* = 0$. We differentiate with respect to $\sqrt{(\text{var } V^*)}$, holding the expectation and the correlation constant.

$$\frac{\partial F}{\partial \sqrt{(\text{var } V^*)}} = \frac{-b\bar{B} \, \text{corr}(V, V^*)\sqrt{(\text{var } V)}}{EV - b\bar{B}[\text{var } V + (EV)^2]} < 0.$$

An increase in var V is more complicated but raises F if the correlation between V and V^* is low enough. If outside debt is foreign denominated, an increase in var V raises F; an increase in var V^* lowers F if the correlation is low enough.

This completes the demonstration of proposition (2): the conventional presumption holds, provided foreign indebtedness is identical to the stock of outside assets issued in foreign currency. To restate the conventional presumption: an increase in foreign indebtedness (holding total wealth constant) or a decrease in the variability of the value of the domestic currency when there is net foreign indebtedness, causes a rise in the risk premium and a fall in the current forward exchange rate.

9.5   When Real Income Is Correlated with Currency Values

Now we consider the case where the value of real assets, such as human and nonhuman capital, is correlated with the value of the currencies. For simplicity, we revert to the assumption that there are no outside assets, so $\bar{B} = \bar{B}^* = 0$. From equation (2),

$$F = \frac{EV^* - bEV^*X}{EV - bEVX},$$

where X is the sum of domestic and foreign real non-nominal wealth. Substituting $\text{cov}(V, X) - EVEX$ for $E(VX)$, and similarly for V^*,

$$F = \frac{EV^*(1 + bEX) - b\,\text{cov}(V^*, X)}{EV(1 + bEX) - b\,\text{cov}(V, X)}.$$

We can substitute $\text{corr}(V, X)\sqrt{(\text{var } V)}\sqrt{(\text{var } X)}$ for $\text{cov}(V, X)$, and similarly for V^*:

$$F = \frac{EV^*(1 + bEX) - b\,\text{corr}(V^*, X)\sqrt{(\text{var } V^*)}\sqrt{(\text{var } X)}}{EV(1 + bEX) - b\,\text{corr}(V, X)\sqrt{(\text{var } V)}\sqrt{(\text{var } X)}}.$$

We can see again the result that when X is uncorrelated with V and V^*, $F = EV^*/EV$ as in the risk-neutral case.

In general, there is a risk premium. The current forward exchange rate is less than the expected future spot rate (i.e., there is a positive risk premium) iff the following condition is met:

$$\text{corr}(V^*, X) \frac{\sqrt{(\text{var } V^*)}}{EV^*} > \text{corr}(V, X) \frac{\sqrt{(\text{var } V)}}{EV}.$$

Let us assume that the domestic country is the larger country, so V is more highly correlated (in absolute value) with X than is V^*. Assume also that the currency values are equally variable. Then what we might call the "naive presumption," that there is always a positive risk premium from the viewpoint of the domestic country, is upheld if X is positively correlated with V and V^*, but is reversed if X is negatively correlated with V and V^*.

The effects of changes in the variability of the currency values can be read directly from the formula for F. When X is positively correlated with V^*, an increase in the variability of V^* causes F to fall, that is, causes the foreign currency to depreciate. Similarly, when X is positively correlated with V, an increase in the variability of V causes F to rise, that is, causes the domestic currency to depreciate. Thus the conventional presumption that increased variability of a currency's future value causes a fall in its current value[8] holds true when real nonfinancial wealth is positively correlated with the currency values. The reasoning is intuitively clear: holders of domestic currency, the value of which is positively correlated with other forms of wealth, must be compensated for increased variability for the same reason that the holder of a stock, the value of which is positively correlated with the market basket, must be compensated for increased variability.

But when X is *negatively* correlated with V^*, an increase in the variance of V^* causes F to *rise*, and when X is negatively correlated with V, an increase in the variance of V causes F to *fall*. The conventional presumption is reversed because a currency the value of which is negatively correlated with other forms of wealth affords a valuable opportunity for hedging against risk, much like a stock the value of which is negatively correlated with the market basket.

Which case, a positive or negative correlation between non-nominal wealth and the inverse of the price level, is more likely? Assume that the value of real assets can be represented by next period's real income. Assume furthermore, that the correlation between total (domestic plus foreign) real income and the domestic price level is dominated by the correlation between *domestic* real income and the domestic price level.[9] Then the answer is given by a graph with an aggregate demand curve and aggregate supply curve describing the domestic economy. If supply shocks dominate, then real output is negatively correlated with the price level and thus positively correlated with its inverse: the conventional presumption holds. But if demand shocks dominate, then real output is positively correlated with the price level and thus negatively correlated with its inverse: the conventional presumption is reversed. Keynesian economics concentrated on demand shocks, such as fluctuations in exogenous investment or in government fiscal and monetary policy. But we know that supply shocks, such as fluctuations in the terms of trade or the weather, are very important. The question of which shocks dominate cannot be settled a priori. Possibly the correlation is close to zero over the time range that is relevant (say three months), suggesting a risk premium close to zero.

9.6   Conclusion

The statements made in the literature regarding the risk premium on foreign exchange have here been shown to assume implicitly that a country's net indebtedness consists of outside assets denominated in its own currency. It cannot be denied that governments do issue outside assets and that they are generally denominated in their own currency. But two questions arise:

1. Can residents truly be indifferent to an increase in their government's indebtedness? This controversy is well known under the heading "Are government bonds net wealth?" and will not be discussed here.

2. If the risk premium that a government must pay on its debt issues (the amount by which the value of the proceeds is less than the expected future value of the money it will have to pay back) is significant in magnitude, then why doesn't the government denominate its debt in a basket of currencies, so as to allow foreign investors to diversify the risk away and thus obviate the need to pay a risk premium?[10] To the extent that governments (especially those of small countries) do denominate their debt in foreign currencies, they allow exchange risk to be diversified away. The extent to which this practice is not common suggests that exchange risk is not important.

As to correlation between currency values and real income, it appears a priori as likely that the conventional presumption is reversed as that it is upheld. Increased exchange rate variability could very well mean decreased overall real risk, if the value of the currency is negatively correlated with the value of real assets.

The obvious moral is that care must be taken in reasoning from the portfolio choices facing individual risk-averse investors to general market equilibrium. But a possible second moral is that, even if we do not believe that the assumptions necessary for a zero risk premium (no true outside assets and no correlation between currency values and real output) are literally true, we may believe that they are close enough to true to make the assumption of no risk premium a useful simplification. If perfect markets are assumed (perfect information, rational expectations, and no transactions costs), then the additional assumption of no nondiversifiable exchange risk may be acceptable.

On the other hand, if perfect markets are not assumed, then nondiversifiable exchange risk regains its importance. Transactions costs may prevent individuals from diversifying away all risk in practice even if they could do so in theory.

Acknowledgment

I thank Rudiger Dornbusch, Stanley Fischer, Donald Lessard, Franco Modigliani, and Hal Varian for comments and suggestions.

10

In Search of the Exchange Risk Premium: A Six-Currency Test Assuming Mean-Variance Optimization

There has been a great deal of interest in the portfolio-balance approach to modeling international financial behavior.[1] The investor is assumed to balance his portfolio among the assets of various countries as a function of their relative expected returns. An implication is that an increase in the supply of one country's assets requires something like an increase in its interest rate or in the expected appreciation of its currency, in order for the assets to be willingly held.

The empirical work under this approach has not been as successful as the theoretical work. In particular, no one has yet been able to reject statistically the hypothesis that countries' bonds are perfect substitutes, so that expected returns are equalized.

All of the many tests of unbiasedness in the forward exchange market are joint tests of efficiency and the absence of a risk premium (i.e., perfect substitutability). Tests of unconditional biasedness in the forward rate fail to find any such bias persisting over the length of the floating rate period.[2] Other tests, such as those for serial correlation in the prediction errors, do sometimes reject the joint null hypothesis. Some authors, such as Hansen and Hodrick (1980) and Cumby and Obstfeld (1981), interpret the results as evidence against perfect substitutability and for a risk premium.[3] To do so one must argue that the risk premium fluctuates frequently between positive and negative, in order to account for the absence of persistent unconditional bias.

If the imperfect substitutability interpretation were correct, one would expect the relative returns to be systematically related to asset supplies as required by the portfolio-balance equation. Dooley and Isard (1979) and Frankel (1982c) fail to find a significant positive relationship between expected returns and bond supplies. Of course, this failure to reject perfect substitutability between domestic and foreign bonds could be due to the low power of the test as easily as to the virtue of the null hypothesis.

Recently the application of finance theory, by which I mean the principles of expected utility maximization, to the international portfolio-balance model has given the model additional impetus. This application was pioneered by Kouri (1976b, 1977), and more recently formulated in a manner simple enough to be directly usable in macroeconomic models by Dornbusch (1983a).[4] The parameters in the asset-demand functions, rather than being determined arbitrarily, are seen to depend in a simple way on the coefficient of risk aversion and the return variance-covariance matrix.

Kouri and de Macedo (1978), de Macedo (1982), and Dornbusch (1980), have used the finance theory to estimate the optimal portfolio from statistical variances and covariances. These analyses are not intended as formal tests of the hypothesis that actual asset-demand functions are in fact equal to the optimizing portfolio-balance functions. Indeed the results would not hold up under such testing since the optimal demand is computed to be negative in some cases (such as the yen and French franc in Kouri and de Macedo's estimates), even though the actual supply is known to be positive. Nevertheless, the authors' motivation in estimating optimal portfolios is clearly to explain actual investor behavior, rather than, for example, to improve their personal investment portfolio planning.

Roll and Solnik (1977), Cornell and Dietrich (1978), and Robichek and Eaker (1978) look for a significant positive relationship between expected returns of currencies and their covariances ("betas") with a market portfolio. But these papers share with the estimates of optimal portfolios an important limitation. They implicitly assume that expected returns (i.e., interest rates and expected appreciation) are constant over time.[5] This assumption is inconsistent with recent exchange rate history, with the lack of persistent unconditional bias in the forward rate, and with the macroeconomic models in which one would want to use a successfully estimated portfolio-balance equation. The limitation is related to the fact that the papers make no use of data on asset supplies: changes in expected returns are the result of changes in asset supplies.

The aim of this chapter is to test whether asset demands are properly described by the portfolio-balance equation, as against the null hypothesis of perfect substitutability. The chapter goes beyond previous attempts to relate expected rates of return (or exchange rates) to bond supplies, by bringing to bear the additional knowledge we have gained from the finance literature that the coefficients are related to the variance-covariance matrix. Imposing these restrictions should give us a more powerful test. On the other hand, the technique used here dominates that of previous empirical finance studies in that it uses the asset supply data. It thus allows the estimate of the expected relative return or risk premium to fluctuate over time, rather than requiring it to be constant over time.

The technique used is maximum likelihood estimation of the *arguments* of the portfolio-balance function (the expected returns) at the same time as the *parameters* of the function (the coefficient of risk-aversion and the vari-ance-covariance matrix.[6] The likelihood for the zero value of risk aversion turns out to be very close to the likelihood for reasonable positive values. This finding implies failure to reject the null hypothesis of perfect substitut-ability once again.

10.1   Derivation of the Portfolio-Balance Equation from Mean-Variance Optimization

In this section we derive the form that a multicurrency asset-demand equa-tion should take if the investor maximizes a function of the mean and variance of his end-of-period real wealth.[7] The results are familiar from Kouri (1977) and Dornbusch (1980).

Let $\tilde{W}_t$ be real wealth. The investor must choose the vector of portfolio shares that he wishes to allocate to marks, pounds, yen, francs, and Cana-dian dollars: $x_t' \equiv [x_t^{DM} x_t^{\pounds} x_t^{Y} x_t^{F} x_t^{C\$}]$. The residual is the share allocated to U.S. dollars: $(1 - x_t'\iota)$, where ι is a column vector of five ones. End-of-period real wealth depends on the portfolio allocation and on real returns:

$$\tilde{W}_{t+1} = \tilde{W}_t + \tilde{W}_t x_t' r_{t+1} + \tilde{W}_t (1 - x_t'\iota) r_{t+1}^{\$}$$

$$= \tilde{W}_t [x_t'(r_{t+1} - \iota r_{t+1}^{\$}) + 1 + r_{t+1}^{\$}] \tag{1}$$

where $r_{t+1}' \equiv [r_{t+1}^{DM} \ldots r_{t+1}^{C\$}]$ is a vector of the real returns realized on the five countries' assets. The real return on the jth asset is:

$$1 + r_{t+1}^{j} \equiv \frac{1 + i_t^{j}}{(1 + \pi_{t+1}^{\$})(1 + \Delta s_{t+1}^{j})} \approx 1 + i_t^{j} - \pi_{t+1}^{\$} - \Delta s_{t+1}^{j} \tag{2}$$

where i_t^{j} is the one-period interest rate on j-bonds, $\pi_{t+1}^{\$}$ is the rate of inflation during the period for the appropriate basket of goods, expressed in dollars, and Δs_{t+1}^{j} is the rate of depreciation during the period of cur-rency j against the dollar. Similarly, the real return on dollar assets is

$$1 + r_{t+1}^{\$} \equiv \frac{1 + i_t^{\$}}{1 + \pi_{t+1}^{\$}} \approx 1 + i_t^{\$} - \pi_{t+1}^{\$}. \tag{3}$$

If we use the approximations, the five-currency vector of returns *relative* to the dollar is very simple:

$$r_{t+1} - ir^{\$}_{t+1} \approx i_t - ui^{\$}_t - \Delta s_{t+1}$$

where i_t and Δs_{t+1} are five-currency vectors. The real return on an asset relative to the dollar is simply the interest differential minus depreciation of the currency, because the inflation rate drops out. Thus,

$$\tilde{W}_{t+1} = \tilde{W}_t[x_t'(i_t - ui^{\$}_t - \Delta s_{t+1}) + 1 + i^{\$}_t - \pi^{\$}_{t+1}]. \tag{4}$$

We define α to be a vector of consumption shares allocated to goods produced by Germany, the United Kingdom, Japan, France, and Canada. The residual $[1 - \alpha' \iota]$ is the consumption share allocated to U.S. goods. Then the dollar inflation index is computed as follows:

$$\pi^{\$}_t = \alpha'(\bar{\pi}_t - \Delta s_t) + (1 - \alpha' \iota)\bar{\pi}^{\$}_{US_t}$$

where elements of

$$\bar{\pi}_t' \equiv (\pi^{DM}_{G_t}, \pi^{£}_{UK_t}, \pi^{Y}_{J_t}, \pi^{F}_{F_t}, \pi^{C\$}_{C_t}) \quad \text{and} \quad \bar{\pi}^{\$}_{US_t}$$

represent the rates of inflation in the goods of the six countries, each expressed in terms of its own currency. The "bars" represent an important assumption that is made at this point: goods prices are nonstochastic when expressed in the currency of the producing country. Only the exchange rate is uncertain.[8]

The expected value and variance of end-of-period wealth (4), conditional on current information, are as follows:

$$E(\tilde{W}_{t+1}) = \tilde{W}_t x_t'(i_t - ui^{\$}_t - E\Delta s_{t+1}) + 1 + i^{\$}_t - \alpha'(\bar{\pi}_{t+1} - E\Delta s_{t+1})$$

$$- (1 - \alpha' \iota)\bar{\pi}^{\$}_{US_{t+1}}$$

$$V(\tilde{W}_{t+1}) = \tilde{W}_t^2[V(-x_t'\Delta s_{t+1} + \alpha'\Delta s_{t+1})]$$

$$= \tilde{W}_t^2[(-x_t' + \alpha')\Omega(-x_t + \alpha)] \tag{5}$$

where we have defined the variance-covariance matrix of currency depreciation: $\Omega \equiv E(\Delta s_{t+1} - E\Delta s_{t+1})(\Delta s_{t+1} - E\Delta s_{t+1})'$.

Investors maximize a function of the mean and variance:

$$F[E(\tilde{W}_{t+1}), V(\tilde{W}_{t+1})].$$

We differentiate with respect to x_t, the vector of portfolio shares:

$$\frac{dF}{dx_t} = F_1 \frac{dE(\tilde{W}_{t+1})}{dx_t} + F_2 \frac{dV(\tilde{W}_{t+1})}{dx_t} = 0$$

$$F_1 \tilde{W}_t(i_t - ui^{\$}_t - E\Delta s_{t+1}) + F_2 \tilde{W}_t^2 2\Omega(x_t - \alpha) = 0$$

We define the coefficient of relative risk aversion $\rho \equiv -F_2 \tilde{W}_t 2/F_1$, which is assumed to be constant. (The Arrow-Pratt measure of relative risk aversion is defined as $\rho \equiv -U''\tilde{W}/U'$, where $U(\tilde{W})$ is the utility function the expectation of which is to be maximized. One can take a Taylor-series approximation to $EU(\tilde{W})$ and differentiate it with respect to $E(\tilde{W})$ and $V(\tilde{W})$ to show that the two definitions of ρ are equivalent.)[9] Then we have our result:

$$i_t - \tilde{u}_t^{\$} - E\Delta s_{t+1} = \rho\Omega(x_t - \alpha) \tag{6}$$

Equation (6) is the portfolio-balance system that is estimated in the following section. Particularly important is the case of risk neutrality. If $\rho = 0$, then the expected relative return on all assets is zero; perfect substitutability and uncovered interest parity hold.

Inverting equation (6) to solve for the portfolio shares provides further economic intuition:

$$x_t = \alpha + (\rho\Omega)^{-1}(i_t - \tilde{u}_t^{\$} - E\Delta s_{t+1}). \tag{7}$$

The asset demands consist of two parts. The first term α represents the "minimum-variance" portfolio. If an investor is extremely risk averse ($\rho = \infty$), or if exchange rates are very uncertain ($|\Omega| = \infty$), the investor will hold countries' assets in the same proportions as the "liabilities" represented by his consumption patterns. The second term represents the "speculative portfolio". A higher expected return on a given asset induces investors to hold more of that asset than is in the minimum-variance portfolio, to an extent limited only by the degree of risk-aversion and the uncertainty of the exchange rate. Again, in the case of risk neutrality ($\rho = 0$), the assets become perfect substitutes and arbitrage ensures that the expected relative returns are zero.

Before we proceed to estimate equation (6) econometrically, two points must be noted. First, the derivation of the equation was phrased in terms of the behavior of a single investor. We should have been thinking of the x variable as having a subscript representing the investor. In Section 10.2, we assume that all investors in the market have the same expectations, the same degree of risk aversion, and the same consumption patterns. Thus they have the same asset-demand functions (7), so we can simply aggregate across the entire market and think of the equations as applying to the aggregate world portfolio. We will relax this assumption in section 10.3.

The second point is due to Krugman. The approximations made in equations (2) and (3) contain errors that, though they may be small if the variances are small, are of the same order of magnitude as the risk premium itself. If the derivation is done rigorously, a term of $\Omega\alpha - \sigma^2/2$ must be added to equation (6). To the extent that the investor consumes the goods of a given country, an increase in the variance of its exchange rate will raise the expected purchasing power of *other* countries' assets due to Jensen's inequality. Appendix 10A repeats the theoretical derivation of the present section, with due attention paid to this point. The ultimate econometric result, a failure to reject risk neutrality, is unchanged.

10.2   Econometric Results

In the past, the stumbling block in econometric estimation of portfolio-balance equations or in testing the perfect substitutability hypothesis has been the measurement of expected returns. Here we are willing to assume that expectations are formed rationally, but require that they be conditional on current information, rather than being formed unconditionally and thus being estimable from sample means. We define ε_{t+1} to be the expectational error, which is independent of all information known at time t:

$$E\Delta s_{t+1} = \Delta s_{t+1} + \varepsilon_{t+1}, \qquad E(\varepsilon_{t+1}|I_t) = 0.$$

We combine the rational expectations definition with equation (6):

$$i_t - u_t^\$ - \Delta s_{t+1} = \rho\Omega(x_t - \alpha) + \varepsilon_{t+1}. \tag{8}$$

Two important aspects of equation (8) are that (1) with the substitution of ex post depreciation for expected depreciation, all variables are observable, and that (2) the error term is independent of the right-hand-side variable x_t. Thus we could estimate the system regressing the relative returns against x_t, equation by equation.[10] However, this technique would waste the information that the coefficient matrix is $\rho\Omega$ and the vector of constant terms is $-\rho\Omega\alpha$. *The key insight of this chapter is that Ω is precisely the variance-covariance matrix of the error term, and the system should be estimated subject to this constraint.* The imposition of a constraint between coefficients and variances, as opposed to among coefficients, is unusual in econometrics, and requires nonlinear Maximum Likelihood estimation.[11]

Appendix 10B derives the first-order conditions to maximize the likelihood function. Appendix 10C describes the method used to solve the (nonlinear) first-order conditions. And Appendix 10D (which appears only in the original published article) describes the data and calculation of the variables, which required some care. The time sample consisted of monthly observations from June 1973 to August 1980.

We constrain α to reflect actual consumption shares (in 1977) since these data are readily available. But the question whether ρ is equal to or greater than zero is central, so it is not constrained but rather estimated simultaneously with Ω and with the time-varying vector of expected returns that will be the fitted values of the equations.

In the dimension of ρ, the likelihood function turns out to be very flat but monotonically decreasing over the relevant range ($\rho \geq 0$); its maximum occurs at $\rho = 0$. This finding constitutes a failure to reject at any desired degree of significance the hypothesis that investors are risk neutral and that domestic and foreign assets are thus perfect substitutes.

It is important to realize the very limited nature of this claim. In the first place, the model employed here makes several simplifying assumptions. It assumes that goods prices are nonstochastic. It assumes that the relevant assets are limited to the bonds of the six countries (omitting equities, for example), and that the supplies of these bonds are properly measured. It assumes that the variance-covariance matrix is stationary. Finally, it assumes that investors optimize with respect to the mean and variance of their wealth one period at a time. Each of these simplifications could, in theory, invalidate the results, and it would be desirable to relax each of them in future research.

A second, and perhaps more important, respect in which the conclusions of this chapter are limited is that a failure to reject the null hypothesis does not entitle us to assert the null hypothesis. In the present case, the power of the test is especially low because the likelihood function is so flat. We are also unable to reject such plausible values for ρ as 1.0, 2.0, or higher numbers. (The log likelihoods are 947.01 for $\rho = 0$, 946.93 for $\rho = 1.0$, and 946.85 for $\rho = 2.0$.)[12]

The reader who is a priori favorably disposed to the notion of a risk premium may prefer to put the technique developed in this chapter to an alternative use, especially given the flatness of the likelihood function. If one believes that the risk premium exists and that asset demands depend on it according to a portfolio-balance function like equation (7), one can obtain the most efficient estimator of the variance-covariance matrix Ω, and thus of the parameters in the function, by imposing a plausible value of ρ and taking the maximum likelihood estimate subject to it. De Macedo (1980) and Krugman (1981) refer to the "Samuelson presumption" that $\rho = 2$. Thus table 10.1 reports the estimated parameters of the asset-demand functions $(\rho\Omega)^{-1}$ for the case of $\rho = 2$. By checking the signs of the off-diagonal elements we see that all pairs of currencies are substitutes,

Table 10.1
The parameters of the asset demand function: $(\rho\Omega)^{-1}$ for the constraint $\rho = 2$ with preferences assumed uniform across investors

The demand for the assets of:	Depends on the expected return (relative to the dollar) on the assets of:				
	Germany	UK	Canada	France	Japan
Germany	0.283	−0.110	0.086	−0.168	−0.085
UK	−0.110	0.867	−0.118	−0.283	−0.146
Canada	0.086	−0.118	2.061	−0.126	−0.007
France	−0.168	−0.283	−0.126	0.842	−0.166
Japan	−0.085	−0.146	−0.007	−0.166	0.628

Note: All coefficients have been divided by 1200 so that they can be used to multiply interest rates quoted on a percent per annum basis.

except that the Canadian dollar and the mark are complements. We can compute row sums to find the demand for the missing sixth asset, the U.S. dollar: the mark is the weakest substitute for the dollar, and the Canadian dollar, not surprisingly, is the strongest. One must keep in mind that the speculative portfolio is given by the matrix in table 10.1 multiplied by the expected relative returns, which are the fitted values of our equation, and that the total portfolio is the speculative portfolio plus the minimum variance portfolio α, which is the consumption share vector. There is not much point reporting the total portfolio demand at any particular point in time, since it is by construction precisely equal to the actual portfolio supply at that point in time.

10.3   The Test with Consumption Patterns Varying across Countries

In the closed-economy Capital Asset Pricing Model, investors are often allowed to have different ρ's, with those who are less risk averse "insuring" those who are more risk averse. In the international context, allowing investors to have different α's is surely the highest priority. Kouri and de Macedo (1978), Dornbusch (1983a), and Krugman (1981) presume, realistically, that each country's investors have a relatively greater preference for its own goods, and thus, given equation (7) (and given sufficient risk aversion; see Krugman), a relatively greater demand for its own assets. An implication is that current account imbalances that redistribute wealth from deficit countries to surplus countries will raise net world demand for the assets of the latter. Indeed this result accounts for much of the renewed popularity of the portfolio-balance model. In this section we allow residents of different countries to have different consumption patterns (α's), and thus different asset-holding preferences.

We repeat the asset-demand equation (7), with a subscript j denoting the country of residence of the investor whose holdings are being described (the United States, Germany, the United Kingdom, France, Japan, Canada, and the Rest of the World):

$$X_{jt}/W_{jt} = x_{jt} = \alpha_j + (\rho\Omega)^{-1}(i_t - \iota i_t^\$ - E\Delta s_{t+1}). \tag{9}$$

We multiply each of the equations ($j = 1, \ldots, 7$) by w_{jt}, defined to be the country's share (W_{jt}/W_t) of world wealth:

$$X_{jt}/W_t = \alpha_j w_{jt} + (\rho\Omega)^{-1}(i_t - \iota i_t^\$ - E\Delta s_{t+1})w_{jt}.$$

We add up the seven equations, and use

$$\sum_{j=1}^{7} w_{jt} = 1,$$

to get our equation for the aggregate world portfolio:

$$x_t = \alpha w_t + (\rho\Omega)^{-1}(i_t - \iota i_t^\$ - E\Delta s_{t+1}) \tag{10}$$

where we have defined α to be a matrix whose seven columns ($\alpha_j, j = 1, \ldots, 7$) indicate the consumption preferences of residents of the seven countries. (Recall that there are five elements in each of the α_j, as there are in the vector $x_t \equiv X_t/W_t$.) Intuitively, the demand for a given country's asset depends positively not only on its expected relative return but also on the wealth of those investors who have a relatively greater preference for that country's goods and thus for its assets. Notice that in the special case when all investors have the same preferences ($\alpha_1 = \alpha_2 = \ldots \alpha_7$), this equation reduces to equation (7); the distribution of wealth has no effect.

We invert the asset-demand equation (10) and add the rational expectations assumption to get the equation in regression form:

$$i_t - \iota i_t^\$ - \Delta s_{t+1} = \rho\Omega(x_t - \alpha w_t) + \varepsilon_{t+1}. \tag{11}$$

As far as the Maximum Likelihood Estimation problem described in appendixes 10B and 10C is concerned, this equation is the same as (7). The independent variable has simply changed from being a vector of asset supplies minus constants ($x_t - \alpha$) to a vector of asset supplies minus linear combinations of the distribution of wealth ($x_t - \alpha w_t$).

As in section 10.2, the likelihood function is very flat, and we technically cannot reject $\rho = 0$. In this case, however, the likelihood function is slightly

Table 10.2
The parameters of the asset demand function: $(\rho\Omega)^{-1}$ for the constraint $\rho = 2$ with preferences varying across country of residence

The demand for the assets of:	Depends on the expected return (relative to the dollar) on the assets of:				
	Germany	UK	Canada	France	Japan
Germany	0.289	−0.112	0.104	−0.185	−0.074
UK	−0.112	0.869	−0.137	−0.261	−0.141
Canada	0.104	−0.137	2.315	−0.167	0.047
France	−0.185	−0.261	−0.167	0.837	−0.187
Japan	−0.074	−0.141	0.047	−0.187	0.631

Note: All coefficients have been divided by 1200 so that they can be used to multiply interest rates quoted on a percent per annum basis.

increasing in ρ; the log likelihoods are 987.33 for $\rho = 0.0$, 987.44 for $\rho = 1.0$, and 987.54 for $\rho = 2.0$, and the maximum occurs somewhere above $\rho = 30$. As before, we report the matrix $(\rho\Omega)^{-1}$, which tells us the responsiveness of asset demands to expected rates of return, for the case $\rho = 2$. The parameter estimates in table 10.2 are similar to those in table 10.1.

10.4   Conclusion

What conclusion can be drawn from our failure to reject the null hypothesis? These results carry some weight against those who believe that the case for a risk premium has been firmly established. The existence of deviations of exchange rate changes from the forward discount, even if serially correlated, does not in itself constitute evidence for a risk premium. Only a systematic relationship between these deviations, on the one hand, and variables on which the risk premium is theoretically supposed to depend— such as asset supplies and the variance-covariance matrix—on the other hand, would constitute evidence of a risk premium. This chapter has shown that no such systematic relationship exists. And while the power of the test may be low, imposing mean-variance optimization has given us greater power than previous tests.

Appendix 10A: Derivation of the Krugman Version

As mentioned at the end of section 10.1, Krugman points out in a continuous-time model that Jensen's inequality is not merely a mathematical annoyance that can be swept away with an appeal to approximation, but is substantive to the question of how the parameters of the asset-demand functions depend on Ω.

Assume that the spot exchange rate of currency j against the dollar follows a continuous-time diffusion process in proportional terms:

$$\frac{dS^j}{S^j} = \delta_j dt + \sigma_j dZ. \tag{12}$$

Kouri (1977) and Kouri and de Macedo (1978) derive the optimal portfolio allocation among k assets. When prices are nonstochastic, the vector of expected real returns relative to the dollar depends on asset supplies as follows:

$$E(r - \iota r^\$) = \rho\Omega(x - \alpha). \tag{6'}$$

This equation would be identical to our equation (6) estimated in the text if one could validly approximate the real return on a bond as its interest rate minus expected currency depreciation and dollar inflation, as in equations (2) and (3).

Krugman shows (in a two-currency model) that the correct expected relative return on the assets of country j in (6') is:

$$E(r^j - r^\$) = i^j - i^\$ - \delta_j - \Omega^j\alpha + \sigma_j^2.$$

where Ω^j is the jth row of Ω that gives the variance σ_j^2 of exchange rate j and its covariances with the other dollar exchange rates. This is the same as in our equation (6) but for the presence of the $-\Omega^j\alpha + \sigma_j^2$ term. The intuitive explanation for the presence of this term is as follows. If all of the investor's consumption falls on the goods of a particular country ($\alpha^j = 1$), then there is no extra term for the relative return on that country's assets ($\Omega^j\alpha = \sigma_j^2$); changes in its exchange rates (the prices of foreign currencies in terms of domestic) are unambiguous indicators of changes in the real value of foreign assets, because the real value of domestic currency is certain. But an increase in the variance of exchange rate j raises the expected purchasing power of asset j over foreign goods due to Jensen's inequality. Thus, to the extent that foreign goods enter the relevant consumption basket ($\alpha^j < 1$), the variance raises the expected real return on asset j.

For empirical purposes, we must translate this result from continuous time to discrete time. By Ito's lemma, the *log* of the spot rate s^j follows a diffusion process related to that describing the *level* in equation (12):

$$ds' = \mu_j dt + \sigma_j dZ \qquad \text{where} \qquad \mu_j \equiv \delta_j - \sigma_j^2/2.$$

The nice thing about diffusion processes is that changes observed over a discrete unit time interval are normally distributed with known mean and variance:

$$E(s_{t+1}^j - s_t^j) = \mu_j \qquad \text{and} \qquad V(s_{t+1}^j - s_t^j) = \sigma_j^2.$$

Therefore if the continuous-time rates of return are constant over the time interval,

$$i_t^j - i_t^\$ - E\Delta s_{t+1}^j = i_t^j - i_t^\$ - \delta_j + \sigma_j^2/2$$

$$= E(r^j - r^\$) + \Omega^j\alpha - \sigma_j^2/2.$$

Equation (6') now translates into discrete time as:

$$i_t - u_t^\$ - E\Delta s_{t+1} = \rho\Omega(x_t - \alpha) + \Omega\alpha - \sigma^2/2 \qquad (6'')$$

where $\sigma^2/2$ is a vector whose j^{th} element is $\sigma_j^2/2$. This equation supports the seemingly ad hoc practice, common especially in joint tests of forward market efficiency and risk neutrality ($\rho = 0$), of defining exchange rates in logs to "get around the Siegal paradox." Careful treatment of Jensen's inequality gives rise only to a constant in the expected prediction error; time-varying expected prediction errors would require the existence of risk premia or the failure of rational expectations.

Unlike the Dornbusch form (6) estimated in the text, the Krugman form (6'') is not homogeneous in $\rho\Omega$. This turns out to make estimation of the Krugman form more difficult than the maximum likelihood estimation (MLE) for the simpler Dornbusch form, described in the next two appendixes. Use of a "canned" maximum likelihood package for the Krugman form produced results very similar to those for the Dornbusch form: over the range from $\rho = 0$ to $\rho = 30$ the maximum occurred at zero, and point estimates of the Ω^{-1} matrix were similar to those in table 10.1. When the consumption preferences in equation (6'') are allowed to vary across countries, the equation can be aggregated in a way analogous to that in section 10.3 for the Dornbusch form. The maximum now occurs at the more reasonable value of 13. But we are still unable statistically to reject zero, and the point estimates of Ω^{-1} are very similar to those in table 10.2.

Appendix 10B: MLE First-Order Conditions for Dornbusch Equation 6

In this appendix we write down the likelihood function for the Dornbusch model of the risk premium, equation (6), and derive the first-order conditions for the maximization of the function, which are represented by equations (16) and (18). The derivation of (16) and (18) is described in some detail in this appendix, as is the method of solving (16) and (18) in the following appendix, because the problem is a general one. The estimation technique could be applied to other contexts such as a closed-economy model of money, bonds, and capital, in which the data might turn out to be more hospitable to the portfolio-balance hypothesis than they are in the present context.

We repeat the Dornbusch equation with the expectational error term ε_{t+1}:

$$z_{t+1} = \rho\Omega(x_t - \alpha) + \varepsilon_{t+1} \tag{13}$$

where we have defined the vector of relative ex post returns $z_{t+1} \equiv i_t - i_t^\$ - \Delta s_{t+1}$. Assuming that the errors are normally distributed (see note 7), the likelihood function is:

$$L = (2\pi)^{-NT/2}|\Omega|^{-T/2} \exp\left[-\frac{1}{2}\sum_{t=1}^{T} \varepsilon'_{t+1}\Omega^{-1}\varepsilon_{t+1}\right] \tag{14}$$

where T is the number of observations and N is the number of exchange rates (five, in our case) and $\varepsilon_{t+1} = z_{t+1} - \rho\Omega(x_t - \alpha)$. To find the values of ρ and Ω that maximize L given the data, we first take the log of the likelihood:

$$\ln L = -\frac{NT}{2}\ln 2\pi - \frac{T}{2}\ln|\Omega| - \frac{1}{2}\sum z'_{t+1}\Omega^{-1}z_{t+1}$$

$$-\frac{\rho^2}{2}\sum (x_t - \alpha)'\Omega(x_t - \alpha) + \rho\sum z'_{t+1}(x_t - \alpha) \tag{15}$$

From this expression it can be seen that three moment matrices are sufficient statistics:

$$\sum z_{t+1}z'_{t+1}, \qquad \sum (x_t - \alpha)(x_t - \alpha)', \qquad \text{and} \qquad \sum z'_{t+1}(x_t - \alpha).$$

We take the derivative of the log likelihood, first with respect to ρ, and set it equal to zero:

$$\frac{\partial \ln L}{\partial \rho} = -\rho\sum (x_t - \alpha)'\Omega(x_t - \alpha) + \sum z'_{t+1}(x_t - \alpha) = 0. \tag{16}$$

From (16) it can be seen that if Ω were known, the MLE of ρ would just be the GLS estimate of ρ in equation (8).[13,14]

More complicated is the derivative of the log likelihood with respect to Ω. Henri Theil (1971, p. 33), shows that

$$\frac{\partial \Omega^{-1}}{\partial \omega_{bk}} = -(\Omega^{-1} i_h)(i'_k \Omega^{-1})$$

where ω_{hk} is element h, k of Ω, and vectors i_h and i'_k select out column h and row k of Ω^{-1}.

It follows that

$$\frac{\partial x' \Omega^{-1} y}{\partial \omega_{hk}} = -(x' \Omega^{-1} i_h)(i'_k \Omega^{-1} y)$$

$$= -(i'_k \Omega^{-1} y)(x' \Omega^{-1} i_h)$$

This is element h, k of the matrix $\Omega^{-1'} x y' \Omega^{-1'}$. So we have

$$\frac{\partial x' \Omega^{-1} y}{\partial \Omega} = -\Omega^{-1} x y' \Omega^{-1} \quad (\Omega \text{ being symmetric}).$$

We use this, and the facts

$$\frac{\partial \ln |\Omega|}{\partial \Omega} = \Omega^{-1} \quad \text{and} \quad \frac{\partial (x' \Omega x)}{\partial \Omega} = x x'$$

(also from Theil (1971), equations (6.14) and (6.8), respectively), to differentiate (15).

$$\frac{\partial \ln L}{\partial \Omega} = 0 = -\frac{T}{2} \Omega^{-1} + \frac{1}{2} \sum \Omega^{-1} z_{t+1} z'_{t+1} \Omega^{-1} - \frac{\rho^2}{2} \sum (x_t - \alpha)(x_t - \alpha)'.$$

(17)

Pre- and post-multiplying (17) by Ω gives

$$0 = -\frac{T}{2} \Omega + \frac{1}{2} \sum z_{t+1} z'_{t+1} - \frac{\rho^2}{2} \sum \Omega(x_t - \alpha)(x_t - \alpha)' \Omega,$$

(18)

which together with (16) characterizes the MLE.

Appendix 10C: Method of Solution of MLE First-Order Condition for Ω

The coefficient of risk aversion ρ, whose MLE first-order condition is given by (16), is easily estimated because it is a scalar. In this case, we simply conducted a grid search over the relevant range of ρ.

It is much less straightforward to estimate the variance-covariance matrix Ω. The problem is that the first-order condition (18) is quadratic in Ω, preventing a closed-form solution that might translate into a GLS framework on which one could use a packaged program. If we define the moment matrices

$$D \equiv \frac{1}{T} \sum z_{t+1} z'_{t+1} \quad \text{and} \quad C \equiv \frac{\rho^2}{T} \sum (x_t - \alpha)(x_t - \alpha)' \tag{19}$$

then (18) is

$$\Omega C \Omega + \Omega - D = 0. \tag{20}$$

The trick is to transform the quadratic system (20) into a system of equations *in scalars* that can be solved by the ordinary quadratic formula.[15]

As argued by C. R. Rao (1973, p. 41), since C^{-1} is symmetric positive definite, there exists a nonsingular matrix T such that $C^{-1} = T'T$, and since D is also symmetric, there exists a matrix P and a diagonal matrix of eigenvalues Λ such that

$P'GP = \Lambda$, $P'P = I$, where $G \equiv T^{-1'}DT^{-1}$. Define $R \equiv T^{-1}P$. Then

$R'DR = \Lambda$ and $R'C^{-1}R = I$, or $C = RR'$.

The point is to pre- and post-multiply (20) by R to diagonalize D:

$R'\Omega C \Omega R + R'\Omega R - R'DR = 0$

$R'\Omega R R'\Omega R + R'\Omega R - \Lambda = 0$

We can write this

$Y^2 + Y - \Lambda = 0$, where $Y \equiv R'\Omega R$.

Y has multiple solutions. There will exist one that is diagonal.[16] Its elements are given by a set of N quadratic equations: $Y_{ii}^2 + Y_{ii} - \lambda_i = 0$. In solving these equations we take the positive root: $Y_{ii} = (1 + \sqrt{1 + 4\lambda_i})/2$. Once Y is calculated, Ω is formed as

$\Omega = R^{-1'}YR^{-1}$.

The value of the log likelihood function is found by substituting the calculated Ω directly into (15).

The computer program to perform these calculations was written in Fortran by Tony Rodrigues and uses the IMSL package of mathematical subroutines. It takes as data the number of equations, the sample size, the absolute moment matrices of z_{t+1} and $x_t - \alpha$, and the sum

$$\sum z'_{t+1}(x_t - \alpha).$$

The range of ρ in the grid search is specified (in this case 0.0–30.0) but easily changed. The program calculates separately the likelihood for $\rho = 0$, a special case in which

$$\Omega = \sum z_{t+1} z'_{t+1} / T$$

as can be seen in (18).

Acknowledgment

I thank Tony Rodrigues for capable research assistance; the Institute of Business and Economic Research at the University of California at Berkeley and the National Science Foundation under Grant No. SES 8007162 for research support; and Charles Engel, Robert Hodrick, and Paul Ruud for comments.

11

Recent Estimates of Time-Variation in the Conditional Variance and in the Exchange Risk Premium

A variety of empirical evidence suggests that conditional variances of exchange rates vary over time. Examples based on observed second moments of exchange rates are Cumby and Obstfeld (1984), Hsieh (1984, 1989), Domowitz and Hakkio (1985), Diebold and Pauly (1986), Diebold and Nerlove (1986), and Manas-Anton (1986). Lyons (1988) and Hsieh and Manas-Anton (1986) have extracted implicit variances from foreign exchange options data, and they confirm that investors' perceived variances vary over time.

The behavior of investors in the foreign exchange market depends on the conditional variance. In past work on the implications of mean-variance optimization by investors, I explicitly assumed that the conditional variances and covariances of returns were constant over time: "[The] model employed here makes several simplifying assumptions.... It assumes that the variance-covariance matrix is stationary.... Each of these simplifications could, in theory, invalidate the results, and it would be desirable to relax each of them in future research" (1986a, p. 260). I recognized that second moments can in fact change over time; but I argued that it was more important to begin by focusing on how *first* moments vary over time with asset quantities, such variation being crucial, for example, to the question of the effects of foreign exchange intervention:

It is certainly true that parameters such as the variances in our asset demand functions can change over time.... But this paper is written under the supposition that fluctuations in expected returns are more of a problem than fluctuations in variances. After all, the former are the variables in the asset demand functions, and the latter are the parameters. Allowing expected returns to vary was first priority. Allowing the parameters to vary is a subject for future research.[1]

The major thrust of these papers was that mean-variance optimization, because it implies a linear relationship between the exchange risk premium and the variance of the exchange rate, implies three propositions about the risk premium:

1. It is small in absolute magnitude.

2. Foreign exchange intervention, and other changes in the supply of assets, have a small effect on it.

3. It does not vary much over time.

Several recent papers, inspired by empirical findings that the conditional variance does indeed vary over time, explore what happens to arguments like mine regarding the magnitude of the risk premium when one relaxes the assumption that the variance is constant. This direction of research is a welcome one.

11.1   The Upper Bound on the Conditional Variance

Adrian Pagan (1988) challenges my earlier (1986a, p. S63) use of the sample variance, as an upper bound on the conditional variance which investors use to think about risk. The variance for monthly changes in, for example, the pound/dollar rate around the forecasts of the forward rate is 0.010 on an annualized basis (1986a, p. S56; col. (4) ÷ 2). Given a coefficient of relative risk aversion of 2 and the assumption that only the exchange rate is stochastic, mean-variance optimization can be seen to imply that the risk premium rp is given by $-V[\alpha + \frac{1}{2}] + 2Vx$, where V is the conditional variance, α is the share of foreign goods in consumption, and x is the share of foreign assets in the portfolio.[2] To simplify, assume that α, which is in any case between 0 and 1, is $\frac{1}{2}$. Then

$$rp = -V + 2Vx. \tag{1}$$

I used 0.010 as the upper bound for V. Thus my argument was that if the supply of marks is increased by 1 percent ($\Delta x = 0.01$), then an upper bound on the change in the risk premium Δrp is 0.02 percent per annum, or two basis points. If the level of x is close to 1 or 0 (even though it is unlikely that x would in fact be that different from α), then the magnitude of the risk premium could still be only as large as $V = 1$ percent. (See the preceding chapter, particularly equation (6) or (6'), for the necessary assumptions, the derivation, and other citations.)

Pagan gives an example of a statistical distribution that can have a conditional variance, for a particular realization in the preceding period, that is larger than the unconditional variance. The upshot of his comment is that I have not succeeded in putting an upper bound on the variance of the exchange rate and therefore have not succeeded in putting an upper bound on the risk premium.

I would have thought uncontroversial my statement that the conditional variance "should be smaller than the unconditional variance," which is estimated by the sample variance. Let e_{t+1} be the *change* in the spot rate (in excess of the forward discount) in period $t + 1$, $\text{Var}(e)$ be the unconditional variance, $E_t e_{t+1}$ be the conditional expectation and ε_{t+1} be the expectational error. Then

$$e_{t+1} = E_t e_{t+1} + \varepsilon_{t+1}$$

$$\text{Var}(e_{t+1}) = E(e_{t+1} - Ee_{t+1})^2$$

$$= E(\varepsilon_{t+1} + E_t e_{t+1} - Ee_{t+1})^2.$$

If we expand, use the fact that the conditional and unconditional expectations of ε_{t+1} are zero and use $E(E_t e_{t+1}) = Ee_{t+1}$, then we get

$$\text{Var}(e_{t+1}) = E(\varepsilon_{t+1}^2) + \text{Var}(E_t e_{t+1}). \tag{2}$$

The unconditional variance is equal to the variance of the expectational error plus the variance of the conditional expectation. If the conditional variance $V_t \equiv E_t(\varepsilon_{t+1}^2)$ is constant over time, then it is equal to $E(\varepsilon_{t+1}^2)$, which from the equation above is clearly less than $\text{Var}(e)$.

How then is Pagan's counterexample possible? His concocted distribution is in fact an instance of a much more fundamental point. If the conditional variance is at some times bigger than at other times, then the risk premium will also be correspondingly bigger. A more transparent example than Pagan's is the case where the variance itself follows an autoregressive process, as in Robert Engle's (1982) ARCH model, so that a large squared realization in one period implies a large conditional variance in the following period. When I used the unconditional variance, estimated by the sample variance, as an upper bound on the conditional variance, I was thinking of both as constant over time, in which case my claims hold. If the conditional variance varies over time, then it is evident that my bound can be exceeded in those periods when the variance is especially large. Estimates in Engel and Rodrigues (1987), explained below, indeed show the conditional variance at times during the 1973–85 sample period substantially exceeding the bound of the unconditional variance (Figures 1A–1D).

If we allow the conditional variance V_t to vary over time, then we can still apply the upper bound both to the *average* conditional variance, $EV_t \equiv E[E_t(\varepsilon_{t+1}^2)] = E(\varepsilon_{t+1}^2)$, which appears in the above equation, and to the average risk premium. If the conditional variance is ten times larger than 0.010 one period in ten (for example, when the preceding squared realization was particularly large), then it is true that a 1 percent change in the portfolio in that period will change the risk premium by as much as 0.2 percent per annum and that the risk premium could theoretically be as large as 10 percent per annum (if close to 100 percent of the portfolio is in one asset or the other). But in the other nine periods out of ten, these magnitudes would have to be zero for the variance to average out to 0.010.

Hence, the conclusion is that if we allow for the variance to vary over time, propositions (1) and (2) above remain true if interpreted in the appropriate sense of averages over time. A consequence of allowing the variance to vary over time, however, is that variation in asset supplies x is not the only source of variation in the risk premium rp, so that proposition (3) above is now suspect. This point is made by Giovannini and Jorion (1987), to whom I now turn.

11.2   Conditioning on the Interest Rate

To evaluate the implications for the variation of the risk premium, as in proposition (3), we need to quantify somehow the variation of the conditional variance. The total variation in daily or weekly squared exchange rate changes is very large. Giovannini and Jorion (1987) report a variance of weekly squared changes equal to 0.001725 (a standard deviation of 4.2 percent) for the mark/dollar rate, 1979–84 (p. 111). Even when squared daily changes are averaged within a month, the monthly variances still vary greatly. For 100 months from December 1977 to April 1986, the mark/dollar variances of daily changes appear to range from 0.00074 (a standard deviation of 2.72 percent) in the most stable month to as large as 0.2487—a standard deviation of 49.87 percent. (The source is Frankel and Meese, 1987.)[3] The question is what fraction of the total variation in these squared exchange rate changes could investors have foreseen based on available information. Different authors have conditioned the variance on different information sets.

Giovannini and Jorion (1987) model the conditional variance by assuming a linear dependence on domestic and foreign interest rates.[4] They obtain an R^2 of 0.063 for squared weekly exchange rate changes, using mark/dollar data for 1979–84 (p. 111). The implication is that the variance of the predictable component of squared weekly exchange rate changes is $0.063 \times 0.001725 = 1.1 \times 10^{-4}$. (It was mistakenly reported as 1.1 in their original paper.) Thus the Giovannini-Jorion estimate implies that 1.1×10^{-4} is also the variance of the risk premium on a per-week basis, which is a large standard deviation of 54.5 percent ($0.545 = 52 \times \sqrt{1.1 \times 10^{-4}}$) on a per annum basis.[5]

11.3   Conditioning on Lagged Volatility

A number of papers estimate the conditional variance time series by conditioning on lagged variability, as in the ARCH model of the variance, instead of on interest rates. Let this period's conditional variance depend linearly on last period's squared error:

$$V_t = V_0 + \rho \varepsilon_{t-1}^2. \tag{3}$$

Hsieh (1985) finds that after an innovation in the variance of the mark/dollar rate, the peak effect on the conditional variance occurs eight days later.[6] Mark (1987, table 2) estimates a first-order ARCH process on monthly exchange rate data for four currencies; the estimate of ρ for the mark/dollar rate is 0.240. Engel and Rodrigues (1987, table 2) estimate a first-order ARCH process on monthly data for five currencies; their largest estimate of ρ for the mark/dollar rate is a somewhat smaller $0.384^2 = 0.148$. Allowing for longer ARCH lags tends to give an estimated variance process that dies out more slowly. Domowitz and Hakkio (1985), also working with monthly data, estimate a fourth-order ARCH process; the sum of the four (squared) lag coefficients for the mark/dollar rate is 0.521. Diebold and Nerlove (1986, table 7) estimate lags that go back almost as far, but on weekly data; the sum of the lags on their twelfth-order ARCH process is 0.766 for the mark/dollar rate. Given that some of the 0.766 effect on the first week's variance must die out by the fourth week, the estimate seems roughly in line with the Domowitz and Hakkio estimate. But the weekly ARCH estimates in Manas-Anton (1986, table 7) show an effect of only about 0.27.

We now derive the relationship between the (unconditional) variance of the conditional variance and the autoregressive parameter ρ from the ARCH process (3). First we need an expression for the (unconditional) *mean* of the conditional variance.[7]

Since

$$V \equiv EV_t = V_0 + \rho E \varepsilon_{t-1}^2,$$

and

$$= V_0 + \rho V,$$

$$V_0 = V(1 - \rho). \tag{4}$$

We use equation (3) again in deriving an expression for the variance of the variance:

$$\mathrm{Var}(V_t) = E(V_t^2) - (EV_t)^2$$

$$= E(V_0 + \rho \varepsilon_{t-1}^2)^2 - V^2$$

$$= V_0^2 + 2V_0\rho V + -V^2 + \rho^2 E\varepsilon_{t-1}^4.$$

Using (4) and the expression immediately above, we see that:

$$\mathrm{Var}(V_t) = V^2(1 - \rho)^2 + 2V^2(1 - \rho)\rho - V^2 + \rho^2 E\varepsilon_{t-1}^4$$

$$= \rho^2(E\varepsilon_{t-1}^4 - V^2). \tag{5}$$

We cannot eliminate the fourth-power term without additional information. But if we are willing to assume that the conditional distribution of ε_{t-1} is normal (we already know that it has mean zero and variance V_{t-1}), then we can use a well-known property of the normal distribution:[8]

$$E_{t-2}\varepsilon_{t-1}^4 = 3E_{t-2}\varepsilon_{t-1}^2 = 3V_{t-1}^2. \tag{6}$$

Thus

$$E\varepsilon_{t-1}^4 = EE_{t-2}\varepsilon_{t-1}^4 = 3EV_{t-1}^2.$$

We use (3) again, with the result that:

$$E\varepsilon_{t-1}^4 = 3E[(V_0 + \rho\varepsilon_{t-2}^2)^2]$$

$$= 3[V_0^2 + 2V_0\rho E\varepsilon_{t-2}^2 + \rho^2 E\varepsilon_{t-2}^4],$$

and

$$E\varepsilon_t^4(1 - 3\rho^2) = 3V_0(V_0 + 2\rho V).$$

Via (4),

$$E\varepsilon_t^4(1 - 3\rho^2) = 3V(1 - \rho)(V - V\rho + 2\rho V)$$

$$= 3V(1 - \rho)V(1 + \rho),$$

and

$$E\varepsilon_t^4 = 3V^2(1 - \rho^2)/(1 - 3\rho^2). \tag{7}$$

Now we substitute (7) into (5):

$$\text{Var}(V_t) = \rho^2 \left(\frac{3V^2(1 - \rho^2)}{1 - 3\rho^2} - V^2 \right)$$

$$= \rho^2 2V^2/(1 - 3\rho^2). \tag{8}$$

The monthly sample variance of the forward rate prediction error is about 0.001.[9] Even assuming that this is an accurate estimate of the unconditional variance of the forward rate prediction error, Ee_t^2, we must remember that it is only an upper bound on $\text{Var}(\varepsilon_t^2) = EV_t$. We repeat equation (2) using $E_t e_{t+1} = rp_t$:

$$\text{Var}(e_t) = EV_t + \text{Var}(rp_t). \tag{2'}$$

Even though the mean of ε_t is zero under rational expectations, the mean of e_t is not zero unless the mean of the risk premium is zero (which is what we are trying to discover). The question is how much of the sample variance of e_t (0.001) is due to the variance of the risk premium and how much to the conditional variance.

To state the strongest possible case for the risk premium, subject to our assumptions regarding risk aversion and consumption, let us take the portfolio share $x = 1$. Then, equation (1) becomes

$$rp_t = V_t; \tag{1'}$$

the risk premium is given very simply by the conditional variance V_t.

Equation (1') and our ARCH equation (8) give us

$$\text{Var}(rp_t) = \text{Var}(V_t)$$

$$= 2\rho^2 V^2/(1 - 3\rho^2). \tag{9}$$

On a monthly basis, if we take the Mark (1987) estimate of the ARCH parameter $\rho = 0.240$ and the estimate of the unconditional variance of the forward discount prediction error $\text{Var}(e_t) = 0.001$, it follows that the variance of the risk premium is on the order of

$$\text{Var}(rp_t) = 2(0.058)(0.001)^2/(1 - 3(0.058))$$

$$= 0.140 \times 10^{-6}$$

and the standard deviation is 0.374×10^{-3}, on a monthly basis. This implies that the standard deviation of the risk premium on a per annum basis is 0.00449 (0.45 percent). The estimates in Diebold and Nerlove

(1986) imply a strikingly similar annualized standard deviation of $52\sqrt{0.85788 \times 10^{-8}} = 0.0048$.[10] The latest Engel-Rodrigues estimate ($\rho = 0.148$) implies a somewhat smaller standard deviation. On the other hand, the standard deviation of the risk premium implied by the Giovannini and Jorion (1988) estimate appears much larger.

11.4 Variances Extracted from Options Prices

Estimates of implicit variances extracted from options prices are potentially superior to the ARCH and other statistical methods in that they do not depend on any specific assumptions about what information investors use to forecast squared errors.[11] Lyons (1988) reports annual variances for the log mark/dollar rate that vary over time over a range of approximately 0.01 to 0.04 (1983–86), implying in our framework a risk premium that varies over a similar range. Hsieh and Manas-Anton (1986, table 4) find that the estimated implicit volatilities differ considerably between put and call options and depending on the strike price and maturity of the contract.[12] But the daily variance implicit in a typical call contract maturing in September 1984 showed a standard deviation across 81 price observations of 0.00094. In our framework this implies a per day risk premium with a standard deviation of the order of 0.00094. The standard deviation of the per annum risk premium is then 0.343, somewhat smaller than the Giovannini and Jorion estimate but still much larger than the ARCH estimates. It is a little disturbing that such different estimates of the variability of the conditional variance emerge, depending upon whether the variances are conditioned on the interest rate (Giovannini and Jorion), conditioned on lagged squared errors (Mark, Diebold and Nerlove, Engel and Rodrigues, and other ARCH estimates), or estimated from options prices. Melino and Turnbull (1987) also find that the variances implied by options prices are significantly larger than those estimated from exchange rate data.

11.5 Can Risk Premiums Derived from Mean-Variance Optimization Explain the Behavior of the Forward Discount?

How can we judge whether these numbers represent large or small variation in the risk premiums? A relevant standard of comparison for deciding what is "small" is the variation in the forward discount. Regressions of ex post spot rate changes against the forward discount commonly produce coefficient estimates closer to 1/2 or 0 than to the unit value implied by the null hypothesis of forward rate unbiasedness. The many authors who assume that investors' expectations can be represented by ex post exchange rate changes in finite samples (up to a random error) thus infer that most, or even all, of the variation in the forward discount constitutes variation in the risk premium. See, for example, Fama (1984), Hodrick and Srivastava (1986), and Bilson (1985). (For elaboration, see the subsequent chapter.) The forward discount of the dollar against the mark has moved in the range of 1 percent per annum to 5 percent per annum in recent years. The one-month forward discount had a standard deviation of 1.7 percent per annum over the period January 1981 to December 1986 (2.4 percent over the period January 1974 to December 1986). Thus some of the standard deviations of the conditional variances estimated above do seem big enough potentially to explain the bias in the forward discount.[13]

Saying that movements in the variance are *big* enough to explain movements in the forward discount is not the same thing, however, as saying that these two variables do in fact move together, as they would need to if the risk premiums were to explain the forward discount's systematic prediction errors. Domowitz and Hakkio (1985) have used the ARCH estimates of the variance to try to explain the errors made by the forward discount in predicting spot rate changes, and Lyons (1988) has used the option-price estimates for the same purpose. Each has some (limited) success with some currencies. But one needs a hypothesis as to whether an increase in the variance should in theory raise the risk premium on the *foreign currency* or should raise the risk premium on the *dollar*. This requires some idea of what the supply of the foreign asset is relative to the minimum-variance portfolio. The asset whose supply exceeds the minimum-variance portfolio is the one that needs to pay a positive risk premium to be willingly held. Finding statistical evidence that the apparent effect of the variance is of the correct sign is more difficult than finding that it is nonzero.

Probably the most careful econometric study of mean-variance optimization across currencies that both uses asset supply data and allows for time-varying variances is Engel and Rodrigues (1987). Their use of the ARCH model of the variance-covariance matrix is to introduce it into the Maximum Likelihood technique used in chapter 9, which imposes a constraint between the matrix of substitutability coefficients on the one hand, and the variance-covariance matrix of the error term in the same regression equation on the other hand.[14] As in earlier papers, Engel and Rodrigues reject the hypothesis that the systematic prediction errors in the forward discount can be explained by mean-variance optimization. We are thus not yet at the point where we can claim to have found the risk variables that explain the behavior of the forward discount prediction errors.

Acknowledgment

I thank Francis Diebold, Charles Engel, and Ken Froot for useful comments and discussion, and the Alfred Sloan Foundation and the Institute of International Studies at the University of California at Berkeley for research support. Effort has been made to ensure that the authors cited here would agree that the computations based on their parameter estimates are appropriate, but it is always possible that errors remain.

12

Forward Discount Bias: Is It an Exchange Risk Premium?

with Kenneth A. Froot

12.1 Introduction

There is by now a large literature testing whether the forward discount is an unbiased predictor of the future change in the spot exchange rate.[1] Most of the studies that test the unbiasedness hypothesis reject it, and they generally agree on the direction of bias. They tend to disagree, however, about whether the bias is evidence of a risk premium or of a violation of rational expectations. Some studies assume that investors are risk neutral, so that the systematic component of exchange rate changes in excess of the forward discount is interpreted as evidence of a failure of rational expectations. On the other hand, others attribute the same systematic component to a time-varying risk premium that separates the forward discount from expected depreciation.

Investigations by Fama (1984) and Hodrick and Srivastava (1986) have recently gone a step further, interpreting the bias not only as evidence of a nonzero risk premium, but also as evidence that the variance of the risk premium is greater than the variance of expected depreciation. Bilson (1985) expresses the extreme form of this view, which he calls a new "empirical paradigm": expected depreciation is always zero, and changes in the forward discount instead reflect changes in the risk premium. Often cited in support of this view is the work of Meese and Rogoff (1983a) and others, who find that a random walk model consistently forecasts future spot rates better than alternative models, including the forward rate.

But one cannot address without additional information the basic issues of whether systematic expectational errors or the risk premium are responsible for the repeatedly biased forecasts of the forward discount, let alone whether the risk premium is more variable than expected depreciation. In this chapter we use survey data on exchange rate expectations in an attempt to help resolve these issues. The data come from three surveys: one conducted by American Express Banking Corporation of London irregularly between 1976 and 1985; another conducted by the *Economist's Financial Report*, also from London, at regular six-week intervals since 1981; and a third conducted by Money Market Services (MMS) of Redwood City, California, every two weeks beginning in November 1982 and every week beginning in October 1984. Frankel and Froot (1985, 1987) discuss the data and estimate models of how investors form their expectations.[2] In this chapter we use the surveys to divide the forward discount into its two components—expected depreciation and the risk premium—in order to shed new light on the large literature that finds bias in the predictions of the forward rate.

We want to be skeptical of the accuracy of the survey data, to allow for the possibility that they measure true investor expectations with error. Such measurement error could arise in a number of ways. We shall follow the existing literature in talking as if there exists a single expectation that is homogeneously held by investors, which we measure by the median survey response.[3] But, in fact, different survey respondents report different answers, suggesting that if there is a single true expectation, it is measured with error. Another possible source of measurement error in our expected depreciation series is that the expected future spot rate may not be recorded by the survey at precisely the same moment as the contemporaneous spot rate is recorded.[4]

Our econometric tests allow for measurement error in the data, provided that the error is random. There is a formal analogy with the standard rational expectations methodology, which uses ex post exchange rate changes rather than survey data and assumes that the error in measuring true expected depreciation, usually attributed to "news," is random. One of our findings below is that the expectational errors made in predicting ex post sample exchange rate changes are correlated with the forward discount. This, of course, could be consistent with a failure of investor rationality, but it is also consistent with "peso problems," nonstationarities in the sample (such as a change in the process governing the spot rate), and learning on the part of investors. But there is an important respect in which the origin of these systematic expectational errors is immaterial: our results imply that widespread econometric practice—inferring from ex post data what investors must have expected ex ante—tends to give misleading answers.

The chapter is organized as follows. In section 12.2 we reproduce the standard regression test of forward discount bias. We then use the surveys to separate the bias into a component attributable to systematic expectational errors and a component attributable to the risk premium. Sections 12.3 and 12.4 in turn test the statistical significance of the component attributable to the risk premium and the component attributable to systematic expectational errors, respectively. Section 12.5 concludes.

12.2 The Regression of Forward Discount Bias

The most popular test of forward market unbiasedness is a regression of the future change in the spot rate on the forward discount:[5]

$$\Delta s_{t+k} = \alpha + \beta f d_t^k + \eta_{t+k}^k, \tag{1}$$

where Δs_{t+k} is the percentage depreciation of the currency (the change in the log of the spot price of foreign exchange) over k periods and fd_t^k is the current k-period forward discount (the log of the forward rate minus the log of the spot rate). The null hypothesis is that $\beta = 1$. Some authors include $\alpha = 0$ in the null hypothesis as well. In other words, the realized spot rate is equal to the forward rate plus a purely random error term, η_{t+k}^k. A second but equivalent specification is a regression of the forward rate prediction error on the forward discount:

$$fd_t^k - \Delta s_{t+k} = \alpha_1 + \beta_1 fd_t^k + \eta_{t+k}^k, \tag{2}$$

where $\alpha_1 = -\alpha$ and $\beta_1 = 1 - \beta$. The null hypothesis is now that $\alpha_1 = \beta_1 = 0$: the prediction error is purely random.

Most tests of (1) have rejected the null hypothesis, finding β to be significantly less than one. Often the estimate of β is close to zero or negative.[6] Authors disagree, however, on the reason for this finding of bias. Longworth (1981) and Bilson (1981b), for example, assume that there is no risk premium, so that the forward discount accurately measures investors' expectations; they therefore interpret the bias as a rejection of the rational expectations hypothesis. Bilson describes the finding of β less than one as a finding of "excessive speculation," meaning that investors would do better to reduce the absolute magnitude of their expected exchange rate changes. In the special case of $\beta = 0$, the exchange rate follows a random walk, and investors would do better to choose $\Delta s_{t+k}^e = 0$. On the other hand, Hsieh (1984) and most others assume that investors did not make systematic prediction errors in the sample; they interpret the bias as evidence of a time-varying risk premium.

Standard Results Reproduced

We begin by reproducing the standard OLS regression results for (1) on sample periods that correspond precisely to those that we shall be using for the survey data.[7] We report these results, in part, to show that the results obtained when we use the survey data below cannot be attributed to small sample size, unless one is also prepared to attribute the usual finding of forward discount bias to small sample size.[8] Table 12.1 presents the standard forward discount unbiasedness regressions (equation (1)) for our sample periods.[9] All of the coefficients fall into the range reported by previous studies. There is ample evidence to reject unbiasedness: coefficients are significantly less than one. More than half of the coefficients are even significantly less than zero, a finding of many other authors as well. The F-tests also indicate that the unbiasedness hypothesis fails in most of the data sets.

Are the commonly found results in table 12.1 the consequence of a risk premium or systematic expectational errors?

Decomposition of the Forward Discount Bias Coefficient

The survey data allow us to answer the question directly. We can now allocate part of the deviation from the null hypothesis of $\beta = 1$ to each of

Table 12.1
Standard test of forward rate bias: OLS regression of $\Delta s_{t+1} = \alpha + \beta fd_t + u_{t+1}$ (*Economist* survey, June 1981–August 1988)

Term (k)	3-Month	6-Month	12-Month
b estimate	-1.916	-2.539	-2.080
Standard error	0.580	0.467	0.458
GMM s.e. (homos.)	0.907	0.875	1.065
GMM s.e. (hetero.)	0.979	1.010	0.766
$t: \beta = 0$	-2.11^*	-2.90^{**}	-1.95
$t: \beta = 0.5$	-2.66^{**}	-3.47^{**}	-2.42^*
$t: \beta = 1$	-3.21^{**}	-4.04^{**}	-2.89^{**}
$F: \alpha = 0, \beta = 1$	3.14^{**}	10.00^{**}	x
R^2	0.05	0.12	0.11
DW (lower bound)	1.01	0.54	0.24

Note: 309 observations.
x: F statistic not reported, because GMM covariance matrix not positive definite.
* Significant at 95 percent level.
** Significant at 99 percent level.

the alternatives: systematic errors and the presence of a risk premium. The probability limit of the coefficient β in (1) is

$$\beta = \frac{\text{cov}(\eta^k_{t+k}, fd^k_t) + \text{cov}(\Delta s^e_{t+k}, fd^k_t)}{\text{var}(fd^k_t)}, \tag{3}$$

where η^k_{t+k} is market participants' expectational error, and Δs^e_{t+k} is the market expectation. We use the definition of the risk premium,

$$rp^k_t = fd^k_t - \Delta s^e_{t+k}, \tag{4}$$

and a little algebra to write β as equal to 1 (the null hypothesis) minus a term arising from any failure of rational expectations, minus another term arising from the risk premium:

$$\beta = 1 - b_{re} - b_{rp}, \tag{5}$$

where

$$b_{re} = \frac{-\text{cov}(\eta^k_{t+k}, fd^k_t)}{\text{var}(fd^k_t)}; \qquad b_{rp} = \frac{\text{var}(rp^k_t) + \text{cov}(\Delta s^e_{t+k}, rp^k_t)}{\text{var}(fd^k_t)}.$$

With the help of the survey data, both terms are observable. By inspection, $b_{re} = 0$ if there are no systematic prediction errors in the sample, and $b_{rp} = 0$ if there is no risk premium (or, somewhat more weakly, if the risk premium is uncorrelated with the forward discount).

The decomposition was computed for sample periods up to 1985.[10] First, b_{re} is very large in size when compared with b_{rp}, often by more than an order of magnitude. In most of the regressions, the lion's share of the deviation from the null hypothesis consists of systematic expectational errors. For example, in the *Economist* data $b_{re} = 1.49$ and $b_{rp} = 0.08$. Second, while b_{re} is greater than zero in all cases, b_{rp} is sometimes negative, implying in (5) that the effect of the survey risk premium is to push the estimate of the standard coefficient β in the direction above one. Indeed, for the MMS one-month data, our largest survey sample with 740 observations, $b_{re} = 4.81$, and $b_{rp} = -2.07$. In these cases, risk premiums do not explain a positive share of the forward discount's bias. The positive values for b_{re}, on the other hand, suggest the possibility that investors tended to overreact to other information, in the sense that respondents might have improved their forecasting by placing more weight on the contemporaneous spot rate and less weight on the forward rate. Third, to the extent that the surveys are from different sources and cover different periods of time, they provide independent information, rendering their agreement on the relative importance and sign of the expectational errors all the more force-ful. In sum, the risk premium appears to have little economic importance for the bias of the forward discount.[11]

While the qualitative results above are of interest, we would like to know whether they are statistically significant, whether we can formally reject the two obvious polar hypotheses: (a) that the results are attributable to expectational errors, that is, that the point estimates of b_{re} are statisti-cally significant; and (b) that they are attributable to the presence of the risk premium, i.e., that the point estimates of b_{re} are statistically significant. We test these two (and several subsidiary) hypotheses in turn in sections 12.3 and 12.4.

The Variance of Expected Depreciation Versus Variance of the Risk Premium

Notice that in table 12.1 β is significantly less than $1/2$. It is precisely on the basis of such estimates that Fama (1984) and Hodrick and Srivastava (1986) have claimed that expected depreciation is less variable than the exchange risk premium. We state the Fama-Hodrick-Srivastava (FHS) inter-pretation of the results as

$$\text{var}(\Delta s_{t+k}^e) < \text{var}(rp_t^k). \tag{6}$$

To see how they arrive at this inequality, we use the definition of the risk premium in (4) to write the FHS proposition as

$$\text{var}(\Delta s_{t+k}^e) < \text{var}(rp_t^k) + \text{var}(fd_t^k) - 2\,\text{cov}(fd_t^k, \Delta s_{t+k}^e),$$

or

$$\frac{\text{cov}(fd_t^k, \Delta s_{t+k}^e)}{\text{var}(fd_t^k)} < \frac{1}{2}. \tag{6'}$$

The regression coefficient β, as given by (3), is

$$\beta = \frac{\text{cov}(\Delta s_{t+k}, fd_t^k)}{\text{var}(fd_t^k)}. \tag{7}$$

Under the assumption that the prediction error, η_{t+k}^k, is uncorrelated with fd_t^k, the coefficient β becomes the same as the ratio in the inequality (6'). Thus, a finding of $\beta < 1/2$ satisfies the variance inequality in (6). Added intuition is offered by recalling the special case $\beta = 0$. This is the case identified by Bilson (1985): the variation in fd_t^k consists entirely of variation in rp_t^k, and not at all variation in Δs_{t+k}^e.

Table 12.2
Comparison of variances of expected depreciation and the risk premium ($\times 10^2$ per annum)

Forecast horizon	Source survey	Dates	N	(1) Variance of Δs_{t+1}	(2) Variance of fd_t	(3) Variance of $\Delta \hat{s}_{t+1}^e$	(4) Variance of rp_t	(3)−(4)
1 week	MMS	10/84–2/86	247	2.756	NA	0.346	NA	NA
2 weeks	MMS	1/83–10/84	187	0.703	NA	0.113	NA	NA
1 month	MMS	11/82–11/88	740	0.831	0.008	0.249	0.222	0.027
3 months	MMS	1/83–10/84	187	0.610	0.014	0.067	0.062	0.005
	Economist	6/81–12/85	190	1.651	0.051	0.178	0.121	0.056
6 months	Economist	6/81–12/85	190	2.004	0.093	0.173	0.082	0.091
	AMEX	1/76–8/85	51	1.658	0.111	0.134	0.084	0.051
12 months	Economist	6/81–12/85	195	1.368	0.155	0.215	0.092	0.123
	AMEX	1/76–8/85	51	1.446	0.192	0.195	0.129	0.066

We can use expectations as measured by the survey data to investigate the FHS claim directly, without having to assume that there is no systematic component to the prediction errors. Table 12.2 shows the variance of expected changes in the spot rate, as measured by the surveys, and the variance of the risk premiums, for each data set. The variance of expected depreciation (column 3) is of the same order of magnitude as the variance of the risk premium (column 4), but is nevertheless larger in each of the samples. Although random measurement error in the survey data would tend to overstate each of these variances individually, it does not affect the estimate of their difference. Thus, "random walk" expectations ($\Delta s^e_{t+k} = 0$) do not appear to be supported by the survey data. We test formally the FHS hypothesis that the variance of expected depreciation is less than the variance of the risk premium in section 12.3.

12.3 Does the Risk Premium Explain Any of the Forward Discount's Bias?

In the previous section we offered point estimates of the bias in the forward discount, which suggested that more of the bias was due to systematic expectations errors than to a time-varying risk premium. In this section we formally test whether the risk premium is correlated with the forward discount. In the next section we shall formally test for systematic expectations errors.

Analogously to the standard regression equation, we regress our measure of expected depreciation against the forward discount:

$$\Delta \hat{s}^e_{t+k} = \alpha_2 + \beta_2 f d^k_t + \varepsilon^k_t. \tag{8}$$

The null hypothesis that the correlation of the risk premium with the forward discount is zero implies that $\beta_2 = 1$. By inspection, $\beta_2 = 1 - b_{rp}$, so that a finding of $\beta_2 = 1$ would imply that the estimates of b_{rp} are not statistically different from zero.

Besides the hypothesis that there is no time-varying risk premium, (8) also allows us to test the hypothesis of a mean-zero risk premium: $\alpha_2 = 0$. The hypothesis that the risk premium is identically zero is given by $\Delta s^e_{t+k} = f d^k_t$. How then should we interpret the regression error ε^k_t? It is the random measurement error in the surveys. That is, $\Delta \hat{s}^e_{t+k} = \Delta s^e_{t+k} + \varepsilon^k_t$, where Δs^e_{t+k} is the unobservable market-expected change in the spot rate. Note also that in a test of (8) using the survey data, the properties of the error term, ε^k_t, will be invariant to any "peso problems," which affect, rather,

Table 12.3
Test for time-varying risk premium: OLS regression of $\Delta s_t^e = \alpha_2 + \beta_2 fd_t + e_t$

Term (k)	3-Month	6-Month	12-Month
β_2 estimate	1.123	1.113	1.005
Standard error	0.143	0.096	0.099
GMM s.e. (homoskedastic)	0.196	0.146	0.185
GMM s.e. (correcting for heteroskedasticity)	0.198	0.122	0.169
t: $\beta_2 = 0$	5.73**	7.61**	5.44**
t: $\beta_2 = 0.5$	3.18**	4.20**	2.73**
t: $\beta_2 = 1$	0.63	0.77	0.03
F: $\alpha_2 = 0$, $\beta_2 = 1$	20.9*	41.8*	x
R^2	0.36	0.58	0.53
DW (lower bound)	1.60	1.29	0.90

Notes: GMM standard errors are calculated using the generalized method of moments; although overlapping observations are not an issue because ex post spot rate changes do not enter in, pooling across currencies creates a correlation across exchange rates.

Correcting for possible heteroskedasticity makes little difference; the reported test statistics assume homoskedasticity. Separate constant terms were estimated for each currency, but are not reported, to save space. The five currencies are the pound, mark, Swiss franc, yen and French franc.

308 observations.

x: F stat not reported, because GMM covariance matrix not positive definite.
* Significant at 95 percent level.
** Significant at 99 percent level.

the ex post distribution of actual spot rate changes. Another way of stating the null hypothesis is the proposition that domestic and foreign assets are perfect substitutes in investors' portfolios.[12]

Table 12.3 reports the OLS regressions of (8). In some respects the data provide evidence in favor of perfect substitutability of assets denominated in different currencies. Contrary to the hypothesis of a risk premium that is correlated with the forward discount, the estimates of β_2 are statistically indistinguishable from one.[13] Expectations seem to move very strongly with the forward rate. In addition, the coefficients are estimated with much greater precision than the corresponding estimates in table 12.1.

In terms of our decomposition of the forward discount bias coefficient, table 12.3 shows that the values of b_{rp} are statistically far from one but are not significantly different from zero. Thus, the rejection of unbiasedness found in the previous section cannot be explained entirely by the risk premium, at any reasonable level of confidence. Indeed, we cannot reject the hypothesis that the risk premium explains no positive portion of the bias.

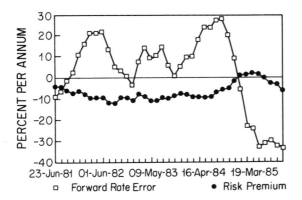

Figure 12.1
Forward rate errors and risk premium from the three-month *Economist* survey. Note: Data have been smoothed.

There is strong evidence of a constant term in the risk premium, however: α_2 is large and statistically greater than zero. The F-tests reject the parity relation at a high level of significance. Figures 12.1–12.4 make apparent the high average level of the risk premium (as well as its lack of correlation with the usual measure of the risk premium, the forward discount prediction errors).[14] Thus, the qualitatively small values of b_{rp} should not be taken to imply that the survey responses include no information about investors' expectations beyond that contained in the forward rate.[15]

We can also use (8) to test formally the FHS hypothesis that the variance of the risk premium is greater than the variance of expected depreciation. This is the inequality (6), which we found to be violated by point estimates in table 12.2. The probability limit of the coefficient β_2 is

$$\beta_2 = \frac{\text{cov}(\Delta \hat{s}^e_{t+k}, fd^k_t)}{\text{var}(fd^k_t)} = \frac{\text{cov}(\Delta s^e_{t+k}, fd^k_t)}{\text{var}(fd^k_t)}, \tag{9}$$

where we have used the assumption that the measurement error ε^k_t is uncorrelated with the forward discount fd^k_t. It follows from (9) that only if $\beta_2 < 1/2$ does the FHS inequality (6') hold; if β_2 is significantly greater than 1/2, the variance of expected depreciation exceeds that of the risk premium.

Table 12.3 also reports a t-test of the hypothesis that $\beta_2 = 1/2$. The data strongly reject the hypothesis that the variance of the true risk premium is greater than or equal to that of true expected depreciation. We have rather

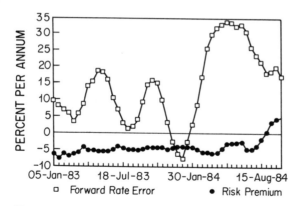

Figure 12.2
Forward rate errors and risk premium from the three-month MMS survey. Note: Data have been smoothed.

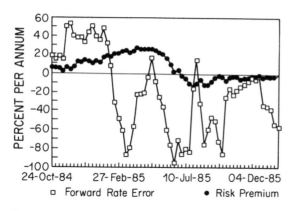

Figure 12.3
Forward rate errors and risk premium from the one-month MMS survey. Note: Data have been smoothed.

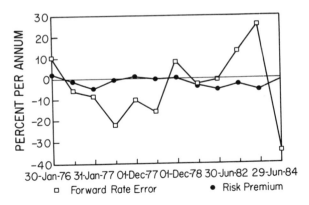

Figure 12.4
Forward rate errors and risk premium from the six-month AMEX data. Note: Data have been smoothed.

$\text{var}(\Delta s_{t+k}^e) > \text{var}(rp_t^k)$. Indeed, the finding that $\beta_2 = 1$ implies that the risk premium is uncorrelated with the forward discount:

$$\text{var}(rp_t^k) + \text{cov}(\Delta s_{t+k}^e, rp_t^k) = 0. \tag{10}$$

Thus, we cannot reject the hypothesis that the covariance of true expected depreciation and the true risk premium is negative (as Fama found), nor can we reject the extreme hypothesis that the variance of the true risk premium is zero.

Under the null hypothesis that there is no time-varying risk premium and the regression error ε_t^k in (8) is random measurement error, we can use the R^2s from the regressions to obtain an estimate of the relative importance of the measurement error component in the survey data. The R^2 statistics in table 12.3 are relatively high, suggesting that measurement error is relatively small. For example, under this interpretation of the R^2s, measurement error accounts for about 40 percent of the variability in expected depreciation from the six-month *Economist* data. For a standard of comparison, the corresponding R^2 in table 12.1, which uses ex post exchange rate changes as a noisy measure of expectations, implies that about 90 percent of the variability in the measure is noise.[16] This suggests that the survey data are a better measure of investors' expectations than are the ex post exchange rate changes, for those contexts where it is desirable to have an accurate measure of investors' expectations (e.g., estimating asset demand equations).

12.4 Do Expectational Errors Explain Any of the Forward Discount's Bias?

In the previous section we formally tested the hypothesis that there exists no time-varying risk premium that could explain the findings of bias in the forward discount. In this section we formally test the hypothesis that there exist systematic expectational errors that can explain those findings.

A Test of Excessive Speculation

Perhaps the most powerful test of rational expectations is one that asks whether investors would do better if they placed more or less weight on the contemporaneous spot rate as opposed to all other variables in their information set.[17] This test is performed by a regression of the expectational prediction error on expected depreciation:

$$\Delta \hat{s}^e_{t+k} - \Delta s_{t+k} = a + d\Delta \hat{s}^e_{t+k} + v^k_{t+k}, \tag{11}$$

where the null hypothesis is $a = 0$, $d = 0$, and the error term is the measurement error in the surveys less the unexpected change in the spot rate, $v^k_{t+k} = \varepsilon^k_t - \eta^k_{t+k}$. This is the equation that Bilson (1981b) and others had in mind, which we already termed a test of "excessive" speculation (see equation (2)), with the difference that we are now measuring investors' expected depreciation by the survey data instead of by the ambiguous forward discount.

The test findings consistently indicate that $d > 0$, so that investors could on average do better by giving more weight to the contemporaneous spot rate.[18] In other words, the excessive speculation hypothesis is upheld. F-tests of the hypothesis that there are no systematic expectational errors, $a = d = 0$, reject at the 1 percent level for all of the survey data sets. The results would appear to constitute a resounding rejection of rationality in the survey expectations.

Up until this point, our test statistics have been robust to the presence of random measurement error in the survey data because the surveys have appeared only on the left-hand side of the equation. But now the surveys appear also on the right-hand side; as a result, under the null hypothesis, measurement error biases toward one our estimate of d in (11). In the limiting case in which the measurement error accounts for all of the variability of expected depreciation in the survey, the parameter estimate would be statistically indistinguishable from one. In the tests of equation

(11), twelve of fifteen estimates of d are greater than one; in five cases the difference is statistically significant. This result suggests that measurement error is not the source of our rejection of rational expectations. However, we shall now see that stronger evidence can be obtained.

Another Test of Excessive Speculation

Another test of rational expectations, which is free of the problem of measurement error, is to replace $\Delta \hat{s}^e_{t+k}$ on the right-hand side of (11) with the forward discount fd^k_t:

$$\Delta \hat{s}^e_{t+k} - \Delta s_{t+k} = \alpha_1 + \beta_1 fd^k_t + v^k_{t+k}. \tag{12}$$

There are several reasons for making the substitution in (12). We know from our results in section 12.3 that expected depreciation is highly correlated with fd^k_t. Because fd^k_t is free of measurement error, it is a good candidate for an "instrumental variable." Indeed, if we as econometricians can look up the precise forward discount in the newspaper, we can also do so as prospective speculators. A finding of $\beta_1 > 0$ in either equation (9) or (13) suggests that a speculator could have made excess profits by betting against the market. But the strategy to "bet against the market" is far more practical if expressed as "bet against the (observable) forward discount" than as "do the opposite of whatever you would have otherwise done."

Equation (12) has additional relevance in the context of our decomposition of the forward rate unbiasedness regression in section 12.2: the coefficient β_1 is precisely equal to the deviation from unbiasedness due to systematic prediction errors, b_{re}. Thus, (12) can tell us whether the observed large positive values of b_{re} are statistically significant.

Table 12.4 reports OLS regressions of (12).[19] We now see that the point estimates of b_{re} described in section 12.2 are measured with precision. The data continue to reject statistically the hypothesis of rational expectations, $\alpha_1 = 0$, $\beta_1 = 0$. They reject $\beta_1 = 0$ in favor of the alternative of excessive speculation. The result that b_{re} is significantly greater than zero seems robust across different forecast horizons and different survey samples. In terms of the decomposition of the typical forward rate unbiasedness test, we can now reject statistically the hypothesis that all of the bias is attributable to the survey risk premium. Also, we cannot reject the hypothesis that all of the bias is due to repeated expectational errors made by survey respondents. This finding need not mean that investors are irrational. If they are learning about a new exchange rate process, or if there is a "peso

Table 12.4
Test for biased expectations ("overexcitability"): OLS regression of
$\Delta s^e_{t+1} - \Delta \hat{s}_t = \alpha_1 + \beta_1 f d^k_t + v^k_{t+1}$

Term (k)	MMS survey, Oct. 1984–Jan. 1988		Economist survey, June 1981–Aug. 1988	
	4-Week	3-Month	6-Month	12-Month
Estimate of underexcitability parameter c	−0.006	−2.992	−3.586	−3.129
Standard error	0.615	0.609	0.505	0.479
GMM s.e. (homoskedastic)	0.863	0.930	0.926	1.040
GMM s.e. (heteroskedastic)	0.809	1.053	1.083	0.820
$t: \beta_1 = 0$	−1.17	−3.22**	−3.875**	−3.007**
$F: \alpha_1 = \beta_1 = 0$	3.24*	2.33	4.36*	182.64**
DF	(5,659)	(6,308)	(6,308)	(6,308)
DW (lower bound)	1.04	0.89	0.48	0.29
R^2	0.001	0.08	0.15	0.14

* Significant at 95 percent level.
** Significant at 99 percent level.

problem" with the distribution of the error term, then one could not expect them to foresee errors in the sample period, even though the errors appear to be systematic ex post.

12.5   Conclusions

Our general conclusion is that, contrary to what is assumed in conventional practice, the systematic portion of forward discount prediction errors does not capture a time-varying risk premium. This result was qualitatively clear from the point estimates in section 12.2 or from the figures. But we can now make several statements that are more precise statistically.

1. We reject the hypothesis that all of the bias in the forward discount is due to the risk premium. This is the same thing as rejecting the hypothesis that none of the bias is due to the presence of systematic expectational errors.

2. We cannot reject the hypothesis that all of the bias is attributable to these systematic expectational errors, and none to a time-varying risk premium.

3. The implication of (1) and (2) is that changes in the forward discount reflect, one-for-one, changes in expected depreciation, as (for example)

perfect substitutability among assets denominated in different currencies would imply.

4. We reject the claim that the variance of the risk premium is greater than the variance of expected depreciation. The reverse appears to be the case: the variance of expected depreciation is large in comparison with the variance of the risk premium.

5. Because the survey risk premium appears to be uncorrelated with the forward discount, we cannot reject the hypothesis that the market risk premium we are trying to measure is constant. We do find a substantial *average* level of the risk premium. But, to repeat, the premium does not vary with the forward discount as conventionally thought.

Acknowledgment

This is an extensively revised version of NBER Working Paper No. 1963. We would like to thank Alberto Giovannini, Robert Hodrick, and many other participants at various seminars for helpful comments; Barbara Bruer, John Calverley, Lu Cordova, Kathryn Dominguez, Laura Knoy, Stephen Marris, and Phil Young for help in obtaining data, Joe Mullally for expert research assistance, the National Science Foundation (under grant no. SES-8218300), the Institute for Business and Economic Research at U. C. Berkeley, and the Alfred P. Sloan Foundation for research support.

IV

**Exchange Rate
Expectations**

Introduction to Part IV

The key role afforded to investor expectations was from the beginning a cornerstone of the "asset-market approach" to exchange rates. Indeed, it may rank as a more important cornerstone than the condition of perfect capital mobility, since the latter assumption dates from the famed Mundell-Fleming model of the 1960s.

It is easy, especially for practitioners, to fall into the habit of thinking that the high volatility of exchange rates, which is both observed in practice and predicted by the asset-market models, is a consequence of speculation, that is, of investors' making bets on the basis of their expectations. The use of phrases such as "overshooting" seems to encourage this habit. But as a closer reading of the literature makes clear, the property of high variability is rather a consequence of the condition of perfect capital mobility. In the overshooting model and the other rational-expectations models described in part II, speculation is stabilizing rather than destabilizing. Volatility is in fact lower than in the Mundell-Fleming model.

The first three chapters in part IV continue my fruitful collaboration with Ken Froot. The first (chapter 13), "Using Survey Data to Test Standard Propositions Regarding Exchange Rate Expectations," employs the same data as in the last chapter of part III. The application here is to how investors form expectations. The finding is that investors respond to an appreciation today by expecting—at horizons of three to twelve months—future depreciation. Speculation is stabilizing.

This relatively benign view of how expectations are formed was soon disturbed, however, by the evidence that there are in fact a variety of competing models that are reflected in investors' positions. The models that are most popular among foreign exchange market participants, particularly those taking positions at short horizons, go under the name of "technical analysis" or "chartism." These tend to forecast by extrapolating past trends, and thus to be destabilizing, as is confirmed by investigation of survey data at horizons of one week to one month. This is the reverse of the tendency reported at longer horizons.

Chapter 14, "Understanding the U.S. Dollar in the Eighties: The Expectations of Chartists and Fundamentalists," came out of the frustrations of trying to explain the dollar's behavior in 1985. This is the model of "speculative bubbles that did *not* fully obey the rules of rational expectations" that was alluded to at the end of the introduction to part II. It would be a misunderstanding of this chapter to think that it says that bubbles get started because speculators irrationally extrapolate past trends. The dynamics of the model come, rather, from changes over time in the weights assigned by the marketplace to the two classes of forecasters. The weights, in turn, are determined by portfolio managers in quite a reasonable way: by adjusting in response to evidence on which class of forecaster is performing better. For the record, figure 14.3 was generated in 1985, with the dollar still near its peak.

This train of thought is continued in chapter 15, "Chartists, Fundamentalists, and Trading in the Foreign Exchange Market," which includes Granger-causality tests suggesting that dispersion of beliefs among forecasters has an effect on volume of trade in the market, which in turn has an effect on the volatility of the market rate.

If one concludes that some part of exchange rate movement is unnecessary, one might next wonder if the authorities could not usefully intervene in the foreign exchange market. This question is addressed in chapter 16, "Foreign Exchange Intervention: An Empirical Assessment (with Kathryn Dominguez). The portfolio effect of changes in asset supplies is the effect on the risk premium for which the evidence was so elusive in part III. This chapter uses the survey data to measure investor expectations. It also ties in methodologically with chapter 5 in that announcements, in this case public reports of intervention, turn out to have the greatest effects in the marketplace by means of their impact on expectations.

I have long considered myself a supporter of floating exchange rates among major countries. Many in the profession have reacted to the last twenty years of floating rates by losing their affection for them. I suppose I have moved somewhat in the same direction, beginning especially in 1985. But there is a middle ground between simple advocacy of fixed or floating rates, and even between simple advocacy of more or less government activism. It is a middle ground that I think has been the right answer all along: attempts to stabilize the exchange rate are appropriate only to the extent that the country is politically willing to give up independence of its macroeconomic policies. A possible lesson from the U.S. experience in the early 1980s is that, even if markets are not always rational and optimizing, neither are governments.[1] Although a fixed exchange rate can often discipline monetary policy (or even fiscal policy) in a small country, it would be no match for the American political process. The United States has always been big enough to do what it wants and it thinks that it still is. Indeed, the ability to borrow huge sums on internationalized financial markets has allowed the United States to defer the fiscal constraint for ten years.

In a smaller, more open country, on the other hand, stabilizing the exchange rate can make sense, providing again that the people are willing to give up macroeconomic independence. This is, of course, the point of the optimum currency area literature introduced by Mundell (1961) and McKinnon (1963). It is applicable in many parts of the world today, but especially to Europe, where some countries may be willing to give up independence. Chapter 17, "The European Monetary System: Credible in 1988–91?" (with Steven Phillips) uses a new source of survey data, which is available for smaller countries as well as larger, to examine whether market participants expect European exchange rates to stay within the target zones specified by the EMS. It finds that by 1991, the year of the Maastricht Agreement, the system had indeed gained a measure of credibility, particularly among the Deutschemark, Dutch guilder, and Belgian Franc. One expects that a Northern subset, at least, of the European countries in the 1990s will continue their journey back to exchange rate stability; it may be fitting to end the book on this note.

13

Using Survey Data to Test Standard Propositions Regarding Exchange Rate Expectations

with Kenneth A. Froot

No variable is as ubiquitous in international financial theory and yet as elusive empirically as investors' expectations regarding exchange rates. In the past, expectations have been modeled in an ad hoc way, often by using the forward exchange rate. There is, however, a serious problem with using the forward discount as the measure of the expected change in the exchange rate, in that the two may not be equal. The gap that may separate the forward discount and expected depreciation is generally interpreted as a risk premium. Most of the large empirical literature testing the unbiasedness of the forward exchange rate, for example, has found it necessary either arbitrarily to assume away the existence of the risk premium, if the aim is to test whether investors have rational expectations, or else to assume that expectations are in fact rational, if the aim is to test propositions regarding the behavior of the risk premium.

We offer a new source of data to measure exchange rate expectations that avoids such problems: three independent surveys of the expectations held by exchange market participants. Between 1976 and 1985, American Express Banking Corporation (Amex) polled a sample of 250–300 central bankers, private bankers, corporate treasurers, and economists, regarding their expectations of major exchange rates six months and twelve months into the future, approximately once a year. Since 1981, the *Economist Financial Report*, a newsletter associated with the *Economist*, has conducted at regular six-week intervals a survey of fourteen leading international banks regarding their expectations at three, six, and twelve-month horizons. And since 1983, Money Market Services, Inc. (MMS) has conducted a similar survey on a weekly or biweekly basis, at a variety of short-term horizons. The first two surveys record expectations of five currencies against the dollar (the pound, French franc, mark, Swiss franc, and yen), and the MMS data have been collected for four currencies (the pound, mark, Swiss franc, and yen). In each survey, it is the median response that is reported.

In this chapter, we are interested principally in two questions: how best to describe the survey expectations in terms of simple models of investors' expectations formation; and whether investors' expectations are unbiased forecasts of the actual spot exchange rate process. Our aim here is not to develop any special new hypotheses of our own. But a theme which runs throughout our investigation is the stabilizing role of expectations. Do the data confirm the suspicions of some critics of floating exchange rates that expectations are characterized by bandwagon effects? Or, in line with many macro models of exchange rate determination, does a current appreciation of the currency by itself generate expectations of future depreciation?

The chapter is organized as follows. Section 13.1 discusses the exchange rate survey data. In section 13.2, we present some simple but enlightening summary statistics from the surveys. In section 13.3, we attempt to describe the survey data by using several popular formulations for exchange rate expectations: extrapolative, adaptive, and regressive models. Section 13.4 then investigates the behavior of the actual spot process and the rationality of the various expectations mechanisms considered in section 13.3. In section 13.5, we offer some thoughts on heterogeneity of exchange rate expectations, and section 13.6 gives our conclusions.

13.1   The Survey Data

Economists generally distrust survey data. It is a cornerstone of "positive economics" that we learn more by observing what people do in the marketplace than what they say. Nevertheless, alternative measures of expectations all have their own drawbacks. For this reason, closed-economy macro and financial economists have found survey data useful, in studies of expected inflation (where the Livingston survey has been the most popular), expected official announcements of the money stock and other macroeconomic variables (where MMS is the source), and firm inventory behavior and related topics (see Michael Lovell, 1986). To our knowledge, there had been no studies prior to this one using survey data on exchange rate expectations.[1] This might be considered surprising in light of the great interest in the subject, evident in the large literature on the forward market. One could even argue that the case for using survey data on exchange rate expectations is on firmer ground than the case for using survey data on inflation expectations. The respondents to the surveys participate more directly in the spot and forward exchange markets than the respondents to the Livingston survey participate in the goods markets: they are economists in the foreign exchange trading room or the traders themselves in major international banks who have up-to-the-minute information on the values of the currencies covered. At the very least, these exchange rate survey data contain some useful information that warrants study. It seems likely that economists have not used the data in the past only because they have been unaware of their existence.

One limitation to the survey data should be registered from the start, the relatively small number of times the surveys were conducted as of early 1986: twelve dates for the Amex data, thirty-eight for the *Economist* data, forty-seven for the 1983–84 MMS survey.[2] By pooling the cross section of four or five currencies at each survey date, however, we achieve respectable sample sizes. The obvious contemporaneous correlation of error terms across currencies may be exploited, and we do so with two techniques. Seemingly unrelated regressions are used in cases where the error terms are serially uncorrelated, while method of moments estimators are employed when under the null hypothesis there is serial correlation.[3] In addition, there is considerable variety of forecast horizon in the data we employ. We estimate equations for the pooled data at three-, six-, and twelve-month horizons for the *Economist* data, three-months for the MMS data, and six- and twelve-months for the Amex data.

13.2 Preliminary Results

Before we set out to test the hypotheses of interest, some descriptive statistics and preliminary tests are in order.

The Magnitude of Expected Depreciation

First, the survey data can be used to shed some light on questions concerning the size of expected depreciation relative to the forward discount. In general, the forward discount can be decomposed into expected depreciation and the risk premium:

$$fd_t = \Delta s^e_{t+1} + rp_t,$$

where fd_t is the log of the forward rate minus the log of the spot rate at time t (expressed in dollars per unit of foreign currency), and Δs^e_{t+1} is the log of the expected future spot rate minus the log of the current spot rate. Many models of exchange rate determination have made the simplifying (but extreme) assumption that expectations are static, for lack of a better alternative, that is, that expected depreciation is zero:

$$\Delta s_{t+1}^e = 0. \tag{1}$$

For example, William Branson, Hannu Halttunen, and Paul Masson did so, giving as a reason that "we have very little empirical evidence on alternative, more complicated expectations mechanisms" (1977, p. 308). The immortal Mundell-Fleming model of exchange rates under conditions of perfect capital mobility can be interpreted as having assumed static expectations, so that international arbitrage equated domestic and foreign interest rates.

More recently, this point of view has been, in a sense, vindicated by the work of Richard Meese and Kenneth Rogoff (1983a). They have shown that the current spot exchange rate is a better predictor of the future rate than are standard monetary models, more elaborate time-series models, or the current forward exchange rate; that is, that the exchange rate seems to follow a random walk. Similar empirical findings have turned up in other contexts. Many papers, such as John Bilson (1981b) and Roger Huang (1984), have reported evidence that the rational expectation is closer to zero depreciation than to the forward discount. These authors did not explicitly conclude that the same is necessarily true of investors' expectations; they found support for the random walk model of the spot rate, but were relatively agnostic on investors' expectations.

Nevertheless, this work seems to imply that investors' expected depreciation is not a very interesting variable—that it does not differ very much from zero and is not very responsive to changes in the contemporaneous information set. Bilson (1985) seems to express this point of view, holding that "actual or market forecasts of exchange rates" are unrelated to the forward discount. The position in the Bilson paper is, in effect, that the random walk holds not only as a description of the actual spot rate process but also as a description of investors' expectations formation. It follows that the risk premium constitutes the entire forward discount.

A very different impression of the relative importance of expected depreciation as a component of the forward discount is given by all three of our surveys. Table 13.1a shows, for each of the surveys, expected depreciation of the dollar against all currencies for which data are available. Most striking is that the survey-expected depreciation is not only consistently positive, but is larger (often several times larger) than the expected depreciation implied by the contemporaneous forward discounts reported in table 13.1b. An important feature of table 13.1a is the apparent agreement across different surveys and forecast horizons. The corroboration of such large expected depreciation numbers suggests that the results are not due to the

Table 13.1a
Survey expected depreciation of the dollar against five currencies

Data set	1976–79	1981	1982	1983	1984	1985
MMS 3-month				8.17	7.26	
Economist 3-month		9.95	13.44	10.17	10.68	1.56
Economist 6-month		8.90	10.31	10.42	11.66	3.93
Amex 6-month	1.20	7.60	10.39	4.19	9.93	1.16
Economist 12-month		7.17	8.33	7.65	10.02	4.24
Amex 12-month	−0.20	5.67	6.86	5.18	8.47	3.60

Note: MMS data are the average of four currencies (the pound, mark, Swiss franc, and yen) and do not include the French franc.

Table 13.1b
Forward discount of the dollar against five currencies

Time sample	1976–79	1981	1982	1983	1984	1985
MMS 3-month				3.05	4.60	
Economist 3-month		3.94	2.95	1.17	3.20	1.22
Economist 6-month		3.74	3.01	1.10	3.21	0.84
Amex 6-month	1.06	4.49	5.21	1.48	4.39	0.02
Economist 12-month		3.40	3.02	1.25	3.29	0.89
Amex 12-month	0.93	3.70	4.65	1.28	4.45	0.31

Notes: Forward discounts were recorded at the time each survey was conducted. See the Data Appendix for more detail. MMS data are the average of four currencies (the pound, mark, Swiss franc, and yen) and do not include the French franc.

particularities of each survey's respondents. Table 13.2 shows the averages of alternative measures of expected depreciation by survey *and* by country. The forward discount numbers seem to imply that, on average, the dollar was expected to depreciate against the mark, Swiss franc, and yen, to remain approximately unchanged against the pound, and to appreciate against the franc. The survey expectations, on the other hand, suggest that the results in table 13.1a do not mask a great deal of variation across countries. Table 13.2 shows that the surveys consistently predicted substantial depreciation of the dollar against all five currencies surveyed. In every survey, expected depreciation is considerably smaller, however, for currencies that were selling forward at a smaller discount (or a larger premium).

These simple results provide some indication that market expectations are positively correlated, at least cross sectionally, with the forward discount. Such systematic relationships between expected depreciation and

Table 13.2
Various measures of expected depreciation over the following months (percent per annum)

Forecast horizon	Survey source	Dates	Survey data		Forward discount	Actual change	
			N	$s^e(t+1) - s(t)$	$f(t) - s(t)$	N	$s(t+1) - s(t)$
1 Week							
Total	MMS	10/84–2/86	247	1.03		247	20.20
UK			62	−12.84		62	14.96
WG			62	2.84		62	21.36
SW			61	8.84		61	20.10
JA			62	5.40		62	24.39
2 Weeks							
Total	MMS	1/83–10/84	187	4.22		187	−12.35
UK			47	−2.66		47	−16.15
WG			47	5.09		47	−15.19
SW			46	6.10		46	−13.86
JA			47	8.40		47	−4.23
1 Month							
Total	MMS	10/84–2/86	176	−2.63	1.23	176	20.82
UK			44	−11.91	−3.85	44	10.13
WG			44	−2.26	3.23	44	23.82
SW			44	0.67	3.74	44	21.76
JA			44	2.99	1.68	44	27.55
3 Months							
Total	MMS	1/83–10/84	187	7.76	3.75	187	−10.77
UK			47	4.46	0.37	47	−13.92
WG			47	8.33	4.68	47	−13.68
SW			46	9.62	6.13	47	−12.61
JA			47	8.68	3.85	47	−2.90

Table 13.2 (continued)

Total	*Economist*	6/81–12/85	190	9.13	2.20	195	−0.84
UK			38	3.66	−0.06	38	−6.43
FR			38	5.17	−3.94	38	−4.43
WG			38	11.84	4.36	38	0.81
SW			38	12.30	5.99	38	1.47
JA			38	12.66	4.67	38	4.37
6 Months							
Total	*Economist*	6/81–12/85	190	9.30	2.22	180	−2.18
UK			38	4.19	0.14	36	−6.79
FR			38	4.69	−4.03	36	−6.29
WG			38	12.39	4.35	36	−0.96
SW			38	12.27	5.89	36	−0.36
JA			38	12.94	4.74	36	3.52
Total	Amex	1/76–8/85	51	3.87	2.07	51	5.98
Early Period		1/76–12/78	26	1.20	1.06	26	8.98
Later Period		6/81–8/85	25	6.66	3.12	25	2.86
12 Months							
Total	*Economist*	6/81–12/85	195	7.77	2.31	155	−6.42
UK			38	3.38	0.36	31	−9.47
FR			38	3.72	−3.63	31	−11.20
WG			38	10.67	4.24	31	−5.60
SW			38	10.41	5.91	31	−5.75
JA			38	10.67	4.66	31	−0.08
Total	Amex	1/76–8/85	51	2.81	1.88	46	2.02
Early Period		1/76–12/78	26	−0.20	0.93	26	8.85
Later Period		6/81–8/85	25	5.95	2.88	20	−6.86

other contemporaneous variables suggest that there is more to investor expectations than is revealed by the random walk model of expectations.[4]

Unconditional Bias

The simplest possible test of rational expectations is to see whether expectations are unconditionally biased, that is, whether investors systematically overpredict or underpredict the future spot rate. Tests performed in the 1970s clearly failed to find any unconditional bias.[5] But in the 1980s, the dollar consistently sold at a discount in the forward exchange market against the most important currencies, as is shown in tables 13.1b and 13.2b, and yet it was not until 1985 that the great, long-anticipated dollar depreciation began to materialize. Indeed, George Evans (1986) uses a nonparametric sign test on the forward rate prediction errors over the 1981–84 period and finds significant unconditional bias against the pound. Could there be unconditional bias in the survey data for this period as well?

Table 13.3 reports formal tests of unconditional bias. The MMS three-month data, available for the period January 1983 to October 1984, show statistically significant bias for all four currencies, even more than do the three-month forward discount data during the same period. The *Economist* data are available through 1985, the first year of dollar decline. The bias is not quite statistically significant at the three- and six-month horizons, but it is significant at the one-year horizon.[6] The general rule seems to be that when the forward discount is biased, the survey data are also biased, with the implication that the finding cannot be attributed to a risk premium. The presence of bias in the 1980s clearly arose from the episode of dollar appreciation that ended in February 1985. Respondents consistently overpredicted the future value of foreign currencies against the dollar in this period.

One explanation that could be suggested for such findings of bias is that the surveys measure investors' expectations with error. But it should be noted that if one is willing to assume that the measurement error is random, then the conclusions are unaffected. Under the null hypothesis, positive and negative measurement errors should average out, just like positive and negative prediction errors by investors.

Short of concluding that investors' expectations are not equal to the rationally expected value, one major possible explanation for findings of biasedness remains. It is that the standard errors in our tests are invalidated by the "peso problem" of nonnormality in the distribution of the test statistic. The peso problem arises when there is a small probability of a large change in the exchange rate each period—such as results from a devaluation, a bursting of a speculative bubble, or a big change in fundamentals—and when the sample size is not large enough to invoke the central limit theorem with confidence.[7]

The sensitivity of the direction and magnitude of the bias in prediction error to the choice of sample period is evident in the Amex survey, the only one available in 1976–79. These data show unconditional bias in the opposite direction in the earlier period, as do the forward rate data: respondents consistently underpredicted the value of foreign currencies against the dollar. When the entire Amex data set from 1976 to 1985 is used, prediction errors show no unconditional bias for either the survey data or the forward rate.

13.3 Tests of Expectations Formation

The question of what mechanisms investors use to form expectations is of interest independent of the question of whether these mechanisms are rational, that is, whether they coincide with the mathematical expectation of the actual spot process. In this section we investigate alternative specifications of expectations, and in section 13.4 we test for their rationality.

A number of simple formulations have traditionally been used. A general framework for expressing them comes from writing the investors' expected future (log) spot rate as a weighted average of the current (log) spot rate with weight $1 - \beta$ and some other element, x_t, with weight β:

$$s_{t+1}^e = \beta x_t + (1 - \beta)s_t. \tag{2}$$

In examining different versions of equation (2), our null hypothesis will be that expectations are in fact static, that is, that $\beta = 0$ (investors believe in the random walk). We choose interesting candidates for the "other element," x_t, as alternative hypotheses. The models we will consider are extrapolative expectations, adaptive expectations, and regressive expectations. They feature as the other element x_t, respectively: the lagged spot rate, s_{t-1}, the lagged expectation, s_t^e, and some notion of a long-run equilibrium level of the spot rate, $\bar{s}_t$.

One characterization of expectations formation often claimed by market participants themselves is that the most recent trend is extrapolated: if the currency has been depreciating, then investors expect that it will continue to depreciate.[8] Such "bandwagon" expectations are represented:

Table 13.3
Unconditional bias in predictions of future exchange rates (percent per annum)

Forecast horizon	Survey source	Dates	N	Survey error $s^e(t+1) - s(t+1)$			Forward discount error $f(t) - s(t+1)$		
				Mean	SD of Mean	t-Statistic	Mean	SD of Mean	t-Statistic
1 Week									
Total	MMS	10/84–2/86	247	−19.17	8.17	−2.35			
UK			62	−27.79	19.87	−1.40			
WG			62	−18.52	15.25	−1.21			
SW			61	−11.27	17.82	−0.63			
JA			62	−18.99	10.97	−1.73			
2 Weeks									
Total	MMS	1/83–10/84	187	16.57	3.37	4.92			
UK			47	13.49	6.70	2.01			
WG			47	20.28	7.43	2.73			
SW			46	19.95	6.42	3.11			
JA			47	12.63	6.25	2.02			
1 Month									
Total	MMS	10/84–2/86	176	−23.44	6.78	−3.46	−19.59	6.31	−3.10
UK			44	−22.04	15.19	−1.45	−13.98	13.26	−1.05
WG			44	−26.08	12.62	−2.07	−20.59	11.77	−1.75
SW			44	−21.09	13.96	−1.51	−18.02	13.12	−1.37
JA			44	−24.57	12.27	−2.00	−25.88	12.10	−2.14
3 Months									
Total	MMS	1/83–10/84	187	18.53	2.88	6.44	14.51	2.86	5.08
UK			47	18.38	5.91	3.11	14.29	5.90	2.42
WG			47	22.01	5.89	3.73	18.36	5.99	3.07
SW			46	22.23	5.20	4.28	18.74	4.85	3.86
JA			47	11.58	5.14	2.25	6.75	4.97	1.36

Table 13.3 (continued)

Total	Economist	6/81–12/85	190	9.97	2.92	3.42	3.04	2.73	1.12
UK			38	10.09	6.66	1.51	6.37	5.88	1.08
FR			38	9.61	6.47	1.48	0.49	5.98	0.08
WG			38	11.02	6.45	1.71	3.55	5.90	0.60
SW			38	10.83	7.03	1.54	4.52	6.73	0.67
JA			38	8.29	5.95	1.39	0.30	5.84	0.05
6 Months									
Total	Economist	6/81–12/85	180	11.70	3.20	3.66	4.48	3.03	1.48
UK			36	11.32	6.71	1.69	7.10	6.24	1.14
FR			36	11.08	7.13	1.55	2.15	6.71	0.32
WG			36	13.56	7.16	1.89	5.36	6.63	0.81
SW			36	12.77	7.80	1.64	6.37	7.37	0.86
JA			36	9.76	6.84	1.43	1.41	6.65	0.21
Total	Amex	1/76–8/85	51	−2.11	2.82	−0.75	−3.92	2.61	−1.50
Early Period		6/76–12/78	26	−7.78	2.94	−2.65	−7.93	2.80	−2.83
Later Period		6/81–8/85	25	3.79	4.59	0.83	0.26	4.30	0.06
12 Months									
Total	Economist	6/81–12/85	155	14.83	2.23	6.64	9.00	2.39	3.77
UK			31	13.73	4.96	2.77	10.39	5.46	1.90
FR			31	15.10	4.75	3.18	7.20	5.09	1.41
WG			31	17.02	4.72	3.60	10.02	4.82	2.08
SW			31	16.73	5.06	3.31	12.13	5.41	2.24
JA			31	11.59	5.02	2.31	5.15	5.27	0.98
Total	Amex	1/76–8/84	46	0.71	2.52	0.28	0.04	2.30	0.02
Early Period		6/76–12/78	26	−9.05	3.20	−2.83	−7.92	3.36	−2.36
Later Period		6/81–8/84	20	13.40	1.07	12.52	10.38	1.10	9.42

Note: Degrees of freedom used to estimate standard deviation (SD) of the mean are the number of nonoverlapping observations of each data set.

$$\Delta s_{t+1}^e = -g\Delta s_t, \tag{3}$$

where Δs_t is the most recent observed change in the log of the exchange rate and g is hypothesized to be less than zero. (Again, static expectations would be the special case where $g = 0$.) It has long been a concern of critics of floating exchange rates that bandwagon expectations would render the system unstable. For example, Ragnar Nurkse argued:

[Speculative] anticipations are apt to bring about their own realization. Anticipatory purchases of foreign exchange tend to produce or at any rate to hasten the anticipated fall in the exchange value of the national currency, and the actual fall may set up or strengthen expectations of a further fall.... Exchange rates under such circumstances are bound to become highly unstable, and the influence of psychological factors may at times be overwhelming. (1944, p. 118)

Nurkse's view was challenged by Milton Friedman (1953), who argued that speculation would be stabilizing. "Speculation" can be defined as buying and selling of currency in response to expectations of exchange rate changes, as compared to the counterfactual case of static expectations. A property of bandwagon expectations is that the expected future spot rate as a function of the observed current spot rate has an elasticity that exceeds unity, as contrasted to static expectations, in which the elasticity is equal to unity. Because investors sell a currency that they expect to depreciate, it follows that under bandwagon expectations, speculation is destabilizing.

The remaining three models we discuss go in the opposite direction. They can all be subsumed under the label inelastic, or *stabilizing, expectations*: a change in the current spot rate induces a revision in the expected future level of the spot rate that, though it may be positive, is less than proportionate. An observed appreciation of the currency generates an anticipation of a future depreciation of the currency back, at least partway, toward its previously expected level. If speculators act on the basis of the expected future depreciation, they will put downward pressure on the price of the currency today; in other words, speculation will be stabilizing. One case of stabilizing expectations is equation (3) with g greater than zero. An equivalent representation would be

$$s_{t+1}^e = (1 - g)s_t + gs_{t-1}, \tag{4}$$

where s_t is the logarithm of the current spot rate and g is hypothesized to be positive. The hypothesis is a simple form of *distributed lag expectations*. Obviously we could have longer lags as well.

In tables 13.4 through 13.11, we can interpret the regression error as random measurement error in the survey data. Under the joint hypothesis

Table 13.4
Extrapolative expectations (independent variable: $s(t-1) - s(t)$)

Seemingly unrelated regressions[a] of survey expected depreciation:
$s^e(t+1) - s(t) = a + g(s(t-1) - s(t))$

Data set	Dates	g^c	$D\text{-}W^b$	DF	$t: g = 0$	R^2
Economist 3-month	6/81–12/85	0.0416	1.81	184	1.98[d]	0.30
		(0.0210)				
with AR(1) correction		0.0463		179	2.37[e]	0.38
		(0.0195)				
MMS 3-month	1/83–10/84	−0.0391	1.49	179	−2.32[e]	0.37
		(0.0168)				
with AR(1) correction		−0.0298		194	−1.46	0.19
		(0.0203)				
Economist 6-month	6/81–12/85	0.0730	1.36	184	3.25[f]	0.54
		(0.0225)				
with AR(1) correction		0.0832		179	3.53[f]	0.58
		(0.0236)				
Amex 6-month	1/76–8/85	0.2994	1.89	45	6.15[f]	0.81
		(0.0487)				
Economist 12-month	6/81–12/85	0.2018	1.47	184	6.82[f]	0.84
		(0.0296)				
with AR(1) correction		0.2638		179	10.51[f]	0.92
		(0.0251)				
Amex 12-month	1/76–8/85	0.3796	0.94	45	4.76[f]	0.72
		(0.0798)				

Notes: Asymptotic standard errors are shown in parentheses.
a. Amex 6 and 12-month regressions use OLS due to the small number of degrees of freedom.
b. The D-W statistic is the average of the equation-by-equation OLS Durbin-Watson statistics for each data set.
c. All equations are estimated allowing each currency its own constant term. To conserve space, estimates of these constant terms are omitted here, but are reported in Froot and Frankel (1986) and Frankel and Froot (1985).
d. Significant at the 10 percent level.
e. Significant at the 5 percent level.
f. Significant at the 1 percent level.

that the mechanism of expectations formation is specified correctly and that the measurement error is random, the parameter estimates are consistent. It should be noted that this joint hypothesis is particularly restrictive because the spot rate appears on the right-hand side; if a change in expected depreciation feeds back to affect both the contemporaneous spot rate and any element of the regression error, then the parameter estimates will be biased and inconsistent. Such simultaneous equation bias, however, is not a problem under our null hypothesis that expected depreciation is constant.

Table 13.4 reports the results of the Seemingly Unrelated Regressions (SUR)[9] of the survey expected depreciation on the recent change in the spot rate, equation (3), which we label under the general title of extrapolative expectations, where $g > 0$ represents the case of distributed lag and $g < 0$ represents the case of bandwagon expectations.[10] Most of the slope parameters in the column labeled g in table 13.4 are positive and significant at the 1 percent level. The evidence suggests that expectations are less than unit elastic with respect to the lagged spot rate, that is, expectations are stabilizing. For example, the point estimate of 0.04 in the three-month *Economist* data set implies that an appreciation of 10 percent today generates an expectation of a 0.4 percent depreciation over the next three months, a rate of 1.6 percent per year.

The Durbin-Watson (D-W) tests for serial correlation reported in table 13.4 (except those for the Amex data sets) are the averages of the equation-by-equation OLS regressions used in the first step of the SUR procedure. For this reason, and since the Amex data are irregularly spaced and thus are not true time-series, values of the D-W test must be interpreted with caution. Nevertheless, the null hypothesis of no "serial" correlation is still appropriate, and the low reported values of the statistic suggest that the standard errors are suspect. To correct for serial correlation in the residuals, we used a generalized three-stage least squares estimator that allows for contemporaneous as well as first-order serial correlation of each country's residual.[11] These results for the *Economist* and MMS data sets are reported beneath the uncorrected SUR estimates in table 13.4.[12] While we find some evidence of serial correlation in the data, the corrected coefficients are similar in size, and the standard errors are even more unfavorable to the bandwagon hypothesis than in the uncorrected seemingly unrelated regressions. The lone case of a negative point estimate for g, in the three-month MMS sample, loses its statistical significance under the correction for serial correlation.

Despite the rejection of bandwagon expectations in favor of the stabilizing distributed lag, it may still be true that psychological factors are important in foreign exchange markets. The absence of bandwagon effects in the data does not rule out the possibility of speculative bubbles. For example, rational bubbles which are constantly forming and popping would not yield systematic bandwagon effects in the spot rate.

Adaptive expectations are an old standby in the economist's arsenal of expectations models. The expected future spot rate is formed adaptively, as a weighted average of the current observed spot rate and the lagged expected rate:

$$s_{t+1}^e = (1 - \gamma_1)s_t + \gamma_1 s_t^e, \tag{5}$$

where γ_1 is hypothesized between 0 and 1 for expectations to be inelastic.[13]

We report the results of regressing expected depreciation on the lagged survey prediction error in table 13.5:

$$\Delta s_{t+1}^e = \gamma_1(s_t^e - s_t). \tag{5'}$$

Three of the six coefficients in the column labeled γ_1 are statistically significant. All three are positive, implying that expectations place positive weight on the previous prediction. The results in table 13.5 provide evidence in favor of the hypothesis that expectations are stabilizing.[14] The D-W statistics are again very low, particularly in the twelve-month data. When we use the three-stage least squares correction for serial correlation, the coefficient is significant in three out of four data sets.

The *regressive expectations* model was made popular by Rudiger Dornbusch (1976c). It is a more elegant specification, consistent with dynamic models in which variables such as goods prices converge toward their long-run equilibrium values over time in accordance with differential equations, or, in discrete time, in accordance with difference equations:

$$s_{t+1}^e = (1 - \vartheta)s_t + \vartheta \bar{s}_t. \tag{6}$$

Here $\bar{s}_t$ is the long-run equilibrium exchange rate, and ϑ (a number between 0 and 1 in this discrete-time version) is the speed at which s_t is expected to regress toward $\bar{s}_t$, as can perhaps be seen more clearly in the equivalent representation,

$$\Delta s_{t+1}^e = -\vartheta(s_t - \bar{s}_t). \tag{7}$$

The long-run equilibrium $\bar{s}_t$ can itself change. It is often assumed to obey

Table 13.5
Adaptive expectations (independent variable: $s^e(t) - s(t)$)

Seemingly unrelated regressions[a] of survey expected depreciation:
$s^e(t + 1) - s(t) = a + \gamma_1(s^e(t) - s(t))$

Data set	Dates	γ_1[c]	D-W[b]	DF	$t: \gamma_1 = 0$	R^2
Economist 3-month	6/81–12/85	0.0798	2.01	169	3.93[f]	0.63
		(0.0203)				
with AR(1) correction		0.0716		164	3.97[f]	0.64
		(0.0180)				
MMS 3-month	1/83–10/84	−0.0272	1.29	159	−1.26	0.15
		(0.0215)				
with AR(1) correction		−0.0234		154	−1.00	0.10
		(0.0234)				
Economist 6-month	6/81–12/85	0.0516	1.12	159	3.20[f]	0.53
		(0.0161)				
with AR(1) correction		0.0783		154	3.52[f]	0.58
		(0.0223)				
Amex 6-month	1/76–8/85	−0.0702	2.10	15	−0.58	0.04
		(0.1200)				
Economist 12-month	6/81–12/85	−0.0093	1.10	139	−0.38	0.02
		(0.0244)				
with AR(1) correction		0.1890		134	6.28[f]	0.81
		(0.0301)				
Amex 12-month	1/76–8/85	0.0946	0.55	31	4.47[f]	0.69
		(0.0212)				

Notes and footnotes: See table 13.4.

purchasing power parity, increasing proportionately in response to a change in the domestic money supply and price level.

In the econometric tests below, we try out two alternate formulations for $\bar{s}_t$. The simplest possible description of the long-run equilibrium is that it is constant over our sample. Thus we regress expected depreciation on the spot rate and constant terms for each country. The results are presented in table 13.6. A second specification for the long-run value of the exchange rate is that given by purchasing power parity (PPP). In this case, $\bar{s}_t$ moves with relative inflation differentials instead of remaining constant:

$$\bar{s}_t = s_0 + \log\left(\frac{P_t/P_0}{P_t^*/P_0^*}\right), \tag{8}$$

where s_0 is the log of the average nominal value of the foreign currency in terms of dollars, 1973–79, P_t and P_t^* are the current monthly levels of the

Table 13.6
Regressive expectations I (independent variable: $s(t)$; long-run equilibrium constant)

Seemingly unrelated regressions[a] of survey expected depreciation:
$s^e(t + 1) - s(t) = a - \theta s(t)$

Data set	Dates	θ^c	D-W[b]	DF	$t: \theta = 0$	R^2
Economist 3-month	6/81–12/85	0.0359	1.56	184	3.55[f]	0.58
		(0.0101)				
with AR(1) correction		0.0226		179	2.07[e]	0.32
		(0.0109)				
MMS 3-month	1/83–10/84	0.0100	1.46	179	0.63	0.04
		(0.0159)				
with AR(1) correction		0.0061		174	0.31	0.01
		(0.0195)				
Economist 6-month	6/81–12/85	0.0764	1.14	184	6.00[f]	0.80
		(0.0127)				
with AR(1) correction		0.0807		179	4.73[f]	0.71
		(0.0170)				
Amex 6-month	1/76–8/85	−0.0000	1.19	45	−0.00	0.00
		(0.0235)				
Economist 12-month	6/81–12/85	0.1724	1.03	184	10.70[f]	0.93
		(0.0161)				
with AR(1) correction		0.1905		179	10.48[f]	0.92
		(0.0182)				
Amex 12-month	1/76–8/85	0.0791	0.48	45	2.29[e]	0.37
		(0.0346)				

Notes and footnotes: See table 13.4.

U.S. and foreign CPIs, respectively, and P_0 and P_0^* are the average levels of the U.S. and foreign CPIs, 1973–79.

The general conclusions that come out of tables 13.6 and 13.7 are identical. Four of the six data sets give significant weight to the long-run equilibrium, in each case positive. Investors expect the spot rate to regress toward its long-run equilibrium. Note that this is a stronger property than the fact, which we discovered in tables 13.1a and 13.2, that investors forecast large depreciation on average throughout the 1980s. Regressivity requires not only that investors expect a currency that is above its long-run level to depreciate, but also that they expect it to depreciate by more the further it is above its equilibrium value. In table 13.7, the Economist regressions at three-, six-, and twelve-month horizons show that deviations from PPP are expected to decay at annual rates of $(1 - 0.9881^4) \approx 5$ percent, $(1 - 0.9218^2) \approx 15$ and 24 percent, respectively. This last figure implies that the expected half-life of PPP deviations is 2.5 years.

Table 13.7
Regressive expectations II (independent variable: $\bar{s}(t) - s(t)$; long-run equilibrium *PPP*)

Seemingly unrelated regressions[a] of survey expected depreciation:
$s^e(t+1) - s(t) = a + \theta(\bar{s}(t) - s(t))$

Data set	Dates	θ[c]	D-W[b]	DF	$t: \theta = 0$	R^2
Economist 3-month	6/81–12/85	0.0223 (0.0126)	1.66	184	1.78[d]	0.26
with AR(1) correction		0.0119 (0.0133)		179	0.89	0.08
MMS 3-month	1/83–10/84	−0.0207 (0.0146)	1.55	179	−1.41	0.18
with AR(1) correction		0.0083 (0.0194)		174	0.43	0.02
Economist 6-month	6/81–12/85	0.0600 (0.0159)	1.32	184	3.77[f]	0.61
with AR(1) correction		0.0782 (0.0221)		179	3.54[f]	0.58
Amex 6-month	1/76–8/85	0.0315 (0.0202)	1.22	45	1.56	0.21
Economist 12-month	6/81–12/85	0.1750 (0.0216)	1.25	184	8.10[f]	0.88
with AR(1) correction		0.2449 (0.0274)		179	8.93[f]	0.90
Amex 12-month	1/76–8/85	0.1236 (0.0276)	0.60	45	4.48[f]	0.69

Notes and footnotes: See table 13.4.

Clearly, if a high R^2 were our goal, more complicated models could have been reported. We estimated a more general specification for expectations, expanding the information set to include simultaneously the current and lagged spot rates, the long-run equilibrium rate, and the lagged expected spot rate. We then tested the entire set of nested hypotheses, beginning with this general specification and going all the way to static expectations. In particular, we considered as alternatives to the simple models discussed above hybrid specifications such as "adaptive-bandwagon":

$$\Delta s^e_{t+1} = \gamma(s^e_t - s_t) - g\Delta s_{t+1}.$$

The R^2s of these more complex permutations were higher than those reported in tables 13.4 through 13.7. However, the best fits were for models which are unfamiliar compared with the popular formulations above. Furthermore, the strongest statistical rejections were those reported here, of static expectations against the simpler extrapolative, adaptive, and regressive models; when estimating the hybrid models, by contrast, we were able statistically to accept the constraints implied by the simple models. For these reasons we do not report the results.

The central point of our analysis is to investigate the robustness of a rejection of static expectations, not to settle on any single model of expectations. The goodness of fit statistics in tables 13.4 through 13.7, however, give us an opportunity to compare the fits of these simple alternative specifications. From this set of alternatives, the best model appears to be the distributed lag.

13.4   Are Expectations Formed Rationally?

Now that we have an idea of the parameters describing the formation of investor expectations, we will see how well they correspond to the parameters describing the true process governing the spot rate. We could estimate first the mathematical expectation of the actual spot process conditional on each of the information sets considered in section 13.3, and only then test for equality with the process governing investors' expectations. Here we report directly regressions of the difference between investor expectations and the realized spot rate ($\Delta s^e_{t+1} - \Delta s_{t+1}$ or, equivalently, $s^e_{t+1} - s_{t+1}$) against the same variables as in the preceding section. Under the null hypothesis the coefficient should be zero, and the error term should be uncorrelated with the right-hand-side variables, that is, the spot rate prediction error should be purely random, as should be the case for any right-hand-side variables observed at time t. Furthermore, under the null hypothesis, the error term should be serially uncorrelated, which makes the econometrics easier. The logic is the same as in the existing literature of rational expectations tests, where expectations are measured by the forward rate rather than survey data, except that we are free of the problems presented by the risk premium.[15] Because a statistical rejection of the null hypothesis could in theory be due to the failure of the error term to have the proper normal distribution (the peso problem mentioned in section 13.2), or could be due to a learning period following a "regime change," rather than to a failure of investors to act rationally, we will use the terms "systematic expectational errors" or "bias in the sample" to describe the alternative hypothesis, in preference over a "failure of rational expectations."

In testing whether expectations are biased in the sample, there are added advantages in having first tested models of what variables matter for expectations. For those cases in which we fail to reject the null hypothesis, it helps to have an idea whether the right-hand-side variable is relevant to determining Δs_{t+1}^e and Δs_{t+1}; if not, the test for the presence of bias is not very powerful. For those cases when we do reject the null hypothesis, we will have a ready-made description of the nature of investors' bias. An explicit alternative hypothesis is lacking in most standard tests.

Econometric Issues

The tests of rational expectations below were performed by *OLS*, with standard errors calculated using a method of moments procedure. The usual *OLS* standard errors are inappropriate because of the contemporaneous correlation across countries, and a sampling interval many times smaller than the forecast horizon. In the previous section, where expected depreciation is the regressand, a long forecast horizon and short sampling interval do not themselves imply that the error term is serially correlated, since expectations are formed using only contemporaneous and past information. When the prediction error is on the left-hand side, however, we have the usual problem induced by overlapping observations: under the null hypothesis the error term, consisting of new information that becomes available during the forecast interval, is a moving average process of an order equal to the number of sampling intervals contained in the forecast horizon minus one.[16] The *OLS* point estimates remain consistent in spite of the serially correlated residuals. The method of moments estimate of the sample covariance matrix of the *OLS* estimate, $\hat{\beta}$ is

$$\hat{\Theta} = (X'_{NT}X_{NT})^{-1}X'_{NT}\hat{\Omega}X_{NT}(X'_{NT}X_{NT})^{-1}, \tag{9}$$

where X_{NT} is the matrix of regressors of size N (countries) times T (time). The (i,j)th element of the unrestricted covariance matrix, $\hat{\Omega}$ is

$$\hat{\omega}(i,j) = \frac{1}{NT-k} \sum_{l=0}^{N-1} \sum_{t=k+1}^{T} \hat{u}_{t+lT}\hat{u}_{t-k+lT}$$

$$\text{for } mT - n \leq k \leq mT + n; \quad m = 0, \ldots, N-1$$

$$= 0 \text{ otherwise,} \tag{10}$$

where n is the order of the MA process, $\hat{u}_{t+lT}$ is the *OLS* residual, and $k = |i - j|$. Such an unrestricted estimate of Ω uses many degrees of freedom; in the case of the *Economist* twelve-month data, $N = 5$ and $n = 8$, so that the covariance matrix has $N(N+1)n/2$ or 120 independent parameters. We instead estimated a restricted covariance matrix, $\tilde{\Omega}$, with typical element:

$$\tilde{\omega}(t + lT, t - k + pT) = \frac{1}{N-1} \sum_{l=0}^{N} \hat{\omega}(t + lT, t - k + pT)$$

$$\text{if } l = p \text{ and } -n \le k \le n$$

$$= \frac{2}{N(N-1)} \sum_{p=0}^{N-1} \sum_{l=0}^{N-1} \hat{\omega}(t + lt, t - k + pT)$$

$$\text{if } l \ne p \text{ and } -n \le k \le n$$

$$= 0 \text{ otherwise.} \tag{11}$$

These restrictions have the effect of averaging the own-currency and cross-currency autocorrelation functions of the OLS residuals, respectively, bringing the number of independent parameters down to $2n$.

A problem with our estimate of $\tilde{\Omega}$ is that it need not be positive definite in small samples. Whitney Newey and Kenneth West (1985) offer a consistent estimate of Ω that discounts the jth order autocovariance by $1 - (j/(m + 1))$, and is positive definite in finite samples. For any given sample size, however, there is still a question of how large m must be to guarantee positive definiteness. In the subsequent regressions we tried $m = n$ (which Newey and West themselves suggest) and $m = 2n$. We report standard errors using the latter value of m because they were consistently larger than those using the former.

The Results

We now turn to the results of our tests of rationality within the three models examined in section 13.3.

In table 13.4, we found that if investors' expected future spot rate is viewed as a distributed lag of the actual spot rate, then the weight on the current spot rate is less than one and the weight on the lagged spot rate greater than zero. Is this degree of inelasticity of expectations rational? Or is the future spot rate more likely to lie in the direction of the current spot rate, as would be the case if the actual spot rate followed a random walk?

Table 13.8 shows highly significant rejections for three of the six data sets of the hypothesis that expectations exhibit no systematic bias. As in the case of unconditional bias, the results are immune to measurement error in the survey data, provided the error is orthogonal to the regressors. The *Economist* twelve-month data significantly overestimate the tendency for the spot rate to keep moving in the same direction as it had been, while

Table 13.8
Rationality of extrapolative expectations (independent variable: $s(t-1) - s(t)$)

OLS regressions of survey prediction errors: $s^e(t+1) - s(t+1) = a + g(d(t-1) - s(t))$

Data set	Dates	g	DF	$t: g = 0$	R^2	F test $a = 0, g = 0$
Economist 3-month	6/81–12/85	0.2501 (0.1695)	184	1.48	0.19	1.06
MMS 3-month	1/83–10/84	−0.2084 (0.1506)	182	−1.38	0.18	6.67[c]
Economist 6-month	6/81–12/85	0.2449 (0.2904)	174	0.84	0.07	0.97
Amex 6-month	1/76–8/85	1.0987 (0.3776)	45	2.91[c]	0.48	3.32[c]
Economist 12-month	6/81–12/85	−0.6516 (0.2564)	149	−2.54[b]	0.42	8.09[c]
Amex 12-month	1/76–8/85	2.0001 (0.3667)	40	5.45[c]	0.77	5.28[c]

Notes: All equations are estimated allowing each currency its own constant term. To conserve space, estimates of the constants are omitted here, but are reported in our paper (1986). Methods of moments standard errors are shown in parentheses.
a. Significant at the 10 percent level.
b. Significant at the 5 percent level.
c. Significant at the 1 percent level.

the Amex data *underestimate* the tendency to keep moving in the same direction. The diversity of results is not primarily attributable to a difference between the two surveys. Table 13.4 showed similar parameters of expectations formation in the two surveys. Rather the difference is primarily attributable to the behavior of the actual spot process during the two different sample periods for which data are available. If one includes in the sample the years 1976–78, during which the Amex data are available, then more extrapolative expectations would have been correct, because the dollar had a long run of declines followed by a long run of appreciation. But if one considers the period 1981–85 alone, *less* extrapolative expectations would have been correct, because first differences of the actual spot rate (though usually negative) were not positively serially correlated.[17] The conclusion is that the actual spot process is significantly different from investors' expectations, but it is also more complicated than a simple distributed lag with constant weights, whether correctly perceived by investors or not.

In table 13.5, we found that investors' expectations can be viewed as adaptive. When investors make a prediction error, they revise their previ-

Table 13.9
Rationality of adaptive expectations (independent variable: $s^e(t) - s(t)$)

OLS regressions of survey prediction errors: $s^e(t + 1) - s(t + 1) = a + \gamma(s^e(t) - s(t))$

Data set	Dates	γ	DF	$t: \gamma = 0$	R^2	F test $a = 0, \gamma = 0$
Economist 3-month	6/81–12/85	0.4296 (0.1395)	169	3.08ᶜ	0.51	3.39ᶜ
MMS 3-month	1/83–10/84	−0.2289 (0.2207)	158	−1.04	0.11	6.35ᶜ
Economist 6-month	6/81–12/85	0.0884 (0.2488)	149	0.36	0.01	1.52
Amex 6-month	1/76–8/85	0.5571 (0.5227)	15	1.07	0.11	1.04
Economist 12-month	6/81–12/85	−1.0310 (0.2452)	109	−4.20ᶜ	0.66	10.27ᶜ
Amex 12-month	1/76–8/85	0.5972 (0.1007)	25	5.93ᶜ	0.80	8.05ᶜ

Notes and footnotes: See table 13.8.

ous expectations most, though not all, of the way to the new observed spot rate. Would they do better to revise their expectation even further, or less far? Assume that the true best predictor of the future spot rate is a weighted average of the current spot rate and the lagged expectation:

$$s_{t+1} = (1 - \gamma_2)s_t + \gamma_2 s_t^e + \varepsilon_{t+1}. \tag{12}$$

Then investors' expectations would be rational if and only if γ_1 from equation (5) were equal to γ_2 from equation (12). Taking the difference of the two equations,

$$s_{t+1}^e - s_{t+1} = (\gamma_1 - \gamma_2)(s_t^e - s_t) + \varepsilon_{t+1}. \tag{13}$$

In table 13.9, we regress the expectational error against the lagged expectational error as in equation (13). Such tests of serial correlation are a common way of testing for efficiency in the forward market.[18] In the context of adaptive expectations, we can see clearly what the alternative hypothesis is. Positive serial correlation is precisely the hypothesis that expectations are insufficiently adaptive; investors could avoid making the same error repeatedly if they revised their expectations all the way to the new spot rate. Negative serial correlation is the hypothesis that expectations are overly adaptive. Table 13.9 shows that expectations are insufficiently adaptive in four of six data sets. In two cases, the tendency for investors to put too little weight on the current spot rate is highly signifi-

Table 13.10
Rationality of regressive expectations I (independent variable: $s(t)$; long-run equilibrium constant)

OLS regressions of survey prediction errors: $s^e(t + 1) - s(t + 1) = a - \theta s(t)$

Data set	Dates	θ	DF	$t: \theta = 0$	R^2	F test $a = 0, \theta = 0$
Economist 3-month	6/81–12/85	−0.1686 (0.0934)	184	−1.80[a]	0.27	1.20
MMS 3-month	1/83–10/84	−0.0288 (0.1431)	182	−0.20	0.00	6.02[c]
Economist 6-month	6/81–12/85	−0.3582 (0.1936)	174	−1.85[a]	0.28	1.40
Amex 6-month	1/76–8/85	−0.0427 (0.1647)	45	−0.26	0.01	2.07[a]
Economist 12-month	6/81–12/85	−0.4167 (0.1895)	149	−2.20[c]	0.35	6.54[c]
Amex 12-month	1/76–8/85	0.1904 (0.2919)	40	0.65	0.05	0.36

Notes and footnotes: See table 13.8.

Table 13.11
Rationality of regressive expectations II (independent variable: $\bar{s}(t) - \bar{s}(t)$; long-run equilibrium PPP)

OLS regressions of survey prediction errors: $s^e(t + 1) - s(t + 1) = a + \theta(\bar{s}(t) - \bar{s}(t))$

Data set	Dates	θ	DF	$t: \theta = 0$	R^2	F test $a = 0, \theta = 0$
Economist 3-month	6/81–12/85	−0.2041 (0.1100)	184	−1.86[a]	0.28	1.24
MMS 3-month	1/83–10/84	−0.0335 (0.1387)	182	−0.24	0.01	6.01[c]
Economist 6-month	6/81–12/85	−0.4344 (0.2252)	174	−1.93[a]	0.29	1.49
Amex 6-month	1/76–8/85	0.0343 (0.1643)	45	0.21	0.00	1.78
Economist 12-month	6/81–12/85	−0.5090 (0.2227)	149	−2.29[b]	0.37	6.48[c]
Amex 12-month	1/76–8/85	0.4278 (0.2412)	40	1.77[a]	0.26	0.85

Notes and footnotes: See table 13.8.

cant statistically. In one case (the *Economist* twelve-month data), investors put too much weight on the current spot rate relative to the weight they place on the lagged expectation: these expectations appear to be overly adaptive.[19]

In tables 13.6 and 13.7 we found that investors expected the spot rate to regress over the subsequent year toward a long-run equilibrium, at a rate of up to 24 percent of the existing gap. In tables 13.10 and 13.11 we test whether this regressive expectation is borne out by reality. An earlier version of this chapter that included data only up to March 1985 showed that the *Economist* data were overly regressive. But now in both the *Economist* and MMS data the actual spot rate on average regressed toward equilibrium to an even greater extent than investors expected. In the case of the *Economist* twelve-month data, the highly significant coefficient is evidence that investors systematically underestimated the degree of regressivity. But the results are dominated by the peaking of the dollar in 1985. When the years 1976–78 are included (the Amex sample), there is on average no tendency for the spot rate to regress toward equilibrium. Again, the finding of systematic expectational errors is fairly robust, but the sign is sensitive to the precise sample period.

13.5   Thoughts on "The" Expected Exchange Rate

Several considerations suggest that, if we were to reject the hypothesis of rational expectations, the alternative hypothesis would have to be more complex than the simple models considered above. In table 13.3, we found that investors systematically overpredicted the depreciation of the dollar in the 1980s and systematically underpredicted its depreciation in the late 1970s. Similarly, there was a consistent tendency for investors to overestimate the speed of regression before 1985 and to underestimate it thereafter. Such findings suggest the possibility that the nature of the forecasting bias changes over time. Investors could even be rational, and yet make repeated mistakes of the kind detected here, if the true model of the spot process is evolving over time. There is nothing in our results to suggest that it is easy to make money speculating in the foreign exchange markets.

Another puzzle is that the gap between the forward discount and the expected rate of depreciation in the survey data is so large, an average of 7 percent for the *Economist* six-month data. To explain the gap as a risk premium would require (1) that assets denominated in other currencies were perceived in the early 1980s as riskier than assets denominated in dollars, and (2) that investors are highly risk averse. An alternative is the possibility that investors do not base their actions on a single homogeneous expectation such as regressive expectations. If expectations are heterogeneous, then the forward discount that is determined in market equilibrium could be a convex combination of regressive expectations and other forecasts that are closer to static expectations.

There is a third clue that expectations are more complex than a simple homogeneous model such as those estimated above. In our results the three-month survey data exhibit a lower speed of regression toward the long-run equilibrium, even when annualized, than do the six-month data, and the six-month survey data exhibit a lower speed of regression than do the twelve-month data. This pattern in the term structure suggests the possibility that those investors who think longer term tend to be the ones who subscribe to regressive expectations, and those who think shorter term tend to be the ones who subscribe to forecasts that are closer to static expectations.

In this chapter we have treated exchange rate expectations as homogeneous, for the simple reason that almost all the literature, both theoretical and empirical, does so. Our goal here has been to test standard propositions about "the" expected rate of depreciation, whether it is nonzero, whether it is inelastic, whether it is rational, and so on. But in fact, each forecaster has his or her own expectation. The *Economist* six-month survey, for example, reports a high-low range around the median response; it averages 15.2 percent for the five exchange rates.[20] Different models may be in use at one time. We believe that heterogeneous expectations and their role in determining market dynamics are important areas for future research.[21]

13.6 Conclusions

To summarize our findings:

1. Exchange rate expectations are not static. The observed nonzero forward discount numbers, far from being attributable to a positive risk premium on the dollar during the recent period, have *understated* the degree of expected dollar depreciation, which was consistently large and positive.

2. Exchange rate expectations do not exhibit bandwagon effects. We find that the elasticity of the expected future spot rate with respect to the current spot rate is in general significantly less than unity; expectations put positive weight on the "other factor," regardless of whether it is the lagged spot rate (distributed lag expectations), lagged expected rate (adaptive

expectations), or the long-run equilibrium rate (regressive expectations). The general finding of inelastic expectations is important because it implies that a current increase in the spot exchange rate itself generates anticipations of a future decrease, as in the overshooting model, which should work to moderate the extent of the original increase. Speculation is stabilizing.

3. While expected depreciation is large in magnitude, the actual spot exchange rate process may be close to a random walk, giving rise to unconditional bias in the survey forecast errors during the 1980s. In view of point 2, a spot process that is close to a random walk would suggest that expectations are less elastic than is rational. Indeed, we find statistically significant bias conditional on, for example, lagged expectational errors. This is the same finding common in tests of efficiency in the forward exchange market, but it now cannot be attributed to a risk premium.

4. The nature of the rejection of rational expectations strongly depends on the sample period. During the 1981–85 period, the actual spot process did not behave according to investors' expectations that the currency would return toward its previous equilibrium, but, after February 1985, the dollar depreciated at a rate in excess of what was expected. It seems likely that the actual spot rate process is more complicated than any of the models tested here.

5. While this chapter adopted the standard theoretical and empirical framework that assumes homogeneous expectations, a number of clues suggest that investigating heterogeneous investor expectations would be a useful avenue for future research.

Appendix 13A

Here we describe the construction of the *Economist*, Amex, and MMS data sets more specifically.

The *Economist Financial Review* conducted thirty-eight surveys beginning in June 1981 through December 1985. Surveys took place on a specific day on which the foreign exchange markets were open. Respondents were asked for their expectations of the value of the five major currencies against the dollar in three-, six-, and twelve-months' time. We carefully matched a given day's survey results with that day's actual spot and forward rates, and with actual spot rates as close as possible to 90, 180, and 365 days into the future.

The *Amex Bank Review* conducted twelve surveys beginning in January 1976 through July 1985. Respondents were asked for their expectations of the value of the same five currencies in six- and twelve-months time. The first three surveys, however, included only the pound and the mark. Future foreign exchange market realizations were matched in a manner similar to that used for the *Economist* data. Amex Bank surveys were conducted by mail, and hence it was impossible to pick specific days which were used by all respondents as reference points with any degree of certainty. Since exchange rates vary so much within a month, two methods of choosing the contemporaneous spot rate (and the corresponding future rates respondents were predicting) were employed. First, single days within the survey period were selected. Second, thirty-day averages of daily rates were constructed to encompass the entire survey period. Since both methods yielded very similar quantitative results in the body of the chapter, the results from the latter Amex data set are reported only in the NBER working paper version.

Between January 1983 and October 1984, MMS conducted forty-seven surveys (one each two weeks) of the value of the dollar against the pound, mark, Swiss franc, and yen in three-months' time. Matching of actual spot and forward rates was done in a manner similar to that used for the *Economist* survey.

Actual market spot and forward rates were taken from DRI. They represent the average of the morning bid and ask rates from New York. Lagged exchange rates (used for extrapolative expectations) are market rates approximately ninety days before survey dates.

Specific dates on which the surveys were conducted, and for which actual market data was obtained, are contained in Tables A1, A2, and A3 in Frankel and Froot (1985).

Acknowledgment

This is an extensively revised version of NBER Working Paper No. 1672. We thank Barbara Bruer, John Calverly, Louise Cordova, Kathryn Dominguez, Laura Knoy, Stephen Marris, and Money Market Services, Inc. for help in obtaining data, the National Science Foundation (under grant no. SES-8218300), the Institute for Business and Economic Research at UC-Berkeley, and the Alfred P. Sloan Foundation's doctoral dissertation program for research support.

14

Understanding the U.S. Dollar in the Eighties: The Expectations of Chartists and Fundamentalists

with Kenneth A. Froot

14.1 Introduction

There is general agreement that the large appreciation of the dollar from 1980 to February 1985 was attributable to an increase in the demand for dollar assets relative to other currencies. The only alternative hypothesis would be a decrease in the supply of dollar assets relative to other currencies. Given the rapid rate of increase in the supply of U.S. assets as measured by the federal government deficit, and the related current account deficit, it does not seem that asset supplies moved the right way to explain the rise in the value of the dollar.

There is less agreement about why investors suddenly found dollar assets so much more attractive after 1980. One set of explanations based on fundamentals is that there was an increase in the expected rate of return on dollar assets—a decline in the U.S. expected inflation rate, increase in the interest rate, or combination of the two—relative to other countries' assets.

A second set of explanations would attribute the increased demand for dollar assets to a self-confirming increase in expected future appreciation of the dollar (or decrease in expected future depreciation). By self-confirming we mean that the change in expectations is not driven by fundamentals; the dollar may have been on a rational speculative bubble path.

A third set of explanations is that there was an increase in the perceived safety of U.S. assets relative to other countries. This is the so-called safe-haven explanation.

We have concluded elsewhere (for example, Frankel and Froot, 1986a) that the increase in the real interest differentials between the United States and its trading partners readily explains most of the 1981–84 appreciation of the dollar but that this standard explanation misses some of the dynamics, particularly the last 20 percent or so of the appreciation up to

February 1985.[1] We have also argued that the alternatives which have been proposed, the safe-haven and rational speculative bubble hypotheses, are even less capable of explaining how the appreciation could have persisted for four years. It thus seems that a new theory is called for.

In this chapter we propose the outlines of a model of a speculative bubble that is not constrained by the assumption of rational expectations. The model features three classes of actors: fundamentalists, chartists, and portfolio managers. None of the three acts utterly irrationally, in the sense that each performs the specific task assigned him in a reasonable, realistic way. Fundamentalists think of the exchange rate according to a model—say, the Dornbusch overshooting model for the sake of concreteness—that would be exactly correct if there were no chartists in the world. Chartists do not have fundamentals such as the long-run equilibrium rate in their information set; instead they use autoregressive models—say, simple extrapolation for the sake of concreteness—that have only the time series of the exchange rate itself in the information set. Finally, portfolio managers, the actors who actually buy and sell foreign assets, form their expectations as a weighted average of the predictions of the fundamentalists and chartists. The portfolio managers update the weights over time in a rational Bayesian manner, according to whether the fundamentalists or the chartists have recently been doing a better job of forecasting. Thus each of the three is acting rationally subject to certain constraints. Yet the model departs from the reigning orthodoxy in that the agents could do better, in expected value terms, if they knew the complete model. When the bubble takes off agents are irrational in the sense that they learn about the model more slowly than they change it. Furthermore, the model may be unstable in the neighborhood of the fundamentals equilibrium but stable around a value for the dollar that is far from that equilibrium.

14.2   Fundamentalists and Chartists

In Frankel and Froot (1986a) we presented evidence supporting the following five propositions, each with elements of paradox.

1. The dollar continued to rise after mid-1984, even after all fundamentals (the interest differential, current account, etc.) apparently began moving the wrong way. The only explanation left would seem to be, almost tautologically, that investors were responding to a rising expected rate of change in the value of the dollar. In other words, the dollar was on a bubble path.

2. Evidence suggests that the investor-expected rate of depreciation reflected in the forward discount is not equal to the rationally expected rate of depreciation. The failure of a fall in the dollar to materialize in four years implies that the rationally expected rate of depreciation was less than the forward discount.

3. On the other hand, current account calculations in the spirit of Krugman (1985) and Marris (1985) suggested that the rationally expected rate of depreciation was greater than the current forward discount.

4. Data from surveys show that the respondents during 1981–85 did indeed hold an expected rate of depreciation substantially greater than the forward discount.[2] But interpreting their responses as true investor expectations, and interpreting the excess over the forward premium as a negative risk premium, raises several problems. First, if investors seriously expected the dollar to depreciate so fast, why did they buy dollars? Second, the theory of exchange risk says that the risk premium should generally be small and, for the dollar in the 1980s, that it probably moved in the positive direction.

5. In the safe-haven theory, a perceived shift in country risk rather than exchange risk might seem to explain many of the foregoing paradoxes. However, the covered differential between European and U.S. interest rates actually fell after 1982, suggesting that perceptions of country risk, if anything, shifted against the United States.

The model of fundamentalists and chartists that we are proposing has been designed to reconcile these conflicting conclusions. To begin with, we hypothesize that the views represented in the American Express and *Economist* six-month surveys are primarily fundamentalist, like the views of Krugman and Marris (and most other economists). But it may be wrong to assume that investors' expectations are necessarily the ones reported in the six-month surveys or that they are even homogeneous (as most of our models do). Expectations are heterogeneous. Our model suggests that the market gives heavy weight to the chartists, whose expected rate of change in the value of the dollar has been on average much closer to zero, perhaps even positive. Paradox (4) is answered if fundamentalists' expectations are not the only ones determining positions that investors take in the market.

The increasing dollar overvaluation after the interest differential peaked in 1982 or 1984 would be explained by a falling market-expected rate of future depreciation (or rising expected rate of appreciation), with no necessary basis in fundamentals. The market-expected rate of depreciation declined over time, not necessarily because of any change in the expectations held by chartists or fundamentalists, but rather because of a shift in the weights assigned to the two by the portfolio managers, who are the agents who take positions in the market and determine the exchange rate. They gradually put less and less weight on the big-depreciation forecasts of the fundamentalists, as these forecasts continue to be proven false, and more and more weight on the chartists.

Before we proceed to show how such a model works, we offer one piece of evidence that there is not a single homogeneous expected rate of depreciation reflected in the survey data: the very short-term expectations (one-week and two-week) reported in a third survey of market participants, by Money Market Services, Inc., behave very differently from the medium-term expectations (three, six, or twelve month) reported in any of the three surveys.[3]

Table 14.1 shows expected depreciation (from all three surveys) at a variety of time horizons. Perhaps most striking is a large fall in the standard deviation of the mean as the forecast horizon increases. At the short end of the spectrum, none of the means from the one-week forecasts is significantly different from zero at the 1 percent level, and the standard deviations are large, ranging from 4.2 percent to 9.1 percent.[4] At the other extreme, the one-year forecast horizon, all of the means are highly significant with t statistics approaching 30, and the standard deviations are below 0.6 percent. The intermediate horizons conform to this pattern of decline.

A second striking fact is that the one-week and one-month surveys, which were conducted only for 10/84 to 9/85, indicate that respondents on average expected the dollar to appreciate, often at a rapid annual rate. During the comparable period for which twelve-month forecasts are available (1/85 to 4/84), expected depreciation was still large and positive at 7.32 percent as well as significant ($t = 8.29$). For more on the different behavior of long-term and short-term expectations in the survey data, see Frankel and Froot (1987b).

These two facts suggest that there are far more consistent views about the value of the dollar in the longer run than in the shorter run. While short-run expectations may predict appreciation or depreciation at different times, longer run forecasts consistently call for substantial depreciation. It is as if there are actually two models of the dollar operating, one at each end of the spectrum, and a blend in between. The fundamentalist model, for which we specify a Dornbusch overshooting model, can be identified with the longer run expectations. The chartist model, a simple ARIMA forecasting equation such as a random walk, might be identified with the shorter run. Under this view, respondents use some weighted average of the two models in formulating their expectations for the value of the dollar at a given future date, with the weights depending on how far off that date is.

These results suggest an alternative interpretation of how chartist and fundamentalist views are aggregated in the marketplace, an aggregation that takes place without the benefit of portfolio managers. It is possible that the chartists are simply people who tend to think short term and the fundamentalists are people who tend to think long term. For example, the former may by profession be "traders," people who buy and sell foreign exchange on a short-term basis and have evolved different ways of thinking than the latter, who may by profession buy and hold longer term securities.[5]

In any case, one could interpret the two groups as taking positions in the market directly, rather than merely issuing forecasts for the portfolio managers to read. The market price of foreign exchange would then be determined by demand coming from both groups. But the weights that the market gives to the two change over time, according to the groups' respective wealths.[6] If the fundamentalists sell the dollar short and keep losing money, while the chartists go long and keep gaining, in the long run the fundamentalists will go bankrupt and there will only be chartists in the marketplace. The model that we develop in the next section pursues the portfolio managers' decision-making problem instead of the marketplace-aggregation idea, but the two are similar in spirit.

Yet another possible interpretation of the survey data is that the two ways of thinking represent conflicting forces within the mind of a single representative agent. When respondents answer the longer term surveys, they give the views that their economic logic tells them are correct. When they get into the trading room, they give greater weight to their instincts, especially if past bets based on their economic logic have been followed by ruinous "negative reinforcement." A respondent may think that when the dollar begins its plunge, he or she will be able to get out before everyone else does. This opposing instinctual force comes out in the survey only when the question pertains to the very short term—one or two weeks. It would be too big a contradiction for his conscience if a respondent were to report a one-week expectation of dollar depreciation that was (proportionately) just as big as the answer to the six-month question, at the same time that he or she was taking a long position in dollars. Again, we prefer the interpretation where the survey reflects the true expectations of the respondent, and the market trading is done by some higher authority; but others may prefer the more complex psychological interpretation.

Table 14.1
The term structure of expected depreciation and prediction errors (in percent per annum)

Forecast horizon	Survey source	Dates	N	Expected depreciation $s^e(t+1) - s(t)$			Survey prediction error $s^e(t+1) - s(t+1)$			Forward discount $f(t) - s(t)$			Forward rate prediction error $f(t) - s(t+1)$		
				Mean	SD of Mean	t stat	Mean	SD of Mean	t stat	Mean	SD of Mean	t stat	Mean	SD of Mean	t stat
1 week															
Total	MMS	10/84–9/85	183	−8.13	4.23	−1.92	−23.36	10.55	−2.21						
UK			46	−24.26	9.08	−2.67	−41.13	25.70	−1.60						
WG			46	−3.81	7.58	−0.50	−19.40	20.23	−0.96		NA			NA	
SW			45	−0.75	9.96	−0.07	−13.88	23.58	−0.59						
JA			46	−3.53	6.74	−0.52	−18.81	13.41	−1.40						
2 weeks															
Total	MMS	1/83–10/84	187	−4.22	1.26	3.36	16.57	3.38	4.91						
UK			47	−2.66	2.48	−1.07	13.49	6.77	1.99						
WG			47	5.08	2.59	1.96	20.28	7.51	2.70		NA			NA	
SW			46	6.09	2.54	2.40	19.95	6.49	3.07						
JA			47	8.40	2.21	3.79	12.63	6.32	2.00						
1 month															
Total	MMS	10/84–9/85	48	−10.25	2.88	−3.56	−23.80	7.76	−3.07	−0.16	0.87	−0.18	−13.71	7.49	−1.83
UK			12	−25.06	6.07	−4.13	−38.95	20.29	−1.92	−5.63	2.09	−2.69	−19.52	19.52	−1.00
WG			12	−6.91	6.10	−1.13	−19.91	14.82	−1.34	1.56	1.47	1.06	−11.44	13.93	−0.82
SW			12	−6.38	5.15	−1.24	−19.59	17.09	−1.15	1.99	1.52	1.31	−11.22	16.76	−0.67
JA			12	−2.66	3.65	−0.73	−16.76	8.84	−1.90	1.45	0.77	1.87	−12.65	9.95	−1.27

Table 14.1 (continued)

3 months

Total	MMS	1/83–10/84	187	7.76	0.38	20.53	18.53	2.89	15.52	3.75	0.17	21.52	14.51	2.87	5.07
UK			47	4.46	0.55	8.08	18.38	5.98	3.07	0.37	0.19	1.96	14.29	5.97	2.40
WG			47	8.33	0.62	13.45	22.01	5.96	3.69	4.68	0.14	34.37	18.36	6.05	3.03
SW			47	9.62	1.01	9.51	22.23	5.26	4.23	6.13	0.14	43.69	18.74	4.91	3.82
JA			47	8.68	0.54	15.95	11.58	5.20	2.23	3.85	0.16	23.77	6.75	5.02	1.35
Total	Economist	6/81–8/85	165	10.03	0.63	15.80	15.54	2.75	5.64	2.47	0.36	6.82	7.98	2.59	3.09
UK			33	5.16	1.34	3.84	14.38	6.80	2.11	0.47	0.36	1.34	9.69	6.07	1.60
FR			33	5.57	1.08	5.17	15.88	5.80	2.74	−4.23	0.70	−6.07	6.08	5.42	1.12
WG			33	12.79	1.17	10.91	17.19	5.86	2.93	4.54	0.21	21.26	8.94	5.41	1.65
SW			33	12.96	1.11	11.68	16.16	6.95	2.33	6.39	0.33	19.30	9.58	6.63	1.45
JA			33	13.67	1.51	9.04	14.10	5.16	2.73	5.16	0.46	11.25	5.59	5.17	1.08

6 months

Total	Economist	6/81–8/85	165	9.88	0.45	21.76	18.07	2.27	7.30	2.47	0.35	7.16	10.24	2.44	4.20
UK			33	5.03	0.74	6.81	16.82	5.52	3.05	0.64	0.29	2.20	11.99	5.38	2.23
FR			33	4.77	0.80	5.95	17.98	4.97	3.61	−4.30	0.57	−7.54	8.45	4.84	1.75
WG			33	12.97	0.68	19.17	20.33	5.20	3.91	4.52	0.19	24.22	11.35	5.06	2.24
SW			33	12.77	0.70	18.12	19.35	6.58	2.94	6.27	0.28	22.65	12.47	6.26	1.99
JA			33	13.86	0.69	19.98	15.86	5.07	3.13	5.21	0.42	12.51	6.93	5.32	1.30
Total	AMEX	7/81–8/84	20	8.03	0.90	8.88	13.01	3.34	3.89	3.89	0.93	4.19	8.88	3.13	2.84

The fragments of empirical evidence in table 14.1 are the only ones we will offer by way of testing our approach. The aim in what follows is to construct a model that reconciles the apparent contradictions discussed above. There will be no hypothesis testing.

We think of the value of the dollar as being driven by the decisions of portfolio managers who use a weighted average of the expectations of fundamentalists and chartists. Specifically

$$\Delta s_{t+1}^m = \omega_t \Delta s_{t+1}^f + (1 - \omega_t)\Delta s_{t+1}^c \tag{1}$$

where Δs_{t+1}^m is the rate of change in the spot rate expected by the portfolio managers, Δs_{t+1}^f and Δs_{t+1}^c are defined similarly for the fundamentalists and chartists, and ω_t is the weight given to fundamentalist views. For simplicity we assume $\Delta s_{t+1}^c = 0$. Thus equation (1) becomes

$$\Delta s_{t+1}^m = \omega_t \Delta s_{t+1}^f \tag{2}$$

or

$$\omega_t = \Delta s_{t+1}^m / \Delta s_{t+1}^f.$$

If we take the six-month forward discount to be representative of portfolio managers' expectations and the six-month survey to be representative of fundamentalists' expectations we can get a rough idea of how the weight, ω_t, varies over time.

Table 14.2 contains estimates of ω_t from the late 1970s to 1985. (There are, unfortunately, no survey data for 1980.) The table indicates a preponderance of fundamentalism in the late seventies; portfolio managers gave almost complete weight to this view. But beginning in 1981, as the dollar began to rise, the forward discount increased less rapidly than fundamentalists' expected depreciation, indicating that the market (or the portfolio

Table 14.2
Estimated weight given to fundamentalists by portfolio managers

	1976–79	1981	1982	1983	1984	1985
Forward discount (1)	1.06	3.74	3.01	1.10	3.07	−0.16
Survey expected depreciation (2)	1.20	8.90	10.31	10.42	11.66	4.00
$\omega = (1)/(2)$	0.88	0.42	0.29	0.11	0.26	−0.04

Note: Forward discount 1976–85 is at six months and includes data through September 1985 for the average of five currencies: the pound, French franc, mark, Swiss franc, and yen. Survey expected depreciation 1981–85 is from the *Economist* six-month survey data, and for 1976–79 is from the AMEX survey data for the same five currencies.

managers in our story) was beginning to pay less attention to the fundamentalists' view. By 1985 the market's expected depreciation had fallen to about zero. According to these computations, fundamentalists were being completely ignored.

While the above scenario solves the paradox posed in proposition (4), it leaves unanswered the question of how the weight ω_t, which appears to have fallen dramatically since the late 1970s, is determined by portfolio managers. Furthermore, if portfolio managers have small risk premia, and thus expect depreciation at a rate close to that predicted by the forward discount, we still must account for the spectacular rise of the dollar (proposition (1)), and resolve how the rationally expected depreciation differs from the forward discount (propositions (2) and (3)).

14.3   Portfolio Managers and Exchange Rate Dynamics

We have characterized the chartist and fundamentalist views of the world, and hinted at the approximate mix that portfolio managers would need to use if the market risk premium is to be near zero. We now turn to an examination of the behavior of portfolio managers, and of the determination of the equilibrium spot rate. In particular, we first focus exclusively on the dynamics of the spot rate which are generated by the changing expectations of portfolio managers. We then extend the framework to include the evolution of fundamentals that eventually must bring the dollar back down.

A general model of exchange rate determination can be written

$$s_t = c\Delta s_{t+1}^m + z_t \tag{3}$$

where $s(t)$ is the log of the spot rate, Δs_{t+1}^m is the rate of depreciation expected by "the market" (portfolio managers) and z_t represents other contemporaneous determinants. This very general formulation, in which the first term can be thought of as speculative factors and the second as fundamentals, has been used by Mussa (1976) and Kohlhagen (1979). An easy way to interpret equation (3) is in terms of the monetary model of Mussa (1976), Frenkel (1976) and Bilson (1978a). Then c would be interpreted as the semielasticity of money demand with respect to the alternative rate of return (which could be the interest differential, expected depreciation, or expected inflation differential; the three are equal if uncovered interest parity and purchasing power parity hold), and z_t would be interpreted as the log of the domestic money supply relative to the foreign (minus the log of relative income, or any other determinants of real money demand). An interpretation of equation (3) in terms of the portfolio-balance approach is slightly more awkward because of nonlinearity. But we could define

$$z_t = d_t - f_t - c(i_t - i_t^*) \tag{4}$$

where d_t is the log of the supply of domestic assets (including not only money but also bonds and other assets), f_t is the log of the supply of foreign assets, and $i_t - i_t^*$ is the nominal interest differential. Then equation (3) can be derived as a linear approximation to the solution for the spot rate in a system where the share of the portfolio allocated to foreign assets depends on the expected return differential or risk premium, $i_t - i_t^* - \Delta s_{t+1}^m$. If investors diversify their portfolios optimally, c can be seen to depend inversely on the variance of the exchange rate and the coefficient of relative risk-aversion.[7] In any case, the key point behind equation (3), common throughout the asset-market view of exchange rates, is that an increase in the expected rate of future depreciation will reduce demand for the currency today, and therefore will cause it to depreciate today.

This chapter imbeds in the otherwise standard asset pricing model given by equation (3) a form of market expectations that follows equation (1). That is, we assume that portfolio managers' expectations are a weighted average of the expectations of fundamentalists, who think the spot rate regresses to long-run equilibrium, and the expectations of chartists who use time-series methods. We define $\bar{s}$ to be the logarithm of the long-run equilibrium rate and v to be the speed of regression of s_t to $\bar{s}$. In the view of fundamentalists

$$\Delta s_{t+1}^f = \theta(\bar{s} - s_t). \tag{5}$$

In the context of some standard versions of equation (3)—the monetary model of Dornbusch (1976c) in which goods prices adjust slowly over time or the portfolio-balance models in which the stock of foreign assets adjusts slowly over time—it can be shown that equation (5) might be precisely the rational form for expectations to take if there were no chartists in the market, $\omega_t = 1$. (Unfortunately for the fundamentalists, the distinction is crucial; equation (5) will not be rational given the complete model.)

For example, if we define z_t in equation (3) as the interest differential we have

$$s_t = \alpha + c\theta(\bar{s} - s_t) - b(i_t - i_t^*). \tag{6}$$

Uncovered interest parity, $i_t - i^* = v(\bar{s} - s_t)$, implies that $\theta = 1/(b - c)$

and $\alpha = \bar{s}$. It is then straightforward to show that v can be rational within the Dornbusch (1976c) overshooting model.[8]

In the second group of models (Kouri, 1976a, and Rodriguez, 1980, are references), overshooting occurs because the stock of net foreign assets adjusts slowly through current account surpluses or deficits. A monetary expansion creates an imbalance in investors' portfolios which can be resolved only by an initial increase in the value of net foreign assets. This sudden depreciation of the domestic currency sets in motion an adjustment process in which the level of net foreign assets increases and the currency appreciates to its new steady state level. In such a model (which is similar to the simulation model below), the rate of adjustment of the spot rate, v, may also be rational, if there are no chartists. Repeating equation (6) but using the log of the stock of net foreign assets instead of the interest differential as the important fundamental, we have in continuous time

$$s(t) = \alpha + c\theta(\bar{s} - s(t)) - df(t). \tag{7}$$

Suppose the actual rate of depreciation is $\dot{s}(t) = v(\bar{s} - s(t))$. Equation (7) then can be rewritten in terms of deviations from the steady state levels of the exchange rate and net foreign assets, $\bar{s}$ and $\bar{f}$,

$$\dot{s}(t) = (-v/c\theta)(\bar{s} - s(t)) - (dv/c\theta)(\bar{f} - f(t)) \tag{8}$$

where rationality implies that $v = \theta$. Following Rodriguez (1980), the normalized current account surplus may also be expressed in deviations from steady state equilibrium:

$$\dot{f} = -q(\bar{s} - s(t)) + \gamma(\bar{f} - f(t)) \tag{9}$$

where q and γ are the elasticities of the current account with respect to the exchange rate and the level of net foreign assets, respectively. The system of equations (8) and (9) then has the rational expectations solution:

$$\theta = [c\gamma - 1 + ((1 - c\gamma)^2 + 4c(\gamma + dq))^{1/2}]/2c. \tag{10}$$

14.4 The Model with Exogenous Fundamentals

We now turn to describe the model, assuming for the time being that important fundamentals remain fixed. Regardless of which specification we use for the fundamentals, the existence of chartists whose view are given time-varying weights by the portfolio managers complicates the model. For simplicity we study the case in which the chartists believe the exchange rate follows a random walk, $\Delta s_{t+1}^c = 0$. Thus equation (1) becomes

$$\Delta s_{t+1}^m = \omega_t \theta(\bar{s} - s_t).$$ (1a)

Since the changing weights by themselves generate self-sustaining dynamics, the expectations of fundamentalists will no longer be rational, except for the trivial case in which fundamentalist and chartist expectations are the same, $\theta = 0$.

The "bubble" path of the exhange rate will be driven by the dynamics of portfolio managers' expected depreciation. We assume that the weight given to fundamentalist views by portfolio managers, ω_t, evolves according to

$$\Delta \omega_t = \delta(\hat{\omega}_{t-1} - \omega_{t-1}).$$ (11)

$\hat{\omega}_{t-1}$ is in turn defined as the weight, computed ex post, that would have accurately predicted the contemporaneous change in the spot rate, defined by the equation

$$\Delta s_t = \hat{\omega}_{t-1} \theta(\bar{s} - s_{t-1}).$$ (12)

Equations (11) and (12) give

$$\Delta \omega_t = \delta \Delta s_t / [\theta(\bar{s} - s_{t-1})] - \delta \omega_{t-1}.$$ (13)

The coefficient δ in equation (13) controls the adaptiveness of ω_t.

One interpretation for δ is that it is chosen by portfolio managers who use the principles of Bayesian inference to combine prior information with actual realizations of the spot process. This leads to an expression for δ which changes over time. To simplify the following anaylsis we assume that δ is constant; in appendix 14A, we explore more precisely the problem that portfolio managers face in choosing δ. The results that emerge there are qualitatively similar to those that follow here.

Taking the limit to continuous time, we can rewrite equation (13) as

$$\dot{\omega}(t) = \delta[\dot{s}(t)/[\theta(\bar{s} - s(t))] - \omega(t)] \quad \text{if } 0 < \omega(t) < 1;$$ (14)

if $\omega(t) = 0$ then

$$\begin{bmatrix} \dot{\omega}(t) = 0 & \text{if } \dot{s}(t) \leqslant 0 \\ \dot{\omega}(t) = (\delta\dot{s}(t)/[\theta(\bar{s} - s)] & \text{if } \dot{s}(t) > 0; \end{bmatrix}$$ (14a)

if $\omega(t) = 1$ then

$$\begin{bmatrix} \dot{\omega}(t) = 0 & \text{if } \dot{s}(t) \geqslant \theta(\bar{s} - s(t)) \\ \dot{\omega}(t) = (\delta\dot{s}(t)/[\theta(\bar{s} - s(t)] - \delta & \text{if } \dot{s}(t) < \theta(\bar{s} - s(t)) \end{bmatrix}$$ (14b)

where a dot over a variable indicates the total derivative with respect to time. The restrictions that are imposed when $\omega(t) = 0$ and $\omega(t) = 1$ are to keep $\omega(t)$ from moving outside the interval $[0,1]$. These restrictions are in the spirit of the portfolio manager's choice set: the portfolio manager can at most take one view or the other exclusively.

The evolution of the spot rate can be expressed by taking the derivative of equation (3) (for now holding z and the long-run equilibrium, $\bar{s}$, constant)

$$\dot{s}(t) = \dot{\omega}(t)(c\theta/[1 + c\theta\omega(t))](\bar{s} - s(t)). \tag{15}$$

Equations (14) and (15) can be solved simultaneously and rewritten, for interior values of ω, as

$$\dot{\omega}(t) = -[\delta\omega(t)(1 + c\theta\omega(t))]/[1 + c\theta\omega(t) - \delta c]; \quad \text{if } 0 < \omega(t) < 1 \tag{16}$$

$$\dot{s}(t) = [-\delta\omega(t)c\theta]/[1 + c\theta\omega(t) - \delta c](\bar{s} - s(t)). \tag{17}$$

In principle, an analytic solution to the differential equation (16) could be substituted into (17), and then (17) could be integrated directly.[9] For our purposes it is more desirable to use a finite difference method to simulate the motion of the system. In doing so we must pick values for the coefficients, c, v and δ, and starting values for $\omega(t)$ and $s(t)$.

To exclude any unreasonable time paths implied by equations (16) and (17), we impose the obvious sign restrictions on the coefficients. The parameter v must be positive and less than one if expectations are to be regressive, that is, if they are to predict a return to the long-run equilibrium at a finite rate. By definition, δ and $\omega(t)$ lie in the interval $[0,1]$ since they are weights. The coefficient c measures the responsiveness of the spot rate to changes in expected depreciation and must be positive to be sensible.

These restrictions, however, are not enough to determine unambiguously the sign of the denominator of equations (16) and (17). The three possibilities are that: $1 + cv\omega(t) - \delta c < 0$ for all ω; $1 + cv\omega(t) - \delta c < 0$ for all ω; and

$$1 + c\theta\omega(t) - \delta c \lesseqgtr 0 \quad \text{as} \quad \omega(t) \lesseqgtr \omega^*, \quad \text{where} \quad 0 < \omega^* < 1.[10]$$

If $1 + c\theta\omega(t) - \delta c < 0$, the system will be stable and will tend to return to the long-run equilibrium from any initial level of the spot rate. This might be the case if portfolio managers use only the most recent realization of the spot rate to choose $\omega(t)$, that is, if $\delta \approx 1$. If, on the other hand, portfolio managers give substantial weight to prior information so that δ is small, the expression $1 + c\theta\omega(t) - \delta c$ will be positive. In this case the spot rate will tend to move away from the long-run equilibrium if it is perturbed.

Let us assume that portfolio managers are slow learners.[11] What does this assumption imply about the path of the dollar? If we take as a starting point the late 1970s, when $s(t) \approx \bar{s}$ and when $\omega_t \approx 1$ (as the calculations presented in table 14.2 suggest), equation (17) says that the spot rate is in equilibrium, that $\dot{s}(t) = 0$. From equation (14b), we see that $\dot{\omega}(t) = 0$ as well. Thus the system is in a steady state equilibrium, with market expectations exclusively reflecting the views of fundamentalists.

But given that $1 + c\theta\omega(t) - \delta c > 0$, this equilibrium is unstable, and any shock starts things in motion. Suppose that there is an unanticipated appreciation (the unexpected persistence of high long-term U.S. interest rates in the early 1980s, for example). The sign restrictions imply that $\omega(t)$ is unambiguously falling over time. Equation (16) says that the chartists are gaining prominence, since $\dot{\omega}(t) < 0$. The exchange rate begins to trace out a bubble path, moving away from long-run equilibrium; equation (17) shows that $\dot{s}(t) < 0$ when $\bar{s} > s(t)$. This process cannot, however, go on forever, because market expectations are eventually determined only by chartist views. At this point the bubble dynamics die out since both $\omega(t)$ and $\dot{\omega}(t)$ fall to zero. From equation (17), $s(t)$ then stops moving away from long-run equilibrium, as it approaches a new, lower equilibrium level where $\dot{s}(t) = 0$. In the words of Dornbusch (1983d), the dollar is both high and stuck.

Figures 14.1 and 14.2 trace out a "base-case" simulation of the line profile of the spot rate and ω. They are intended only to suggest that the

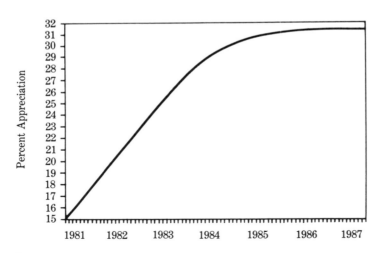

Figure 14.1
Simulated value of the dollar above its long-run equilibrium

model can potentially account for a large and sustained dollar appreciation. The figures assume that the dollar is perturbed out of a steady state equilibrium where $\bar{s} = s(t)$ and $\omega(0) = 1$ in October 1980. The dollar rises at an decreasing rate until sometime in 1985, when, as can be seen in Figure 14.2, the simulated weight placed on fundamentalist expectations becomes negligible. A steady state obtains at a new higher level, about 31 per cent above the long-run equilibrium implied by purchasing power parity. Although we tried to choose reasonable values for the parameters used in this example, the precise level of the plateau and the rate at which the currency approaches it are sensitive to different choices of parameters. (Appendix 2 in the originally-published paper gives more detail on values used in the simulation.)

It is worth emphasizing that the equilibrium spot rate appreciates along its bubble path even though none of the actors expects appreciation. This result is due to the implicit stock adjustment taking place. As portfolio managers reject their fundamentalist roots, they reshuffle their portfolios to hold a greater share in dollar assets. For fixed relative asset supplies, a greater dollar share can be obtained in equilibrium only by additional appreciation. This unexpected appreciation, in turn, further convinces portfolio managers to embrace chartism. The rising dollar becomes self-sustaining. In the end, when the spiral finally levels off at $\omega(t) = 0$, the level at which the currency becomes stuck represents a fully rational equilibrium:

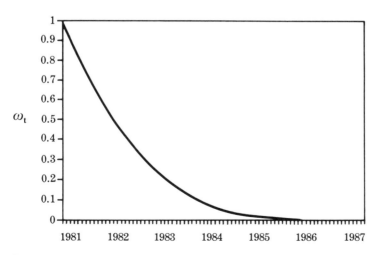

Figure 14.2
Simulated weight placed on fundamentalist expectations by portfolio managers

portfolio managers expect zero depreciation and the rate of change of the exchange rate is indeed zero.

What some would term the irrationality of the model can be seen by inspecting equation (17). Recall that market-expected depreciation, that of portfolio managers, is a weighted average of chartist and fundamentalist expectations, $\omega(t)\theta(\bar{s} - s(t))$. But the actual, or rational, expected rate of depreciation is given by $[-\delta c/[1 + c\theta\omega(t) - \delta c]]\omega(t)\theta(\bar{s} - s(t))$. The two are not equal, unless $\omega = 0$.[12] The problem we gave portfolio managers was to pick $\omega(t)$ in a way that best describes the spot process they observe (together with the prior confidence they had in fundamentalist predictions). But theirs is an impossible task, since the spot process is more complicated.

14.5   The Model with Endogenous Fundamentals

The results so far offer an explanation for the paradox of proposition (1), that sustained dollar appreciation occurs even though all agents expect depreciation. But a spot rate that is stuck at a disequilibrium level is an unlikely end for any reasonable story. The next step is to specify the mechanism by which the unsustainability of the dollar is manifest in the model.

The most obvious fundamental which must eventually force the dollar down is the stock of net foreign assets. Reductions in this stock, through large current account deficits, cannot take place indefinitely. Sustained borrowing would, in the long run, raise the level of debt above the present discounted value of income. But long before this point of insolvency is reached, the gains from a U.S. policy aimed at reducing the outstanding liabilities (either through direct taxes or penalties on capital, or through monetization) would increase in comparison to the costs. If foreigners associate large current account deficits with the potential for moral hazard, they would treat U.S. securities as increasingly risky and would force a decline in the level of the dollar.

To incorporate the effects of current account imbalances, we consider the model, similar to Rodriguez (1980), given in equation (7):

$$s_t = \alpha + c\Delta s_{t+1}^m - df \tag{18}$$

where Δs_{t+1}^m is defined in equation (1a) and where f represents the log of cumulated U.S. current account balances. The coefficient, d, is the semi-elasticity of the spot rate with respect to transfers of wealth, and must be positive to be sensible. The differential equations (16) and (17) now become

$$\dot{\omega}(t) = [\delta/[1 + c\theta\omega(t) - \delta c]][-\omega(t)(1 + c\theta\omega(t)) - (d\dot{f})/(\theta(\bar{s} - s(t))]$$

$$\text{if } 0 < \omega(t) < 1 \quad (19)$$

$$\dot{s}(t) = [-\delta\omega(t)c\theta(\bar{s} - s(t)) + d\dot{f}]/[1 + c\omega(t)\theta - \delta c]. \quad (20)$$

If we were to follow the route of trying to solve analytically the system of differential equations, we would add a third equation giving the "normalized" current account $\dot{f}$, as a function of $s(t)$. (See, for example, equation (9) above.) But we here instead pursue the simulation approach.

In the simulation we use actual current account data for $\dot{f}$, the change in the stock of net foreign assets. Figures 14.3 and 14.4 trace out paths for the differential equations (19) and (20). During the initial phases of the dollar appreciation, the current account, which responds to the appreciation with a lag, does not noticeably affect the rise of the dollar. But as ω becomes small, the spot rate becomes more sensitive to changes in the level of the current account, and the external deficits of 1983–85 quickly turn the trend. When ω is small and portfolio managers observe an incipient depreciation of the dollar, they begin to place more weight on the forecasts of fundamentalists, thus accelerating the depreciation initiated by the current account deficits. There is a "fundamentalist revival." Ironically, fundamentalists are initially driven out of the market as the dollar appreciates, even though they are ultimately right about its turn to $\bar{s}$.

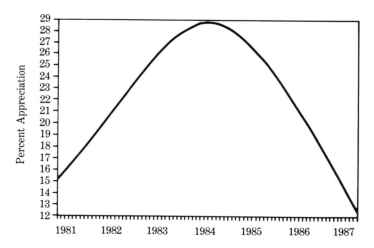

Figure 14.3
Simulated value of the dollar above its long-run equilibrium with endogenous current account

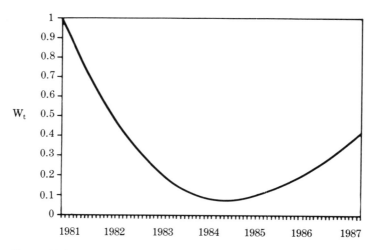

Figure 14.4
Simulated weight placed on fundamentalist expectations by portfolio managers with endogenous current account

Naturally, all of our results are sensitive to the precise parameters chosen. To gain an idea of the various sensitivities, we report in table 14.3 results using alternative sets of parameter values in the simulation corresponding to appendix 14A. While there is some variation, the qualitative pattern of bubble appreciation, followed by a slow turn-around and bubble depreciation, remains evident in all cases.

Recall that one of the main aims of the model is to account for the two seemingly contradictory facts given by propositions (2) and (3): first that market efficiency tests results imply that the rationally expected rate of dollar depreciation has been less than the forward discount, and second that the calculations based on fundamentals, such as those by Krugman and Marris, imply that the rationally expected rate of depreciation, by 1985, became greater than the forward discount.

Table 14.4 clarifies how the model resolves this paradox. The first two lines show the expectations of our two forecasters, the chartists and fundamentalists. The third line repeats the six-month survey expectations to demonstrate that they may in fact be fairly well described by the simple regressive formulation we use to represent fundamentalist expectations in line two. The fourth line contains the depreciation expected by the portfolio managers. Note that these expectations are close to the forward discount in line 6, even though the forecasts of the fundamentalists and of the chartists are not. Since only the portfolio managers are hypothesized to

Table 14.3
Sensitivity analysis for the simulation of the dollar

	Parameter	Values		Maximum appreciation of the dollar above the initial shock	No. of months until peak
δ	c	θ	d	%	
0.04	25	0.045	−0.005	11.4	41
0.06	25	0.045	−0.005	26.9	27
0.02	25	0.045	−0.005	5.8	44
0.04	15	0.045	−0.005	6.4	38
0.04	35	0.045	−0.005	18.1	40
0.04	25	0.03	−0.005	8.8	36
0.04	25	0.06	−0.005	13.5	44
0.04	25	0.045	0	16.4	80
0.04	25	0.045	−0.0025	11.6	45
0.04	25	0.045	−0.0075	11.4	38

Notes: These estimates correspond to the simulation depicted in figure 8 in Frankel and Froot (1990a). The parameter delta falls over time according to equation (A3) in appendix 14A.

Table 14.4
Alternative measures of expected depreciation (in percent per annum)

Expectation from:	Line	1981	1982	1983	1984	1985	1986
Chartists in the simulation	(1)	0	0	0	0	0	0
Fundamentalists in the simulation	(2)	7.63	9.82	11.68	11.98	10.33	7.69
Economist six-month survey	(3)	8.90	10.31	10.42	11.66	4.89	NA
Weighted average expected depreciation in the simulation	(4)	5.29	3.31	1.59	0.99	1.49	2.08
Rationally expected depreciation in the simulation	(5)	−2.97	−5.16	−4.38	−0.72	3.89	6.22
Actual forward discount	(6)	3.74	3.01	1.10	3.07	−0.74	NA

Note: Fundamentalists in the simulation use regressivity parameter of .045, implying that about 70 percent of the contemporaneous overvaluation is expected to remain after one year. The *Economist* six-month survey includes data through December 1985. Weighted average expected depreciation in the simulation is a weighted average of chartists and fundamentalists, where the weights are those of portfolio managers. Rationally expected depreciation is the perfect foresight solution given by equations (19) and (20). The actual six-month forward discount includes data through December 1985.

take positions in the market, we can say that the magnitude of the market risk premium is small (as mean-variance optimization would predict). Finally, line 5 shows the actual depreciation in the simulation, which is equivalent to the rationally expected depreciation given the model above. (Of course, none of the agents has the entire model in his or her information set.) Notice that during the 1981–84 period, the rationally expected depreciation is not only significantly less than the forward discount, but less than zero. This pattern agrees with the results of market efficiency tests discussed earlier. But the rationally expected depreciation is increasing over time. Sometime in late 1984 or early 1985, the rationally expected rate of depreciation becomes positive and crosses the forward discount. As calculations of the Krugman-Marris type would indicate, as of 1985 or 1986 rationally expected depreciation is greater than the forward discount. The paradox of propositions (2) and (3) is thus resolved within the model.

All this comes at what might seem a high cost: portfolio managers behave irrationally in that they do not use the entire model in formulating their exchange rate forecasts. But another interpretation of this behavior is possible, in that portfolio managers are actually doing the best they can in a confusing world. Within this framework they cannot have been more rational; abandoning fundamentalism more quickly would not solve the problem in the sense that their expectations would not be validated by the resulting spot process in the long run. In trying to learn about the world after a regime change, our portfolio managers use convex combinations of models which are already available to them and which have worked in the past. In this context, rationality is the rather strong presumption that one of the prior models is correct. It is hard to imagine how agents, after a regime change, would know the correct model.

14.6   Conclusions and Extensions

This chapter has posed an unorthodox explanation for the aerobatics of the dollar. The model we use assumes less than fully rational behavior in the sense that none of the three classes of actors (chartists, fundamentalists, and portfolio managers) conditions their forecasts on the full information set of the model. In effect, the bubble is the outcome of portfolio managers' attempt to learn the model. When the bubble takes off (and when it collapses), they are learning more slowly about the model than they are changing it by revising the linear combination of chartist and fundamentalist views they incorporate in their own forecasts. But as the weight given to fundamentalists approaches zero or one, portfolio managers' estimation of the true force changing the dollar comes closer to the true one. These revisions in weights become smaller until the approximation is perfect: portfolio managers have "caught up" by learning more rapidly than they change the model. The inability of agents with prior information to bring about immediate convergence to a rational expectations equilibrium may provide a framework in which to view "bubbles" in a variety of asset markets.

Several extensions of the model in this chapter would be worthwhile. First, it would be desirable to allow chartists to use a class of predictors richer than a simple random walk. They might form their forecasts of future depreciation by using ARIMA models, for example. Simple bandwagon or distributed lag expectations for chartists would be the most plausible since they capture a wide range of effects and are relatively simple analytically. Second, we might want to consider extensions which give the model local stability in the neighborhood of $\omega = 1$. Small perturbations from equilibrium would then not instantly cause portfolio managers to begin losing faith in fundamentalist counsel. Only sufficiently large or prolonged perturbations would upset portfolio managers' views enough to cause the exchange rate to break free of its fundamental equilibrium.

Appendix 14A

In this section we consider the problem portfolio managers face: how much weight should they give to new information concerning the "true" level of $\omega(t)$. We obtain an explicit formulation for these optimal Bayesian weights, thus replacing equation (11) and supplying firmer foundations for the results reported in the text.

Even though in the model of the spot rate given by equation (3) the value of the currency is fully deterministic, individual portfolio managers who are unable to predict accurately ex-ante changes in the spot rate may view the future spot rate as random. They would then form predictions of future depreciation on the basis of observed exchange rate changes and their prior beliefs. At each point in time, portfolio managers therefore view future depreciation as the sum of their current optimal predictor and a random term.

$$\Delta s_{t+1} = \omega_t \theta(\bar{s} - s_t) + \varepsilon_{t+1} \tag{A1}$$

where ε_{t+1} is a serially uncorrelated normal random variable with mean 0 and variance $\theta(\bar{s} - s_{t-1})/\tau$.[13] Using Bayes' rule, the coefficient ω_t may be written as a weighted average of the previous period's estimate, ω_{t-1}, and information obtained from the contemporaneous realization of the spot rate,

$$\omega_t = [T_t/(T_t + \tau)]\omega_{t-1} + [\tau/T_t + \tau)][\Delta s_t/(\theta(\bar{s} - s_{t-1}))] \qquad (A2)$$

where $T_t = T_{t-1} + \tau$ where T_0 is the precision of portfolio managers' prior information.[14] Thus, if portfolio managers use Bayesian techniques, the weight they would give to the current period's information may be expressed as

$$\delta_t = \tau/(\tau t + T_0) \qquad (A3)$$

Equation (A3) shows that the weight portfolio managers give to new information would fall over time as decison makers gain more confidence in their prior distribution, or as the prior distribution for the future change in the spot rate converges to the actual posterior distribution. If, however, portfolio managers suspect that the spot rate is nonstationary, past information would be discounted relative to more recent observations. Instead of combining prior information in the form of an OLS regression of actual depreciation on fundamentalist expectations (as they do above), portfolio managers might use a varying parameter technique to take into account the nonstationarity. In this case, the weight they put on new information might not decline over time to zero.

As we have shown in appendix I of Frankel and Froot (1990a), computing δ_t using equation (A3) does not change substantially the results of the simulations presented in the text.

15

Chartists, Fundamentalists, and Trading in the Foreign Exchange Market

with Kenneth A. Froot

The overshooting theory of exchange rates seems ideally designed to explain some important aspects of the movement of the dollar in recent years. Over the period 1981–84, for example, when real interest rates in the United States rose above those among trading partners (presumably due to shifts in the monetary/fiscal policy mix), the dollar appreciated strongly. It was the higher rates of return that made U.S. assets more attractive to international investors and caused the dollar to appreciate. The overshooting theory would say that, as of 1984, for example, the value of the dollar was so far above its long-run equilibrium that expectations of future depreciation were sufficient to offset the higher nominal interest rate in the minds of international investors. Figure 15.1 (b) shows the correlation of the real interest differential with the real value of the dollar, since exchange rates began to float in 1973.

15.1 Bubble Episodes

At times, however, the path of the dollar has departed from what would be expected on the basis of macroeconomic fundamentals. The most dramatic episode is the period from June 1984 to February 1985. The dollar appreciated another 20 percent over this interval, even though the real interest differential had already begun to fall. The other observable factors that are suggested in standard macroeconomic models—money growth rates, real growth rates, the trade deficit—at that time were also moving in the wrong direction to explain the dollar rise.

It is now widely accepted that standard observable macroeconomic variables are not capable of explaining, much less predicting ex ante, the majority of short-term changes in the exchange rate. But economists divide into two camps on what this means. One view is that the unexplained short-term changes must be rational revisions in the market's perception of the

(a) Nominal and real long term interest rates

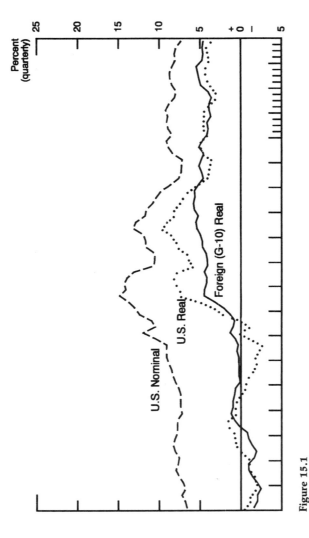

Figure 15.1

(a) Nominal and real long-term interest rates. (b) The dollar and real interest rates. Notes: The CPI-adjusted dollar is a weighted-average index of the dollar against the currencies of the non-U.S. G-10 countries plus Switzerland, where nominal exchange rates are multiplied by relative levels of CPIs. Weights are proportional to each foreign country's share in world exports plus imports from 1978 through 1983. The long-term real interest differential is the U.S. rate minus the weighted average of foreign country weights. Source: Peter Hooper and Catherine Mann, Board of Governors of the Federal Reserve System.

(b) The dollar and real interest rates

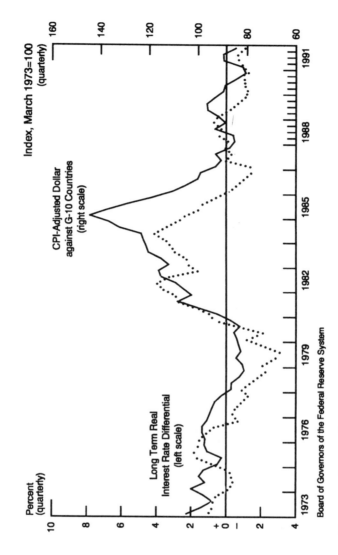

Figure 15.1 (continued)

equilibrium exchange rate due to shifts in "tastes and technologies," even if the shifts are not observable to macroeconomists in the form of standard measurable fundamentals. A major difficulty with this interpretation is that it is difficult to believe that there could have been an increase in the world demand for U.S. goods (or in U.S. productivity) sufficient to increase the equilibrium real exchange rate by more than 20 percent over a nine-month period and that such a shift could then have been reversed over the subsequent nine months.

This brings us to the second view, which is that the 1984–85 appreciation may have been an example of a speculative bubble: that it was not determined by fundamentals but rather was the outcome of self-confirming market expectations. The dollar in 1985 "overshot the overshooting equilibrium." Some have suggested that the appreciation of 1988–89, on a smaller scale, may also have been of this nature.

There exist elegant theories of "*rational* speculative bubbles," in which all participants know the correct model. Some observers have suggested that 1984–85 may best be described as a bubble that was not characterized by rational expectations.[1] We have suggested that such episodes may best be described by models of bubbles in which market participants do not agree on the model for forecasting the exchange rate.[2]

While the conventional approach in the literature, theoretical as well as empirical, is to assume that there is such a thing as "the" market expectation of the future exchange rate, there is evidence that investors have heterogeneous expectations. For one thing, surveys of the forecasts of participants in the foreign exchange market show wide dispersion at any point in time. One conducted by the *Financial Report* (affiliated with the *Economist*) reports a high-low range of six-month forecasts that averages 15.2 percent. Data in a survey conducted by MMS International show a dispersion of opinion (as measured by the standard deviation across respondents) at the one-month horizon that averaged 2.2 percent for the yen/dollar rate. The dispersion was slightly higher for the mark, pound, and Swiss franc rates.

15.2 Trading in the Foreign Exchange Market

The tremendous volume of foreign exchange trading is another piece of evidence that reinforces the idea of heterogeneous expectations, since it takes differences among market participants to explain why they trade. Every three years, the Federal Reserve Bank of New York counts transaction in the U.S. foreign exchange market. In April 1989, foreign exchange trading (adjusted for double counting) totaled $129 billion a day. Simultaneous counts in London and Tokyo reported $187 billion and $115 billion a day, respectively. Thus, the three-country total was over $430 billion of foreign exchange trading a day. The next set of surveys was released in September 1992, covering the preceding April. It showed that U.S. trading had increased by another 49 percent, to $192 billion, London trading by 62 percent, to $303 billion, and Japanese trading by 10.8 percent, to $128 billion. Adding in other markets, the worldwide total is thought to be about $1,000 billion a day.

Interestingly, the banks in the 1989 New York Federal Reserve Bank census reported that only 4.9 percent of their trading was with a nonfinancial firm and the nonbanks only 4.4 percent; in other words, 95 percent of the trading takes place among the banks and other financial firms rather than with customers, such as importers and exporters. Clearly, trading among themselves is a major economic activity for banks.

What is the importance of trading volume (beyond supporting the case for the importance of heterogeneous expectations)? There are three possible hypotheses, with regard to implications for movements in the market price:

1. The greater the liquidity or "depth" of the markets, the more efficient the processing of news regarding economic fundamentals and the smaller "unnecessary volatility" in the exchange rate.

2. The foreign exchange market is already perfectly efficient, so that trading volume is irrelevant to price movements and therefore uninteresting.

3. Much trading is based on "noise" rather than "news" and leads to excessive volatility.

Choosing convincingly among these three hypotheses may be too large a task to accomplish here. But there is evidence that trading volume, exchange rate volatility, and the dispersion of expectations among forecasters are all positively related. We have developed a weekly data set for four currencies (British pound, German mark, Japanese yen, and Swiss franc), covering the period October 1984 to February 1988. Trading volume is measured by the weekly number of futures contracts (nearest-term) traded on the IMM of the Chicago Mercantile Exchange, volatility is measured by the squared percentage fifteen-minute-changes in the futures price, averaged over the week, and dispersion is measured by the percentage standard deviation of forecasts across respondents in the survey conducted weekly by MMS International.

Table 15.1
Cross-correlation Tests for Causality
Volume (vol) and one-week dispersion of opinion (disp):

	Q1: disp causal to vol	Q2: vol causal to disp	Q3: disp and vol are causally related
British pound	8.9824**	6.1753**	15.2343**
Deutsche mark	5.1219**	0.0736	9.3893**
Swiss franc	2.5873	0.2451	9.5726**
Japanese yen	9.3782**	0.2815	17.0853**

Volume (vol) and one-month dispersion of opinion (disp):

British pound	7.6687**	0.1304	56.3448**
Deutsche mark	0.5934	0.6339	2.2189
Swiss franc	3.7731*	3.1839*	7.5340**
Japanese yen	3.3784*	0.2170	6.6081**

Volume (vol) and price volatility (var):

	Q1: var causal to vol	Q2: vol causal to var	Q3: var and vol are causally related
British pound	0.0183	4.6030**	59.7655**
Deutsche mark	0.0045	0.0972	20.8328**
Swiss franc	0.8481	2.3921	38.5250**
Japanese yen	0.1159	1.1872	37.4416**

Price volatility (var) and one-week dispersion of opinion (disp):

	Q1: disp causal to var	Q2: var causal to disp	Q3: disp and var are causally related
British pound	4.9982**	4.1458**	14.5069**
Deutsche mark	7.1153**	4.4469**	17.5255**
Swiss franc	4.8134**	2.9839*	12.1650**
Japanese yen	3.5491*	5.8905**	27.4114**

Table 15.1 (continued)

Price volatility (var) and one-month dispersion of opinion (disp):

	Q1: disp causal to var	Q2: var causal to disp	Q3: disp and var are causally related
British pound	6.7898**	1.5047	10.6410**
Deutsche mark	3.4790*	5.0540**	15.6198**
Swiss franc	5.9060**	3.4279*	18.0211**
Japanese yen	2.2187	4.3179**	10.2997**

Notes: Q1 and Q2 are Chi-square with 1 degree of freedom.
Q3 is Chi-square with 3 degrees of freedom.
** Denotes significance at the 5 percent level.
* Denotes significance at the 10 percent level.

Granger-causality tests on prewhitened data, reported in table 15.1, show that the degree of dispersion has strong effects in the market. Dispersion Granger-causes volume at the 90 percent level in three currencies out of four, whether dispersion is measured in one-week or one-month forecasts. Dispersion also Granger-causes volatility, in three out of four currencies at the one-week horizon, and four out of four at the one-month horizon. We also find that the contemporaneous correlation between volume and volatility is high: .515 for the pound, .316 for the mark, .412 for the Swiss franc, and .417 for the yen.

One interpretation of these results is that the existence of conflicting forecasts leads to noise-trading—the causation runs from dispersion to the volume of trading, and then from trading to volatility—though there probably exist other interpretations as well. The Granger test does not show statistically significant causation running directly from volume to volatility. But one would expect any such causality to be purely contemporaneous, and it is important to keep in mind that the Granger test cannot detect this type of causality.

It should be noted that the tests in table 15.1 also show that volatility Granger-causes dispersion: volatility Granger-causes one-week dispersion for all four currencies and one-month dispersion for three out of four. We think that this apparent effect may be partly spurious: the MMS survey catches different respondents at different times of the day, so their forecasts of the expected future level of the exchange rate will differ more if the level of the spot rate on that day moves around more. On the other hand, it is easy to see how higher lagged volatility could cause higher dispersion of expectations because forecasters use different models to interpret the data.

15.3   The Rising Importance of Chartists

We now turn to the question of how the existence of different forecasting techniques might lead to "excess volatility." It has long been remarked that if there exist traders who tend to forecast by extrapolating recent trends—that is, who have "bandwagon expectations"—then their actions can exacerbate swings in the exchange rate. Many so-called chartist forecasters, or technical analysts, are thought to use rules that are extrapolative, such as, "Buy when the one-week moving average crosses above the twelve-week moving average."

How do speculators form expectations in practice? Frankel and Froot (1990a) offered evidence from the survey data that, at short horizons, respondents tend to forecast by extrapolating recent trends, while at long horizons they tend to forecast a return to a long-run equilibrium such as PPP. Table 15.2 reports an update of these estimates. The coefficients reported are to be interpreted as answers to the question, "For every 1 percent that the dollar appreciates in a given week, what percentage change does the median respondent forecast for the dollar thereafter?" The answer at the one-week horizon is another .13 percent in the same direction. At the four-week horizon, the extrapolation is smaller. Respondents expect that, by the time three months have passed, the dollar will be *lower* than at the day when they are formulating their forecasts, and lower still at six months. One year out, they expect the dollar to be .33 percent lower, for every 1 percent that the dollar has appreciated this week.

Table 15.2
Do forecasters extrapolate? OLS regressions of expected future rate of depreciation against most recent actual depreciation

Survey data source	MMS International		*Economist Financial Report*		
Sample period	Oct. 1984–Jan. 1988		June 1981–Aug. 1988		
Term of forecast	1-week	4-week	3-month	6-month	12-month
Estimate of extrapolative parameter	.13	.08	−.08	−.17	−.33
Standard error (GMM)	.03	.05	.03	.03	.06
t-statistic	4.32*	1.60	−2.98*	−4.98*	−5.59*

* Significant at 99 percent confidence level.

This leads to the question: which kind of forecasters dominate the market—those who think short-term and appear to have bandwagon expectations, or those who think long-term and have regressive expectations? Since Milton Friedman (1953), the standard argument against the importance of destabilizing speculators is that they will on average lose money and be driven out of the market in the long run. A number of special counter-examples to the Friedman argument have been constructed over the years, most involving heterogeneous actors (e.g., "suckers" who lose money and "sharpies" who win). The simplest counter-example would be based on the theory of rational speculative bubbles, where each market participant loses money if he *doesn't* go along with the herd. The problem with this theory, which identifies speculative bubbles with the unstable paths in a rational-expectations saddle-path problem, is that it has nothing to say about what causes a bubble to start. What, for example, generated a speculative bubble in the period leading up to February 1985, if that is what the dollar surge evident in figure 15.1 was?

The model of speculative bubbles developed in chapter 14 of this book says that over the period 1981–85, the market shifted weight away from the fundamentalists, and toward the technical analysts or "chartists." This shift was a natural Bayesian response to the inferior forecasting record of the former group, as their forecasts of dollar depreciation continued to be proved wrong month after month. The change in the weighted-average forecast of future dollar depreciation in turn changed the demand for dollars, and therefore its price in the foreign exchange market.

Table 15.3
Techniques used by forecasting services

Year	No. of services surveyed	No. using technical models	No. using fundamentals	No. using both models
1978	23	3	19	0
1981	13	1	11	0
1983	11	8	1	1
1984	13	9	0	2
1985	24	15	5	3
1986	34	20	8	4
1987	31	16	6	5
1988	31	18	7	6

Note: When a forecasting firm offers more than one service, each is counted separately. Some services did not indicate the nature of their technique.
Source: *Euromoney*, August issues.

Is there any sort of evidence for such a theory? *Euromoney* magazine runs a yearly August review of between ten and twenty-seven foreign exchange forecasting services. Summary statistics are reported in table 15.3. The trend is very clear. In 1978, eighteen forecasting firms described themselves as relying exclusively on economic fundamentals, and only two on technical analysis. By 1985, the positions had been reversed: only one firm reported relying exclusively on fundamentals and twelve on technical analysis.[3]

In short, it may indeed be the case that shifts over time in the weight that is given to different forecasting techniques are a source of changes in the demand for dollars and that large exchange rate movements may take place with little basis in macroeconomic fundamentals.

Acknowledgment

The authors thank MMS International for data and Lu Cordova and Joseph Mullally for valuable research assistance.

16

Foreign Exchange Intervention: An Empirical Assessment

with Kathryn M. Dominguez

16.1   Introduction

Can intervention policy effectively influence market expectatons of current and future foreign exchange rates? The conventional wisdom offers an unequivocal answer. Intervention in the foreign exchange market has little or no effect, except to the extent that it implies changes in countries' money supplies. In the latter case, intervention is just a particular variety of monetary policy. The conventional wisdom thus says that intervention does not offer the authorities an *independent* policy tool for influencing the foreign exchange market.

In the early 1980s, the belief that intervention was not an effective policy tool was widely shared among academic economists, central bankers, and market participants. In the first Reagan administration, the ineffectiveness of intervention was an article of faith, and the U.S. government accordingly refrained from buying or selling foreign exchange (with some minor exceptions). In 1985, however, attitudes at the U.S. Treasury shifted abruptly. The U.S. authorities began to intervene again in the markets, in collaboration with other country's central banks, most visibly as decided at the meeting of G-5 economic leaders at the Plaza Hotel in September of that year. Since that time, intervention has taken place regularly. Foreign exchange traders have taken note of it. They are observed to react to reports of intervention as vigorously as to any other sort of news. Most traders, and most involved central bankers, believe that this intervention has at times had important effects. We believe that the time is right for a reconsideration of the conventional wisdom as to the ineffectiveness of foreign exchange intervention.

In this chapter we examine the two possible channels through which intervention can influence the foreign exchange rate: the portfolio and the expectations channels. Intervention can influence exchange rates through the *portfolio channel* provided foreign and domestic bonds are considered imperfect substitutes in investors' portfolios. Intervention operations that, for example, increase the current supply of mark relative to dollar assets, which private investors are obliged to accept into their portfolios, will force a decrease in the relative price of deutsche mark assets.[1] Intervention can also influence exchange rates, regardless of whether foreign and domestic bonds are imperfect substitutes, through the *expectations channel*. The public information that central banks are intervening in support of a currency (or are planning to intervene in the future) may, under certain conditions, cause speculators to expect an increase in the price of that currency in the future. Speculators react to this information by buying the currency today, bringing about the change in the exchange rate today.

While some previous empirical studies of foreign exchange intervention operations have found evidence from daily data that central banks have had a statistically significant effect on exchange rates (Loopesko 1984; Dominguez 1990, 1992), the studies were not able to distinguish whether the effect was coming through the portfolio or the expectations channel. The goal of this study is to disentangle the influence of the two potential channels during the most recent experience with central bank intervention operations.

16.2   Intervention Policy in Practice

Intervention operations by central banks involve the purchase of foreign assets with domestic assets (or sale), which, if not *sterilized* will result in an increase (or decrease) in the domestic monetary base. For example, when the Fed intervenes against the dollar, the Fed's portfolio of foreign assets (typically deutsche mark and yen-denominated assets) increases while its dollar deposits decrease. At the same time, dollar deposits of commercial banks at the Fed increase. As a consequence, the U.S. monetary base (commercial bank deposits at the Fed plus currency in circulation) is increased. The Fed can sterilize this increase by selling the appropriate number of dollar-denominated assets in open-market operations.

The Federal Reserve Bank of New York reportedly fully and automatically sterilizes its intervention operations on a daily basis. In practice, the foreign exchange trading room immediately reports its dollar sales to the open market trading room, which then buys that many fewer bonds, so that the daily money supply is unaffected. The Bundesbank also claims to sterilize its foreign exchange intervention operations routinely as a techni-cal matter. Nevertheless, the general view is that both banks have at times allowed intervention operations to influence monetary aggregates. The degree of monetary accommodation is, however, limited, to the extent that they both target money supply growth. In this chapter we do not concen-trate on the distinction between sterilized and nonsterilized intervention. We study the intervention operations that actually took place between 1982 and 1988, regardless of whether they were sterilized.

Central banks have not routinely made daily intervention data avail-able to the public. Quarterly data on monetary authorities' international reserves are available both from central bank publications and the Interna-tional Monetary Fund's *International Financial Statistics*. Quarterly changes in these data have commonly been used by researchers as proxies for intervention flows.[2] These data, however, can differ significantly from ac-tual official purchases of foreign exchange in the open market. The level of a country's reserves can change even if the central bank does not transact in the foreign exchange market. Reserves increase with interest accruals on offical portfolio holdings and fluctuate with valuation changes on existing nondollar reserves.

Apart from the fact that reserve data do not provide good approxima-tions to official intervention activity, quarterly and monthly data obscure important daily information. Intervention operations are implemented on a minute-to-minute basis. Net daily intervention information at a minimum is necessary for study of intervention's effects. Data on daily official central bank purchases and sales in the foreign exchange market have rarely been made available to researchers outside the government.[3]

The U.S. Treasury has recently agreed to change its long-standing policy and has allowed the Board of Governors of the Federal Reserve System to make its daily intervention data publicly available, with a one-year lag. At this time none of the other G-7 central banks has a general policy of releasing its intervention data to the public. We are fortunate to have available for purposes of this study, in addition to the recently released Fed data, daily Bundesbank intervention data from 1982 through 1988.

Although contemporaneous intervention operations are not published on a daily basis by the central banks, daily intervention operations are frequently reported in newspapers and over the wire services. So although current official data are unavailable, there exist numerous unofficial sources of the data. How do traders and reporters learn about intervention operations? Although each central bank has its own particular set of practices, they generally undertake intervention directly with the foreign exchange desk of a large commercial bank. As with any other foreign exchange transaction, trades are officially anonymous. If the Fed decides to intervene in support of the dollar, the Fed trader can either call a broker or deal directly with another trader at a commercial bank to place an order for dollars. If the Fed would like the market to know the source of the dollar purchase, the Fed trader will call one of a number of selected commercial banks that the Fed traditionally does business with. Unless the Fed trader says otherwise, the bank trader will understand that not only does the Fed want to purchase dollars but that it would like the market to know this. This information is reportedly disseminated among traders in the market within minutes of the original Fed call.

Given the speed at which information flows in the foreign exchange market, more remarkable than the revelation of intervention operations are the occasions when operations are kept secret. In the U.S. case, the Fed is more likely to intervene secretly through the broker market, although it can also do so using a commercial bank with which it does not traditionally do business. The Fed also, on occasion, intervenes secretly through the major banks with which it traditionally does business. In any case, if the Fed trader says that the intervention operation is to remain secret, then the broker or bank trader has an incentive not to disclose the Fed's presence in the market if he or she ever wants to be privy to future intervention information and business.

What is the relative frequency of "secret" interventions? Secret interventions are not differentiated in central banks' official data, but one can roughly infer which operations were secret by comparing the official data with published reports of intervention activity in the financial press. Although traders may sometimes know that central banks are intervening without its showing up in the financial press, this relatively conservative accounting for reported intervention reveals that the bulk of recent intervention is not secret.[4] In the econometric analysis to follow, we include secret and reported intervention separately in order to determine whether the distinction is important.

16.3 A Two-Equation System: The Portfolio and Expectations Channels

The traditional theoretic explanation for how intervention operations influence exchange rates is based on the portfolio balance approach to exchange rate determination. The central assumption is that foreign and domestic bonds are imperfect substitutes for each other in investors' portfolios. Investors hold both foreign and domestic bonds in their portfolios and optimize a function of the mean and variance of their end-of-period wealth.[5] The monetary authority can influence the relative prices of foreign and domestic bonds by changing their relative supply in investors' portfolios. For example, if the Fed increases the relative supply of dollar-denominated bonds in the market, then investors will demand a dollar risk premium to compensate them for the risk that they bear holding the additional dollar assets.

The first equation in our two-equation system is a modified version of the traditional portfolio-balance model. (We introduced this form of the equation in Dominguez and Frankel 1993.) The main modification relative to the previous literature is that we assume that exchange rate expectations can be measured more precisely using survey data than by assuming rational expectations and using ex post changes in the exchange rate. Intuitively, the equation lets the expected risk premium on mark-denominated assets depend on the relative quantity of mark-denominated assets in investors' portfolios.

$$i_{t,k}^{DM} - i_{t,k}^{\$} + \Delta\hat{s}_{t,k}^{e} = \beta_0 + \beta_1 v_t + \beta_2 v_t x_t + u_{t,k} \tag{1}$$

where $i_{t,k}^{DM}$ is the k-period-ahead EuroDM interest rate, $i_{t,k}^{\$}$ is the k-period-ahead eurodollar interest rate, $\Delta\hat{s}_{t,k}^{e}$ is the expected change in the spot rate between period t and $t + k$ measured by the survey data, v_t is the daily variance of exchange rate changes over the preceding week, x_t is the share of mark-denominated assets in investors' portfolios, and the error term, $u_{t,k}$, reflects any measurement error in the data. If the sole (random) measurement error occurs in the survey data, OLS estimates of (1) will be appropriate. However, if the asset data are measured with error or if asset demands are given by the mean-variance specification *plus* an error term, then the regression will be subject to simultaneity bias and (1) should be estimated using instrumental variables. We do both.

The second equation in the two-equation system is our expectations equation. Regardless of whether the portfolio balance channel is operative, intervention operations may influence exchange rates if they provide relevant news to market participants.[6] The expectations equation therefore lets the change in investors' expectation of the future exchange rate be a function of past changes in the spot exchange rate and intervention policy news.

$$(\hat{s}^e_{t,k} - \hat{s}^e_{t-j,k}) = \alpha_0 + \alpha_1(s_t - s_{t-j}) + \alpha_2(s_t - \hat{s}^e_{t-j,k})$$

$$+ \alpha_3 ANNOC_t + \alpha_4 REPINT_t + \alpha_5 SECINT_t + \varepsilon_t \qquad (2)$$

where $(\hat{s}^e_{t,k} - \hat{s}^e_{t-j,k})$ is the revision in the log of the MMS survey prediction of the k-period ahead dollar/mark spot rate from time $t - j$ to time t, s_{t-j} is the log of the spot rate on the day of the last MMS survey, $ANNOC_t$ and $REPINT_t$ are $(1, 0, -1)$ dummy variables that capture reports of exchange rate policy news since the last survey date, $SECINT_t$ is a $(1, 0, -1)$ dummy variable for nonreported intervention operations since the last survey date, and ε_t is the error term.[7]

Our specification of the expectation equation is general in that it allows for both extrapolative and adaptive expectations. At the four-week horizon, respondents have been observed to put negative weight on the lagged spot rate and more-than-unit weight on the contemporaneous spot rate, so that they are extrapolating the recent trend into the future to get their forecast.[8] Our extrapolative parameter is α_1. Bandwagon expectations are the special case $\alpha_1 > 0$ and $\alpha_2 = 1$. Previous work has also found evidence that respondents form their predictions adaptively, putting positive weight on the lagged survey prediction (Frankel and Froot 1987, reproduced here as chapter 13). Our speed-of-adaptation parameter is $(1 - \alpha_2)$. Adaptive expectations are the special case $\alpha_1 = 0$ and $\alpha_2 < 1$. Static expectations are the special case $\alpha_1 = 0$, $\alpha_2 = 1$. Expectations are stabilizing overall if $\alpha_1 + \alpha_2 < 1$, and destabilizing overall if $\alpha_1 + \alpha_2 > 1$.

We also include two news variables in our expectations equation in order to capture information appearing in the newspaper about changes in central banks' exchange rate policy since the last survey date. $ANNOC_t$ is set equal to $+1$ if there were central bank announcements in support of the dollar (including, for example, announcements of G-7 meetings to deal with dollar weakness), -1 if there were official announcements against the dollar, and 0 if there were no such announcements. $REPINT_t$ is set equal to $+1$ if there were reports of central bank intervention in support of the dollar, -1 if there were reports of intervention against the dollar, and 0 if there were no such reports. The fifth independent variable included in the regression is secret intervention, denoted $SECINT_t$. $SECINT_t$ is set equal to $+1$ if there were no reports of intervention when a central bank in fact intervened in support of the dollar, -1 if interventions against the dollar were not reported, and 0 otherwise. We expect the two news variables, $ANNOC_t$ and $REPINT_t$ to have a negative effect on expectations of the future dollar/mark rate. If nonreported intervention is truly secret, we expect the coefficient on $SECINT_t$, α_5, to be zero.

The survey data used in both the portfolio balance and expectations equations are four-week-ahead survey forecasts of the mark-dollar exchange rate conducted by Money Market Services, International, for the period October 24, 1984 to December 30, 1988.[9] Unlike some other surveys, it is conducted on a weekly basis (since July 1985; before that it was conducted every two weeks). In addition, we report results for an earlier period November 17, 1982, to October 10, 1984, when the survey pertained to three-month ahead forecasts. One might expect that intervention would have a greater effect in the later period, since the Reagan administration's firm commitment to free-floating began to waver when Donald Regan and Beryl Sprinkel were succeeded at the Treasury by James Baker and Richard Darman in January 1985, and when the Plaza Agreement followed in September.

The intervention data series measure consolidated daily official foreign exchange transactions in millions of dollars at current market values. Positive values denote purchases of dollars and negative values denote official dollar sales. The Fed data distinguish between interventions against the mark and the yen and exclude so-called passive intervention operations. Passive interventions are Fed purchases and sales of foreign currency with customers who would otherwise have dealt with market agents.[10] The Bundesbank data exclude nondiscretionary interventions required by rules of the European Monetary System.

The daily intervention data provided by the central banks measure official net purchases or sales of dollars in the foreign exchange market. Central bank interest payments and receipts on reserve assets are not included in the data. Intervention is measured in three ways in these regressions. *One-day* intervention is Fed and Bundesbank purchases of dollars on the day before the survey. *Two-week* or *one-week* intervention is cumulated between survey dates, so that it measures total Fed and Bundesbank dollar purchases since the last survey. *Cumulative* intervention is cumulated from the beginning of the sample period and therefore measures the relative stock supplies of outside assets denominated in dollar and mark currencies.

Equations (1) and (2) make up our two-equation system. The two endogenous variables are the current period spot rate and survey expectation of the future spot rate. We are able to deal with the potential simultaneity problems in both equations by using the exogenous variables from each equation as instruments for the other equation. The instruments for equation (1) include last period's spot exchange rate, s_{t-j}, last period's survey expectation of the future spot rate, $\hat{s}^e_{t-j,k}$, and the news variables, $ANNOC_t$ and $REPINT_t$, from equation (2). The instruments for equation (2) include the variance of spot changes since the last survey date, v_t, and the total quantity of marks sold in foreign exchange intervention (measured in marks), x_t, from equation (1).

16.4   The Estimation Results

Table 16.1 presents the expectations equation regression results for the early sample period. News reports appear to have had no effect on expecta-

Table 16.1
Sample: November 1982–October 1984
$$(\hat{s}^e_{t,k} - \hat{s}^e_{t-j,k}) = \alpha_0 + \alpha_1(s_t - s_{t-j}) + \alpha_2(s_t - \hat{s}^e_{t-j,k}) + \alpha_3 ANNOC_t + \alpha_4 REPINT_t + \alpha_5 SECINT_t + \varepsilon_t$$

Biweekly three-month-ahead survey expectation equation (Obs = 54, $k = 90$, $j = 14$) instruments: v_t, IDM_t

	One-day[a]		Two-week[b]		Cumulative[c]	
α_0	0.005	(0.006)	0.006	(0.006)	0.008	(0.008)
α_1	0.414	(0.400)	0.328	(0.367)	−0.069	(0.609)
α_2	0.406	(0.210)[†]	0.420	(0.217)[†]	0.432	(0.279)
α_3	−0.002	(0.008)	−0.002	(0.008)	−0.005	(0.010)
α_4	0.002	(0.007)	0.003	(0.006)	0.008	(0.009)
α_5	−0.001	(0.004)	−0.001	(0.004)	0.003	(0.006)
$\chi^2(1)$	7.990**		7.177**		4.123*	
$\chi^2(2)$	7.822**		9.272**		1.984	
D.W.	2.09		2.05		1.90	
R^2	0.72		0.70		0.51	

a. Intervention instrumental variable (IDM) is measured at the end-of-day prior to the survey.
b. Intervention instrumental variable is an accumulated measure between survey forecasts.
c. Intervention instrumental variable is an accumulated measure from the beginning of the sample period.
Note: Standard errors are in parentheses. [†] denotes significance at the 90% level; * denotes significance at the 95% level; ** denotes significance at the 99% level.
The $\chi^2(1)$ statistic pertains to the hypothesis that $\alpha_2 = 1$ (expectations are not adaptive); and $\chi^2(2)$ pertains to the hypothesis that $\alpha_1 = \alpha_2 = 0$ (expectations are not extrapolative, but are completely adaptive).

tions in the early period 1982 through 1984. However, the instrumental variable estimates for the same regression over the 1985–1988 subperiod, presented in table 16.2, indicate a marked change in regime. The coefficients on the news variables appear with the correct sign and are statistically significant in all the regressions for the latter sample: newspaper reports of exchange rate policy announcements and central bank intervention in support of the dollar tend to lower expectations of the future dollar/mark exchange rate. The average effect of reported intervention on the one-month ahead expectations of the dollar/mark exchange rate ranged between .4 and .6 percent. The effect of other official announcements was twice as large, ranging between .9 and 1.1 percent.

In table 16.2 the coefficient on the lagged spot rate, $-\alpha_1$, and the coefficient on the lagged expectation, $(1 - \alpha_2)$, are each statistically different from both zero and one. In other words, there is evidence of extra-

Table 16.2
Sample: October 1984–December 1988
$(\hat{s}^e_{t,k} - \hat{s}^e_{t-j,k}) = \alpha_0 + \alpha_1 (s_t - s_{t-j}) + \alpha_2 (s_t - \hat{s}^e_{t-j,k}) + \alpha_3 ANNOC_t + \alpha_4 REPINT_t + \alpha_5 SECINT_t + \varepsilon_t$

Weekly one-month-ahead survey expectation equation (Obs = 186, $k = 30$, $j = 7$) instruments: v_t, IDM_t

	One-day[a]		One-week[b]		Cumulative[c]	
α_0	0.005	(0.001)**	0.006	(0.001)**	0.005	(0.001)**
α_1	0.394	(0.194)*	0.442	(0.219)*	0.146	(0.253)
α_2	0.559	(0.116)**	0.626	(0.116)**	0.478	(0.134)**
α_3	−0.009	(0.002)**	−0.009	(0.002)**	−0.011	(0.003)**
α_4	−0.005	(0.002)**	−0.004	(0.002)*	−0.006	(0.002)**
α_5	0.005	(0.003)	0.005	(0.003)	0.007	(0.003)*
$\chi^2(1)$	14.362**		10.379**		15.144**	
$\chi^2(2)$	17.821**		18.724**		6.599**	
D.W.	2.24		2.23		2.10	
R^2	0.67		0.67		0.61	

a. Intervention instrumental variable (IDM) is measured at the end-of-day prior to the survey.
b. Intervention instrumental variable is an accumulated measure between survey forecasts.
c. Intervention instrumental variable is an accumulated measure from the beginning of the sample period.
Note: Standard errors are in parentheses. * denotes significance at the 95% level; ** denotes significance at the 99% level. The $\chi^2(1)$ statistic pertains to the hypothesis that $\alpha_2 = 1$ (expectations are not adaptive); and $\chi^2(2)$ pertains to the hypothesis that $\alpha_1 = \alpha_2 = 0$ (expectations are not extrapolative, but are completely adaptive).

polative behavior *and* gradual adaptation. Overall, expectations are neither stabilizing nor destabilizing.

Tables 16.3 and 16.4 present the portfolio equation regression results. The intervention variable (defined as x_t in the text) is measured in millions of dollars in these tables. This approach allows the estimated coefficient to determine the denominator of the portfolio shares and is preferred, to the extent one lacks faith in the reliability of measurements of aggregate wealth.[11] We disaggregate the intervention variable by including Fed and Bundesbank intervention separately. The three separate sets of regressions, therefore, include intervention measured as the sum of Bundesbank and Fed intervention, intervention by the Bundesbank, and intervention by the Fed.

Table 16.4 presents the instrumental variable regressions of equation (1) over the latter subperiod, October 1984 to December 1988. The coefficient on intervention is generally statistically significant, regardless of how it is measured. This result implies that intervention, even if sterilized, had an effect. If mark and dollar assets were perfect substitutes, then the coefficient should have been zero: changes in asset supplies would have no effect on the risk premium.

In order to check that the results reported in table 16.4 are robust, we reestimated equation (1), excluding outliers and the variance constraint. In order to examine the influence of outliers on the results, we searched for regression residuals from equation (1) that were greater than 2.5 times the standard error of the regression estimate. Over the full sample period, two observations met the criterion: September 25, 1985 (the second trading day after the Plaza Accord) and March 5, 1986. Table 16.5 presents regression estimates of equation (1) excluding the two outlying observations over the latter subperiod and including the intervention variable as a percent of wealth, rather than in millions of dollars. If we control for the definition of intervention in the regression, the intervention coefficient estimates excluding the two outliers are virtually identical to those reported in table 16.4. The coefficient estimates on the variance terms, however, are no longer statistically significant except when intervention is cumulated from the beginning of the sample period. In a second set of tests presented in table 16.6 we examine the sensitivity of the reported results to the mean-variance specification by reestimating (1) without constraining the variance and intervention to enter multiplicatively. The estimated coefficients on the intervention variables are qualitatively identical (in terms of statistical significance) to those reported in tables 16.4 and 16.5.

Table 16.3

Sample: November 1982–October 1984

$$i^{DM}_{t,k} - i^{s}_{t,k} + \Delta \hat{s}^{e}_{t,k} = \beta_0 + \beta_1 v_t + \beta_2 v_t I_t + u_{t,k}$$

Biweekly three-month-ahead risk premium equation (Obs = 55, k = 90, j = 14, intervention expressed in millions of \$) instruments: s_{t-j}, $\hat{s}^{e}_{t-j,k}$, $ANNOC_t$, $REPINT_t$

	One-day[a]		Two-week[b]		Cumulative[c]	
I I_t includes Fed and Bundesbank intervention						
β_0	0.009	(0.004)*	0.009	(0.004)*	0.005	(0.003)†
β_1	−28.032	(57.433)	−38.212	(60.749)	372.170	(109.322)**
β_2	0.279	(0.706)	0.012	(0.061)	0.043	(0.009)**
ρ	0.625	(0.197)**	0.621	(0.204)**	0.266	(0.369)
D.W.	2.16		2.15		1.94	
R^2	0.41		0.41		0.39	
II I_t includes only Bundesbank intervention						
β_0	0.009	(0.004)*	0.009	(0.004)*	0.005	(0.003)†
β_1	−55.220	(63.241)	−37.319	(61.343)	371.305	(107.605)**
β_2	−0.784	(1.593)	0.003	(0.066)	0.045	(0.009)**
ρ	0.644	(0.189)**	0.632	(0.198)**	0.251	(0.411)
D.W.	2.15		2.16		1.94	
R^2	0.41		0.42		0.40	
III I_t includes only Fed intervention						
β_0	0.009	(0.004)*	0.009	(0.004)*	0.006	(0.004)
β_1	−27.264	(55.588)	−45.193	(48.008)	369.001	(168.774)*
β_2	1.029	(1.762)	−0.497	(0.647)	0.937	(0.365)*
ρ	0.615	(0.203)**	0.645	(0.191)**	0.544	(0.362)
D.W.	2.17		2.16		2.06	
R^2	0.41		0.39		0.31	

a. Intervention variable is measured at the end-of-day prior to the survey.

b. Intervention variable is an accumulated measure between survey forecasts.

c. Intervention variable is an accumulated measure from the beginning of the sample period.

Note: Standard errors are in parentheses. † denotes significance at the 90% level; ** denotes significance at the 99% level. ρ is the estimated first lag correlation coefficient.

Table 16.4

Sample: October 1984–December 1988

$$i_{t,k}^{DM} - i_{t,k}^{\$} + \Delta \hat{s}_{t,k}^{e} = \beta_0 + \beta_1 v_t + \beta_2 v_t I_t + u_{t,k}$$

Weekly one-month-ahead risk premium equation (Obs $= 185$, $k = 30$, $j = 7$, intervention expressed in millions of \$) instruments: s_{t-j}, $\hat{s}_{t-j,k}^{e}$, $ANNOC_t$, $REPINT_t$

	One-day[a]		One-week[b]		Cumulative[c]	
I I_t includes Fed and Bundesbank intervention						
β_0	0.001	(0.001)	0.002	(0.001)	0.002	(0.002)
β_1	53.851	(17.355)**	39.501	(13.766)**	217.216	(104.010)*
β_2	0.308	(0.128)*	0.067	(0.030)*	0.009	(0.005)†
ρ	0.307	(0.194)	0.344	(0.202)†	0.449	(0.173)**
D.W.	2.12		2.13		2.22	
R^2	0.08		0.14		0.11	
II I_t includes only Bundesbank intervention						
β_0	0.002	(0.001)	0.002	(0.001)†	0.002	(0.002)
β_1	38.803	(14.283)**	32.562	(13.103)*	178.043	(94.692)†
β_2	0.328	(0.184)†	0.083	(0.053)	0.008	(0.005)
ρ	0.343	(0.176)†	0.347	(0.191)†	0.397	(0.068)**
D.W.	2.15		2.15		2.18	
R^2	0.13		0.15		0.16	
III I_t includes only Fed intervention						
β_0	0.001	(0.002)	0.002	(0.001)	0.002	(0.002)
β_1	49.716	(17.780)**	39.809	(14.076)**	64.535	(20.422)**
β_2	0.410	(0.222)†	0.103	(0.055)†	0.018	(0.008)*
ρ	0.335	(0.176)†	0.361	(0.190)†	0.483	(0.177)**
D.W.	2.14		2.15		2.25	
R^2	0.09		0.14		0.05	

a. Intervention variable is measured at the end-of-day prior to the survey.

b. Intervention variable is an accumulated measure between survey forecasts.

c. Intervention variable is an accumulated measure from the beginning of the sample period.

Note: Standard errors are in parentheses. † denotes significance at the 90% level; ** denotes significance at the 99% level. ρ is the estimated first lag correlation coefficient.

Table 16.5

Sample: October 1984–December 1988

(omitting outlying observations on 9/25/85 and 3/5/86)

$$i_{t,k}^{DM} - i_{t,k}^{\$} + \Delta \hat{s}_{t,k}^{e} = \beta_0 + \beta_1 v_t + \beta_2 v_t I_t + u_{t,k}$$

Weekly one-month-ahead risk premium equation (Obs = 183, $k = 30$, $j = 7$, intervention expressed as prcent of wealth) instruments: s_{t-j}, $\hat{s}_{t-j,k}^{e}$, $ANNOC_t$, $REPINT_t$

	One-day[a]		One-week[b]		Cumulative[c]	
I I_t includes Fed and Bundesbank intervention						
β_0	0.003	(0.001)*	0.003	(0.001)*	0.003	(0.002)†
β_1	19.728	(14.734)	18.039	(14.675)	217.351	(71.927)**
β_2	7222.415	(2229.645)**	1565.290	(552.027)**	193.954	(67.694)**
ρ	0.386	(0.177)*	0.393	(0.197)*	0.478	(0.198)*
D.W.	2.20		2.17		2.23	
R^2	0.19		0.20		0.19	
II I_t includes only Bundesbank intervention						
β_0	0.004	(0.002)*	0.004	(0.001)*	0.003	(0.001)*
β_1	16.721	(14.690)	16.744	(14.682)	450.834	(114.997)**
β_2	6867.251	(2882.011)*	1926.778	(915.987)*	459.885	(120.435)**
ρ	0.402	(0.165)*	0.389	(0.188)*	0.429	(0.362)
D.W.	2.22		2.18		2.18	
R^2	0.20		0.19		0.21	
III I_t includes only Fed intervention						
β_0	0.003	(0.002)†	0.003	(0.001)*	0.003	(0.002)
β_1	19.598	(14.952)	17.108	(14.694)	51.374	(22.239)*
β_2	11792.140	(4571.997)**	2557.322	(1059.437)*	372.542	(165.706)*
ρ	0.409	(0.162)*	0.422	(0.180)*	0.533	(0.172)**
D.W.	2.21		2.20		2.28	
R^2	0.18		0.20		0.13	

a. Intervention variable is measured at the end-of-day prior to the survey.

b. Intervention variable is an accumulated measure between survey forecasts.

c. Intervention variable is an accumulated measure from the beginning of the sample period.

Note: Standard errors are in parentheses. † denotes significance at the 90% level; * denotes significance at the 95% level; ** denotes significance at the 99% level. The coefficient on $v_t I_t$ (β_2) and its corresponding standard error are divided by 100 for readability. ρ is the estimated first lag correlation coefficient.

Table 16.6
Sample: October 1984–December 1988
$i_{t,k}^{DM} - i_{t,k}^{5} + \Delta\hat{s}_{t,k}^{e} = \beta_0 + \beta_1 v_t + \beta_2 v_t I_t + u_{t,k}$

Weekly one-month-ahead unconstrained risk premium equation
(Obs $= 185$, $k = 30$, $j = 7$, intervention expressed as percent of wealth)
instruments: s_{t-j}, $\hat{s}_{t-j,k}^{e}$, $ANNOC_t$, $REPINT_t$

	One-day[a]		One-week[b]		Cumulative[c]	
I I_t includes Fed and Bundesbank intervention						
β_0	0.002	(0.001)†	0.003	(0.001)*	0.017	(0.006)**
β_1	30.639	(12.448)*	28.803	(12.295)*	38.850	(13.519)**
β_2	43.774	(12.632)**	12.325	(3.725)**	1.641	(0.574)**
ρ	0.319	(0.196)	0.288	(0.228)	0.459	(0.232)*
D.W.	2.14		2.12		2.24	
R^2	0.15		0.16		0.10	
II I_t includes only Bundesbank intervention						
β_0	0.003	(0.001)†	0.003	(0.001)*	0.028	(0.007)**
β_1	28.118	(12.459)*	26.513	(12.289)*	38.876	(13.124)**
β_2	39.366	(15.466)*	16.161	(6.028)**	2.876	(0.848)**
ρ	0.342	(0.176)†	0.299	(0.208)	0.402	(0.387)
D.W.	2.16		2.12		2.19	
R^2	0.16		0.16		0.13	
III I_t includes only Fed intervention						
β_0	0.002	(0.001)	0.002	(0.001)	0.004	(0.002)†
β_1	32.935	(12.714)**	30.822	(12.532)*	38.944	(14.106)**
β_2	82.379	(28.492)**	17.366	(6.612)**	3.679	(1.651)*
ρ	0.347	(0.179)†	0.334	(0.195)†	0.537	(0.192)**
D.W.	2.15		2.15		2.32	
R^2	0.14		0.15		0.05	

a. Intervention variable is measured at the end-of-day prior to the survey.
b. Intervention variable is an accumulated measure between survey forecasts.
c. Intervention variable is an accumulated measure from the beginning of the sample period.
Note: Standard errors are in parentheses. † denotes significance at the 90% level; * denotes significance at the 95% level; ** denotes significance at the 99% level. ρ is the estimated first lag correlation coefficient.

16.5   A Summary of the Quantitative Effects

Our two-equation system estimates indicate that official announcements about exchange rate policy and reports of intervention influence exchange rate expectations, and intervention operations influence the risk premium. In this section, we make use of some of the parameter estimates from our regression analyses as an example to calculate the effect of intervention on the dollar/mark exchange rate. We assume in these calculations that interest rates in the United States and Germany are held constant. If interest rates were allowed to vary, then the effects in a general portfolio-balance model might be either smaller or larger than those reported here. Sterilized intervention in support of the dollar, for example, might drive down dollar interest rates, reducing the demand for dollar assets and thereby mitigating the effect on the exchange rate.

First, consider the effect of intervention on the exchange rate if it is not known publicly. We begin with the baseline case where expectations are assumed to be neither extrapolative nor adaptive. Under these assumptions, the intervention has no effect at all on the risk premium. If the risk premium does not change, then equation (1) indicates that x_t does not change.

The portfolio share that is allocated to mark assets, x_t, is defined as $S_t M_t / W_t$, where S_t is the spot mark-dollar exchange rate, M_t is the total quantity of mark assets in investors' portfolios (denominated in marks), and W_t is total wealth (denominated in dollars). Analogously, the portfolio share that is allocated to dollar assets, $1 - x_t$, is defined as D_t / W_t where D_t is the total quantity of dollar assets held in investors' portfolios and $S_t M_t + D_t = W_t$. S_t, the spot exchange rate, is thus equal to:

$$S_t = \frac{D_t}{M_t} \frac{x_t}{1 - x_t}. \tag{3}$$

From this expression for S_t, it is evident that the effect of intervention on the exchange rate is in proportion to the supply of mark assets in investors' portfolios. What is the effect of 100 million dollars of intervention? If we are thinking of the special case where only nonsterilized intervention matters, then the definition of M_t is relatively clear: total reserve money supplied to the banking system by the Bundesbank, which, as of the end of 1988, was \$124.19 billion.[12] Thus the effect is only .081 percent. If we are thinking of sterilized intervention, then the effect of 100 million dollars of intervention will be even smaller, because M_t is the total supply of mark-denominated bonds, rather than just mark money. It should be emphasized that these small magnitudes derive solely from the small size of intervention relative to the relevant denominators and not from any parameters that we have estimated. But it is worth recalling that this effect, even if small, is nonetheless not zero, according to our rejection of perfect substitutability between mark and dollar bonds.

To get large effects on the exchange rate, we need the public to hear the news of the intervention. Our second experiment considers the effect of such information in isolation, as reflected in the coefficient on the reported intervention dummy variable, even if such intervention is in fact not taking place. If intervention actually takes place and is publicly reported, then its total effect would be the sum of the (small) effect reported in the preceding paragraph plus the (much larger) effect reported in the next paragraph. Under our baseline case (no change in interest rates and no extrapolative or adaptive expectations), the risk premium simply changes by the coefficient of $REPINT_t$ in the expectation equation. Such a change in the risk premium will have a large effect on the demand for mark-versus-dollar assets.

In order to calculate the effect of a report of intervention on the exchange rate we need to return to equation (3). The log form of equation (3) is:

$$\log S_t = \log\left(\frac{D_t}{M_t}\right) + \log(x_t) - \log(1 - x_t). \tag{4}$$

The derivative of the log of the spot exchange rate with respect to reported intervention can be calculated using (4) and the knowledge that x_t is a function of the risk premium, rp_t, which in turn is a function of expected depreciation, $\Delta \hat{s}^e_{t,k}$, which in turn is a function of the news variables $REPINT_t$ and $ANNOC_t$.

$$\frac{d \log S_t}{dREPINT_t} = \left[\frac{1}{x_t} + \frac{1}{1 - x_t}\right]\frac{dx_t}{drp_t}\frac{drp_t}{dREPINT_t}. \tag{5}$$

The derivative of x_t with respect to the risk premium is $(v_t \beta_2)^{-1}$ from equation (1). If we rearrange equations (1) and (2), hold interest rates constant and set $\alpha_1 = 1$ and $\alpha_2 = 0$, we see that the derivative of the risk premium with respect to reported intervention is equal to the derivative of the expected depreciation with respect to reported intervention, which is α_4 from equation (2). As an example, if we take $x = .5$ and take our parameter estimates from I_t defined as cumulative intervention, the effect of an intervention report on the exchange rate is 2.7 percent.[13] If we measure x_t at the end of the sample period (.112),[14] the effect is approximately twice as large. If we take β_2 estimates from one-day or one-week intervention equations, the effect is much smaller.

The expectations effect of news on the exchange rate seems high. One's intuition that the effect should, in reality, be smaller can easily be fit into any of several categories. First, it is possible, even if we are talking about intervention that is sterilized in the sense that there is no change in the money supply, that the interest rates will absorb some of the impact of the decreased demand for mark assets (the German interest rate rising and the U.S. interest rate falling), so that the depreciation of the mark will be smaller. One would need to specify a complete portfolio-balance model to answer how big the changes in the interest rates would be. But the effect on the nominal interest differential need not be large to damp significantly the reported effect on the spot rate.

Second, if one wishes to depart from the baseline case to consider the possibility of extrapolative expectations, then the effects reported above obtain only in the long-run equilibrium in which $s_t - s_{t-1}$ is zero. The short-run impact effect could be smaller.[15] For some readers an intuitively appealing implication of extrapolative expectations is that, after the first-week impact of the news, market forecasters react further to the observed change in the exchange rate by jumping on the bandwagon, so that the effect grows in subsequent weeks. Others may prefer to believe that expectations are regressive rather than extrapolative or that newspaper reports or other random disturbances to the level of the spot rate, to the extent that they are not confirmed subsequently by actual observed changes in macroeconomic fundamentals, will gradually lose their effect on the spot rate as time passes, and that this "unwinding factor" is not adequately captured in our equations. This last possibility would constitute a third factor that could reduce the effect on the spot rate in long-run equilibrium below that reported above.[16]

Our own inclination is to believe that expectations only tend to be extrapolative in occasional periods: speculative bubble environments, when the foreign exchange market loses its moorings and forecasters forget about fundamentals. Of course, these are precisely the periods in which central bankers might be most interested in using the tool of intervention.[17]

The last circumstance in which the effect on the spot rate would be less than that estimated here is if the event occurs during a period when the variance is higher than it is on average. Again, this might be precisely the sort of period in which central bankers would be most interested in using intervention as a short-term tool, to smooth disorderly markets.[18]

Our results cannot be viewed as definitive. Nevertheless, to sum up, the findings for the dollar/mark rate during our mid-1980s sample period are generally favorable for the effectiveness of intervention. There appear to be statistically significant effects both through the expectations channel and through the portfolio channel. The quantitative effects can vary, depending both on the particular estimates chosen for the key parameters and on the precise experiment that one wishes to consider. But we hope that the statistical significance of the effects that we find will contribute to a reevaluation of the conventional wisdom as to the ineffectiveness of intervention.

Appendix 16A: Variable Definitions and Data Sources

s_t — log of the \$/DM spot exchange rate at time t (source: DRI)

$\hat{s}^e_{t,k}$ — log of Money Market Services median k-period-ahead expectation for the \$/DM rate at time t (source: MMS)

v_t — daily variance of \$/DM exchange rate changes over the preceding week

$i^{DM}_{t,k}$ — Euro-DM k-period-ahead interest rate at time t (source: DRI)

$i^{\$}_{t,k}$ — Euro-\$ k-period-ahead interest rate at time t (source: DRI)

I_t — central bank intervention, in millions of \$, known at time t[19] (sources: Fed and Bundesbank)

IDM_t — central bank intervention, in millions of DM, known at time t

$ANNOC_t$ — +1 for official central bank announcements in support of the dollar since the last MMS survey date (source: newspapers[20])
−1 for official central bank announcements against the dollar since the last MMS survey date (source: newspapers)
0 for no relevant central bank announcements (except intervention)

$REPINT_t$ — +1 for reported central bank intervention in support of the dollar since the last MMS survey date (source: newspapers)
−1 for reported central bank intervention against the dollar since the last MMS survey date (source: newspapers)
0 for no reports of central bank intervention

$SECINT_t$ — +1 if $I_t > 0$ and $REPINT_t = 0$
−1 if $I_t < 0$ and $REPINT_t = 0$
0 otherwise

Acknowledgment

This chapter is one of several joint papers to follow from our first work on this subject, which was NBER Working Paper No. 3299. Another is forthcoming in the *American Economic Review*. Frankel would like to thank the Center for International and Development Economics Research (funded at U.C. Berkeley by the Ford Foundation) for support.

17

The European Monetary System: Credible in 1988–1991?

with Steven Phillips

The European Monetary System has been in operation since 1979. At its inception, it was greeted skeptically by many. The break-up of the prior "Snake" regime did not inspire confidence in governments' willingness or ability to keep major European currencies together, and there was considerable divergence in the policies and performance of the participants. Sure enough, realignments were recurrent during the first eight years—eleven altogether. Only the Dutch guilder was able to maintain a nearly fixed rate against the DM, undergoing just two small devaluations.

A period of exchange rate stability dates from January 1987, the month of the twelfth realignment and extends through December 1991, the date of the Maastricht Agreement. Giavazzi and Spaventa (1990) argue that 1987 marked the beginning of a "New EMS." A series of policy steps and institutional reforms were undertaken during these five years with the aim of enhancing exchange rate stability.[1] But the question arose whether there might not be a future realignment. Most relevant to such issues as interest rate convergence, the question arises whether investors *thought* that there might be a future realignment. These questions are particularly interesting in light of the crisis of September 1992, in which the Italian lira, pound sterling, and Spanish peseta were in fact devalued despite past assurances to the contrary. We test here the recent credibility of the EMS with participants in the foreign exchange market.

Recent research on the EMS takes off from the theory of the target zone introduced by Krugman (1991). He examined the case where the commitment of the authorities to intervene to defend the target zone was completely credible, showing the effect of investor awareness that the foreign exchange market would become a one-way bet as the exchange rate neared the target zone boundary. Empirical studies, such as Flood, Rose, and Mathieson (1991), show that the European data of the 1980s do not fit the standard target zone model. The simplest test of target zone credibility is that proposed by Svensson (1991): expected future exchange rates were found to lie nearly always outside contemporaneous EMS target zones for the period 1979 through early 1990. This result suggested that the market during this period usually perceived a strong probability of realignment. Expectations were inferred from interest rates using the assumption of uncovered interest parity (requiring that there exist no risk premium).

Our goal here is to update the tests of exchange rate expectations, to see in particular if the credibility of the EMS was enhanced over the period 1988–91 and for what currencies. Our main methodological innovation is the use of the *Currency Forecasters' Digest* survey data, supplementing interest differentials as a measure of market expectations.[2] The potentially important advantage of using survey data is immunity to errors introduced by exchange risk premiums. If the existence of a large exchange risk premium meant that the apparent finding of expected rates outside the band was spurious, this would still be a piece of evidence that investors had little faith in exchange rate stability; after all, they would not demand a risk premium if they were confident that the exchange rate would not change. Nevertheless, we wish to distinguish empirically between the exchange risk premium, and expectations of exchange rate changes.

As noted in part III of this volume, it is a controversial question whether the exchange risk premium is large enough and variable enough to render the forward discount or interest differential deficient measures of the expected future spot rate. Recent tests using the survey data for a number of minor currencies[3] turn up more evidence of a time-varying risk premium than did earlier studies of the major currencies.

In addition to the question of EMS credibility per se, we are also interested in whether the empirical failure of the standard target zone model might reflect simply an erroneous assumption of uncovered interest parity. The alternative explanation of the empirical results, advanced by Bertola and Svensson (1993), is based on time-varying credibility. Our analysis suggests particularly good reason to believe that EMS credibility changed over this period.

17.1   The First Eight Years

We begin by reviewing the standard evidence on EMS credibility based on interest differentials. If there is no risk premium and uncovered interest parity holds, we can use interest rates and contemporaneous spot rates to construct expected future exchange rates and see whether they lie within the bands.[4] Figure 17.1 plots expected future exchange rates at the one-

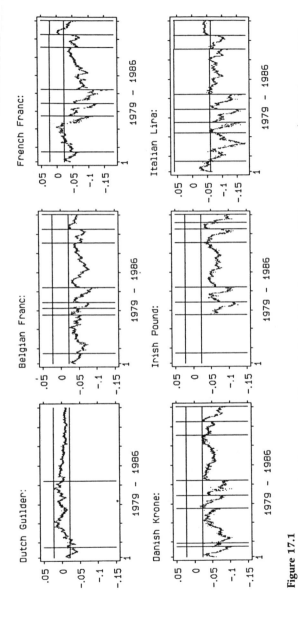

Figure 17.1
One-year expectations, based on interest differentials (as deviations from current DM central rate), March 1979–January 1987

year horizon, as deviations from then-current central rates. Vertical lines indicate dates of realignment against the DM, and the horizontal lines indicate the target zone boundaries. The period is March 1979 through the January 1987 realignment.

Figure 17.1 provides striking evidence on the historical credibility of the EMS. Only the Dutch guilder is nearly always expected to remain inside its contemporaneous band. The other five currencies are nearly always expected to violate the limits against the DM. The evidence supports the view that the EMS had low credibility during its first eight years. The many devaluations during this period apparently did not come as a surprise.

17.2   Did Expected Future Exchange Rates Fall inside the Bands during 1988–91?

We now proceed to the period February 1988 to December 1991, the date of the Maastricht meeting on European Monetary Union. We add to the original set of six currencies two late joiners, the Spanish peseta and British pound.

To assess the credibility of the current EMS target zones, we update in figure 17.2 the interest rate test, presenting the twelve-month expectations implied by uncovered interest parity. It may be compared to figure 17.1 for the earlier period. All eight currencies show smaller expected deviations from current central rates than pre-1987. Table 17.1 compares sample means from the two periods; t-statistics indicate a statistically significant increase in credibility for all five currencies tested.

We note an upward trend in the twelve-month expectations within the 1988–91 period. During the second half of the sample, most values were within the target zones, a remarkable finding by earlier EMS standards. However, these results are valid only under the assumption of uncovered interest parity. We therefore turn to our alternative measure of expectations, the survey data.

Figure 17.3 presents plots of the forecasts at the one-month horizon for the period February 1988 to December 1991.[5] They typically lie within the official limits. Figure 17.4 shows the forecasts at a three-month horizon; they too come to lie within the bands by the second quarter of 1988. At both horizons, however, forecasts (with the exception of the guilder) have often been close to the lower limits of the band, a possible symptom of imperfect credibility.

A more stringent test comes with consideration of longer horizons. Figure 17.5 shows twelve-month expectations, which were often outside

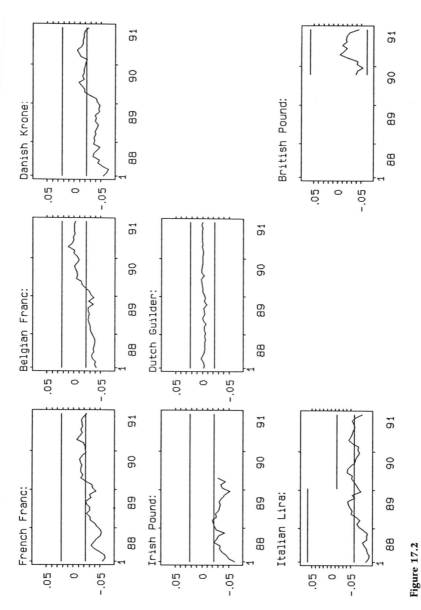

Figure 17.2
Twelve-month expectations, using interest differentials (as log deviation from DM central rate), February 1988–December 1991

Table 17.1
Mean 12-month expectations (from interest rates) as deviations from DM central rates

Currency	Mar. 1979– Dec. 1986	Feb. 1988– Dec. 1991	Difference of means	*t*-test of inequality
France	−5.570%	−2.870%	+2.700	+5.98
Belgium	−4.950	−1.940	+3.010	+11.60
Denmark	−5.170	−3.140	+2.030	+6.27
Netherlands	−0.531	−0.162	+0.369	+2.24
Italy	−8.400	−7.420	+0.980	+1.49
		−2.130**	+6.270	+14.46
Ireland	−6.500*	NA	NA	NA

Notes: Percentages approximated as log deviations times 100.
* Irish interest rate data available for 1982–1986 only.
** The central rate of the lira shifted with the narrowing of the target zone in January 1990. February 1988–December 1989 mean was −7.42%; January 1990–December 1991 mean was −2.13%.

the target zone: prior to 1990, the forecasts for the currencies of France, Denmark, Belgium, and Italy were typically 1 to 3 percentage points below their lower DM limits. In January 1990, however, forecasts for these four currencies began to strengthen, crossing inside the band limits by the second quarter of that year. In 1991, the twelve-month forecasts were typically inside the target zone.

Notice that the survey-based forecasts of figure 17.5 are similar to the interest-rate-based forecasts of figure 17.2. for the same period and horizon. The exception is the Irish pound, where the *CFD* data show greater credibility: since mid-1988, most of its twelve-month forecasts are inside the DM target zone.

Figure 17.6 presents (quarterly) forecasts at a horizon of five years. Although most have been several percentage points below the lower limits, some show an upward trend. Several draw near to the zone during 1990–91 or cross into it (most clearly the Belgian franc). With credibility apparently greater than before, the 1988–91 EMS might seem more likely to conform to the basic target zone model developed by Krugman and others. We now reexamine this question using the recent data.

17.3 Reassessing the Performance of Target Zone Models

The standard target zone model is built on an equation that determines the exchange rate as a function of economic fundamentals, such as the money supply and real income, and rationally expected depreciation. The funda-

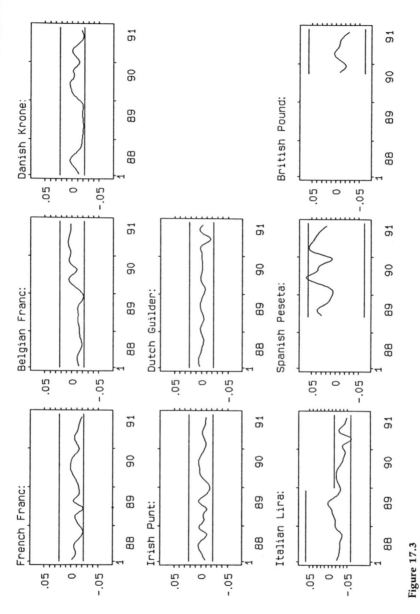

Figure 17.3
One-month forecasts, computed from CFD Survey (as log deviation from DM central rate), February 1988–December 1991

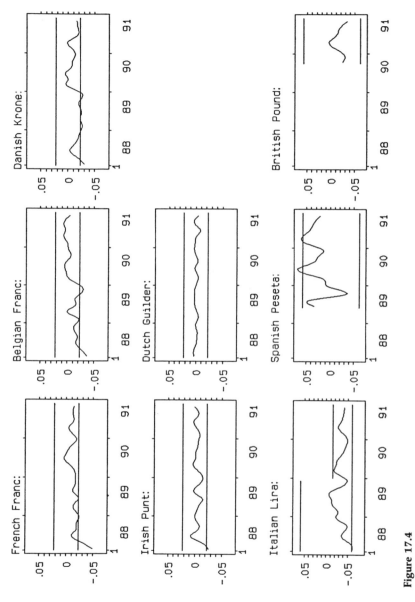

Figure 17.4

Three-month forecasts, computed from CFD Survey (as log deviation from DM central rate), February 1988–December 1991

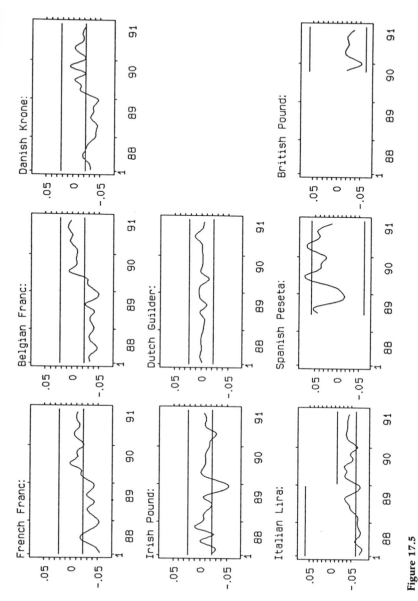

Figure 17.5
Twelve-month forecasts, computed from CFD Survey (as log deviation from DM central rate), February 1988–December 1991

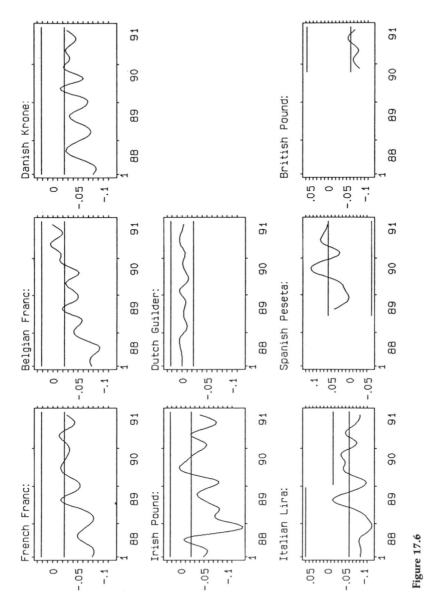

Figure 17.6
Five-year forecasts, computed from quarterly CFD Survey (as log deviation from DM central rate)

Table 17.2
Correlation coefficients: spot position in band and expected change over 12-month horizon

	February 1988–December 1991		January 1990–December 1991	
	Survey data	Interest differential	Survey data	Interest differential
Belgium	+.716	+.823	+.476	+.760
	(.000)	(.000)	(.025)	(.000)
Denmark	+.106	−.196	−.014	−.392
	(.493)	(.186)	(.954)	(.058)
France	+.067	+.006	−.308	−.519
	(.665)	(.965)	(.163)	(.009)
Ireland	+.105	NA	+.077	NA
	(.498)		(.732)	
Netherlands	−.232	−.262	−.346	−.316
	(.129)	(.075)	(.115)	(.133)
Italy	−.059*	+.491*	−.414	−.360
	(.794)	(.017)	(.056)	(.084)

Notes: Marginal significance levels in parentheses.
* Through December 1989 only.

mentals are assumed to evolve exogenously, in accordance with a continuous-time stochastic process (analogous to a random walk), except that discrete changes in the money supply occur when the authorities intervene to defend the band. The mathematical solution for the exchange rate has the important property that, near the bands, speculation will help stabilize the exchange rate, lessening and postponing the need for actual intervention. This phenomenon has been called the "honeymoon effect." The model is predicated on the assumption that the commitment to defend the band is entirely credible.[6]

The first rigorous empirical evaluation of the target zone model is the study of the EMS through May 1990 by Flood, Rose, and Mathieson (1991). Such tests require a number of questionable auxiliary assumptions in addition to the basic assumption of target zone credibility: the absence of a risk premium, flexibility of goods prices, and a reliable estimate of the money demand elasticity with respect to the interest rate. We focus here on a key prediction of the theory that does not depend on these assumptions: a negative relationship between the *level* of the exchange rate (within the band) and its *expected rate of change*. This relationship is the basis for the stabilizing honeymoon effect.

Table 17.2 presents correlations between the exchange rate and its own expected rate of change, using both measures of expectations. For the entire four-year period, there are more positive coefficients than negative, and none of the latter is statistically significant. Indeed, that of the Belgian franc is significantly positive. We also report results for the second half of the period. Signs are negative during 1990–91 for Denmark, Netherlands, Italy, and France (and significantly so for the interest rate test on the last). These results suggest that credibility increased between the first half of the sample and the second.

17.4   The Bertola-Svensson Model: Time-Varying Credibility

While a good fit of a target zone model does not require perfect credibility, it does require that the degree of credibility be stable over the sample period. In the Bertola-Svensson framework, credibility is imperfect *and* time varying; there is then no general implication for the relationship between the exchange rate's position within the zone and its own expected rate of change. If the probability of realignment is nonzero but fairly stable, their analysis yields the standard prediction of a negative correlation between s_t and $E_t(ds/st)$. However, if the realignment probability is highly variable, a positive correlation may emerge. Intuitively, a change in the perceived probability of a realignment is, of course, reflected in the overall expected rate of change of s_t, but it also moves the current level of s_t in the same direction. Thus, the pattern of covariation between these variables will depend on the relative variability of the probability of realignment.

The Bertola-Svensson framework is appealing for several reasons. First, the usual assumption of constant credibility seems implausible. Indeed, the statistics reported here suggest that credibility of the EMS target zones generally improved in the period leading up to Maastricht. Second, the Bertola-Svensson model is consistent with the failure to find a deterministic negative relationship between s_t and $E_t(ds/dt)$ and the occasional findings of a positive correlation (as in table 17.2). It is particularly encouraging that the best evidence of a negative correlation is found for the guilder. In the light of our earlier analysis, a plausible explanation is that the guilder's target zone is nearly perfectly credible and has remained so over the sample period. On the other hand, the positive correlation found for the French franc suggests that credibility has been changing (presumably improving) over the period.

17.5   Summary and Conclusions

We have used recent evidence from a survey of exchange rate forecasts to examine a number of aspects of the EMS target zones. In the light of recent institutional developments within the European Community, we have been particularly interested in the hypothesis that the EMS target zones experienced an important increase in credibility.

The analysis suggests the following conclusions. The guilder's DM target zone is clearly the most credible. For most other EMS currencies, the survey data confirm earlier findings that their DM target zones have been less than perfectly credible. On the other hand, the survey evidence suggests that credibility increased over the 1988–91 period, especially after early 1990. Consideration of exchange rate expectations constructed from interest differentials corroborates these findings and allows a comparison with earlier regimes: the 1988–91 regime was significantly more credible. However, we still find some evidence against perfect credibility of most EMS target zones, even in 1991, for all currencies but the Dutch guilder and Belgian franc.

Turning attention to the previously documented failure of the standard target zone model to conform to EMS data, the question arises whether mismeasurement of expectations is to blame. Estimation results based on survey data are no more supportive of that idea than those based on uncovered interest parity. In our view, a more likely source of the model's failure is its implicit assumption of constant credibility. Frankel and Phillips (1992), which elaborates on the analysis of the survey data, estimates a time-varying measure of credibility. We are therefore attracted to the Bertola-Svensson model in which expected rate of *realignment* is permitted to vary over time.

Acknowledgment

This chapter is a revised and condensed version of NBER Working Paper No. 3819. We thank Robert Flood, Alberto Giovannini, David Romer, Andrew Rose, Lars Svensson, and Rudiger Dornbusch for helpful comments. For support, we thank the Institute for International Economics and the Institute for Business and Economic Research at the University of California at Berkeley.

Notes

Chapter 1

1. Steady-state inflation was introduced into the Dornbusch model in Frankel (1979b) and Buiter and Miller (1982).

2. Dornbusch (1980). Hacche and Townend (1981), Meese and Rogoff (1983a). Backus (1984), and Frankel (1984b).

3. The criticisms made here are spelled out in Frankel and Meese (1987) and Froot (1987).

4. The literature began with Hamada (1985). A number of contributions appear in Buiter and Marston (1985).

5. The consequences of coordination when policy-makers subscribe to conflicting models, such as the twelve in question, are explored in Frankel and Rockett (1986). A related point, which emerges also in Oudiz and Sachs (1984) and other empirical studies of coordination, is that the magnitude of the transmission effects, whatever their sign, is in any case so small that it is difficult to see how coordination could be important.

6. For a survey, see Dornbusch (1985).

7. On the other hand, a statistically significant tendency for the real exchange rate to regress to PPP is more apparent when 116 years of U.S.-U.K. data are used. The speed of adjustment is estimated at 15 percent a year in Frankel (1986d) and 9 percent a year in Edison (1987). Given parameters so small in size, and the large magnitude of the disturbances to the real exchange rate in the floating-rate data, it is not surprising that most studies on the short post-1973 period have been statistically unable to reject zero.

8. Examples where a statistical failure to reject a random walk on the real exchange rate is claimed as evidence in favor of an equilibrium theory include Roll (1979), Adler and Lehmann (1983), and Stockman (1987).

9. This disturbing trend in modern macroeconometrics is an extreme case of the old problem that a statistical failure to reject a null hypothesis does not entitle one

to claim an interesting finding. The failure to reject may simply be due to low power in the test, especially if the null hypothesis is a weak one, as Summers (1986, pp. 593–94) reminds us in the context of testing for efficient financial markets. Traditionally in econometrics, the goal is supposed to be to *succeed* in statistically rejecting one economically interesting hypothesis in favor of another, i.e., to get results that are "statistically significant at the 95 percent level,' rather than the reverse.

10. Survey data on the expectations of market participants suggest that they expected the exchange rate to regress to PPP at a rate of 12 to 17 percent per annum (Frankel and Froot, 1987a, 1988).

11. Of course, one or two empirical observations do not constitute a statistical test. A number of studies on monthly data claim a degree of success using the long-term real interest differential to explain the real exchange rate: Shafer and Loopesko (1983), Sachs (1985), Hutchison and Throop (1985), Golub et al. (1985), and Feldstein (1985). But it must be remembered that repeatedly in the past a version of the monetary approach that has appeared to work well for the sample period on which it was estimated has subsequently gone awry.

12. Krugman (1985). Marris (1985), and Frankel and Froot (1988).

13. Schulmeister (1987) offers a useful description of the various rules of technical analysis that are in widest use and calculates that all of the rules would have made money over the period 1973–86 as a whole (table 9) as well as over each of the nine eighteen-month subperiods. He also cites a 1985 statistic from the Group of 30 that 97 percent of banks and 87 percent of securities houses report the belief that "the use of technical models has had an increasingly significant impact on the market" (p. 14), and expresses disapproval that economists have not seriously studied such rules that are actually used by traders. Reszat (1987) also reports that technical analysis is in widespread use. Goodman (1979) finds that the forecasts of technical analysts perform relatively well (for example, beating the forward rate), but Blake, Beenstock, and Brasse (1986) find the reverse.

14. In their model there exists a riskier asset, which must pay a higher expected return to compensate the rational investors to hold it. The "noise traders" hold more of this asset because they have a mistaken idea of the risk-return trade-off (they "rush in where wise men fear to tread"), and so their share of wealth can grow over time.

15. See Ito and Roley (1987).

16. Federal Reserve Bank of New York (1986).

17. The source is Bank of England (1986). See also Goodhart (1987, p. 59).

18. Reportedly, a minority of traders are allowed to take positions overnight, at the discretion of superiors.

19. The survey was conducted by the *Economist*, at a six-month horizon, for five exchange rates, June 1981–December 1985.

20. According to *Euromoney*, August, 1987, p. 113, one forecasting service makes forecasts every fifteen minutes. Another gives its customers beepers so they can be contacted at short notice. Many of the services refused to give *Euromoney* forecasts at a horizon as long as six months, saying their systems "were orientated [sic] towards a shorter-term horizon" (p. 119). De Long et al. (1987) call this the "Wojnilower problem."

21. The survey data suggest that investors, while expecting a gradual return to equilibrium at six- or twelve-month horizons, tend to extrapolate at one-week or one-month horizons. This pattern is itself a violation of the principle of rationality that the long run is the sum of iterated short runs; it is as if each trader thinks he can ride the current trend a little longer and at the first sign of a reversal will be quick enough to get out before everyone else does. (At any horizon, a comparison with actual ex post facto changes suggests that a rational expectation would be closer to zero depreciation.)

22. Summers (1986) argues that, because variability is so great, neither the econometrician nor the investor can tell if there are expected excess profits to be made from buying an asset whose market price appears to exceed its fundamental price due to a slow-disappearing "fad." Arrow (1982) argues similarly. Both cite the work of Tversky and Kahneman (1981) that individuals overreact to current, visible information, which in this context means putting too much weight on the current spot price in forming their expectations and not enough weight on long-term fundamentals. Dornbusch (1982) shows how investors' extraneous beliefs, such as an imagined future influence of the current account on the exchange rate, can cause the spot rate to deviate far from the fundamentals rate; yet if the current account changes slowly over time, again, neither the investor nor the econometrician could detect the deviation except in very large samples.

23. See Helpman (1981), Helpman and Razin (1979, 1982), Stockman (1979, 1980, 1983, 1987), Miller and Wallace (1985) for some of the most influential papers in this tradition.

24. The 1936 article by Simons—"Rules versus Authorities in Monetary Policy" —reproduced in Simons (1948), already advances a sophisticated discussion of a proposal for constant money.

25. We abstract entirely from dynamics and expectations. For a different formulation see Dornbusch (1987a).

26. We noted above the need to decide whether income or spending should be targeted. The point is significant for world consistency since an individual country can achieve a nominal income target by an improvement in the external balance, thus possibly using beggar-thy-neighbor policy.

27. See the discussion in Cuddington (1983), Dornbusch (1986b, 1987a), and McKinnon (1984a, 1984b).

28. For an assessment of apparent deviations from full market fundamentals, see the collection of eassays in Hogarth and Reder (1986).

Chapter 2

1. Despite the increased attention to inward foreign direct investment in the United States in recent years, it continues to be a smaller component of the capital inflow than portfolio investment. As of the end of 1987, foreign direct investment accounted for only 17 percent of the total stock of foreign-held assets in the United States.

2. There were relatively large differentials separating U.S. interest rates from the Eurodollar rates; at the long-term end of the spectrum, well-known U.S. corporations could borrow more cheaply in the Euromarket than domestically. These differentials fell steadily toward zero between 1982 and 1986, probably as the outcome of innovation that occurred in the Euromarkets—partly in response to these differentials—making it easier for U.S. corporations to borrow there. Much of this innovation went under the name of securitization. See Frankel (1988) for documentation and further references. (It appears that the securitization trend suffered a setback in 1987 and 1988, in part associated with the October 1987 stock market crash; it was then said to be slightly *more* costly for U.S. corporations to issue bonds in the Euromarket than domestically. It remains to be seen whether this reversal of the trend toward perfect integration is serious or lasting.)

3. And even if this relationship does not break down in the future under pressure from fears of international creditors that U.S. indebtedness is becoming excessive.

4. There is a fifth possible—yet more narrowly defined—criterion for the degree of integration of financial markets: the size of transactions costs as measured directly by the bid-ask spread in, for example, the foreign exchange market. Surprisingly, the covered interest differential does not appear to be statistically related to the bid-ask spread (MacArthur 1988).

5. Obstfeld (1986) and Summers (1988) argue that the saving-investment correlation may be due to the common influence of growth rates.

6. Sinn (1991), on the other hand, points out that the practice of averaging saving rates over a longer period may eliminate some of the international capital movements that one is looking for: current accounts must average out to zero in the sufficiently long run.

7. Obstfeld (1986) makes the large-country point in a time-series context, where it properly belongs. But even in a time-series regression for a single country such as the United States, one can correct for the large-country problem by expressing saving and investment rates as deviations from the *rest-of-world* rates of saving and investment, respectively. Under the null hypothesis, an exogenous fall in the U.S. saving rate may drive up the world real interest rate and crowd out investment, but there is no evident reason for the crowding out to be reflected in U.S. investment *to any greater extent* than in rest-of-the-world investment. In Frankel (1986, pp. 44–45), I found that the close correspondence between U.S. saving and investment for 1970–85 remains, even with this adjustment.

8. Obstfeld (1986) finds that the coefficient fell after 1973, in time-series correlations for most of his countries, but Obstfeld (1989) finds that it has risen over

time (1967—84 versus 1956—66), with the United States showing the highest correlation.

9. In a U.S. time-series context, Frankel (1986) used two instrumental variables: the fraction of the population over 65 years of age and the ratio of military expenditure to GNP. The former is considered a determinant of private saving and the latter of public saving, and both have some claim to exogeneity. In the context of cross-sections of developing and industrialized countries, Dooley, Frankel, and Mathieson (1987) used the dependency ratio and, again, the military expenditure variable.

10. Other studies that reject real interest parity for major industrialized countries include Mishkin (1984a. 1984b), Cumby and Obstfeld (1984), Mark (1985), and Cumby and Mishkin (1986). Glick (1987) examines real interest differentials for six Pacific Basin countries vis-à-vis the United States.

11. The ten-year real interest differential vis-à-vis a weighted average of G-5 countries was about 3 percent in 1984, whether expected inflation is measured by a distributed lag, by OECD forecasts, or by DRI forecasts. In 1980, by contrast, the differential was about — 2 percent (Frankel, 1986, pp. 35—36).

12. Gross investment was 16.0 percent of GNP in 1980, which was itself considered a low number (down 0.5 percent from 1971—80).

13. The instrumental variables used are the dependency ratio (the sum of those older than 64 and those younger than 21, divided by the working-age population in between), which is a determinant of private saving, and military expenditure as a share of GNP, which is a determinant of the federal budget deficit. A data appendix in NBER working paper no. 2856 gives details on these and the other variables.

14. Regressions for yearly data beginning in 1930 were reported in table 2 of the original published version of this chapter.

15. There are two other potential sources of differences from the results in Frankel (1986): the Commerce Department released revised national accounts data for the entire period in 1986, and we now use the dependency ratio as the demographic instrumental variable in place of the ratio of the over-65 to the over-20 population. But the years 1985—87 are indeed the source of the fall in the coefficient; when these three years are omitted, the coefficient is over 1 (as when the 1980s are omitted in table 2.2).

16. If the 1956—87 sample is split at 1974, when the United States and Germany removed capital controls, rather than at 1979, there is still a precipitous decline in the cyclically adjusted saving-investment coefficient over time: from .87 (statistically, no difference from 1) to .31 (borderline difference from 0). (Table 3a in the working paper version.) If the 1930—87 sample is split at 1958, when many European countries restored currency convertibility, there is a small increase in the coefficient over time: from .83 (statistically different from 1) to 1.14 (no difference from 1). (Table 2a.) But this is no doubt because the saving and investment rates are not cyclically adjusted for this period (the BEA series is not available back to 1930). Only when expressed on a cyclically adjusted basis is the U.S. national saving rate of 1985—90 especially low.

17. Feldstein and Bacchetta (1989) and Bayoumi (1992) find similar drops in the saving-investment coefficient in the 1980s, for cross-sections of industrialized countries (though they do not use instrumental variables and are thus liable to the econometric criticisms that others have raised concerning the endogeneity of national saving).

18. Measuring barriers to integration by differences in rates of return has the problem that a given degree of integration can appear smaller or larger depending on the disturbances to saving (or to other variables) during the sample period in question. For example, the greater degree of variability in the U.S. real interest differential in the 1980s, as compared to the 1970s or 1960s, may be attributable to the greater swings in variables such as the structural budget deficit, rather than to a lower degree of capital mobility. All we can say for sure is that if the barriers to integration are essentially zero (the degree of capital mobility is essentially perfect), then differentials in rates of return should be essentially zero.

19. For example, Krugman (1978) found that the standard deviation for the real mark/dollar exchange rate during the German hyperinflation, February 1920–December 1923, was much larger (20.8 percent) than during the 1970s, even though the serial correlation was no higher (.765).

20. Cumby and Obstfeld (1984, p. 146) used a Q-statistic to test for higher-order serial correlation in monthly real exchange rate changes and found none. However, they also found that expected inflation differentials were unrelated to expected exchange rate changes, rejecting the random walk characterization of the real exchange rate. Huizinga (1987) was also able to reject the random walk in some cases.

21. As already noted, an AR coefficient of .7 on a yearly basis corresponds to an AR of .97 on a monthly basis ($.97^{12} = .70$). Thus, it might take 564 months of data ($2.93^2(1 - .97^2)/(1 - .97)^2 = 563.7$) to be able to reject the null hypothesis of AR = 1. This is forty-seven years—very little gain in efficiency over the test on yearly data. Summers (1986) demonstrates the low power of random walk tests in the context of stock market prices.

22. DeJong et al. (1988, table II) offer power tables for the Dickey-Fuller test, which show that when the true AR parameter is .8, even a sample size of 100 is sufficient to reject a random walk only about 65 percent of the time.

23. As the sample period covers a number of changes in exchange rate regime, it would be desirable to allow for shifts in the coefficient (and in the variance of the disturbance term). But many of the proponents of a random walk in the real exchange rate claim it as evidence in favor of an "equilibrium" hypothesis, under which fluctuations in the real exchange rate are caused only by real, as opposed to monetary, factors. Under this null hypothesis, changes in regime should not matter for the real exchange rate. Thus our statistical test is a valid rejection of the null hypothesis, even though it lumps together all 119 years of observations.

24. Sticky goods prices are only one of a number of possible sources of deviations from ex ante relative PPP. Another is the existence of the prices of nontraded goods in the relevant price index. Dornbusch (1983) shows how movement in the

relative price of nontraded goods affects the real interest rate, saving, and borrowing from abroad, while Engel and Kletzer (1987) show specifically how such movement can give rise to the Feldstein-Horioka finding. Bovenberg (1989) too shows how imperfect substitutability of goods can give rise to the finding.

25. The rationally expected rate of real depreciation estimated from a specific time-series process is not necessarily the same as the actual expectation of real depreciation held by investors. Frankel (1986, pp. 58–59) used survey data on expectations of exchange rate changes (collected by the *Economist*-affiliated *Financial Report*) and forecasts of price level changes (by DRI) to compute a direct measure of expected real depreciation for the dollar against five currencies. The numbers showed an expectation that the real exchange rate tends to regress back toward PPP at a statistically significant rate of 8 to 12 percent a year.

26. Obstfeld (1986) shows, in a life-cycle model of saving with actual OECD data on the functional distribution of income and on population growth, that the coefficient in an investment regression can be similar to those estimated by Feldstein and Horioka. (Similar claims based on models of intertemporal optimization are made by Ghosh, 1988, Roubini, 1988, Tesar, 1991, and Leiderman and Razin, 1989.) But Feldstein and Bacchetta (1989) argue that the growth rate is not in fact responsible for the observed coefficient.

27. Some of these data were also analyzed in Frankel and MacArthur (1988). Some forward rate observations for Italy, Austria, and Belgium in the Barclay's data looked suspicious. In addition, Barclay's does not quote a rate for Portugal. For this study, forward exchange rates for Italy and Belgium are taken from the Bank of America (also obtained via DRI) and for Austria and Portugal from the *Financial Times*. The Barclay's data for Ireland also appear suspect (1986–88).

28. The data appendix to NBER Working Paper 2309 gives details.

29. The standard errors for individual country means are usable, indeed are conservative, despite the use of overlapping observations, because they are calculated as if there were $T/3$ observations rather than the actual T observations used.

30. Saving-investment regressions, by contrast, show the counterintuitive result: coefficients for LDCs that are lower (suggesting higher capital mobility, in Feldstein and Horioka's terms) than for industrialized countries. Fieleke (1982), Dooley, Frankel and Masson (1987), and Summers (1988).

31. The results were reported in NBER working paper 2856 but were omitted here to save space.

32. It is possible that, for some countries, seasonal variation constitutes one forecastable component.

33. The British liberalization of 1979 is explained and analyzed in Artis and Taylor (1989).

34. As shown, e.g., by Boothe et al. (1985, p. 112).

35. For example, Otani (1983) and Frankel (1984).

36. The frequently large negative covered differential that had been observed for Australia up to mid-1983 (see, e.g., Argy, 1987) largely vanished thereafter.

37. Claasen and Wyplosz (1982), Giavazzi and Pagano (1985, pp. 27–28), Frankel (1982) and Wyplosz (1986), among others.

38. "Capitalism," *Economist*, May 21, 1988, p. 95.

39. The magnitude of the covered interest differential fell sharply in 1987 for these two countries. (See de Macedo and Torres, 1989.)

40. For France, Italy, Ireland, Spain, and Greece (as reported in *World Financial Markets*, September 9, 1988, p. 5). Denmark's covered differential remains quite high in our sample. The country has been reported to have no capital controls left (*Economist*, May 21, 1988), but this evidently applies only to securities: the European Commission reports that deposits and other short-term transactions remained subject to authorization in Denmark as of 1988.

41. Bahrain shows a smaller differential than the others, and even than some of the European countries with controls, like Spain and Ireland. (It should be noted that the forward rate quoted by Barclay's applies to the Saudi riyal; we match it up with the Bahraini interest rate because no local interest rate is available for Saudi Arabia and the two countries are said to be closely tied financially. The riyal is classified by the IMF under the same exchange rate arrangement as Bahrain's currency, the dinar, which would suggest that the same forward rate could be applied to both. But the riyal exchange rate does in fact vary somewhat, so that our measured covered interest differential is not entirely legitimate.)

42. Taylor (1988) studies covered interest parity *within the London Euromarket*. Such studies do not get at the degree of financial market integration *across national boundaries*. When authors find deviations from covered interest parity in such data (e.g., Mishkin, 1984a, p. 1350), it is often due to low quality of the data, e.g., inexact timing. With high-quality data, Taylor finds that covered interest parity held extremely well in 1985, that it held less well in the 1970s, particularly during "turbulent" periods, that the differential had mostly vanished by 1979, and that the differentials that do exist are slightly larger at the longer-term than shorter-term maturities. But, like other studies, Taylor has no data on maturities longer than one year.

43. It is still quite likely, however, that there is a wedge in each country separating the long-term interest rate from the after-tax cost of capital facing firms. Such a wedge could be due either to the corporate income tax system or to imperfect substitutability between bonds and capital. Hatsopoulos, Krugman, and Summers (1988) argue that the cost of capital facing U.S. corporations is higher than that facing Japanese corporations, even when real interest rates are equal, because U.S. companies rely more heavily on equity financing, which is more expensive than debt financing. See also the papers in Feldstein (1987).

44. The results are reported in NBER working paper no. 2856 but are omitted here to save space.

45. Reported in column (1) of table 8 in the originally published version of this chapter.

46. The five exceptions, currencies that depreciated against the dollar at a rate more rapid than predicted by the forward discount, were the Hong Kong dollar, Malaysian ringgit, Singapore dollar, Saudi Arabian riyal, and South African rand.

47. The currencies are the Saudi Arabian riyal and two that appreciated strongly against the dollar, relative to the forward rate: the Japanese yen and the Portuguese escudo.

48. The results are reported in a working paper but are omitted here.

49. Many others have found a highly significant predictable component of (fd-Δs^e), often when regressing against fd, and particularly in-sample. It is possible that such findings are not due to a time-varying premium, as the rational expectations approach would have it, but rather to a time-varying model of spot rate determination (together with insufficiently long sample periods), and learning by investors. Such speculations go outside the scope of this chapter. (See chapters 12 and 14.)

50. The statistics on real depreciation were reported in table 9 of the originally published version of this chapter.

51. The results are reported in a working paper but are omitted here.

52. It seems that in both cases an apparently predictable component of the spot rate changes constitutes most of the variation (as opposed to variation in the forward discount or inflation differential, respectively): the significant coefficients on the forward discount, interest differential, and ex post inflation differential when $(\Delta s - \Delta p - \Delta p^*)$ is the dependent variable are always of opposite sign and similar magnitude as the coefficients when $(fd - \Delta s)$ is the dependent variable.

53. One view is that the high degree of integration of financial markets is one of the *causes* of the high degree of volatility of exchange rates. The issue is discussed, and further references given, in Frankel (1988b).

Introduction to Part II

1. That paper, Frankel and Hardouvelis (1985), extended the test to cover reactions in other foreign exchange, precious metal, and agricultural commodity markets.

2. The argument first appeared in Frankel (1985c).

Chapter 3

1. See papers by Jacob Frenkel (1977, 1980) and by John Bilson (1978a, 1978b).

2. Roots lie in J. Marcus Fleming and Robert Mundell (1964b, 1968b). They argued that if capital were perfectly mobile, a nonzero interest differential would attract a potentially infinite capital inflow, with a large effect on the exchange rate. Victor Argy and Michael Porter (1972), Jürg Niehans (1975), Dornbusch (1976a,

1976b, 1976c), Michael Mussa (1976), and Pentti Kouri (1976a, 1976b) also introduced the role of expectations into the Mundell-Fleming framework.

3. The rates of interest referred to are instantaneous rates per unit of time, i.e., the forces of interest. In the absence of uncertainty (or, in the stochastic case, if the term structures of the interest differential and the forward discount contain no risk premium), equation (1) should also hold when the rates are defined over any finite interval τ, since the left-hand and right-hand sides would be equal to the expected future values of the left-hand side and right-hand side, respectively, of (1) integrated from 0 to τ.

4. For evidence that the deviations from covered interest parity are smaller than transactions costs, see Frenkel and Levich (1975), and pages 58–64 of this book.

5. If there is no long-run growth of real income or technical change in the demand for money, then the rates of monetary growth are π and π^*. If there is long-run real growth or technical change, then we would adjust the monetary growth rates before arriving at the expected long-run inflation rates π and π^*.

6. Note, however, that the assumption of rational expectations or perfect foresight is not required for equation (2) and thus is not required for the model.

7. This would not be quite right because the nominal interest rates are short term while the expected inflation rates are long term. However, it does turn out, with a price-adjustment equation such as is adopted in appendix 3A, that $s - \bar{s}$ is proportional to the short-term real interest differential $[(i - \Delta p^e) - (i^* - \Delta p^{*e})]$.

8. In words, long-run equality between the nominal interest differential and the expected inflation differential follows from interest rate parity (equality between the interest differential and expected depreciation) and long-run relative purchasing power parity (equality between depreciation and the inflation differential). An alternative argument is that in the long run international investment flows ensure that real interest rates are equal across countries: $\bar{i} - \pi = \bar{i}^* - \pi^*$. The investment argument is not necessary, however, nor, if used, does it preclude the possibility of different real rates of interest in the short run, since even the most perfectly classical of economies have fixed capital stocks that earn nonzero varying profit rates in the short run.

9. This assumption rules out the possibility of permanent shifts in the terms of trade and so gives essentially a one-good model. It does allow the possibility of temporary shifts; the existence of large departures from the Law of One Price for international trade even in closely matched categories of goods has been shown in studies by Peter Isard (1977) and by Irving Kravis and Robert Lipsey (1977).

10. Actual money supplies and actual income levels can both easily be allowed to differ from their equilibrium levels, but these extensions of the analysis are omitted here in the interest of brevity.

11. It is not stated here where the errors come from. Probably the most likely source of errors is the money demand equation (5), which would bias the coefficient of $(m - m^*)$ downward if it is not constrained to be one. This possibility is discussed below.

12. See Dornbusch (1976c). The only other differences between the present model and the Dornbusch model are that the former is a two-country model, while the latter is a small-country model, and the latter uses a slightly different price-adjustment equation.

13. In view of the result (A4) in the appendix, that the purchasing power parity gap is proportional to the real interest differential, it is not surprising that a theory which assumes that the former is always zero should also assume that the latter is always zero.

14. Germany is viewed as the domestic country in the econometric equations.

15. The equality of current long-term real rates of interest follows from the result that in the long run the short-term real rates are equal, and the requirement of a rational term structure that the long-term real interest differential be the average of the expected short-term real interest differentials.

16. The semielasticity estimate and an average interest rate of around 6 percent imply an interest elasticity of around $(6.0 \times .06 =) .36$, which is in the range of estimates of the long-run elasticity made by Stephen Goldfeld (1976) and others.

17. Hans Genberg (1978) estimates for Germany that 37 percent of an initial divergence from purchasing power parity disappears after one year.

18. The equation fails to track the continued sharp depreciation of the dollar in January and February 1978. The regressions that were reported in earlier versions of this chapter did not include this period, and consequently appeared more favorable to the real interest differential model.

19. Here we are assuming (for the first time) that the estimated long-run interest semielasticity holds in the short run as well. If money demand is subject to lagged adjustment, then the short-run effect of a monetary contraction on the interest rate and hence on the exchange rate would be *greater* than that calculated here. However, the theory and econometrics behind equation (8) would be completely unaffected.

20. On the other hand, if some of the expansion is expected to be reversed in the following month, then the decrease in the equilibrium rate would be correspondingly *smaller*.

21. The assumption of exogenous output can be relaxed by assuming that output is demand determined. Then a necessary condition for overshooting is that the elasticity of demand with respect to relative prices is less than 1.0. See the appendix to Dornbusch (1976c).

22. The rationalization necessarily implies a disequilibrium formulation of the goods market. More sophisticated price equations give very similar results but are not considered here.

Chapter 4

1. This distinction between capital mobility and substitutability is made precise by Dornbusch and Krugman (1976). Earlier references to it appear in Girton and

Henderson (1976), Girton and Roper (1977), and Dornbusch (1977). The distinction is far from universally accepted (for example, Mundell, 1963, implicitly took perfect mobility to require perfect substitutability) but is useful.

2. Empirical tests have shown covered interest parity to hold to a high degree of approximation, at least in the Eurocurrency market. See, for example, Frenkel and Levich (1977). Covered interest parity holds less well if the interest rates used refer to treasury bills, commercial paper, or other financial securities that differ from the forward contract with respect to tax treatment, default risk, or other factors. However, at the level of aggregation relevant for most macroeconomic models we speak only of "the" interest rate, abstracting from distinctions such as that between the thirty-day Eurodollar interest rate and the thirty-day treasury bill rate. This chapter presumes that level of aggregation and presumes covered interest parity.

3. It is difficult to test uncovered interest parity empirically because expectations are not observable. Uncovered interest parity (and, by implication, perfect substitutability) can be tested *jointly* with market efficiency by examining the ex post excess return on domestic currency. The excess return is defined as the interest differential in excess of ex post depreciation, or alternatively (given covered interest parity) as the forward discount in excess of ex post depreciation. Under the joint null hypothesis, the ex post excess return should be random: the forward rate should be an unbiased predictor of the future spot rate (see figure 4.1).

Some such tests take the perfect substitutability component of the joint hypothesis as given and interpret the results as evidence on efficiency. See, for example, Cornell (1977), Cornell and Dietrich (1978), and chapter 8 here, and Frenkel (1977); the literature is surveyed by Levich (1979a) and Kohlhagen (1978). But others of such tests take the market efficiency component of the joint hypothesis as given and interpret the results as evidence on substitutability. See Stockman (1978), Cumby and Obstfeld (1984), and chapter 10 in this volume.

4. Some of the many examples are Allen and Kenen (1980); Black (1973); Branson (1977); Branson, Halttunen, and Masson (1977); Calvo and Rodriguez (1977); Dooley and Isard (1979); Dornbusch (1983a); Flood (1979); Girton and Henderson (1977); Girton and Roper (1977); Kouri (1976a, 1982); Kouri and de Macedo (1978); McKinnon (1976); Porter (1979); Tobin and de Macedo (1980); and Rodriguez (1980). The antecedents are the portfolio-balance approach under fixed exchange rates, as represented by Branson (1968), and the portfolio-balance model in a closed economy, as represented by Tobin (1969).

5. Examples are Frenkel (1976, 1977, 1980), Mussa (1976), Dornbusch (1976a, 1976c), Girton and Roper (1977), Bilson (1978a, 1978b), Hodrick (1978), and chapter 3 of this volume.

6. Officer (1976) surveys the literature on purchasing power parity. Some other empirical studies are Isard (1977), Genberg (1978), and Krugman (1978).

7. This distinction between the monetary approach to exchange rates and the more restrictive monetarist model follows the distinction made by Whitman (1975) in the theory of fixed exchange rates between the monetary approach to the balance of payments and the more restrictive "global monetarist" model. (In the past—

Frankel (1979b), chapter 3 in this volume—I have used the term "Chicago model" for what I am here calling the monetarist model.)

8. Little published monetarist work asserts this restrictive special case, the monetarists having long ago relaxed the quantity theory of money to study the effect of expected inflation on money demand.

A paper by Caves and Feige (1980) that purports to test the monetary approach to exchange-rate determination uses as its criterion the unusual proposition that the exchange rate is entirely explainable by the past history of the money supplies. Even the most extreme monetarist proponent of the monetary approach recognizes the importance of fluctuations in real income.

In a further confusion, Caves and Feige claim that proponents of the monetary approach "have failed to recognize that one of the consequences of an efficient foreign exchange market is to eliminate the possibility of directly observing a systematic relationship [between] exchange rates and past supplies of national monies. If the foreign exchange market is efficient, all monetary effects on exchange rates will be contemporaneous" (1980, p. 121). But as is well known, market efficiency requires not that changes in the spot rate be independent of past variables such as money supplies, but that changes in the spot rate *in excess of the interest differential* (or forward discount) be independent of past variables. In any monetary model except the restrictive special case described above, the past history of the money supply may contain information on changes in the spot rate without violating efficiency. In the benchmark monetarist model, for example, the interest differential and the rationally expected change in the spot rate are each equal to the relative rate of expected monetary growth; actual changes in the spot rate will be independent of past money supply *changes*, not *levels*. In the Dornbusch overshooting model, changes in the spot rate are not independent of either past money supply changes *or* levels.

9. See Mundell (1964b), Argy and Porter (1972), Niehans (1975), and Dornbusch (1976a, 1976b).

10. The version that follows is based on Dornbusch (1976c) as generalized in Frankel (1979b)—chapter 3 in this volume—to include the case of secular inflation. (In that paper I used the term "Keynesian model" for what I am here calling the "overshooting model." We should also note that overshooting is possible in other models, as shown by Flood [1979].) Investigations of the overshooting properties of the Dornbusch model include Mathieson (1977) and Bhandari (1981).

11. In the appendix to Frankel (1979b)—chapter 3 in this volume—it is proved that the form of exchange rate expectations specified in (12) is rational, assuming an additional equation in which the price level adjusts in the short run in response to excess goods demand (itself a function of relative prices, and possibly income and the real interest rate) and increases in the long run at the secular inflation rate (π).

12. Imposition of this constraint has the added benefit that if the money stocks are endogenous, as they surely are, then it allows consistent estimation of the other coefficients.

13. A third way to obtain still more efficient estimates is to take advantage of the joint distribution that the error terms must have in a world of multilateral floating, through Zellner's technique of seemingly unrelated regressions. The membership of Germany and France in the European Monetary System, for example, provides particularly strong grounds for expecting their exchange rates against the dollar to be highly correlated. However, the results obtained from using Zellner's technique suggest that the gain in efficiency is slight. Of course, the theory may be correct and yet the economic estimation plagued by more serious problems than high standard errors, that is, by inconsistency resulting from misspecification or simultaneity. Haynes and Stone (1981) argue against imposing the constraint that the money demand parameters in equation (1) are equal across countries. But the results are little affected by relaxing the constraints. Driskill and Sheffrin (1981) and others argue that the interest differential is endogenous, requiring simultaneous-equation estimation. In Frankel (1981a) I use the ratio of the monetary base to government debt as an instrumental variable to estimate the coefficient of the interest differential.

14. The turnabout on purchasing power parity is strikingly symbolized by the title of Frenkel (1981b), in contrast to the title of Katseli-Papaefstratiou (1979).

15. The role of an oil shock in determining the real exchange rate is explored by Obstfeld (1980a) and Giavazzi, Odekon and Wyplosz (1982).

16. The table appears in the original 1984 paper, as does a data appendix.

17. The table appears in the original 1984 paper, as does an extensive description of the data in an appendix.

18. Adding the three risk premium variables to the regressions in table 4.2—the monetary model with drift in velocity and the real exchange rate—turns out only to vitiate the relatively positive results. And attempts to relate the risk premium variables directly to the excess return on countries' assets as in equation (19) have not been successful (Dooley and Isard, 1983).

19. It should be noted that Meese and Rogoff's "random walk" finding was that the simple spot exchange rate was a better predictor than the simple forward rate (or the simple forecasts of structural or ARIMA models). This is not quite the same thing as saying that these other predictors are of no help at all in predicting changes in the exchange rate. Meese and Rogoff did not test whether there might exist some *convex combination* of the forward rate (or model forecasts) and the spot rate that would out-predict the simple spot rate. This is what the large literature on bias in the forward discount tests for, and the answer is generally "no." But Somanath (1986) uses updated data sets (to December 1983) to test versions of the monetary models combined with the lagged spot rate, and claims forecasting performance superior to the simple lagged spot rate. See also Woo (1985). Meese and Rogoff (1988) report some ability of the model based on real interest differentials to predict the direction of change in the 1980s.

20. This disturbing trend in modern macroeconometrics is an extreme case of the old problem that a statistical failure to reject a null hypothesis does not entitle one

to claim an interesting finding. The failure to reject may simply be due to low power in the test, especially if the null hypothesis is a weak one. Traditionally in econometrics, the goal is supposed to be to *succeed* in statistically rejecting one economically interesting hypothesis in favor of another, i.e., to get results that are "statistically significant at the 95 percent level," rather than the reverse. What makes the trend away from this principle so remarkable is that the popular null hypothesis of a random walk is so weak that a failure to reject it is nothing other than a failure to explain any movement in the variable of interest. It is true that a problem with the classical econometric criterion is that the author has an incentive to sift through many regressions, and the journal editor has an incentive to sift through many submitted articles, to come up with "good" results. But it is no solution to this problem to redefine the inability to explain something as a "good" result.

21. The ten-year real interest differential, corrected for any risk premium, tells us how far the market expects the dollar to depreciate per year in real terms over the next ten years. The expected real exchange rate in ten years, unlike in three months, can in turn be interpreted as the long-run equilibrium. See, for example, Isard (1983).

22. Frankel (1985b).

Chapter 5

1. The positive effect of unanticipated money announcements on interest rate changes was documented by William Conrad (1981), who used an ARIMA process to measure expected money growth, and J. Grossman (1981), who used the same survey numbers that we do. It has also been documented by Vance Roley (1982), Thomas Urich and Paul Wachtel (1981), Urich (1982), Bradford Cornell (1982a), and Gikas Hardouvelis (1984).

2. This explanation is developed theoretically by Donald Nichols, David Small and C. Webster (1983), as well as by many of the empirical papers listed in note 1.

3. The first version of this paper appeared January 4, 1982. Bradford Cornell (1982b) has written a similar paper.

4. One might legitimately ask how we hope to explain announcement effects on the interest rate if it is tied down by the money demand equation. The rationalization we are using here is that the interest rate i, that gives us instantaneous money market equilibrium is a *very* short-term interest rate—shorter term than the one-month short-term interest rate represented by our data. An announcement that raised or lowered expected future money growth could raise or lower the value that i is expected to have later in the month (when p has had time to adjust fractionally), and thus raise or lower today's one-month rate, without changing today's i. The disadvantage with this rationalization is that announcement effects are in fact observed for interest rates with a term as short as one day, e.g., the Fed funds rate.

A possible alternative solution to the problem is to abandon the requirement that the money demand equation hold exactly in the short run and to model explicitly the money multiplier process as a simultaneous equation in m, the current i, and the i's expected to prevail later in the week or month. Banks react to a monetary announcement by expecting, e.g., contraction and a higher Fed funds rate later in the week, and thus by raising their demand for reserves today, raising the Fed funds rate (and lowering m) today. The fact that banks are allowed to average their reserve holdings out over the week to meet reserve requirements explains why they would drive today's Fed funds rate up to the level expected to prevail later in the week. We are indebted to Dale Henderson for the banking story.

5. Between $t - 1$ and t' the money supply changes occur, and the money demand errors occur. The announcement is made at t. The symbol t' is really only a handy device that designates the values of the variables that would hold at time t, if no money announcement had been made. Thus, $t + 1$ is exactly one period away from t' for purposes, say, of calculating interest rates.

6. We have used the fact that $(m_t - E_{t'} m_t) = (a_t - E_{t'} a_t)$, i.e., that the market's revision of the expected money supply carries with it a matching revision in expected money demand. This follows from the assumptions that prices are sticky, interest rates are observable, and the money demand equation (1) holds.
   Presumably the market has already used changes in the interest rate observed during the week to estimate money supply less money demand, with the breakdown (as to how much each is estimated to have changed) depending rationally on the relative variance of the two. Still, the market gains a lot of information when the true money supply is announced. When it does, the revisions in its estimates of money supply and money demand must be equal.

7. The forecast error is the log of the actual announced money supply minus the log of the predicted money supply. Actually, Money Market Services, Inc., supplied predicted *changes* in the money supply. These figures were added to the current revised figures for the previous week, reported in the *Federal Reserve Bulletin*, to get the predicted money supply.

8. In the light of our finding that the survey data appear to be unbiased predictors of the actual money supply figures, one might be tempted to assume rationality of expectations and to examine the actual money supply process directly. For example, Pierce (1981) has found that the purely transitory component is responsible for a standard deviation of $\pm \$3.3$ billion in the weekly money supply figures. However, the existence of transitory deviations in the money supply is not sufficient to imply the announcement effect on interest rates. We would also need positive autocorrelation in money demand innovations, as in the model of section 5.2 (or in the banking system innovations, as in note 2). Simultaneous estimation of money supply and demand equations might answer the question, but the technique used here is cleaner and easier.

9. The Federal Reserve Board changed its operating procedure on October 6, 1979, abandoning the use of interest rates as a guide to intervention in money markets.

The aim of this policy change, of course, was to enable it to hit its money growth targets in the future, an aim that it had often failed to achieve in the past, and to convince the market of its determination to do so. Thus, it seems appropriate to consider the post-October period alone.

10. For example, Fama (1975) and Frenkel (1981a). Of course, there already exists other evidence against the Fama view. See, for example, Nelson and Schwert (1977).

11. A subsequent paper, Frankel and Hardouvelis (1985), shows that the theoretical and empirical results of this chapter both apply when prices of basic commodities are substituted for prices of foreign exchange. It examines six commodities—gold, silver, sugar, cocoa, cattle, and feeders—for the period December 5, 1980, to November 1, 1982. There is a statistically significant tendency for the commodity prices, like the price of foreign exchange, to fall in response to the announcement of an unexpectedly large money supply. Again this supports the dual claims that (1) the real interest rate varies, because prices of (other) goods are sticky, and (2) the market trusts the Fed to correct deviations from its money growth targets.

12. In other words, our expectation equation (5) is of the form that is rational in a system that includes a price-adjustment equation of the Mussa form.

Chapter 6

1. Contrary to some perceptions, Japan removed most of its controls on capital inflow in 1979. Frankel (1984a) analyzes U.S. pressure, from October 1983 to May 1984, to induce Japan to accelerate liberalization of its financial markets, with the supposed goal of reducing the "undervaluation" of the yen.

2. The overall balance of payments obtained by adding the reported current-account deficit to the reported private capital-account surplus was a large negative number, in the early 1980s. However, the statistical discrepancy, almost all of which belongs in the private balance of payments rather than under official reserve transactions, was approximately as large. In 1982 the statistical discrepancy was the larger of the two, that is, central banks reported net losses of dollar reserve assets. This was not true continuously. In 1984 central banks reported a slight net acquisition of dollar reserve assets. But this was explained by interest earned by foreign central banks on their dollar reserves. Thus, it remains true that central banks sold dollars, not bought them. Such foreign-exchange intervention was increasingly evident in 1985.

3. The dollar was expected to appreciate against the pound and the French franc. It was expected to depreciate against the mark and yen even in the 1970s.

4. Kouri (1976a) introduced rational expectations into the international portfolio-balance model. (Kouri used the term "momentary equilibrium" where Williamson uses "current equilibrium" and this essay uses "the overshooting definition of overvaluation.") If the degree of speculation is defined not as the magnitude of expected depreciation but as the degree of responsiveness to expected deprecia-

tion (i.e., the degree of bond substitutability), its effect on exchange-rate volatility depends on the source of the disturbance (see, e.g., Driskill and McCafferty, 1980).

5. There is always danger of oversimplification. Other factors such as the decline in oil prices played a role in the reduction in inflation. On the other hand, one can view the decline in the dollar price of oil as another effect of the U.S. monetary contraction, via both a fall in worldwide income and the appreciation of the dollar.

6. Overlapping contracts can create the illusion of serial correlation in expectational errors. A small probability of a large change in the exchange rate can skew the error distribution and bias standard errors (the "peso problem"). Variation in the purchasing power of domestic currency can introduce the illusion of bias due to Jensen's inequality. Fortunately, each of these econometric problems can be handled. For one paper addressing each problem, see Hansen and Hodrick (1980), Krasker (1980), and Engel (1984), respectively. The appendix to this essay offers a way of rejecting the hypothesis that rational expectations and "peso problem" conditions describe the 1981–85 appreciation.

7. The a priori argument that the risk premium must be small is made in Krugman (1981) and Frankel (1986a). The latter paper also gives references to the empirical literature.

8. Frankel and Engel (1984) statistically reject the constraints imposed by the hypothesis of mean-variance optimization. Hodrick and Srivastava (1984) reject constraints imposed by the hypothesis of intertemporal expected-utility maximization.

9. Regressions against the forward discount were run by Tryon (1979) and Bilson (1981a), followed by many others. The finding in Meese and Rogoff (1983a) and elsewhere that the forward rate is often no better a predictor than the lagged spot rate is closely related to the finding that the regression coefficient described in the text is less than 1.

10. In Frankel (1983c), I demonstrate formally, in the Dornbusch overshooting model, that if the market overestimates the future rate of change of the exchange rate, the degree of volatility is less than it would be under rational expectations. A smaller increase in the current value of the currency becomes sufficient to generate the expected future depreciation necessary to offset a given interest differential, so overshooting is less extreme.

11. In the literature on exchange-rate determination, examples are Mussa (1976) for the flexible-price monetary model, Dornbusch (1976c) for the sticky-price monetary model, and Kouri (1976a) for the portfolio-balance model. Obstfeld and Rogoff (1983) show that speculative bubbles can be ruled out if the government fractionally backs its currency by standing ready to redeem each dollar for a small amount of gold or real capital, or even if it does so with only small (nonzero) probability.

12. Flood and Garber (1980) conclude that the German hyperinflation of 1921–23 was due to fundamentals—excessive and accelerating money growth—not a speculative bubble. Note, incidentally, that the sort of test used by Meese (1986),

rather than that of Flood and Garber, would be needed to detect a situation in which bubbles are frequently forming and collapsing.

13. If we argue that after a disturbance the exchange rate jumps to another nearby bubble path, we must abandon the framework in which the choice at each point in time is between whatever path we have previously been on and the fundamentals path. In that case, what determines which of the infinite number of bubble paths the market jumps to? We can imagine some variable that is fundamentally irrelevant but that speculators pay attention to nonetheless. Each new bit of information about that variable will then displace the asset price to a new, nearby bubble path. Until someone convincingly models such a process, however, it seems more realistic to assume that when a bubble bursts the asset price returns to the fundamentals path.

14. The term "expected future spot price" is ambiguous owing to Jensen's inequality: in the case where the dollar/pound forward rate is greater than the expected future dollar/pound spot rate, the pound/dollar forward rate will be less than 1 over the expected future dollar/pound spot rate, but not necessarily less than the expected future pound/dollar rate as claimed in the text. There are two ways around this problem. We can measure expected values in terms of purchasing power over a basket of goods assumed common to residents of both countries. Or, in the more realistic case in which residents of each country have a preference for their local currency, we can assume that the risk premium is large enough to outweigh Jensen's inequality, which will be the case if the coefficient of risk aversion exceeds 1 (see, e.g., Krugman, 1981).

15. I have assumed here that exports are denominated in the currency of the producing country. To the extent that they are denominated in the currency of the importing country, it is the exporter who must hedge by selling foreign exchange forward. If U.S. exporters are able to sell pounds at a forward price greater than the expected future spot price, so that the risk premium is a positive factor for U.S. exports, it will go the other way for British exporters. Thus the two effects on trade still go in opposite directions.

16. In the modern stock approach, some participants must be prepared to hold positive open dollar positions in market equilibrium if the net supply of dollar-denominated debt is large relative to pound-denominated debt. This could be interpreted as a positive *cumulative* trade surplus for Britain rather than *flow* trade surplus, assuming Americans deal in assets or liabilities denominated only in dollars. More generally, the net supplies of outside assets—government debts corrected for foreign-exchange intervention—matter most. But cumulated current accounts also enter to the extent that residents of each country prefer to hold their local currency (Dornbusch, 1983a; Krugman, 1981; and pages 108–110 of this book).

17. See Mussa (1979a) for a review of the role of capital mobility and other possible complications in invalidating the old view that floating rates insulate a country from foreign disturbances.

18. If the dollar appreciates enough, the proper policy response for foreigners is not to increase expenditure but to decrease it, as they did. Much attention has been

devoted to the case for international macroeconomic coordination. Oudiz and Sachs (1984) provide an excellent appraisal, with references. There would appear to be a strong case for shifts in the monetary/fiscal *mix*, toward fiscal contraction in the United States and fiscal expansion in Europe and Japan, whether coordinated or not.

19. The decomposition of the deterioration in the U.S. trade balance assumes conventional estimates of trade elasticities with respect to relative prices (1.3) and incomes (2.0). The 1983 base is imports of $260 billion and exports of $200 billion. The figures for real growth in the U.S. versus the rest of the OECD are from the OECD *Economic Outlook*, June 1985.

Chapter 7

1. This seems a more polite label than the alternative possibility, the "know nothing" school.

2. This system was not without drawbacks. Many econometricians adopted the shady practice of trying out many different functional forms, combinations of variables, and sample periods in their regressions until they found results that appeared as statistically significant.

3. If one is a believer in Ricardian equivalence, one looks for an effect of the budget deficit on interest rates or exchange rates, one typically fails to find large and significant effects, and one concludes that therefore Ricardian equivalence holds. If one does not believe in Ricardian equivalence, one looks for an effect of the budget deficit on private saving, one typically fails to find large and significant effects, and one concludes that therefore equivalence does not hold.

4. My comments here pertain, for example, to Alan Stockman (1987). In that paper, like this commentary, the author should be awarded a medal for bravery in taking on the question of what the equilibrium models have to say of use for policy makers. Many authors seek to evade the question altogether.

5. Ibid. Thus most equilibrium theorists do not wish even to hazard a guess as to what profound shifts in consumers' tastes for American products or in workers' productivity occurred over 1980–85 (to double the dollar's value against the yen and mark) or over 1985–87 (to halve it again).

6. As far as I know, he does not offer any evidence of the third kind: things that can be explained by the equilibrium theory but *not* by the sticky-price theory.

7. If the observations are monthly, then forty-seven years of data will do. This calculation and the test results for U.K.-U.S. data from 1869 to 1987 appear in some earlier papers of mine, as well as in Frankel (1991), chapter 2 of this volume.

8. Using the correct Dickey-Fuller test.

9. This sample period mixes different exchange rate regimes, so it would be desirable to allow for heteroskedasticity and for different speeds of adjustment during different subperiods. On the other hand, under the null hypothesis, the

distribution of the real exchange rate is invariant with respect to the regime. (I am indebted to Maurice Obstfeld for this point.)

Introduction to Part III

1. Hodrick (1988) and Levich (1985, 1989) offer surveys.

2. The resolution of the Siegal paradox, wherein the value of a currency is defined in real terms rather than nominal, can be attributed, I believe, to Boyer (1977), Stockman (1978), and Krugman (1977). The test by Engel (1984) takes variable price levels into account directly.

3. The first written (though never published) paper to refer to the distributional problem exemplified by the Mexican peso is believed to have been Rogoff (1977). The problem is also mentioned by Stockman, 1978, pp. 168–72. Neither uses the phrase "peso problem," however. The first published paper with the phrase in the title was Krasker (1980), and for this reason is usually credited.

4. The moving-average process induced by overlapping observations, which was first pointed out by Levich (1976), followed by Stockman (1978, pp. 167–68), Rogoff (1977), and Garber (1978), invalidates OLS statistical tests of unbiasedness. Hakkio (1981) pointed out that the most obvious way of dealing with this problem, GLS, was not in general consistent. The solution adopted in my paper reprinted here was the crude one of simply skipping observations. Hansen and Hodrick (1980) solved the problem by using the method of moments to correct the standard errors; this was also the first paper testing unbiasedness that was published in a top journal. Since then, this solution to the problem of the moving-average process has become so commonplace that it is frequently used automatically in tests on financial market data even where observations are not in fact overlapping and where there is no a priori reason to suspect an error process of the particular moving-average type.

5. Tryon (1979), in a never-published paper, was the first to do this. Meese and Singleton (1982) showed that it was a more powerful test of unbiasedness than the tests performed on levels (as indeed is intuitively clear from comparing columns (4) and (5) in table 8.1 here).

6. For example, this approach was used in the present context, i.e, to show the conditions under which the risk premium could be zero, by Obstfeld (1982).

7. I did this in Frankel (1982b). That paper, "A Test of Perfect Substitutability in the Foreign Exchange Market," is a natural bridge between chapters 8 and 10 here, but the amount of overlap was too great to justify reproducing all three papers.

8. Disturbingly, most international CAPM models continue to assume that dollars are safe assets for all investors in the market, or to make similarly unrealistic assumptions about investors' safe assets, fifteen years after Kouri (1977) and Dornbusch (1983a) showed how to do it right. "Doing it right" when defining real returns means recognizing that residents of each country consume both domestic and foreign goods, with a relative preference for their own, so that what is safe for residents of one country is risky for residents of another.

9. Frankel and Engel (1984).

10. Comprehensive enough, for example, to include either the world's money supplies or its corporate capital (let alone real estate and other assets). It should be noted that the conventional estimates of the coefficient of relative risk aversion come to us primarily from applications outside finance theory.

11. Frankel (1986a).

12. Frankel (1985a) makes this point for a domestic portfolio of stocks, bonds, and other assets, with the same mean-variance framework applied to chapter 10 here.

13. A more recent and more general survey is offered by Bollerslev et al. (1990). Recent references on one of the particular applications of time-varying variances, to the area of foreign exchange options prices, are given in Frankel and Wei (1991).

Chapter 8

1. The data analyzed here are weekly observations of New York rates (on Fridays) in dollars per national currency, obtained from the Harris Bank of Chicago's *Weekly Report*. The one-month forward rates are matched up with the spot rates that appear four weeks later. There may be a discrepancy of one business day, which, it is hoped, will not make much difference.

2. To be more precise, the statistic has the interpretation of an R^2 (in the sense that the unpredicted variation plus the predicted variation equals the total variation in the spot rate) if the prediction errors are orthogonal to a constant ($E(s_{+1} - f) = 0$) and are orthgonal to the contemporaneous forward rates ($E(s_{+1} - f|f) = 0$). These are the first two conditions for rational expectations tested below.

3. Levich (1979a) and Kohlhagen (1978) survey this literature.

4. The proposition that people form expectations rationally is even difficult to evaluate theoretically. A person with apparently irrational expectations can always be considered a rational person who does not have access to the necessary information (either the correct data or the correct model) or for whom an effort to obtain the information would be expensive and unreliable.

5. Levich (1979a) emphasizes this point. In terms of the traditional forward market framework, the supply of speculative funds might fail to be infinitely elastic at the level of the expected future spot rate (Tsiang, 1959).

6. The next chapter demonstrates the proposition that risk aversion is not a sufficient condition for the existence of a risk premium (defined as a discrepancy between the forward rate and what the forward rate would be under risk neutrality). Sufficient conditions are risk aversion *and* any one of the following: transactions costs, the existence of "outside" assets, or a nonzero correlation between the value of currency and the real value of other forms of wealth, such as capital. If none of the latter three conditions holds, then there is no risk premium, because the risk can be completely diversified away; in other words, the supply of speculative funds in the forward market is infinitely elastic at the level of the expected future spot rate.

7. However, they do require that the price of a given future contract follow a random walk (Rogoff, 1978).

8. The log solution is precisely correct—that is, rational expectations will produce a unit coefficient—if the spot rate follows a log normal process in discrete time (see Frankel, 1982d, n.2, or chapter 13, n.7), or a diffusion process in continuous time (see appendix 10A in this volume).

9. Provided the sample period is long enough. For years, the Mexican peso sold at a discount on the forward market, and yet the spot value never changed. The peso during this period would have failed the rational expectations test, even though the market may have been rationally anticipating the possibility of the 50 percent devaluation that in fact occurred in 1976.

10. Stockman (1978) and Cornell (1977) also find no significant mean prediction error over this period. When Stockman divides the period into two-year sub-samples, he does find significant prediction errors for the currencies of two countries out of six and claims this as evidence of nonzero risk premia. But Cornell argues, "It is hard to believe that the premium will change sign over a period as short as four years" (p. 59).

11. This is true even if $E[(s_{+4} - f)|(s - f_{-4})] = 0$ as is required under the null hypothesis of rational expectations, and as is tested below.

12. This first strategy is adopted by Frenkel (1979), Krugman (1977), and Bilson (1981b).

13. This alternative strategy is adopted by Bilson and Levich (1977), who use a Box-Jenkins package to estimate the moving-average process, and Obstfeld (1978), who approximates the moving-average process with a high-order autoregressive process.

14. This point was originally made by Hansen and Hodrick (1980) and Hakkio (1981). These authors suggest their own procedures to get around the problem.

15. Given our previous finding in table 8.2 that the mean forward rate is equal to the mean spot rate, it is not surprising that a constant term that is significantly different from zero is generally associated with a slope coefficient that is significantly different from one.

16. Corrections for possible serial correlation, reported in table VI of the originally published version, have little effect on the results.

17. These results were reported as table IV in the originally published version of this chapter.

18. As we would expect from table 8.2, when the constant alone was in the information set.

19. An intuitive explanation of the joint multivariate distribution of the error terms is as follows. The dollar/pound rate sometimes falls because the pound is weakening on world markets, but it also sometimes falls because the dollar is strengthening on world markets. In the latter case, we would expect the dollar/mark and

dollar/franc rates to fall also. More formally, we can see what the multivariate error distribution might look like by observing that $s(x/z) = s(x/y) + s(y/z)$, where $s(x/z)$ is the log of the value of currency z in terms of currency x, etc. Thus, $\text{var}(s(x/z)) = \text{var}(s(x/y)) + \text{var}(s(y/z)) - 2\text{cov}(s(x/y), s(y/z))$. For example, if we assume complete symmetry in the system (all variances equal to σ, and all covariances between pairs of exchange rates involving four distinct currencies equal to zero), then the covariance between the values of any two currencies, each expressed in the same numeraire, is $\sigma/2$. At the other extreme, if one country is much larger and more stable than the others, so that the variances of exchange rates using that country as numeraire are half the size of the variances of all other exchange rates, then the covariances of the exchange rates with that numeraire will all be zero.

Chapter 9

1. The reference is to the so-called "modern" theory of forward exchange: Tsiang (1959), Feldstein (1968), Grubel (1968), and Leland (1971). This literature ignores the existence of foreign residents, in that the market is assumed to evaluate wealth solely in domestic terms. Thus the ownership of foreign assets carries exchange risk that must be compensated by a risk premium, but the ownership of domestic assets does not. The more recent finance models do include foreign residents in the market for forward exchange. See Solnik (1974), Grauer, Litzenberger, and Stehle (1976), Kouri (1976b, 1977) and Fama and Farber (1979). Some of the conclusions in this chapter are implicit in this literature.

2. See, for example, Dornbusch (1976c) and Frenkel (1976).

3. If the domestic and foreign assets are bonds that pay interest each period of i and i^*, respectively, then the price of assets (payable next period) in terms of this period's currency is $1/(1 + i)$ and $1/(1 + i^*)$, respectively. If S is the current price of foreign currency (payable on the spot) in terms of domestic currency, then covered interest parity says that the current price of foreign assets (payable next period) in terms of domestic assets, F, is equal to $S(1 + i)/(1 + i^*)$.

4. The applicability to the question of tests of the efficiency of the forward market is direct. The application to the question of the determination of the spot rate can be made by assuming that interest rates are held constant. For this purpose, we can imagine that any changes in the stock of assets are made in such a way as to keep interest rates unchanged. If one believes in a portfolio-balance explanation of the demand for money, this means assuming that the stocks of bonds and money are always changed equiproportionately. If one believes in a transactions explanation of the demand for money, this means assuming that only the stock of bonds is changed.

5. The quadratic utility function can only be used over the range $(VW) < (\frac{1}{2}b)$, since the marginal utility for real wealth becomes negative after that point. However, the results can be generalized to the case where utility is any function of the mean and variance of real wealth (whereas in the quadratic case, utility is a *linear* function of the mean and variance). Under the axioms of expected utility maximi-

zation, the underlying stochastic process must have a normal distribution if the function to be maximized is to be an arbitrary function of the mean and variance. To generalize the results, it is sufficient to interpret b_i as $-(\partial U_i/\partial \text{ mean})/(\partial U_i/\partial \text{ var})$, which is not in general constant. I am indebted to Hal Varian for this point.

6. The expression for F jumps from ∞ to $-\infty$ when the denominator is zero, but this is because marginal utility turns negative for the quadratic utility function. The relevant range of $\bar{B}$ and $\bar{B}^*$ lies below this point, so that the denominator of the expression is positive.

7. The measure of absolute risk-aversion is given by

$$-\frac{U''}{U'} = \frac{2b_i}{1 - 2b_i(VW_i)},$$

which increases with real wealth. See Arrow (1970).

8. The proposition should perhaps be called the "naive presumption," since the "conventional presumption" says that the relationship between variability and the risk premium depends on whether the domestic country is a net creditor.

9. In a model where PPP did not always hold, an increase in the domestic price level relative to the foreign price level might lower domestic real income and yet raise foreign real income via a shift in demand. In the extreme, total real income might be unchanged, implying no correlation between X and V and thus no risk premium. But in general, one would expect the correlation between the domestic price level and domestic real income to dominate the correlation between it and foreign real income.

10. There is a distinct issue of moral hazard: if a country or its government is heavily indebted in terms of its own currency, it may be tempted to inflate away the value of the debt. But investors are assumed to be as aware of this possibility as the government. They may demand compensation for the expected inflation, without a necessary increase in risk. If there was an increase in risk from moral hazard, it would be the same as any other increase in risk; it would be to the government's advantage to issue the debt in foreign currency so as not to have to pay a risk premium to investors.

Chapter 10

1. The portfolio-balance model was first applied to the international floating-rate economy by Branson (1976), Kouri (1976a), and Girton and Henderson (1977), followed by many others.

2. Stockman (1978) claims some evidence for nonzero risk premia from unconditional biasedness in the forward rate but only after dividing the sample period into two-year subsamples and only for two countries out of six.

3. Hansen and Hodrick (1983) find the time-series pattern of forward rate prediction errors to be such that they are unable to reject some restrictions implied by an intertemporal model of the time-varying risk premium.

4. Of the many other contributors to this literature, some of the recent ones are chapter 9 this volume, Garman and Kohlhagen (1980), Krugman (1981), Hodrick (1981), Stulz (1981), and Adler and Dumas (1983).

5. Two optimal portfolio studies, von Furstenberg (1981) and de Macedo, Goldstein, and Meerschwam (1984), do allow expected returns to vary gradually over time by estimating them from the time series of actual returns observed up to the period in question.

6. A simple two-currency application of this technique is Frankel (1981b).

7. The assumption that returns are log-normally distributed is sufficient to imply that investors look only at the mean and variance. The normality assumption might be justified by an appeal to geometric Brownian motion observed at discrete intervals, and is necessary for the maximum likelihood estimation in any case.

8. This assumption is made by Krugman but is considered only one special case by Kouri (1976b) and Dornbusch (1983a). The assumption that prices are sticky at least in the short run—and in this case we are talking about one month—is common in macroeconomics.

9. The utility function will have a constant coefficient of relative risk aversion if it is exponential in form:

$$U(\tilde{W}) = \frac{1}{\gamma} \tilde{W}\gamma, \quad \text{where } \rho = 1 - \gamma.$$

The solution to the one-period maximization problem considered here will be the correct solution to the general intertemporal maximization problem, if the utility function is further restricted to the logarithmic form, the limiting case as γ goes to zero, which implies $\rho = 1$, or if events occurring during the period are independent of the expected returns that prevail in the following period as in a stationary log normal process (or, in continuous time, a diffusion process, as in appendix 10A). See Hodrick (1981) or Stulz (1981).

10. Note the importance of the strong assumption that the asset-demand function (7) is correctly specified, so that the only source of regression error in (8) is the expectational error. If the asset stocks are measured with error or if any other determinants of asset demands have been omitted, then a regression of equation (8) would produce estimates that are biased and inconsistent. These considerations justify special care in the calculation of the asset supply variables, described in the data appendix that appeared with the original published version of this article.

11. The idea of estimating asset demand equations by drawing the link between the matrix of coefficients of the expected returns and the variance-covariance matrix of the actual returns is not entirely new. See, for example, Parkin (1970) and Wills (1979).

12. There is good a priori reason to expect high variance of the error term since the regression errors are the expectational errors in predicting exchange rates, which are universally believed to be very large. (See, e.g., Mussa, 1979b.) At first thought, one might expect this to imply low power in the test. But it turns out that

in the present problem, a high error variance implies *high* power in the test. The point can be made intuitively by considering the two-variable case in which the test statistic is a simple t-ratio, with the estimated coefficient in the numerator, and the square root of the variance σ^2 (over the total squared variation of the independent variable) in the denominator. We impose the optimizing hypothesis that the coefficient is equal to $\rho\sigma^2$. Then the t-ratio is proportional to σ, because the coefficient rises with σ^2 while the denominator rises only with σ. Thus the ability to reject zero is *high* if σ is high. A more rigorous argument could be made for the multiple-asset case.

13. I am indebted to Christophe Chamley for this point and for much of my thinking on the MLE first-order conditions.

14. Notice from (16) that we will not get a positive estimate for ρ, as the theory says we should, unless z_{t+1} and $x_t - \alpha$ are positively correlated. In our sample they turn out to be negatively correlated, but z_{t+1} and $x_t - \alpha w_t$, relevant for section 11.3, turn out to be positively correlated.

15. I am indebted to James Demmel, Bruce Char, Beresford Parlett, and Paul Ruud for the solution to (20) described in appendix 11C.

16. Y is real if $I + 4\Lambda > 0$. Reassuringly, G is positive semidefinite because D is, so the elements of Λ, which are the eigenvalues of G, are all positive, and the condition holds.

Chapter 11

1. Frankel (1985a, p. 1062). The other relevant papers include chapter 10.

2. The expression gives the *vector* of risk premiums on n assets if α is the vector of n consumption shares, x the vector of n portfolio shares, and V the $n \times n$ variance-covariance matrix.

3. These are the second moments computed around zero. We will in fact be interested in the second moment computed *around the first moment*. But there is wide agreement that only a very small proportion of exchange rate changes can be explained by either the forward discount, investor expectations, economists' models, or anything else. My argument, addressed in section 11.1, that the sample variance can be taken as an upper bound is again relevant.

4. Giovannini (1987) offers a theoretical justification for the relationship between the level of the interest rate and the time-varying volatility.

5. The variance of the per annum risk premium is 0.297. Another way to get the same answer that is more in keeping with convention in finance is first to multiply the conditional variances at each point in time by 52 to express them in per annum terms. If investors are assumed to determine their portfolios once a year rather than once a week, this might be precisely the correct way to express the variances, on the theory that if the exchange rate process follows geometric Brownian motion in continuous time, then the variance grows linearly with the time interval. In

any case, the estimate of the *variance* of the variances, and therefore the variance of the risk premium, comes out the same: larger (than 1.1×10^{-4}) by 52^2.

6. A unit innovation in V_t is reported to have an effect of 0.225 on the conditional variance V_{t+8}, and an effect 0.087 on V_{t+30}. Similarly, Frankel and Meese (1987, table 3) compute monthly correlations of daily variances for the mark/dollar rate; the autoregressive coefficient on the first month lag is 0.14. But the effect on V_{t+30} of a single observed innovation in ε_t^2, as specified in equation (3), should be less than the effect of an equal innovation in V_t if it could be known with accuracy. Hodrick (1987) estimates a GARCH process (using both ε_t^2 and V_t).

7. In what follows we use the assumption that the *unconditional* moments are constant over time, even though the conditional moments vary.

8. Engel and Rodrigues and the other ARCH estimates generally assume a conditional normal distribution anyway. Note that with a time-varying variance, the unconditional distribution will not be normal. (So $E\varepsilon^4 \neq 3V^2$, for example.) A number of authors have suggested that the common finding of "fat tails" in the unconditional distribution could be explained as such a mixture of normals over time. Boothe and Glassman (1987, table 3) find evidence that the daily distribution of the mark/dollar rate may switch back and forth between a normal with a standard deviation of 0.399 percent and a normal with a standard deviation of 1.103 percent. Similarly, Manas-Anton (1986, table 8) finds that kurtosis drops sharply when exchange rate changes are corrected for an ARCH process.

9. Frankel (1986a).

10. The calculation, reported to the author by Diebold, is based on the model on their p. 18, as estimated in table 7. The time series for the conditional variance is graphed in figure 3.

11. On the other hand, the Black-Scholes option-pricing formula was derived under the assumption that the variance is constant; its applicability to time-varying variances is not clear. Garman and Kohlhagen (1983) show how the Black-Scholes formula must be altered to be correctly applied to foreign currency options, in particular to allow for uncertainty in foreign interest rates in addition to domestic interest rates. See also Melino and Turnbull (1987).

12. This tends to undermine the confidence one has in the option-price method of measuring the conditional variance.

13. Giovannini and Jorion (1988) come to the opposite conclusion once they correct their arithmetic error: that variation in the conditional variance is not big enough, after all, to explain the behavior of the forward discount. But they use a smaller estimate of the share of the portfolio allocated to foreign currency, 0.1 rather than 1.0, so the estimated variance of the risk premium is 100 times smaller than ours. An argument for a larger mark portfolio share such as 0.5 is that, even if marks are only 1/10 of the world portfolio, dollars are far less than 9/10 and the remainder is other currencies with which the mark/dollar rate is correlated. If $x = \alpha = 0.5$ then the risk premium is zero regardless what the variance is (because the supply of marks is equal to the demand arising from the minimum-variance

portfolio). We are using $x = 1.0$ to state the strongest possible case for the risk premium. Indeed, the risk premium standard deviations that then come out of the Giovannini-Jorion or option-pricing estimates, with $x = 1.0$, appear too *large* to be plausible, rather than too small.

14. In addition to using the ARCH model, i.e., conditioning the variance-covariance matrix on lagged squared errors, they also try conditioning on lagged squared innovations in the U.S. money supply and in oil prices. The conclusion regarding the hypothesis of mean-variance optimization is the same.

Chapter 12

1. For a recent survey of the literature, see Hodrick (1988).

2. Dominguez (1986) also uses some of the MMS surveys.

3. For an explicit consideration of heterogeneous expectations, see chapters 14 and 15 in this volume.

4. To measure the contemporaneous spot rate, we experimented with different approximations to the precise survey and forecast dates of the AMEX survey, which was conducted by mail over a period of up to a month. We used the average of the thirty days during the survey and also the mid-point of the survey period to construct reference sets. Both gave very similar results, so that only results from the former sample were reported. In the case of the *Economist* and MMS surveys, which constitute most of our data set, this issue hardly arises to begin with, as they were conducted by telephone on a known day.

5. References include Tryon (1979), Levich (1979a), Bilson (1981b), Longworth (1981), Hsieh (1984), Fama (1984), Huang (1984), Park (1984), and Hodrick and Srivastava (1984, 1986).

6. The finding that forward rates are poor predictors of future spot rates is not limited to the foreign exchange market. In their study of the expectations hypothesis of the term structure, for example, Shiller, Campbell, and Schoenholtz (1983) conclude that changes in the spread between long-term and short-term rates are useless for predicting future changes in short-term interest rates. Froot (1987b) uses survey data on interest rate expectations to test whether the premium's poor predictive power is evidence of a time-varying term premium.

7. DRI provided us with daily forward and spot exchange rates, computed as the average of the noontime bid and ask rates.

8. In these and subsequent regressions, we pool across currencies in order to maximize sample size. (The four currencies in the MMS survey are the pound, mark, Swiss franc, and yen, each against the dollar. The other two surveys include these four exchange rates and the French franc as well.) We must allow for contemporaneous correlation in the error terms across currencies, in addition to allowing for the moving-average error process induced by overlapping observations $(k > 1)$. We report standard errors that assume conditional homoskedasticity, as well as the estimated standard errors that allow for conditional heteroskedasticity.

In the original published version, we also pooled across different forecast horizons to maximize the power of the tests, requiring correction for a third kind of correlation in the errors. We are not aware of this having been done before even in the standard forward discount regression. Each of these econometric issues is discussed at greater length in the NBER working paper version of this chapter.

9. This table, updated to August 1988, is taken from Frankel and Froot (1990b). The original *QJE* paper included data only through December 1985.

10. For all three surveys and four horizons. Table 11 in the original published paper.

11. The results are not a consequence of aggregation. In the NBER working paper version, we report some results by currency for each data set in table 2. There is little diversity in the results across currencies.

12. Assuming that covered interest parity holds, the forward discount fd^k is equal to the differential between domestic and foreign nominal interest rates $i_t^k -$ $\Delta s_{t+k}^e = i_t^k - i_t^{*k}$. In other words, investors are so responsive to differences in expected rates of return as to eliminate them. For tests of uncovered interest parity similar to the tests of conditional bias in the forward discount that we considered in section 12.2, see Cumby and Obstfeld (1981).

13. Table 12.3, updated to August 1988, is taken from Frankel and Froot (1990b). The original *QJE* paper included data only through December 1985, though it reported results from all three surveys: Economics, MMS, and AMEX. In the *Economist* and Amex data sets, which aggregate across time horizons, the estimates were 6.99 and 0.96, respectively.

14. The degree to which the surveys qualitatively corroborate one another is striking. For example, the risk premium in the *Economist* data (figure 12.1) is negative during the entire sample, except for a short period from late 1984 until mid-1985. The MMS three-month sample (figure 12.2) reports that the risk premium did not become positive until the last quarter of 1984, while MMS one-month data (figure 12.3) show the risk premium then remained positive until mid-1985. That the surveys agree on the nature and timing of major swings in the risk premium is some evidence that the particularities of each group of respondents do not influence the results.

15. In table 2 of the NBER working paper version of this study, we reported mean values of the risk premium as measured by the survey data. They were different from zero at the 99 percent level for almost all survey sources, currencies, and sample periods.

16. In table 6 of the NBER working paper version, we correct for the potential serial correlation problem in the *Economist* and MMS data sets by employing a three-stage-least-squares estimator that allows for contemporaneous correlation (SUR) as well as first-order autoregressive disturbances. This procedure does not substantively change the conclusions.

17. Frankel and Froot (1985, 1987) test whether the survey expectations place too little weight on the contemporaneous spot rate and too much weight on specific

pieces of information such as the lagged spot rate, the long-run equilibrium exchange rate, and the lagged expected spot rate. Dominguez (1986) also tests for bias in survey data.

18. Reported as table VI in the original published version of this paper.

19. This table, again, is updated to 1988 and taken from Frankel and Froot (1990b). The original table VI included data from all three surveys.

Introduction to Part IV

1. I have described the history and politics of exchange rate policy formulation in the 1980s elsewhere (Frankel, 1993).

Chapter 13

1. Richard Levich (1979a) studies the predictions of the exchange rate forecasting industry. For a recent study of exchange rate expectations using the MMS survey data, see Kathryn Dominguez (1986).

2. A second limitation of the Amex survey is that it was conducted by mail, and therefore precise dating of expectations was impossible. In response to this problem, we used several alternative methods of dating in all our tests. It turned out that the dating method had a negligible effect on the results. See the data appendix for more detail.

3. In the NBER working paper version of this chapter, we also estimated bootstrap standard errors, which are robust in small samples, with respect to estimators that are nonlinear in the residuals and with respect to a variety of nonnormal distributions. This technique has been omitted here both because the resulting standard errors were not very different from those obtained using more conventional methods and because we now have several times as many observations for the *Economist* data and have added the MMS sample to the analysis.

4. The preceding chapter decomposed the *variance* of the forward discount into expected depreciation and the risk premium. In this chapter, we are concerned only with the first moments.

5. See Bradford Cornell (1977), Alan Stockman (1978), and chapter 8 of this volume.

6. For all data sets but the Amex six-month, prediction errors are overlapping because the surveys are conducted more frequently than the forecast interval. The standard errors reported for each currency in table 13.3 reflect the number of nonoverlapping intervals in each data set and are thus upper bounds. Higher significance levels could be obtained by combining the results for different currencies. But the apparent low standard errors when all observations are simply pooled are misleading, as there is a definite correlation of errors across currencies at any point in time. The proper technique (SUR) for this problem is applied in the following section.

7. It should be noted that a fourth explanation sometimes given for findings of biasedness in the forward rate, after the existence of a risk premium, a failure of rational expectations, and the peso problem, is the convexity term due to Jensen's Inequality (see Charles Engel, 1984). Note, however, that if exchange rates are log normally distributed, this convexity term is bounded above by the unconditional variance of the spot rate and is therefore small. For a lognormally distributed random variable, $X = e^x$, $E[X] = \int e^x f(x)\,dx = \exp[\mu + (1/2)\sigma^2]$ and $E[1/X] = \int e^{-x} f(x)\,dx = \exp[\mu - (1/2)\sigma^2]$, where

$$f(x) = (1/2\pi)\exp[-(x - \mu)^2/2\sigma^2].$$

Thus, $\log(E[X]) - \log(E[1/X]) = \sigma^2$, which is weakly greater than the conditional variance, provided that expectations are formed rationally. During the 1980s, $\sigma^2 = 0.02$ for the spot rate, so that Jensen's Inequality is too small to explain the magnitude of the forward rate prediction errors, let alone the very large shift of about 18 percent between the late 1970s and early 1980s in table 13.3.

8. See, for example, the discussion in Michael Dooley and Jeffrey Shafer (1983, pp. 47–48).

9. Due to the small number of observations in the Amex data sets, OLS rather than SUR was used to conserve degrees of freedom in this case.

10. We take the definition of extrapolative expectations from Jacob Mincer (1969).

11. See R. W. Parks (1967).

12. Because of irregular spacing, we could not correct the estimates for serial correlation in the Amex data sets.

13. Adaptive expectations have been considered by Pentti Kouri (1976a), as a third alternative after static and rational expectations, as well as by Rudiger Dornbusch (1976a) and many other authors.

14. An implication of any measurement error in the survey data is that the lagged prediction errors, which appear as regressors in table 13.5, are also measured with error. Thus we would expect the point estimates of γ_1 to be biased toward zero. However, in view of the fact that the variance of actual spot rate changes is about ten times larger than the variance of the survey-expected depreciation (chapter 12 in this volume, table 2), we suspect that this bias is small.

15. In the NBER working paper version, we reported for purposes of comparison, in all our tests, results both using expectations measured by the forward discount and using expectations measured by the survey data.

16. For the original application of method of moments estimation to exchange rate data with overlapping observations, see Lars Hansen and Robert Hodrick (1980).

17. In the NBER working paper version, we report in each table separate regressions for the actual spot process.

18. See, for example, Dooley-Shafer and Hansen-Hodrick (1980).

19. Stephen Marris (1985, pp. 120–22) uses the *Economist* survey data and argues that expectations are overly adaptive in that a forecasting strategy of putting less

weight on the contemporaneous spot rate would ultimately be vindicated in the long run.

20. Such heterogeneity across investors can still be compatible with a well-defined market expectation. Mark Rubinstein (1974) gives conditions under which agents with different beliefs may be aggregated to form a composite investor with preferences exhibiting rational expectations.

21. Possibilities in this line of research are contained in Roman Frydman and Edmund Phelps (1983). See also the next two chapters.

Chapter 14

1. Calculated using the Federal Reserve's multilateral index of the value of the dollar, from the end of the first quarter, 1984, until February 1985.

2. The Money Market Services survey has been conducted weekly or bi-weekly since 1983. The *Economist* survey covers thirteen leading international banks and has been conducted six times a year since 1981. The American Express survey covers 250 to 300 central bankers, private bankers, corporate treasurers, and economists and has been conducted more irregularly since 1976.

3. For more extensive analyses of the Money Market Services survey data set, see Dominguez (1986), Frankel and Froot (1985a), and chapters 12 and 13 in this volume.

4. For all currencies combined, the standard deviations of the means treat the value of each currency against the dollar as independent. To the extent that all the forecasts contain a common dollar component, these aggregate standard deviations are biased downward, so that the corresponding t statistics are overstated.

5. It sounds strange to describe three to six months as "long term," but such descriptions are common in the foreign exchange markets.

6. Figlewski (1978, 1982) considers an economy in which private information, weighted by traders' relative wealth, is revealed in the market price.

7. See, for example, Frankel (1986a).

8. Assume that prices evolve slowly according to $\dot{p} = \pi(\gamma(s - p) - \sigma(i - i^*))$ (where γ and σ are elasticities of goods demand with respect to the real exchange rate and the interest rate, respectively), that the interest rate differential is proportional to the gap between the current and long-run price levels, $\lambda(i - i^*) = p - \bar{p}$ (where λ is the semielasticity of money demand with respect to the interest rate) and that the long-run equilibrium exchange rate is given by long-run purchasing parity, $\bar{s} = \bar{p}$. Then it can be shown that rationality implies:

$$v = 1/(b - c) = (\pi/2\lambda)(\gamma\lambda + \sigma + (\gamma^2\lambda^2 + 2\lambda\gamma\sigma + \sigma^2 + 4)^{1/2}).$$

9. In this case, however, $\omega(t)$ does not have a closed analytic form.

10. We do not consider the third case, because equations (16) and (17) are not defined at $1 + cv\omega(t) - \delta c = 0$.

11. The following intuition may help us see why the system is stable when portfolio managers are "fast" learners and unstable when they are "slow" learners. Suppose the value of the dollar is above $\bar{s}$, so that the portfolio managers are predicting depreciation at the rate $\omega v(\bar{s} - s(t))$. If the spot rate were to start depreciating at a rate slightly faster than this, portfolio managers would then shift $\omega(t)$ upward, in favor of the fundamentalists. Under what circumstances would these hypothesized dynamics be an equilibrium? Recall from equations (14) and (15) that if δ is big, portfolio managers place substantial weight on new information. The larger is δ, the more quickly the spot rate changes. It is easy to show that if portfolio managers are fast learners (i.e. if $\delta > 1/c + v\omega$), they update ω so rapidly that the resulting rate of depreciation must in fact be greater than $\omega v(\bar{s} - s(t))$. Thus the system is stable. Alternatively, if portfolio managers are "slow" learners, $\delta < 1/c + v\omega$, they heavily discount new information and therefore change $\omega(t)$ too slowly to generate a rate of depreciation greater than $\omega v(\bar{s} - s(t))$. If we instead hypothesize an initial rate of depreciation which is less than $\omega v(\bar{s} - s(t))$, portfolio managers would tend to shift ω downward, more toward the chartists. From equation (15), a negative $\dot{\omega}(t)$ causes the spot rate to appreciate. Thus slow learning will tend to drive the spot rate further away from the long-run equilibrium (given $0 < \omega < 1$), making the system unstable.

12. There is a second root, $\omega = -1/(vc)$, which we rule out since it is less than zero.

13. The assumption that ε_{t+1} exhibits such conditional heteroscedasticity results in a particularly convenient expression for δ_t (equation (A2) below). Under the assumption that ε_{t+1} is distributed normally $(0, \sigma^2)$, δ_t depends on all past values of the spot rate,

$$\delta_t = \tau \bigg/ \left(\tau v \sum_{i=1} (\bar{s} - s_{t-i}) + T_0 \right).$$

14. If the prior distribution is normal, the precision is equal to the reciprocal of the variance.

Chapter 15

1. Paul Krugman (1985) was one of the first to suggest that the market did not appear to realize the extent to which the appreciation of the dollar was not sustainable. Charles Engel and James Hamilton (1990) find that long-term swings are a general characteristic of exchange rates, and that they are not adequately reflected in the forward market. Such findings of predictable excess returns are standardly interpreted as risk premiums. But evidence from survey data on expectations of market participants suggests that the prediction errors of the forward market are *not* due to risk premiums (chapter 12 of this volume).

2. Chapter 14 of this volume.

3. A number of firms combine the two approaches, or else offer a separate serivce of each kind; in this case, usually technical analysis is used for short-term forecast-

ing and fundamentals for long-term forecasting. This pattern matches up well with the regression results from surveys of market participants regarding exchange rate expectations, reported above. The pattern is also confirmed in Taylor and Allen (1992), who report that at short horizons approximately 90 percent of respondents use some chartist input in forming their expectations, and 60 percent judge charts to be as important as fundamentals, while at the horizon of one-year and longer, nearly 30 percent rely purely on fundamentals, and 85 percent judge fundamentals to be more important than charts.

Chapter 16

1. The exchange rate reaction to an increase in the relative supply of outside foreign assets may be reduced if there is an increase in their expected rate of return that induces a corresponding increase in demand.

2. For example, Branson, Halttunen, and Masson (1977), Golub (1989), and Obstfeld (1990).

3. Exceptions include Neumann (1984), Dominguez (1990, 1992), Dominguez and Frankel (1990), and Eijffinger and Gruijters (1991), who were given access to Bundesbank intervention data. There are virtually no exceptions in the case of Federal Reserve data before 1991. At the Versailles Summit in 1982, the G-7 central banks agreed to share daily intervention data with each other as part of a multicountry study of intervention policy. The results of this study are contained in the Jurgensen Report (1983) and summarized in Henderson and Sampson (1983). Three papers by members of the Working Group's research staff that use the confidential data were subsequently published separately—Loopesko (1984), Rogoff (1984), and Wonnacott (1982).

4. In Dominguez and Frankel (1993), we provide a listing of all the news of intervention activity (as well as more general exchange rate policy announcements) by central banks reported in the *Wall Street Journal*, the *London Financial Times* and the *New York Times* over the period 1982 through 1990.

5. References include Kouri and de Macedo (1978), Dornbusch (1983), Adler and Dumas (1983), Branson and Henderson (1985), and Frankel (1982c). This last, which derives the risk-premium equation given below, is reproduced as chapter 10 of this volume.

6. References include Mussa (1981), Henderson (1984), Dominguez (1990, 1992), Obstfeld (1990), and Dominguez and Frankel (1993).

7. Equation (2) does not suffer from the overlapping observation problem familiar from studies of bias in forecasts of future spot rates because the dependent variable is the change in expectations, not the prediction error.

8. Frankel and Froot (1990), reproduced here as chapter 14. Models based on technical analysis (which often essentially extrapolate past trends) are more widely used by professional forecasting services, especially at short horizons, than models based on macroeconomic fundamentals (which could be viewed as regressive ex-

pectations). Of twenty-seven foreign exchange forecasting services reviewed by *Euromoney* magazine in 1988, twelve used only technical models, only one relied exclusively on fundamentals models, and twelve used a combination of the two techniques.

9. These data were introduced in another context by Dominguez (1986) and chapter 13 of this volume.

10. Adams and Henderson (1983) provide detailed discussion and definition of customer transactions.

11. Estimates of equation (1) with intervention measured as a percent of total wealth W_t, rather than in millions of dollars, are presented in Dominguez and Frankel (1990). Wealth, W_t, is measured as the total supply of U.S. and German federal government debt that has been issued and so must be held in investors' portfolios. The estimated coefficients in Dominguez and Frankel (1990) on both the variance and intervention variables are qualitatively similar (in terms of statistical significance) to those reported here in tables 16.3 and 16.4.

12. DM 221.1 billion / 1.7803 DM/$. These numbers are from line 14 and line ae, respectively, for Germany in the *International Financial Statistics*.

13. $[1/x + 1/(1-x)]\alpha_4/(v_t\beta_2) = [1/.5 + 1/.5](.006)/(1.125) = .027$. We use $\alpha_4 = .006$ from table 16.2, the average value of v_t over the latter subperiod, which was .00005803, and $\beta_2 = 19395$ from table 16.5.

14. Total debt issued by the German government divided by the total of German and U.S. debt was .112 at the end of 1988.

15. On the other hand, if market participants are believed to have adaptive or regressive expectations, then the impact in short-run equilibrium will be *higher* than in long-run equilibrium, the familiar overshooting hypothesis.

16. A related point concerns the famous "Lucas critique." If the central bank adopted a policy of routinely making public announcements of its intervention—which is not its practice now—each announcement would not continue to have the same impact as in our estimates (unless, perhaps, it was sufficiently backed up by a correspondingly greater degree of actual changes in asset supplies). Our estimates only purport to say what the effect was during the regime actually in effect during the sample period.

17. References include Krugman (1985), Frankel (1985), Marris (1985), chapter 14 in this volume, and Williamson and Miller (1987).

18. On the other hand, the financial press often talks of central bankers' intervention operations as seeking to have an effect on market behavior precisely by creating extra volatility, and thereby punishing speculators. Our estimates imply that a change in volatility can indeed have a significant impact on investors' asset demands. But, aside from the difficulty of driving out destabilizing speculators without also driving out stabilizing speculators, and aside from the general undesirability of creating needless volatility, there is another problem with this theory. If the supply of dollar assets in the market exceeds the share in the

minimum-variance portfolio, then an increase in the variance will work to *depreciate* the dollar (for a given risk premium), which may not be the direction desired by the authorities.

19. Intervention variable are known at time t (purchases and sales through the end of day $t - 1$) and are defined in terms of number of dollars purchased.

20. Newspapers included the *Wall Street Journal*, the *London Financial Times*, and the *New York Times*.

Chapter 17

1. Appendix B of Frankel and Phillips (1991) presents a chronology.

2. This section in large part replicates Frankel and Phillips (1991). However, the sample there ran only through July 1991, whereas here the sample is updated to December 1991, the month of the Maastricht meeting. (The reader is referred to the earlier paper for some of the technical details of the theory and the tests.)

3. Such as the tests reported in Chinn and Frankel (1991) for twenty-five currencies.

4. This basic test of target zone credibility was first performed by Svensson (1991) for the Swedish krone. Here we replicate the findings of Flood, Rose, and Mathieson (1991) for the EMS. We thank these authors for access to their data. Giovannini (1990) conducts an equivalent test for the French franc and Italian lira.

5. For an extra degree of protection to the confidentiality of the original *Currency Forecasters Digest* data, we have applied a data-smoothing technique to the series plotted in these figures. We believe that the qualitative conclusions are not materially affected by this procedure.

6. The original model featured perfect credibility. However Bertola and Caballero (1992) showed that similar results could obtain with an imperfect, though implicitly constant, degree of credibility.

References

Adams, Donald, and Dale Henderson. 1983. Definition and measurement of exchange market intervention. Board of Governors of the Federal Reserve System Staff Series, no. 126.

Adler, Michael, and Bernard Dumas. 1976. Portfolio choice and the demand for foreign exchange. *American Economic Review* 66, 2 (May): 332–39.

Adler, Michael, and Bernard Dumas. 1983. International portfolio choice and corporation finance: A survey. *Journal of Finance* 38:925–84.

Adler, Michael, and Bruce Lehmann. 1983. Deviations from purchasing power parity. *Journal of Finance* 38, 5 (December): 1471–87.

Akhtar, M. Akbar, and R. S. Hilton. 1984. Effects of exchange rate uncertainty on German and U.S. trade. *Federal Reserve Bank of New York Quarterly Review* 9 (Spring): 7–16.

Allen, Polly, and Peter Kenen. 1980. *Asset Markets, Exchange Rates, and Economic Integration.* New York: Cambridge University Press.

American Express International Banking Corporation. *Amex Bank Review*, London. Various issues, 1976–85.

Argy, Victor. 1987. International financial liberalisation—The Australian and Japanese experiences compared. *Bank of Japan Monetary and Economic Studies* 5, 1:105–68.

Argy, Victor, and M. Porter. 1972. The forward exchange market and the effects of domestic and external disturbances under alternative exchange rate systems. *IMF Staff Papers* 19 (November): 503–32.

Arrow, Kenneth. 1970. *Essays in the theory of risk-bearing.* London: North-Holland.

Arrow, Kenneth. 1982. Risk perception in psychology and economics. *Economic Inquiry* 20 (January): 1–9.

Artis, Michael, and Mark Taylor. 1990. Abolishing exchange control: The UK Experience. In *Private Behaviour and Government Policy in Interdependent Economies.* Edited by A. S. Courakis and M. P. Taylor, pp. 129–158. Oxford: Clarendon Press.

Backus, David. 1984. Empirical models of the exchange rate: Separating the wheat from the chaff. *Canadian Journal of Economics* 17 : 824—26.

Balassa, Bela. 1964. The purchasing-power parity doctrine: A reappraisal. *Journal of Political Economy* 72 : 584—96.

Barro, Robert. 1978. A stochastic equilibrium model of an open economy under flexible exchange rates. *Quarterly Journal of Economics* (February): 149—64.

Bayoumi, Tamim. 1990. Saving-investment correlations: Immobile capital, government policy, or endogenous behavior? *IMF Staff Papers* 37 : 360—87.

Bayoumi, Tamim, and Andrew Rose. 1992. Domestic saving and intra-national capital flows. *European Economic Review*, forthcoming.

Bayoumi, Tamim, and Gabriel Sterne. 1992. Regional trading blocs, mobile capital and exchange rate coordination. Unpublished paper, International Monetary Fund, May.

Bergsten, C. Fred, et al. 1982. *From Rambouillet to Versailles: A Symposium.* Essays in International Finance no. 149. Princeton, N.J.: Princeton University, International Finance Section, December.

Bertola, Giuseppe, and Ricardo Caballero. 1992. Target zones and realignments. *American Economic Review* 82 (June): 520—36.

Bertola, Giuseppe, and Lars Svensson. 1993. Stochastic devaluation risk and empirical fit of target zone models. *Review of Economic Studies*, forthcoming.

Bhandari, Jagdeep. 1981. A simple transnational model of large open economies. *Southern Economic Journal* (April).

Bilson, John. l978a. The monetary approach to the exchange rate—some empirical evidence. *IMF Staff Papers* 25 (March): 48—75.

Bilson, John. 1978b. Rational expectations and the exchange rate. In J. Frenkel and H. G. Johnson, eds., *The Economics of Exchange Rates.* Reading, Mass.: Addison-Wesley.

Bilson, John. 1981a. Profitability and stability in international currency markets. NBER Working Paper no. 664. April.

Bilson, John. 1981b. The speculative efficiency hypothesis. *Journal of Business* 54 (July): 435—51.

Bilson, John. 1985. Macroeconomic stability and flexible exchange rates. *American Economic Review Proceedings* 75 (May): 62—67.

Bilson, John, and Richard M. Levich. 1977. A test of the efficiency of the forward exchange market. New York University Working Paper no. 77—61. June.

Black, Stanley. 1973. International money markets and flexible exchange rates. *Princeton Studies in International Finance* no. 25. Princeton University.

Blake, D., M. Beenstock, and V. Brasse. 1986. The performance of UK exchange rate forecasters. *Economic Journal* (December).

Blanchard, Olivier. 1979. Speculative bubbles, crashes and rational expectations. *Economic Letters*, 387–89.

Blanchard, Olivier, Rudiger Dornbusch, and Richard Layard. 1985. *Restoring Europe's Prosperity*. Cambridge, Mass.: MIT Press.

Board of Governors of the Federal Reserve System. *Federal Reserve Bulletin*. Washington, D.C. Various issues.

Board of Governors of the Federal Reserve System. *Statistical Releases*. Washington, D.C. Various issues.

Bollerslev, T., R. Chou, N. Jayaraman, and K. Kroner. 1990. Applications of ARCH to foreign exchange rate data. In *ARCH Modeling in Finance: A Selective Review of the Theory and Empirical Evidence, with Suggestions for Future Research* (May): 31–41.

Boothe, Paul, K. Clinton, A. Côté, and David Longworth. 1985. *International Asset Substitutability: Theory and Evidence for Canada*. Ottawa: Bank of Canada.

Boothe, Paul and Debra Glassman. 1987. The statistical distribution of exchange rates. *Journal of International Economics* 22 : 153–67.

Boothe, Paul, and David Longworth. 1986. Foreign exchange market efficiency tests: Implications of recent findings. *Journal of International Money and Finance* 5 : 135–52.

Bordo, M., and A. Schwartz, eds. 1985. *A Retrospective on the Gold Standard*. Chicago: University of Chicago Press.

Bovenberg, A. Lans. 1989. The effects of capital income taxation on international competitiveness and trade flows. *American Economic Review* 79, 5 (December): 1045–64.

Boyer, Russell. 1977. The relation between the forward rate and the expected future spot rate. *Intermountain Economic Review* 8 : 14–21.

Branson, William. 1968. *Financial Capital Flows in the U.S. Balance of Payments*. Amsterdam: North-Holland.

Branson, William. 1977. Asset markets and relative prices in exchange rate determination. *Sozialwissenschaftliche Annalen* 1 : 69–89.

Branson, William, Hannu Halttunen, and Paul Masson. 1977. Exchange rates in the short-run: The dollar-deutschemark rate. *European Economic Review* 10 (December): 303–24.

Branson, William, Hannu Halttunen, and Paul Masson. 1979. Exchange rates in the short-run: Some further results. *European Economic Review* 12 (October): 395–402.

Branson, William, and Dale Henderson. 1985. The specification and influence of asset markets. In Ronald Jones and Peter Kenen, eds., *Handbook of International Economics*, vol. 2. Amsterdam: North-Holland.

Buiter, Willem, and Richard Marston, eds. 1985. *International Economic Policy Coordination*. Cambridge: Cambridge University Press.

Buiter, Willem, and Marcus Miller. 1981. Monetary policy and international competitiveness: The problems of adjustment. *Oxford Economic Papers* 33 (July): 143–75.

Buiter, Willem, and Marcus Miller. 1982. Real exchange rate overshooting and the output cost of bringing down inflation. *European Economic Review* 18 (May–June): 85–123.

Business Week. Various issues.

Calvo, Guillermo, and Carlos Rodriguez. 1977. A model of exchange rate determination under currency substitution and rational expectations. *Journal of Political Economy* 85, 3 (June): 617–26.

Campbell, Jonathan, and Richard Clarida. 1987. The dollar and real interest rates. *Carnegie-Rochester Conference on Public Policy* 27. August.

Caprio, G., and D. Howard. 1984. Domestic saving, current accounts, and international capital mobility. International Finance Discussion Paper no. 244. Washington, D.C.: Federal Reserve Board.

Caramazza, F., K. Clinton, A. Côté, and David Longworth. 1986. International capital mobility and asset substitutability: Some theory and evidence on recent structural changes. Technical Report 44. Ottawa: Bank of Canada.

Cardia, Emanuela. 1988. Crowding out in open economies. *Cahier* 8823, Université de Montreal (June).

Caves, Douglas, and Edgar Feige. 1980. Efficient foreign exchange markets and the monetary approach to exchange-rate determination. *American Economic Review* 70 (March): 120–34.

Chinn, Menzie, and Jeffrey Frankel. 1991. Exchange rate expectations and the risk premium: Tests for a cross-section of 17 currencies. NBER Working Paper no. 3806 (August). Forthcoming in *Review of International Economics*.

Claassen, Emil, and Charles Wyplosz. 1982. Capital controls: Some principles and the French experience. *Annales de l'INSEE* 47–48: 237–67.

Conrad, William. 1981. Treasury bill market response to money stock announcements. Unpublished. Federal Reserve Board, Washington, D.C.

Cooper, R. N. 1982. The gold standard: Historical facts and future prospects. *Brookings Papers on Economic Activity* 1: 1–45.

Cooper, R. N. 1986. *Economic Policy in an Interdependent World*. Cambridge, Mass.: MIT Press.

Corden, W. Max. 1983. The logic of the international monetary non-system. In F. Machlup, G. Fels, and H. Müller-Groeling, eds., *Reflections on a Troubled World Economy: Essays in Honour of Herbert Giersch*, pp. 59–74. London: St. Martins Press.

Cornell, Bradford. 1977. Spot rates, forward rates and exchange market efficiency. *Journal of Financial Economics* 5 (August–November): 55–85. Reprinted in D. Lessard, ed., *International Financial Management*. Boston: Warren, Gorham and Lamont, 1979.

Cornell, Bradford. 1982a. Money supply announcements and interest rates: Another view. UCLA Working Paper. March.

Cornell, Bradford. 1982b. Money supply announcements, interest rates, and foreign exchange. *Journal of International Money and Finance* (August): 201–8.

Cornell, Bradford, and J. Kimball Dietrich. 1978. The efficiency of the market for foreign exchange under floating exchange rates. *Review of Economics and Statistics* 60, 1 (February): 111–20.

Council of Economic Advisers. *Economic Report of the President.* Various issues.

Cuddington, John. 1983. Currency substitution, capital mobility and money demand. *Journal of International Money and Finance* 2:111–33.

Cumby, Robert, and Frederic Mishkin. 1986. The international linkage of real interest rates: The European-U.S. connection. *Journal of International Money and Finance* 5:5–24.

Cumby, Robert, and Maurice Obstfeld. 1981. A note on exchange-rate expectations and nominal interest differentials: A test of the Fisher hypothesis. *Journal of Finance* 36 (June): 697–703.

Cumby, Robert, and Maurice Obstfeld. 1984. International interest-rate and price-level linkages under flexible exchange rates: A review of recent evidence. In J. F. O. Bilson and R. C. Marston, eds., *Exchange Rates: Theory and Practice.* Chicago: University of Chicago Press.

Cragg, J., and B. Malkiel. 1982. *Expectations and the Structure of Share Prices.* Chicago: University of Chicago Press.

Cutler, David, James Poterba, and Lawrence Summers. 1990. Speculative dynamics. NBER Working Paper no. 3242. January.

Darby, Michael. 1981. Does purchasing power parity work? *Proceedings of the Fifth West Coast Academic/Federal Reserve Economic Research Seminar,* Federal Reserve Bank of San Francisco.

Darby, Michael. 1986. The internationalization of American banking and finance: Structure, risk and world interest rates. *Journal of International Money and Finance* 5, 4:403–28.

DeJong, David, John Nankervis, Eugene Savin, and Charles Whiteman. 1988. Integration vs. trend-stationarity in macroeconomic time series, Department of Economics Working Paper no. 88-27a, University of Iowa, December.

De Long, J. B., A. Shleifer, L. Summers, and R. Waldmann. 1987. The economic consequences of noise traders. National Bureau of Economic Research Working Papers no. 2395, October.

De Long, J. Bradford, Andrei Shleifer, Lawrence Summers, and Robert Waldmann. 1990. Noise trader risk in financial markets. *Journal of Political Economy* 98, 4:703–38.

Deutsche Bundesbank. Statistical supplements to monthly reports. Bonn. Various issues.

Diba, B. 1987. A critique of variance bounds tests for monetary exchange rate models. *Journal of Money, Credit and Banking* 19:104–11.

Diebold, Francis, and Marc Nerlove. 1986. The dynamics of exchange rate volatility: A multivariate latent factor ARCH model. Special Studies Paper no. 205. Washington, D.C.: Board of Governors of the Federal Reserve System. November.

Diebold, Francis, and Peter Pauly. Endogenous risk in a portfolio-balance rational-expectations model of the deutschemark-dollar rate. Working paper 1986. Board of Governors of the Federal Reserve System. *European Economic Review.*

Dominguez, Kathryn. 1986. Are foreign exchange forecasts rational? New evidence from survey data. *Economics Letters* 21:277–82.

Dominguez, Kathryn. 1990. Market responses to coordinated central bank intervention. *Carnegie-Rochester Series on Public Policy* 32.

Dominguez, Kathryn. 1992. The informational role of official foreign exchange intervention operations: The signalling hypothesis. Chapter 2 in *Exchange Rate Efficiency in the Behavior of International Asset Markets,* N.Y.: Garland Publishing Company.

Dominguez, Kathryn, and Jeffrey Frankel. 1990. Does foreign exchange intervention matter? Disentangling the portfolio and expectations effects for the mark. Revised, 1992. (Part is forthcoming in the *American Economic Review*. More appears as chapter 16 in this volume 3).

Dominguez, Kathryn, and Jeffrey Frankel. 1993. *Intervention Policy Reconsidered.* Washington, D.C.: Institute for International Economics.

Domowitz, Ian, and Craig Hakkio. 1985. Conditional variance and the risk premium in the foreign exchange market. *Journal of International Economics* 19 (August): 47–66.

Dooley, Michael, Jeffrey Frankel, and Donald Mathieson. 1987. International capital mobility: What do saving-investment correlations tell us? *IMF Staff Papers* 34, 3:503–30.

Dooley, Michael, and Peter Isard. 1979. The portfolio-balance model of exchange rates. International Finance Discussion Paper no. 141. Washington, D.C.: Federal Reserve Board, May.

Dooley, Michael, and Peter Isard. 1980. Capital controls, political risk, and deviations from interest-rate parity, *Journal of Political Economy* 88, 2 (April): 370–84.

Dooley, Michael, and Peter Isard. 1982. A portfolio-balance rational-expectations model of the dollar-mark rate. *Journal of International Economics* 12 (May): 257–76.

Dooley, Michael and Peter Isard. 1983. The portfolio-balance model of exchange rates and some structural estimates of the risk premium. *IMF Staff Papers* 30 (December): 683–702.

Dooley, Michael, and Peter Isard. 1985. The appreciation of the dollar: An analysis of the safe-haven phenomenon. Unpublished paper. Washington, D.C.: International Monetary Fund, April.

Dooley, Michael, and Jeffrey Shafer. 1976. Analysis of short-run exchange rate behavior, March 1973 to September 1975. International Finance Discussion Paper no. 76. Washington, D.C.: Federal Reserve Board, February.

Dooley, Michael, and Jeffrey Shafer. 1983. Analysis of short-run exchange rate behavior: March 1973 to November 1981. In D. Bigman and T. Taya, eds., *Exchange Rate and Trade Instability: Causes, Consequences and Remedies.* Cambridge, Mass.: Ballinger.

Dornbusch, Rudiger. 1976a. The theory of flexible exchange rate regimes and macroeconomic policy. *Scandinavian Journal of Economics* 78 (May): 255–79.

Dornbusch, Rudiger. 1976b. Exchange rate expectations and monetary policy. *Journal of International Economics* 6 (August): 231–44.

Dornbusch, Rudiger. 1976c. Expectations and exchange rate dynamics. *Journal of Political Economy* 84, 6 (December): 1161–76.

Dornbusch, Rudiger. 1976d. Capital mobility, flexible exchange rates and macroeconomic equilibrium. In E. Claasen and P. Salin, eds., *Recent Developments in International Monetary Economics.* Amsterdam: North-Holland.

Dornbusch, Rudiger. 1977. Capital mobility and portfolio balance. In R. Aliber, ed., *The Political Economy of Monetary Reform.* London: Macmillan.

Dornbusch, Rudiger. 1978. Monetary policy under exchange rate flexibility. In *Managed Exchange Rate Flexibility,* Federal Reserve Bank of Boston Conference Series. Reprinted in D. Lessard, ed., *International Financial Management.* Boston: Warren, Gorham and Lamont. 1979.

Dornbusch, Rudiger. 1980. Exchange rate economics: Where do we stand? *Brookings Papers on Economic Activity* 1: 143–94.

Dornbusch, Rudiger. 1982. Equilibrium and disequilibrium exchange rates. *Zeitschrift fur Wirtschafts-und Sozialwissenshaften* 102, 6: 573–99. Reprinted in Dornbusch, R., *Dollars, Debts, and Deficits.* Cambridge, Mass.: MIT Press.

Dornbusch, Rudiger. 1983a. Exchange risk and the macroeconomics of exchange rate determination. In R. Hawkins, R. Levich, and C. Wihlborg, eds., *The Internationalization of Financial Markets and National Economic Policy.* Greenwich, Conn.: JAI Press.

Dornbusch, Rudiger. 1983b. Real interest rates, home goods and optimal external borrowing. *Journal of Political Economy* 91, 1 (February): 141–53.

Dornbusch, Rudiger. 1983c. Flexible exchange rates and interdependence. *IMF Staff Papers* (May): 3–38.

Dornbusch, Rudiger. 1983d. Comment on Loopesko and Shafer. *Brookings Papers on Economic Activity* 1: 78–84.

Dornbusch, Rudiger. 1985. Purchasing power parity. NBER Working Paper no. 1591. Also in *The New Palgrave Dictionary of Economics.* London: Macmillan.

Dornbusch, Rudiger. 1986a. Flexible exchange rates and excess capital mobility. *Brookings Papers on Economic Activity* 1: 209–26.

Dornbusch, Rudiger. 1986b. *Dollars, Debts and Deficits.* Cambridge, Mass.: MIT Press.

Dornbusch, Rudiger. 1986c. Special exchange rates for capital account transactions. *World Bank Economic Review* 1, 1:3−33.

Dornbusch, Rudiger. 1987a. External balance correction: Depreciation or protection? *Brookings Papers on Economic Activity* 1:249−69.

Dornbusch, Rudiger. 1987b. Flexible exchange rates 1986. *Economic Journal* 1:1−18.

Dornbusch, Rudiger. 1988. Some doubts about the McKinnon standard. *Journal of Economic Perspectives* 2, 1 (Winter): 105−12.

Dornbusch, Rudiger, and Stanley Fischer. 1980. Exchange rates and the current account. *American Economic Review* 70 (December): 960−71.

Dornbusch, Rudiger, and Jeffrey Frankel. 1988. The flexible exchange rate system: Experience and alternatives. In S. Borner, ed., *International Finance and Trade.* London: Macmillan Press. (Appears as chapter 1 in this volume.)

Dornbusch, Rudiger, and Paul Krugman. 1976. Flexible exchange rates in the short run. *Brookings Papers on Economic Activity* 3:537−84.

Driskill, Robert. 1981. Exchange rate dynamics: An empirical investigation. *Journal of Political Economy* 89, 2 (April): 357−71.

Driskill, Robert, and Stephen McCafferty. 1980. Exchange rate variability, real and monetary shocks, and the degree of capital mobility under rational expectations. *Quarterly Journal of Economics* 94 (November): 577−86.

Driskill, Robert, and Steven Sheffrin. 1981. On the mark: Comment. *American Economic Review* 71 (December): 1068−74.

Dunn, R. 1983. The many disappointments of flexible exchange rates. *Essays in International Finance* no. 154. Princeton: Princeton University.

Economist Newspaper, Ltd. *Financial Report,* London. Various issues, 1981−86.

Edison, H. 1987. Purchasing power parity in the long run: A test of the dollar/ pound exchange rate (1890−1978). *Journal of Money, Credit and Banking* 19, 3 (August): 376−87.

Eichengreen, B., ed. 1986. *The Gold Standard in Theory and History.* New York: Methuen.

Eijffinger, Sylvester C. W., and Noud P. D. Gruijters. 1991. On the effectiveness of daily interventions by the Deutsche Bundesbank and the Federal Reserve System in the U.S. Dollar/Deutsche Mark exchange market. Tilburg University, Research Memorandum FEW394, Tilburg 1989. Forthcoming in E. Baltensperger and H. W. Sinn (eds.) *Exchange Rate Regimes and Currency Union,* London.

Engel, Charles. 1981. Money announcements, interest rates and exchange rates. Paper, University of California at Berkeley.

Engel, Charles. 1984. Testing for the absence of expected real profits in the forward exchange markets. *Journal of International Economics* 17 (November): 299–308.

Engel, Charles, and Jeffrey Frankel. 1984. Why interest rates react to money announcements: An answer from the foreign exchange market. *Journal of Monetary Economics* 13 (January): 31–39. (Appears as chapter 5 in this volume, unabridged.)

Engel, Charles, and James Hamilton. 1990. Long swings in the dollar: Are they in the data and do markets know it? *American Economic Review* 80, 4 (September): 689–713.

Engel, Charles, and Kenneth Kletzer. 1989. Saving and investment in an open economy with non-traded goods. *International Economic Review* (November): 735–52.

Engel, Charles, and Anthony Rodrigues. 1989. Tests of international CAPM with time-varying covariances. *Journal of Applied Econometrics* (April–June): 119–38.

Engle, Robert. Autoregressive conditional heteroskedasticity with estimates of the variance of United Kingdom inflation. *Econometrica* 50 (July): 987–1007.

Evans, George W. 1986. A test for speculative bubbles and the sterling-dollar exchange rate: 1981–84. *American Economic Review* 76 (September): 621–36.

Fama, Eugene. 1970. Efficient capital markets: A review of theory and empirical work. *Journal of Finance* (May): 383–417.

Fama, Eugene. 1975. Short-term interest rates as predictors of inflation. *American Economic Review* 65:269–82.

Fama, Eugene. 1984. Forward and spot exchange rates. *Journal of Monetary Economics* 14:319–38.

Fama, Eugene, and André Farber. 1979. Money, bonds, and foreign exchange. *American Economic Review* 69, 4 (September): 639–49.

Federal Reserve Bank of New York. 1986. Summary of results of U.S. foreign exchange market turnover survey conducted in March 1986. Press release no. 1690. August.

Federal Reserve Bank of New York. 1989. Summary of results of U.S. foreign exchange market survey conducted April 1989. Press release. September 13.

Feldstein, Martin. 1968. Uncertainty and forward exchange speculation. *Review of Economics and Statistics* 50, 2:182–92.

Feldstein, Martin. 1983. Domestic saving and international capital movements in the long run and the short run. *European Economic Review* 21:129–51.

Feldstein, Martin. 1986. The budget deficit and the dollar. *NBER Macroeconomic Annual 1986* (September).

Feldstein, Martin. 1987. *The Effects of Taxation on Capital Accumulation*. Chicago: University of Chicago Press.

Feldstein, Martin, and P. Bacchetta. 1991. National savings and international investment. In D. Bernheim and J. Shoven, eds., *National Saving and Economic Performance*. Chicago: University of Chicago Press.

Feldstein, Martin, and Charles Horioka. 1980. Domestic saving and international capital flows. *Economic Journal* 90:314–29.

Fieleke, Norman. 1981. Foreign-currency positioning by U.S. firms: Some new evidence. *Review of Economics and Statistics* 63, 1 (February): 35–43.

Fieleke, Norman. 1982. National saving and international investment. In *Saving and Government Policy*. Conference Series no. 25. Boston: Federal Reserve Bank of Boston.

Figlewski, Stephen. 1978. Market "efficiency" in a market with heterogeneous information. *Journal of Political Economy* 86:581–97.

Figlewski, Stephen. 1982. Information diversity and market behavior. *Journal of Finance* 37:87–102.

Fleming, J. M. 1962. Domestic financial policies under fixed and under floating exchange rates. *IMF Staff Papers* 9, 3:369–79.

Flood, Robert. 1979. An example of exchange rate overshooting. *Southern Economic Journal* 46:168–78.

Flood, Robert, and Peter Garber. 1980. Market fundamentals versus price-level bubbles: The first tests. *Journal of Political Economy* 88 (August): 745–70.

Flood, Robert, Andrew Rose, and Donald Mathieson. 1991. An empirical exploration of exchange-rate target zones. NBER Working Paper no. 3543. December. *Carnegie-Rochester Series on Public Policy* 35 (Autumn): 7–65.

Frankel, Jeffrey. 1979a. The diversifiability of exchange risk. *Journal of International Economics* 9 (August): 379–93. (Appears as chapter 9 in this volume.)

Frankel, Jeffrey. 1979b. On the mark: A theory of floating exchange rates based on real interest differentials. *American Economic Review* 69 (September): 610–22. (Appears as chapter 3 in this volume.)

Frankel, Jeffrey. 1979c. A test of the existence of the risk premium in the foreign exchange market vs. the hypothesis of perfect substitutability. International Finance Discussion Paper no. 149. Washington, D.C.: Federal Reserve Board, August. (First version of 1982b and 1983b.)

Frankel, Jeffrey. 1980. Tests of rational expectations in the forward exchange market. *Southern Economic Journal* 46 (April): 1083–1101. (Appears as chapter 8 in this volume.)

Frankel, Jeffrey. 1981a. On the mark: Reply. *American Economic Review* 71 (December): 1075–82.

Frankel, Jeffrey. 1981b. Estimation of portfolio-balance functions that are mean-variance optimizing: The mark and the dollar. International Finance Discussion Paper no. 188. Washington, D.C.: Federal Reserve Board, September. Revised 1982. (First version of 1983a.)

Engel, Charles. 1984. Testing for the absence of expected real profits in the forward exchange markets. *Journal of International Economics* 17 (November): 299—308.

Engel, Charles, and Jeffrey Frankel. 1984. Why interest rates react to money announcements: An answer from the foreign exchange market. *Journal of Monetary Economics* 13 (January): 31—39. (Appears as chapter 5 in this volume, unabridged.)

Engel, Charles, and James Hamilton. 1990. Long swings in the dollar: Are they in the data and do markets know it? *American Economic Review* 80, 4 (September): 689—713.

Engel, Charles, and Kenneth Kletzer. 1989. Saving and investment in an open economy with non-traded goods. *International Economic Review* (November): 735—52.

Engel, Charles, and Anthony Rodrigues. 1989. Tests of international CAPM with time-varying covariances. *Journal of Applied Econometrics* (April—June): 119—38.

Engle, Robert. Autoregressive conditional heteroskedasticity with estimates of the variance of United Kingdom inflation. *Econometrica* 50 (July): 987—1007.

Evans, George W. 1986. A test for speculative bubbles and the sterling-dollar exchange rate: 1981—84. *American Economic Review* 76 (September): 621—36.

Fama, Eugene. 1970. Efficient capital markets: A review of theory and empirical work. *Journal of Finance* (May): 383—417.

Fama, Eugene. 1975. Short-term interest rates as predictors of inflation. *American Economic Review* 65 : 269—82.

Fama, Eugene. 1984. Forward and spot exchange rates. *Journal of Monetary Economics* 14 : 319—38.

Fama, Eugene, and André Farber. 1979. Money, bonds, and foreign exchange. *American Economic Review* 69, 4 (September): 639—49.

Federal Reserve Bank of New York. 1986. Summary of results of U.S. foreign exchange market turnover survey conducted in March 1986. Press release no. 1690. August.

Federal Reserve Bank of New York. 1989. Summary of results of U.S. foreign exchange market survey conducted April 1989. Press release. September 13.

Feldstein, Martin. 1968. Uncertainty and forward exchange speculation. *Review of Economics and Statistics* 50, 2 : 182—92.

Feldstein, Martin. 1983. Domestic saving and international capital movements in the long run and the short run. *European Economic Review* 21 : 129—51.

Feldstein, Martin. 1986. The budget deficit and the dollar. *NBER Macroeconomic Annual 1986* (September).

Feldstein, Martin. 1987. *The Effects of Taxation on Capital Accumulation.* Chicago: University of Chicago Press.

Feldstein, Martin, and P. Bacchetta. 1991. National savings and international investment. In D. Bernheim and J. Shoven, eds., *National Saving and Economic Performance*. Chicago: University of Chicago Press.

Feldstein, Martin, and Charles Horioka. 1980. Domestic saving and international capital flows. *Economic Journal* 90:314–29.

Fieleke, Norman. 1981. Foreign-currency positioning by U.S. firms: Some new evidence. *Review of Economics and Statistics* 63, 1 (February): 35–43.

Fieleke, Norman. 1982. National saving and international investment. In *Saving and Government Policy*. Conference Series no. 25. Boston: Federal Reserve Bank of Boston.

Figlewski, Stephen. 1978. Market "efficiency" in a market with heterogeneous information. *Journal of Political Economy* 86:581–97.

Figlewski, Stephen. 1982. Information diversity and market behavior. *Journal of Finance* 37:87–102.

Fleming, J. M. 1962. Domestic financial policies under fixed and under floating exchange rates. *IMF Staff Papers* 9, 3:369–79.

Flood, Robert. 1979. An example of exchange rate overshooting. *Southern Economic Journal* 46:168–78.

Flood, Robert, and Peter Garber. 1980. Market fundamentals versus price-level bubbles: The first tests. *Journal of Political Economy* 88 (August): 745–70.

Flood, Robert, Andrew Rose, and Donald Mathieson. 1991. An empirical exploration of exchange-rate target zones. NBER Working Paper no. 3543. December. *Carnegie-Rochester Series on Public Policy* 35 (Autumn): 7–65.

Frankel, Jeffrey. 1979a. The diversifiability of exchange risk. *Journal of International Economics* 9 (August): 379–93. (Appears as chapter 9 in this volume.)

Frankel, Jeffrey. 1979b. On the mark: A theory of floating exchange rates based on real interest differentials. *American Economic Review* 69 (September): 610–22. (Appears as chapter 3 in this volume.)

Frankel, Jeffrey. 1979c. A test of the existence of the risk premium in the foreign exchange market vs. the hypothesis of perfect substitutability. International Finance Discussion Paper no. 149. Washington, D.C.: Federal Reserve Board, August. (First version of 1982b and 1983b.)

Frankel, Jeffrey. 1980. Tests of rational expectations in the forward exchange market. *Southern Economic Journal* 46 (April): 1083–1101. (Appears as chapter 8 in this volume.)

Frankel, Jeffrey. 1981a. On the mark: Reply. *American Economic Review* 71 (December): 1075–82.

Frankel, Jeffrey. 1981b. Estimation of portfolio-balance functions that are mean-variance optimizing: The mark and the dollar. International Finance Discussion Paper no. 188. Washington, D.C.: Federal Reserve Board, September. Revised 1982. (First version of 1983a.)

Frankel, Jeffrey. 1982a. The mystery of the multiplying marks: A modification of the monetary model. *Review of Economics and Statistics* 64 (August): 515–19.

Frankel, Jeffrey. 1982b. A test of perfect substitutability in the foreign exchange market. *Southern Economic Journal* 49 (October): 406–16.

Frankel, Jeffrey. 1982c. In search of the exchange risk premium: A six-currency test assuming mean-variance optimization. *Journal of International Money and Finance* 1 (December): 255–74. (Appears as chapter 10 in this volume.)

Frankel, Jeffrey. 1982d. On the franc. *Annales de l'INSEE* 47–48: 185–221.

Frankel, Jeffrey. 1983a. Estimation of portfolio-balance functions that are mean-variance optimizing: The mark and the dollar. *European Economic Review* 23: 315–27.

Frankel, Jeffrey. 1983b. Monetary and portfolio-balance models of exchange rate determination. NBER Summer Institute Paper 80-7. In J. Bhandari, ed., *Economic Interdependence and Flexible Exchange Rates*. Cambridge, Mass.: MIT Press. (Incorporated into chapter 4 of this volume.)

Frankel, Jeffrey. 1983c. The effect of excessively elastic expectations on exchange rate volatility in the Dornbusch overshooting model. *Journal of International Money and Finance* 2, 1: 39–46.

Frankel, Jeffrey. 1983d. The desirability of currency apreciation given a contractionary monetary policy and concave supply relationships. NBER Working Paper no. 1110 (April). Also in *Journal of International Economic Integration* 3, 1 (Spring 1988): 32–52.

Frankel, Jeffrey. 1984a. *The Yen/Dollar Agreement: Liberalizing Japanese Capital Markets*. Policy Analyses in International Economics no. 9, Washington, D.C.: Institute for International Economics.

Frankel, Jeffrey. 1984b. Tests of monetary and portfolio-balance models of exchange rate determination. In J. Bilson and R. Marston, eds., *Exchange Rate Theory and Practice*. Chicago: University of Chicago Press. (Incorporated into chapter 4 of this volume.)

Frankel, Jeffrey. 1985a. Comments on Williamson, and Giavazzi and Giovannini. Turin, Italy, June 4–5, 1984. In R. Dornbusch and A. Giovannini, eds. *Europe and the Dollar*. Special issue of *Thema*.

Frankel, Jeffrey. 1985b. Six possible meanings of "overvaluation": The 1981–85 dollar. *Essays in International Finance* no. 159. December. Princeton University. (Appears as chapter 6 in this volume.)

Frankel, Jeffrey. 1985c. The dazzling dollar. *Brookings Papers on Economic Activity* 1: 199–217.

Frankel, Jeffrey. 1985d. Portfolio crowding out empirically estimated. *Quarterly Journal of Economics* 100: 1041–65.

Frankel, Jeffrey. 1986a. The implications of mean-variance optimization for four questions in international macroeconomics. *Journal of International Money and Finance* 5 (March): S53–75.

Frankel, Jeffrey. 1986d. International capital mobility and crowding-out in the U.S. economy: Imperfect integration of financial markets or of goods markets? In R. Hafer, ed., *How Open Is the U.S. Economy?* Lexington, Mass.: Lexington Books.

Frankel, Jeffrey. 1987a. Ambiguous macroeconomic policy multipliers, in theory and in twelve econometric models. In Ralph Bryant, ed., *Empirical Macroeconomics for Interdependent Economies.* Washington, D.C.: Brookings Institute.

Frankel, Jeffrey. 1987b. Obstacles to international macroeconomic policy coordination. International Monetary Fund Working Paper no. 8729. Also *Studies in International Finance* no. 64. Princeton: Princeton University Press, December 1988.

Frankel, Jeffrey. 1988a. International capital flows and domestic economic policies. In M. Feldstein, ed., *The United States in the World Economy.* Chicago: University of Chicago Press.

Frankel, Jeffrey. 1988b. International capital mobility and exchange rate volatility. In *International Payments Imbalances in the 1980's*, pp. 162–88. Edited by Norman Fieleke. Boston: Federal Reserve Bank of Boston.

Frankel, Jeffrey. 1988c. Recent estimates of time-variation in the conditional variance and in the exchange risk premium. *Journal of International Money and Finance* 7 : 115–25. (Appears as chapter 11 in this volume.)

Frankel, Jeffrey. 1989. International financial integration, relations among interest rates and exchange rates, and monetary indicators. In Charles Pigott, ed., *International Financial Integration and the Conduct of U.S. Monetary Policy*, pp. 17–49. New York: Federal Reserve Bank of New York.

Frankel, Jeffrey. 1990. Zen and the art of modern macroeconomics: The search for perfect nothingness. In W. Haraf and T. Willett, eds., *Monetary Policy for a Volatile Global Economy.* Washington, D.C.: American Enterprise Institute. (Appears as chapter 7 in this volume.)

Frankel, Jeffrey. 1991. Quantifying international capital mobility in the 1980s. In D. Bernheim and J. Shoven, eds., *National Saving and Economic Performance.* Chicago: University of Chicago Press (for the National Bureau of Economic Research). (Appears as chapter 2 in this volume.)

Frankel, Jeffrey. 1992. Update to monetary and portfolio balance models of exchange rate determination. In J. Letiche, ed., *International Economic Policies and Their Theoretical Foundations: A Sourcebook*, pp. 826–32. 2d ed. London: Academic Press. (Incorporated into chapter 4 of this volume.)

Frankel, Jeffrey. 1993. The making of exchange rate policy in the 1980s. NBER Working Paper no. 3539, Dec. 1990. Forthcoming in *American Economic Policy in the 1980s*, edited by Martin Feldstein, Chicago: University of Chicago Press.

Frankel, Jeffrey, and Charles Engel. 1984. Do investors optimize over the mean and variance of real returns? A six currency test. *Journal of International Economics* 17 : 309–23.

Frankel, Jeffrey, and Kenneth Froot. 1985. Using survey data to test some standard propositions regarding exchange rate expectations. NBER Working Paper no. 1672. Revised as IBER Working Paper no. 86-11, University of California at Berkeley, 1986. (First draft of 1987a.)

Frankel, Jeffrey, and Kenneth Froot. 1986a. The dollar as a speculative bubble: A tale of chartists and fundamentalists. NBER Working Paper no. 1854 March. Abridged as The dollar as an irrational speculative bubble: A tale of fundamentalists and chartists. In *The Marcus Wallenberg Papers on International Finance*, vol. 1. Washington, D.C.: International Law Institute, 1986.

Frankel, Jeffrey, and Kenneth Froot. 1986b. Understanding the dollar in the eighties: Rates of return, risk premiums, speculative bubbles, and chartists and fundamentalists. Discussion Paper no. 155, Centre for Economic Policy Research, Australian National University, Canberra. Condensed as Understanding the U.S. dollar in the eighties: The expectations of chartists and fundamentalists. *Economic Record* (December): 24–38. (Appears as chapter 14 in this volume.)

Frankel, Jeffrey, and Kenneth Froot. 1986c. Short-term and long-term expectations of the yen/dollar exchange rate: Evidence from survey data. International Finance Discussion Paper no. 292. Washington, D.C.: Federal Reserve Board, September. (First draft of 1987b.)

Frankel, Jeffrey, and Kenneth Froot. 1987a. Using survey data to test standard propositions regarding exchange rate expectations. *American Economic Review* 77, 1 (March): 133–53. (Appears as chapter 13 in this volume.)

Frankel, Jeffrey, and Kenneth Froot. 1987b. Short-term and long-term expectations of the yen/dollar exchange rate: Evidence from survey data. *Journal of the Japanese and International Economies* 1: 249–74.

Frankel, Jeffrey, and Kenneth Froot. 1988. Explaining the demand for dollars: International rates of return, and the expectations of chartists and fundamentalists. In R. Chambers and P. Paarlberg, eds., *Agriculture, Macroeconomics, and the Exchange Rate*. Boulder, Colo.: Westview Press.

Frankel, Jeffrey, and Kenneth Froot. 1990a. Chartists, fundamentalists, and the demand for dollars. In Anthony Courakis and Mark Taylor, eds., *Private Behavior and Government Policy in Interdependent Economies*. Oxford: Clarendon Press.

Frankel, Jeffrey, and Kenneth Froot. 1990b. Exchange rate forecasting techniques, survey data, and implications for the foreign exchange market. International Monetary Fund Working Paper 90/43. May. NBER Working Paper no. 3470. October 1990. *Seminar on the Analysis of Security Prices 36*, no. 1 (May 1991), Center for Research in Security Prices, University of Chicago. (Half appears as 1990c.)

Frankel, Jeffrey, and Kenneth Froot. 1990c. Chartists, fundamentalists and trading in the foreign exchange market. *American Economic Review* 80, 2 (May): 181–85. (Appears as chapter 15 in this volume.)

Frankel, Jeffrey, and Gikas Hardouvelis. 1985. Commodity prices, money surprises, and Fed credibility. *Journal of Money, Credit and Banking* 17, 4 (November, pth. I): 427–38.

Frankel, Jeffrey, and Alan MacArthur. 1988. Political vs. currency premia in international real interest differentials: A study of forward rates for 24 countries. *European Economic Review* 32 (June): 1083–1121. Reprinted in R. MacDonald and M. Taylor, eds., *Exchange Rate Economics*. International Library of Critical Writings in Economics. Cheltenham, U.K.: Edward Elgar Publishing, 1992.

Frankel, Jeffrey, and Richard Meese. 1987. Are exchange rates excessively variable? In S. Fischer, ed., *NBER Macroeconomics Annual 1987*.

Frankel, Jeffrey, and Steve Phillips. 1992. The European Monetary System: Credible at last? NBER Working Paper no. 3819. *Oxford Economic Papers* 44 (April). (Incorporated into chapter 17 of this volume.)

Frankel, Jeffrey, and Katharine Rockett. 1988. International macroeconomic policy coordination when policy-makers do not agree on the model. *American Economic Review* 78, 3 (June): 318–40.

Frankel, Jeffrey, and James Stock. 1987. Regression vs. volatility tests of foreign exchange markets. *Journal of International Money and Finance* 6: 49–56.

Frankel, Jeffrey, and Shang-Jin Wei. 1991. Are the forecasts of exchange rate volatility implicit in options prices excessively variable? NBER Working Paper no. 3910. November.

French, K., and R. Roll. 1986. Stock return variances: The arrival of information and the reaction of traders. *Journal of Financial Economics* 17: 5–26.

Frenkel, Jacob. 1976. A monetary approach to the exchange rate: Doctrinal aspects and empirical evidence. *Scandinavian Journal of Economics* 78 (May): 200–224. Reprinted in J. Frenkel and H. G. Johnson, eds., *The Economics of Exchange Rates*. Reading, Mass.: Addison-Wesley, 1978.

Frenkel, Jacob. 1977. The forward exchange rate, expectations and the demand for money: The German hyperinflation. *American Economic Review* 67, 4 (September): 653–70.

Frenkel, Jacob. 1980. Exchange rates, prices and money: Lessons from the 1920s. *American Economic Review* 70, 2 (May): 235–42.

Frenkel, Jacob. 1981a. Flexible exchange rates, prices, and the role of "news": Lessons from the 1970s. *Journal of Political Economy* 89, 4 (August): 665–705.

Frenkel, Jacob. 1981b. The collapse of purchasing power parities during the 1970s. *European Economic Review* 16: 145–65.

Frenkel, Jacob. 1983a. Flexible exchange rates, prices and the role of "news." In J. Bhandari, and B. Putnam, eds. *Economic Interdependence and Flexible Exchange Rates*. Cambridge, Mass., MIT Press.

Frenkel, Jacob. 1983b. International liquidity and monetary control. In G. von Fursternberg, ed., *International Money and Credit: The Policy Roles*. Washington, D.C.: International Monetary Fund.

Frenkel, Jacob. 1987. The international monetary system: Should it be reformed? NBER Working Paper no. 2163. February.

Frenkel, Jacob, and M. Goldstein. 1986. A guide to target zones. NBER Working Paper no. 2113. December.

Frenkel, Jacob, and H. G. Johnson, eds. 1978. *The Economics of Exchange Rates.* Reading, Mass.: Addison-Wesley.

Frenkel, Jacob, and Richard Levich. 1975. Covered interest arbitrage: Unexploited profits? *Journal of Political Economy* 83 (April): 325–38.

Frenkel, Jacob, and Richard Levich. 1977. Transaction costs and interest arbitrage: Tranquil versus turbulent periods. *Journal of Political Economy* 85, 6: 1209–26. Reprinted in D. Lessard, ed., *International Financial Management.* Boston: Warren, Gorham and Lamont, 1979.

Friedman, Milton. 1953. The case for flexible exchange rates. In M. Friedman, ed., *Essays in Positive Economics*, pp. 157–203. Chicago: University of Chicago Press.

Froot, Kenneth. 1987a. Tests of excess forecast volatility in the foreign exchange and stock markets. NBER Working Paper no. 2362.

Froot, Kenneth. 1987b. New hope for the expectations hypothesis of the term structure of interest rates. NBER Working Paper no. 2363. Revised in *Journal of Finance* 44, June 1989, 283–305.

Froot, Kenneth. 1990. Multinational corporations, exchange rates, and direct investment. In *International Policy Coordination and Exchange Rate Fluctuations*, W. Branson, J. Frenkel, and M. Goldstein, eds. Chicago: University of Chicago Press.

Froot, Kenneth, and Jeffrey Frankel. 1986. Interpreting tests of forward discount unbiasedness using survey data on exchange rate expectations. NBER Working Paper no. 1963 . July. (First draft of 1989.)

Froot, Kenneth, and Jeffrey Frankel. 1989. Forward discount bias: Is it an exchange risk premium? *Quarterly Journal of Economics* 104, 416 (February): 139–61. (Appears as chapter 12 in this volume).

Froot, Kenneth, and Takatoshi Ito. 1989. On the consistency of short-run and long-run exchange rate expectations. *Journal of International Money and Finance* 8, 4 (December): 487–510.

Frydman, Roman, and Edmund Phelps. 1983. *Individual Forecasting and Aggregate Outcomes: "Rational Expectations" Examined.* New York: Cambridge University Press.

Garber, Peter. 1978. Efficiency in foreign exchange markets: Interpreting a common technique. Unpublished paper. University of Virginia.

Garman, Mark, and Steven Kohlhagen. 1980. Inflation and foreign exchange rates under production and monetary uncertainty. Unpublished paper. University of California, Berkeley, June.

Garman, Mark, and Steven Kohlhagen. 1983. Foreign currency option values. *Journal of International Money and Finance* 2, 3 (Dec.): 231–238.

Genberg, Hans. 1978. Purchasing power parity under fixed and flexible exchange rates. *Journal of International Economics* 8 (May): 247–76.

Ghosh, Atish R. 1988. How mobile is capital? Some simple tests. Harvard University.

Giavazzi, Francesco, and Alberto Giovannini. 1984. The dollar and the European Monetary System. Turin, Italy, June 4–5, 1984. In R. Dornbusch and A. Giovannini, eds., *Europe and the Dollar*. Special issue of *Thema*.

Giavazzi Francesco, Mehmet Odekon, and Charles Wyplosz. 1992. Simulating an oil shock with sticky prices. *European Economic Review* 18, 1/2 (May/June): 11–33.

Giavazzi, Francesco, and Marco Pagano. 1985. Capital controls and the European Monetary System. In *Capital Controls and Foreign Exchange Legislation*. Occasional Paper. Milano: Euromobiliare.

Giavazzi, Francesco, and Luigi Spaventa. 1990. The "new" EMS. Centre for Economic Policy Research Paper no. 369. In P. De Grauwe and L. Papademos, eds., *The European Monetary System in the 1990s*. London: Longman.

Giovannini, Alberto. 1987. Uncertainty and liquidity. NBER Working Paper no. 2296. June.

Giovannini, Alberto. 1990. European monetary reform: Progress and prospects. *Brookings Papers on Economic Activity* 2: 217–91.

Giovannini, Alberto, and Philippe Jorion. 1987. Interest rates and risk premia in the stock market and in the foreign exchange market. *Journal of International Money and Finance* 6, 1 (March): 107–24.

Giovannini, Alberto, and Philippe Jorion. 1988. Foreign exchange risk premia volatility once again. *Journal of International Money and Finance* 7, 1 (March): 111–13.

Giovannini, Alberto, and Philippe Jorion. 1989. The time-variation of risk and return in the foreign exchange and stock markets. *Journal of Finance* 44, 2 (June): 307–25.

Girton, Lance, and Dale Henderson. 1976. Financial capital movements and central bank behavior in a two-country, short-run portfolio balance model. *Journal of Monetary Economics* 2: 33–61.

Girton, Lance, and Dale Henderson. 1977. Central bank operations in foreign and domestic assets under fixed and flexible exchange rates. In P. Clark, D. Logue, and R. Sweeney, eds., *The Effects of Exchange Rate Adjustment*, pp. 151–79. Washington, D.C.: Department of the Treasury.

Girton, Lance, and Don Roper. 1977. A monetary model of exchange market pressure applied to the postwar Canadian experience. *American Economic Review* 67, 4 (September): 537–48.

Girton, Lance, and Don Roper. 1981. Theory and implications of currency substitution. *Journal of Money, Credit and Banking* 13, 1 (February): 12–30.

Glick, Reuven. 1987. Interest rate linkages in the Pacific Basin. *Federal Reserve Bank of San Francisco Economic Review* 3: 31–42.

Goldfeld, S. 1976. The case of the missing money. *Brookings Papers on Economic Activity* 3:683–730.

Golub, Stephen. 1989. Foreign-currency government debt, asset markets, and the balance of payments. *Journal of International Money and Finance* 8, 2 (June): 285–94.

Golub, Stephen et al. 1985. Exchange rates and real long-term interest-rate differentials: Evidence for eighteen OECD countries. Economics and Statistics Department Working Paper. Paris: OECD.

Goodhart, Charles. 1988. The foreign exchange market: A random walk with a dragging anchor. *Economica* 55:437–60.

Goodman, S. 1979. Foreign exchange forecasting techniques: Implications for business and policy. *Journal of Finance* 34 (May): 415–27.

Granger, C. 1969. Investigating causal relations by econometric models and cross-spectral methods. *Econometrica* 37 (July): 424–38.

Grauer, F. L. A., R. H. Litzenberger, and R. E. Stehle. 1976. Sharing rules and equilibrium in an international capital market under uncertainty. *Journal of Financial Economics* 3, 3:233–56.

Grauer, F. L. A., R. H. Litzenberger, and R. E. Stehle. 1977. Reply to Bruno Solnik. Unpublished paper.

Gray, M., and S. Turnovsky. 1979. The stability of exchange rate dynamics under perfect myopic foresight. *International Economic Review* 20 (October): 643–60.

Grossman, J. 1981. The "rationality" of money supply expectations and the short-run response of interest rates to monetary surprises. *Journal of Money, Credit and Banking* 13 (November): 409–24.

Grubel, J. B. 1968. Internationally diversified portfolios: Welfare gains and capital flows. *American Economic Review* 58, 5:1299–1314.

Hacche, Graham, and John Townend. 1981. Exchange rates and monetary policy: Modelling sterling's effective exchange rate, 1972–1980. In W. A. Eltis and P. J. N. Sinclair, eds., *The Money Supply and the Exchange Rate*. Oxford: Clarendon Press.

Hakkio, Craig. 1981. Expectations and the forward rate. *International Economic Review* 22:663–78.

Hamada, K. 1985. *The Political Economy of International Monetary Interdependence*. Cambridge, Mass.: MIT Press.

Hansen, Lars, and Robert Hodrick. 1980. Forward exchange rates as optimal predictors of future spot rates: An econometric analysis. *Journal of Political Economy* 88 (October): 829–53.

Hansen, Lars, and Robert Hodrick. 1983. Risk-averse speculation in the forward foreign exchange market: An econometric analysis of linear models. *In Exchange Rates and International Macroeconomics*, Jacob Frenkel, ed. Chicago: University of Chicago Press.

Harberger, Arnold. 1980. Vignettes on the world capital market. *American Economic Review* 70:331–37.

Hardouvelis, Gikas. 1984. Market perceptions of federal reserve policy, and the weekly monetary announcements. *Journal of Monetary Economics* 14 (September): 225–40.

Hardouvelis, Gikas. 1988. Economic news, exchange rates, and interest rates. *Journal of International Money and Finance* 7 (March): 23–25.

Hatsopoulos, George, Paul Krugman and Lawrence Summers. 1988. US competitiveness: Beyond the trade deficit. *Science* 24 (July): 299–307.

Haynes, Steven, and Joe Stone. 1981. On the mark: Comment. *American Economic Review* 71 (December): 1060–67.

Heller, Robert, and Mohsin Khan. 1978. The demand for international reserves under fixed and floating exchange rates. IMF *Staff Papers* Dec.

Helpman, E. 1981. An exploration in the theory of exchange rates. *Journal of Political Economy* 89:865–90.

Helpman, E., and A. Razin. 1979. A consistent comparison of alternative exchange rate regimes. *Canadian Journal of Economics* 12:394–409.

Helpman, E., and A. Razin. 1982. A comparison of exchange rate regimes in the presence of imperfect capital markets. *International Economic Review* 23:365–88.

Henderson, Dale. 1975. Monetary, fiscal and exchange rate policy in a two-country short-run macroeconomic model. Unpublished paper. Federal Reserve Board.

Henderson, Dale. 1980. The dynamic effects of exchange market intervention: Two extreme views and a synthesis. In H. Frisch and G. Schwodiauer, eds., *The Economics of Flexible Exchange Rates*. Supplement to *Kredit und Kapitol* (Heft 6), pp. 156–209. Berlin: Duncker and Humblot.

Henderson, Dale. 1984. Exchange market intervention operations: Their role in financial policy and their effects. In J. Bilson and R. Marston, *Exchange Rate Theory and Practice*. Chicago: University of Chicago Press.

Henderson, Dale, and Kenneth Rogoff. 1981. Negative net foreign asset positions and stability in a world portfolio balance model. International Finance Discussion Paper no. 178. Washington, D.C.: Federal Reserve Board. In *Journal of International Economics* 13 (1982): 85–104.

Henderson, Dale, and Stephanie Sampson. 1983. Intervention in foreign exchange markets: A summary of ten staff studies. *Federal Reserve Bulletin* 69 (November): 830–36.

Hodrick, Robert. 1978. An empirical analysis of the monetary approach to the determination of the exchange rate. In J. Frenkel and H. G. Johnson, eds., *The Economics of Exchange Rates*, pp. 97–116. Reading, Mass.: Addison-Wesley.

Hodrick, Robert. 1981. International asset pricing with time-varying risk premia. *Journal of International Economics* 11 (November): 573–77.

Hodrick, Robert. 1987. Risk, uncertainty, and exchange rates. Northwestern University (September). In *Journal of Monetary Economics* 23 (1989): 433−59.

Hodrick, Robert. 1988. The empirical evidence on the efficiency of forward and futures foreign exchange markets. In *Fundamentals of Pure and Applied Economics*. Chur, Switzerland: Harwood Academic Publishers.

Hodrick, Robert, and Sanjay Srivastava. 1984. An investigation of risk and return in forward foreign exchange. *Journal of International Money and Finance* 3 (April): 5−30.

Hodrick, Robert, and Sanjay Srivastava. 1986. The covariation of risk premiums and expected future spot exchange rates. *Journal of International Money and Finance* 5 : S5−S22.

Hogarth, R., and M. Reder, eds. 1986. *Rational Choice*. Chicago: University of Chicago Press.

Hooper, Peter. 1984. International repercussions of the U.S. budget deficit. International Finance Discussion Paper no. 246. Washington, D.C.: Federal Reserve Board, September.

Hooper, Peter, and Steven Kohlhagen. 1978. The effect of exchange rate uncertainty on the prices and volume of international trade. *Journal of International Economics* 8 (December): 483−511.

Hooper, Peter, and John Morton. 1982. Fluctuations in the dollar: A model of nominal and real exchange rate determination. *Journal of International Money and Finance* 1, 1:39−56.

Hosomi, T. 1985. Toward a more stable international monetary system. In T. Hosomi and M. Fukao, *A Second Look at Foreign Exchange Interventions*. Tokyo: Japan Centre for International Finance.

Hsieh, David. 1984. Test of rational expectations and no risk premium in forward exchange markets. *Journal of International Economics* 17 (August): 173−84.

Hsieh, David. 1985. The statistical properties of daily foreign exchange rates: 1974−1983. Unpublished paper. University of Chicago, October.

Hsieh, David. 1989. Testing for nonlinear dependence in daily foreign exchange rates. *Journal of Business* 62 (July): 339−68.

Hsieh, David, and Luis Manas-Anton. Empirical regularities in the deutsch mark future options. Center for Research in Security Prices Working Paper no. 189. University of Chicago.

Huang, Roger. 1981. The monetary approach to exchange rates in an efficient foreign exchange market: Tests based on volatility. *Journal of Finance* 36:31−41.

Huang, Roger. 1984. Some alternative tests of forward exchange rates as predictors of future spot rates. *Journal of International Money and Finance* 3, 2 (August): 153−67.

Huizinga, John. 1987. An empirical investigation of the long-run behavior of real exchange rates. In Karl Brunner and Allan Meltzer, eds., *Empirical Studies of Veloc-*

ity, Real Exchange Rates, Unemployment and Productivity, pp. 149–214. Carnegie-Rochester Conference Series on Public Policy 27 (Autumn).

Hutchison, Michael, and Adrian Throop. 1985. U.S. budget deficits and the real value of the dollar. *Economic Review* 4 (Fall): 26–43.

International Monetary Fund. *International Financial Statistics*. Washington, D.C. Various issues.

Isard, Peter. 1977. How far can we push the "law of one price"? *American Economic Review* 67 (December): 942–48.

Isard, Peter. 1980. Factors determining exchange rates: The roles of relative price levels, balances of payments, interest rates and risk. International Finance Discussion Paper no. 171. December. Washington, D.C.: Federal Reserve Board.

Isard, Peter. 1983. An accounting framework and some issues for modeling how exchange rates respond to the news. In Jacob Frenkel, ed., *Exchange Rates and International Macroeconomics*. Chicago: University of Chicago Press.

Isard, Peter. 1988. The empirical modelling of exchange rates: An assessment of alternative approaches. In R. Bryant, D. Henderson, G. Holtham, P. Hooper, and S. Symansky, eds., *Empirical Macroeconomics for Interdependent Economies*. Washington, D.C.: Brookings Institution.

Ito, Takatoshi. 1990. Foreign exchange rate expectations: Micro survey data. *American Economic Review* 80 (June): 434–49.

Ito, Takatoshi, and Vance Roley. 1987. News from the U.S. and Japan: Which moves the yen/dollar exchange rate? *Journal of Monetary Economics* 19:255–77.

Johnson, Harry. 1969. The case for flexible exchange rates, 1969. *Federal Reserve Bank of St. Louis Review* 51, 6 (June): 12–24.

Kareken, J., and N. Wallace. 1981. On the indeterminacy of equilibrium exchange rates. *Quarterly Journal of Economics* 156:207–22.

Kasman, Bruce, and Charles Pigott. 1988. Interest rate divergences among the major industrial nations. *Federal Reserve Bank of New York Quarterly Review* (Autumn): 28–42.

Katseli-Papaefstratiou, Louka. 1979. The reemergence of the purchasing power parity doctrine in the 1970s. *Special Papers in International Economics* no. 13. Princeton: Princeton University, December.

Kenen, Peter, and Dani Rodrik. 1986. Measuring and analyzing the effects of short-term volatility in real exchange rates. *Review of Economics and Statistics* 68, 2 (May): 311–15.

Kindleberger, Charles. 1969. The case for fixed exchange rates, 1969. In *The International Adjustment Mechanism*. Boston: Federal Reserve Bank of Boston.

Kling, Arnold. 1985. The dollar and the demand for labor in manufacturing: The case of the missing effect. Unpublished paper. Washington, D.C.: Federal Reserve Board, September.

Koedijk, Kees, and Mack Ott. 1987. Risk aversion, efficient markets and the forward exchange rate. *Federal Reserve Bank of St. Louis Review* (December): 5–13.

Kohlhagen, Steven. 1978. The behavior of foreign exchange markets—A critical survey of the empirical literature. New York University Monograph Series in Finance and Economics no. 3.

Kohlhagen, Steven. 1979. On the identification of destabilizing speculation. *Journal of International Economics* 9:321–40.

Koraczyk, Robert. 1985. The pricing of forward contracts for foreign exchange. *Journal of Political Economy* 93, 2:346–68.

Kouri, Pentti. 1976a. The exchange rate and the balance of payments in the short run and in the long run: A monetary approach. *Scandinavian Journal of Economics* 78 (May): 280–304.

Kouri, Pentti. 1976b. The determinants of the forward premium. Institute for International Economic Studies Seminar Paper no. 62. Stockholm: University of Stockholm, August.

Kouri, Pentti. 1976c. Foreign exchange market speculation and stabilization under flexible exchange rates. Paper presented at Conference on the Political Economy of Inflation and Unemployment in Open Economies, Athens, October.

Kouri, Pentti. 1977. International investment and interest rate linkages under flexible exchange rates. In R. Aliber, ed., *The Political Economy of Monetary Reform*. London: Macmillan.

Kouri, Pentti. 1983. Balance of payments and the foreign exchange market: A dynamic partial equilibrium model. In J. Bhandari, ed., *Economic Interdependence and Flexible Exchange Rates*. Cambridge, Mass.: MIT Press.

Kouri, Pentti, and Jorge de Macedo. 1978. Exchange rates and the international adjustment process. *Brookings Papers on Economic Activity* 1:111–50.

Krasker, William. 1980. The "peso problem" in testing the efficiency of forward exchange markets. *Journal of Monetary Economics* 6:269–76.

Kravis, Irving, and Robert Lipsey. 1977. Export prices and the transmission of inflation. *American Economic Review Proceedings* 67 (February): 155–63.

Kravis, Irving, and Robert Lipsey. 1983. Toward an explanation of national price levels. *Studies in International Finance* no. 52. Princeton: Princeton University.

Krugman, Paul. 1977. The efficiency of the forward exchange markets: Evidence from the twenties and the seventies. Chapter from Ph.D. dissertation, MIT.

Krugman, Paul. 1978. Purchasing power parity and exchange rates: Another look at the evidence. *Journal of International Economics* 8, 3 (August): 397–407.

Krugman, Paul. 1980. Oil and the dollar. NBER Working Paper no. 554. In J. Bhandari, ed., *Economic Interdependence and Flexible Exchange Rates*. Cambridge, Mass.: MIT Press, 1983.

Krugman, Paul. 1981. Consumption preferences, asset demands, and distribution effects in international financial markets. NBER Working Paper no. 651. March.

Krugman, Paul. 1985. Is the strong dollar sustainable? In *The U.S. Dollar—Recent Developments, Outlook and Policy Options*, pp. 103–33. Kansas City, Mo.: Federal Reserve Bank of Kansas City.

Krugman, Paul. 1991. Target zones and exchange rate dynamics. *Quarterly Journal of Economics* 56, 3:669–82. Reprinted in *Currencies and Crises*. Cambridge: MIT Press, 1992.

Laursen, S., and L. Metzler. 1950. Flexible exchange rates for the theory of employment. *Review of Economics and Statistics* 32 (November): 281–99.

Leiderman, Leo, and Assaf Razin. 1989. The saving and investment-balance: An empirical investigation. International Monetary Fund, Washington, D.C. June.

Leland, H. E. 1971. Optimal forward exchange positions. *Journal of Political Economy* 79, 2:257–69.

Levich, Richard. 1979a. On the efficiency of markets for foreign exchange. In R. Dornbusch and J. Frenkel, eds., *International Economic Policy: Theory and Evidence*, pp. 246–67. Baltimore: Johns Hopkins Press.

Levich, Richard. 1979b. Analyzing the accuracy of foreign exchange forecasting services: theory and evidence. In R. Levich and C. Wihlborg, eds., *Exchange Risk and Exposure*. Lexington, Mass.: D.C. Heath.

Levich, Richard. 1985. Empirical studies of exchange rates: Price behavior, rate determination, and market efficiency. In R. Jones and P. Kenen, eds., *Handbook of International Economics*, vol. 2. Amsterdam: North-Holland.

Levich, Richard. 1989. Is the foreign exchange market efficient? *Oxford Review of Economic Policy* 5, 3 (Fall): 40–60.

Liviatan, N. 1980. Anti-inflationary monetary policy and the capital import tax. Warwick Economic Research Papers no. 171.

Logue, Dennis, Richard Sweeney, and Thomas Willett. 1977. Speculative behavior of foreign exchange rates during the current float. Discussion Paper Series, no. 77–2. U.S. Treasury.

Longworth, David. 1981. Testing the efficiency of the Canadian-U.S. exchange market under the assumption of no risk premium. *Journal of Finance* 36:43–49.

Loopesko, Bonnie. 1984. Relationships among exchange rates, intervention, and interest rates: An empirical investigation. *Journal of International Money and Finance* 3 (December): 257–77.

Lovell, Michael C. 1986. Tests of the rational expectations hypothesis. *American Economic Review* 76 (March): 110–24.

Lucas, Robert. 1982. Interest rates and currency prices in a two-country world. *Journal of Monetary Economics* 10 (November): 335–60.

Lyons, Richard. 1988. Tests of the foreign exchange risk premium using the expected second moments implied by options pricing. *Journal of International Money and Finance* 7, 1 (March): 91–108.

MacArthur, Alan. 1988. International financial market integration: Empirical analysis with data from forward and futures currency markets. Ph.D. dissertation, University of California at Berkeley.

de Macedo, Jorge. 1980. Portfolio diversification across countries. Princeton International Finance Section Working Paper. November.

de Macedo, Jorge. 1982. Portfolio diversification across currencies. In R. Cooper, P. Kenen, de Macedo, and J. V. Ypersele, eds., *The International Monetary System under Flexible Exchange Rates*. Cambridge, Mass.: Ballinger.

de Macedo, Jorge, J. Goldstein, and D. Meerschwam. 1984. International portfolio diversification: Short-term financial assets and gold. In J. Bilson and R. Marston, eds., *Exchange Rate Theory and Practice*. Chicago: University of Chicago Press.

de Macedo, Jorge Braga, and Francisco Torres. 1989. Interest differentials, integration, and EMS shadowing: A note on Portugal with a comparison to Spain. In J. da Silva and L. M. Beleza, eds., *Portugal and Internal Market of the EEC*, pp. 173–180. Lisbon: Banco de Portugal.

McKinnon, Ronald. 1963. Optimum currency areas. *American Economic Review* 53 (September): 717–24.

McKinnon, Ronald. 1974. A new tripartite monetary system or a limping dollar standard. *Essays in International Finance* no. 106. Princeton: Princeton University.

McKinnon, Ronald. 1976. Floating exchange rates 1973–74: The emperor's new clothes. In K. Brunner and A. Meltzer, eds., *Institutional Arrangements and the Inflation Problem*. Carnegie-Rochester Series on Public Policy 3 : 79–114.

McKinnon, Ronald. 1984a. *An international standard for monetary stabilization*. Policy Analyses in International Economics no. 8. Washington, D.C.: Institute for International Economics.

McKinnon, Ronald. 1984b. How to coordinate central bank policies. *New York Times*, July 12.

McKinnon, Ronald. 1987a. Currency protectionism: Parity lost. *Wall Street Journal*, February 2.

McKinnon, Ronald. 1987b. A gold standard without gold. Putting a stop to rapid currency swings. *New York Times*, April 12.

McKinnon, Ronald. 1987c. A model for currency cooperation. *Wall Street Journal*, September 21.

McKinnon, Ronald. 1988. Monetary and exchange rate policies for international financial stability: A proposal. *Journal of Economic Perspectives* 2, 1 (Winter): 83–103.

Mañas-Anton, Luis. 1986. Empirical analysis of short-run exchange rate behavior: Statistical evidence and consistent models. Economics and Econometrics Working Paper Series 86-39. University of Chicago. April.

Mathieson, Donald. 1977. The impact of monetary and fiscal policy under flexible exchange rates and alternative expectations structures. *IMF Staff Papers* (November): 535–68.

Mark, Nelson. 1985a. Some evidence on the international inequality of interest rates. *Journal of International Money and Finance* 4:189–208.

Mark, Nelson. 1985b. On time varying risk premia in the foreign exchange market. *Journal of Monetary Economics* 16 (July): 3–18.

Mark, Nelson. 1987. Time varying betas and risk premia in the price of forward foreign exchange contracts, Ohio State University (May). *Journal of Financial Economics* 22 (1988): 335–54.

Marris, Stephen. 1985. Deficits and the dollar: The world economy at risk. *Policy Analyses in International Economics* no. 14. Washington, D.C.: Institute for International Economics. December.

Marris, Stephen. 1987. *Deficits and the Dollar Revisited*. Washington, D.C.: Institute for International Economics.

Marston, R. 1987. Exchange rate policy reconsidered. NBER Working Paper no. 2310. Reprinted in M. Feldstein, ed., *International Economic Cooperation*. Chicago: Univ. of Chicago Press, 1988.

Meese, Richard. 1986. Testing for bubbles in exchange markets: a case of sparkling rates? *Journal of Political Economy* 94, 2 (April): 345–73.

Meese, Richard, and Kenneth Rogoff. 1981. Empirical exchange rate models of the seventies: Are any fit to survive? International Finance Discussion Paper no. 184 Washington, D.C.: Federal Reserve Board, June. (First version of 1983a).

Meese, Richard, and Kenneth Rogoff. 1983a. Empirical exchange rate models of the seventies: Do they fit out of sample? *Journal of International Economics* 14 (February): 3–24.

Meese, Richard, and Kenneth Rogoff. 1983b. The out-of-sample failure of empirical exchange rate models: Sampling error or misspecification? In Jacob Frenkel, ed., *Exchange Rates and International Macroeconomics*, pp. 67–105. Chicago: University of Chicago Press.

Meese, Richard, and Kenneth Rogoff. 1988. Was it real? The exchange rate-interest differential relation over the modern floating-rate period. *Journal of Finance* 43, 4 (September): 933–48.

Meese, Richard, and Kenneth Singleton. 1982. On unit roots and the empirical modeling of exchange rates. *Journal of Finance* 37:1029–37.

Mehra, R., and E. C. Prescott. 1985. The equity premium: A puzzle. *Journal of Monetary Economics* 15:145–161.

Melino, Angelo, and Stuart Turnbull. 1987. The pricing of foreign currency options. University of Toronto, May. *Canadian Journal of Economics* 24, 2 (May 1991): 251–81.

Miles, Marc. 1978. Currency substitution, flexible exchange rates and monetary independence. *American Economic Review* 68, 3 (June): 428–36.

Miller, P. J., and N. Wallace. 1985. International coordination of macroeconomic policies: A welfare analysis. Federal Reserve Bank of Minneapolis *Quarterly Review* 9:14–32.

Mincer, Jacob. 1969. Models of adaptive forecasting. In Jacob Mincer, ed., *Economic Forecasts and Expectations*. New York: Columbia University Press.

Mishkin, Frederic. 1984a. Are real interest rates equal across countries? An empirical investigation of international parity conditions. *Journal of Finance* 39:1345–58.

Mishkin, Frederic. 1984b. The real interest rate: A multicountry empirical study. *Canadian Journal of Economics* 17, 2:283–311.

Money Market Services, Inc. *Currency Market Services*. Various issues, 1983–86.

Morgan Guaranty Trust Co. *World Financial Markets*. New York. Various issues.

Morgan Guaranty Trust Co. 1988. Financial markets in Europe: Toward 1992. *World Financial Markets* 5 (September 9): 1–15.

Mundell, Robert. 1961. The theory of optimal currency areas. *American Economic Review* 51 (November): 509–17.

Mundell, Robert. 1963. Capital mobility and stabilization policy under fixed and flexible exchange rates. *Canadian Journal of Economics and Political Science* 29 (November): 475–85. (Also chapter 18 in Mundell, 1968b.)

Mundell, Robert. 1964a. A reply: Capital mobility and size. *Canadian Journal of Economics* 30 (August): 421–31. (Also appendix to chapter 18 in Mundell, 1968b.)

Mundell, Robert. 1964b. Exchange rate margins and economic policy. In J. Carter Murphy, ed., *Money in the International Order*. Dallas.

Mundell, Robert. 1968a. Towards a better international monetary system. Unpublished paper, University of Chicago.

Mundell, Robert. 1968b. *International Economics*. New York: Macmillan.

Mundell, Robert. 1971. *Monetary Theory*. Pacific Palisades, Calif.: Goodyear.

Murphy, Robert. 1984. Capital mobility and the relationship between saving and investment in OECD countries. *Journal of International Money and Finance* 3:327–42.

Mussa, Michael. 1976. The exchange rate, the balance of payments, and monetary and fiscal policy under a regime of controlled floating. *Scandinavian Journal of Economics* 78 (May): 229–48. Reprinted in J. Frenkel and H. G. Johnson, eds., *The Economics of Exchange Rates*. Reading, Mass.: Addison-Wesley, 1978.

Mussa, Michael. 1977. Real and monetary factors in a dynamic theory of foreign exchange. Unpublished paper, University of Chicago, April.

Mussa, Michael. 1979a. Macroeconomic interdependence and the exchange rate regime. In R. Dornbusch and J. Frenkel, eds., *International Economic Policy*. Baltimore: Johns Hopkins University Press.

Mussa, Michael. 1979b. Empirical regularities in the behavior of exchange rates and theories of the foreign exchange market. In K. Brunner and A. Meltzer, eds., *Policies for Employment, Prices and Exchange Rates*. Carnegie-Rochester Conference Series on Public Policy 11:9–57. Amsterdam: North-Holland.

Mussa, Michael. 1981a. Sticky prices and disequilibrium adjustment in a model of the inflationary process. *American Economic Review* 71 (December): 1020–27.

Mussa, Michael. 1981b. *The Role of Official Intervention*. Group of Thirty Occasional Paper no. 6. New York: Group of Thirty.

Nelson, C., and G. W. Schwert. 1977. Short-term interest rates as predictors of inflation: On testing the hypothesis that the real rate of interest is constant. *American Economic Review* 67 (June): 478–86.

Neumann. Manfred. 1984. Intervention in the Mark/Dollar market: The authorities' reaction function. *Journal of International Money and Finance* 3:223–39.

Newey, Whitney, and Kenneth West. 1985. A simple, positive definite, heteroskedasticity and autocorrelation consistent covariance matrix. Woodrow Wilson School Discussion Paper no. 92. May.

Nichols, Donald A., David H. Small, and C. E. Webster, Jr. 1983. Why interest rates rise when an unexpectedly large money stock is announced. *American Economic Review* 73, 3 (June): 383–88.

Niehans, Jurg. 1975. Some doubts about the efficacy of monetary policy under flexible exchange rates. *Journal of International Economics* 5 (August): 225–81.

Nurkse, Ragnar. 1944. *International Currency Experience: Lessons of the Interwar Period*. Geneva: League of Nations.

Obstfeld, Maurice. 1978. Expectations and efficiency in the foreign exchange market. Unpublished paper. MIT, January.

Obstfeld, Maurice. 1980a. Intermediate imports, the terms of trade, and the dynamics of the exchange rate and current account. *Journal of International Economics* (November) 10, 4:461–80.

Obstfeld, Maurice. 1980b. Portfolio balance, monetary policy, and the dollar-deutsche mark exchange rate. Columbia University Discussion Paper no. 62. March.

Obstfeld, Maurice. 1982. The capitalization of income streams and the effects of open-market policy under fixed exchange rates. *Journal of Monetary Economics* 9 (January): 87–98.

Obstfeld, Maurice. 1986. Capital mobility in the world economy: Theory and measurement. *Carnegie-Rochester Conference Series on Public Policy* 24:55−103.

Obstfeld, Maurice. 1989. How integrated are world capital markets? Some new tests. In R. Findlay et al., eds., *Debt, Stabilization and Development: Essays in Memory of Carlos Diaz-Alejandro.* Oxford: Basil Blackwell.

Obstfeld, Maurice. 1990. The effectiveness of foreign-exchange intervention: Recent experience, 1985−88. In Branson, Frenkel, and Goldstein, eds., *International Policy Coordination and Exchange Rate Fluctuations.* Chicago: University of Chicago Press.

Obstfeld, Maurice, and Kenneth Rogoff. 1983. Speculative hyperinflations in maximizing models: Can we rule them out? *Journal of Political Economy* 91 (August): 675−87.

Obstfeld, Maurice, and Alan Stockman. 1985. Exchange rate dynamics. In R. Jones and P. Kenen, eds., *Handbook of International Economics.* Amsterdam: North-Holland.

Officer, Lawrence. 1976. The purchasing power parity theory of exchange rates: A review article. *IMF Staff Papers* 23 (March).

Oudiz, Gilles, and Jeffrey Sachs. 1984. Macroeconomic policy coordination among the industrial economies. *Brookings Papers on Economic Activity* 1:1−64.

Oudiz, Gilles, and Jeffrey Sachs. 1985. International policy coordination in dynamic macroeconomies. In W. Buiter and R. Marston, eds. *International Economic Policy Coordination.* Cambridge: Cambridge University Press.

Otani, Ichiro. 1983. Exchange rate instability and capital controls: The Japanese experience, 1978−81. In D. Bigman and T. Taya, eds., *Exchange Rate and Trade Instability: Causes, Consequences and Remedies.* Cambridge, Mass.: Ballinger.

Pagan, Adrian. 1988. A note on the magnitude of risk premia. *Journal of International Money and Finance* 7, 1 (March): 109−10.

Park, Keehwan. 1984. Tests of the hypothesis of the existence of risk premium in the forward exchange market. *Journal of International Money and Finance* 3 (August): 169−178.

Parkin, M. 1970. Discount house portfolio and debt selection. *Review of Economic Studies* 37 (October): 469−97.

Parks, R. W. 1967. Efficient estimation of a system of regression equations when disturbances are both serially and contemporaneously correlated. *Journal of the American Statistical Association* 62:500−509.

Pasvolsky, L. 1933. *Current Monetary Issues.* Washington, D.C.: Brookings Institute.

Paul, R., and L. Lehrman. 1982. *The Case for Gold.* Washington, D.C.: Cato Institute.

Penati, A., and Michael Dooley. 1984. Current account imbalances and capital formation in industrial countries, 1949−1981. *IMF Staff Papers* 31:1−24.

Pierce, D. 1981. Trend and noise in the monetary aggregates. In *New Monetary Control Procedures*, vol. 2. Washington, D.C.: Federal Reserve Staff Study, February.

Pigott, Charles, and Richard Sweeney. 1985. Purchasing power parity and exchange rate dynamics: Some empirical results. In S. Arndt, R. Sweeney, and T. Willett, eds., *Exchange Rates, Trade and the U.S. Economy*, pp. 73–89. Washington, D.C.: American Enterprise Institute.

Poole, William. 1967. Speculative prices as random walks: An analysis of ten time series of flexible exchange rates. *Southern Economic Journal* (April): 468–78.

Popper, Helen. 1990. International capital mobility: Direct evidence from long-term currency swaps. International Finance Discussion Papers no. 386 Washington, D.C.: Federal Reserve Board, September.

Porter, Michael. 1979. Exchange rates, current accounts, and economic activity. Unpublished paper. Federal Reserve Board, June.

Reszat, B. 1987. Technical analysis and computer trading. *Intereconomics* (May–June): 107–11.

Robichek. A. A., and M. R. Eaker. 1978. Foreign exchange hedging and the Capital Asset Pricing Model. *Journal of Finance* 33: 1011–1018.

Rodriguez, Carlos Alfredo. 1980. The role of trade flows in exchange rate determination: A rational expectations approach. *Journal of Political Economy* 88, 6: 1145–58.

Rogoff, Kenneth. 1977. Rational expectations in the foreign exchange market revisited. Unpublished paper. MIT, February 1.

Rogoff, Kenneth. 1978. An empirical investigation of efficiency in foreign exchange futures markets. Unpublished paper. MIT, March.

Rogoff, Kenneth. 1979. Anticipated and transitory shocks in a model of exchange rate dynamics. Chapter 2 of Ph.D. dissertation, MIT.

Rogoff, Kenneth. 1984. On the effects of sterilized intervention: An analysis of weekly data. *Journal of Monetary Economics* 14 (September): 133–50.

Rogoff, Kenneth. 1985a. Can international monetary policy coordination be counterproductive? *Journal of International Economies* 18, 3–4: 199–217.

Rogoff, Kenneth. 1985b. Can exchange rate predictability be achieved without monetary convergence? Evidence from the EMS. *European Economic Review* 28: 93–115.

Roley, Vance. 1982. Weekly money supply announcements and the volatility of short-term interest rates. *Federal Reserve Bank of Kansas City Economic Review* (April).

Roll, Richard. 1979. Violations of purchasing power parity and their implications for efficient international commodity markets. In M. Sarnat and G. Szego, eds., *International Finance and Trade*, vol. 1. Cambridge, Mass.: Ballinger.

Roll, Richard, and Bruno Solnik. 1977. A pure foreign exchange asset pricing model. *Journal of International Economics* 7, 2 (May): 161–80.

Rose, Andrew, and Lars Svensson. 1991. Expected and predicted realignments: The FF/DM exchange rate during the EMS. Centre for Economic Policy Research Paper no. 552.

Roubini, Nouriel. 1988. Current account and budget deficits in an intertemporal model of consumption and taxation smoothing: A solution to the Feldstein-Horioka puzzle? Unpublished paper. Yale University, October.

Rubinstein, Mark. 1974. An aggregation theorem for securities markets. *Journal of Financial Economics* 1: 225–44.

Rutledge, David. 1986. Trading volume and price variability: New evidence on the price effects of speculation. In B. A. Gross, ed., *Futures Markets: Their Establishment and Performance*. New York: New York University Press.

Sachs, Jeffrey. 1985. The dollar and the policy mix: 1985. *Brookings Papers on Economic Activity* 1: 117–197.

Schadler, Susan. 1977. Sources of exchange rate variability: Theory and empirical evidence. *IMF Staff Papers* 24, 2: 253–96.

Schulmeister, Stephen. 1987. An essay on exchange rate dynamics. Research Unit Labor Market and Employment Discussion Paper 87–8. Wissenschaftzentrum Berlin fur Sozialforschung, Berlin.

Shafer, Jeffrey. 1979. Flexible exchange rates, capital flows and current account adjustment. Unpublished paper. Federal Reserve Board, October.

Shafer, Jeffrey, and Bonnie Loopesko. 1983. Floating exchange rates after ten years. *Brookings Papers on Economic Activity* 1: 1–70.

Shiller, R., J. Campbell, and K. Schoenholtz. 1983. Forward rates and future policy: Interpreting the term structure of interest rates. *Brookings Papers on Economic Activity*, 223–42.

Siegal, Jeremy. 1972. Risk, interest rates and the forward exchange. *Quarterly Journal of Economics* 86, 2: 303–309.

Simons, Henry. 1948. *Economic Policy for a Competitive Society*. Chicago: University of Chicago Press.

Sinn, Stefan. 1992. Saving-investment correlations and capital mobility: On the evidence from annual data. *Economic Journal* 102 (September): 1162–70.

Solnik, Bruno. 1974. An equilibrium model of the international capital market. *Journal of Economic Theory* 8, 4: 500–524.

Solnik, Bruno. 1977. Sharing rules . . . : A comment. Unpublished paper.

Solomon, Robert. 1985. Effects of the strong dollar. Brookings Discussion Papers in International Economics no. 35. September.

Somonath, V. S. 1986. Efficient exchange rate forecasts: Lagged models better than the random walk. *Journal of International Money and Finance* 5, 2 (June): 195–220.

Stockman, Alan. 1978. Risk, information and forward exchange rates. In J. Frenkel and H. G. Johnson, eds., *The Economics of Exchange Rates*, pp. 193–212. Reading, Mass.: Addison-Wesley.

Stockman, Alan. 1979. Monetary control and sterilization under pegged exchange rates. Unpublished paper. University of Rochester.

Stockman, Alan. 1980. A theory of exchange rate determination. *Journal of Political Economy* 88:673–98.

Stockman, Alan. 1983. Real exchange rates under alternative nominal exchange rate systems. *Journal of International Money and Finance* 2, 2:147–66.

Stockman, Alan. 1987. The equilibrium approach to exchange rates. *Economic Review*, Federal Reserve Bank of Richmond (March–April): 12–30.

Stockman, Alan. 1988. Real exchange rate variability under pegged and floating nominal exchange rate systems: An equilibrium theory. NBER Working Paper no. 2565. April.

Stockman, Alan. 1990. Exchange rates, the current account, and monetary policy. In W. Haraf and T. Willett, eds., *Monetary Policy for a Volatile Global Economy*. Washington, D.C.: American Enterprise Institute.

Stulz, R. December 1981. A model of international asset pricing. *Journal of Financial Economics* 9:383–406.

Summers, Lawrence. 1986. Does the stock market rationally reflect fundamental values? *Journal of Finance* 41, 3 (July): 591–601.

Summers, Lawrence. 1988. Tax policy and international competitiveness. In J. Frenkel, ed., *International Aspects of Fiscal Policies*. Chicago: University of Chicago Press.

Svensson, Lars. 1985. Currency prices, terms of trade, and interest rates: A general equilibrium asset-pricing cash-in-advance approach. *Journal of International Economics* 18:17–41.

Svensson, Lars. 1991. The simplest test of target zone credibility. *IMF Staff Papers* 38 (September): 655–65.

Svensson, Lars. 1992b. The foreign exchange risk premium in a target zone with devaluation risk. *Journal of International Economics* 33 (August): 21–40.

Svensson, Lars. 1992c. Assessing target zone credibility: Mean reversion and devaluation expectations in the EMS 1973–1992. *European Economic Review*, forthcoming.

Taylor, Mark. 1988. Covered interest arbitrage and market turbulence: An empirical analysis. Centre for Economic Policy Research Discussion Paper no. 236.

Taylor, Mark, and Helen Allen. 1992. The use of technical analysis in the foreign exchange market. *Journal of International Money and Finance* 11, 3 (June): 304–314.

Tesar, Linda. 1991. Savings, investment and international capital flows. *Journal of International Economics* 31, 1/2 (August): 55–78.

Theil, Henri. 1971. *Principles of Econometrics.* New York: John Wiley & Sons.

Tobin, James. 1969. A general-equilibrium approach to monetary theory. *Journal of Money, Credit and Banking* 1 (February): 15–29.

Tobin, James. 1978. A proposal for international monetary reform. *Eastern Economic Journal* 3, 3–4 (July–October). Also in his *Essays in Economics: Theory and Policy.* Cambridge, Mass.: MIT Press.

Tobin, James. 1983. Comment on "Domestic saving and international capital movements in the long run and the short run" by M. Feldstein. *European Economic Review* 21:153–56.

Tobin, James, and de Macedo, Jorge Braga. 1980. The short-run macroeconomics of floating exchange rates: An exposition. In J. Chipman and C. P. Kindleberger, eds., *Flexible Exchange Rates and the Balance of Payments: Essays in Memory of Egon Sohmen.* New York: North-Holland.

Tryon, Ralph. 1979. Testing for rational expectations in foreign exchange markets. International Finance Discussion Paper no. 139. Federal Reserve Board, May.

Tsiang, S. C. 1959. The theory of forward exchange and the effects of government intervention in the forward exchange market. *IMF Staff Papers* 4, 1:75–106.

Turnovsky, S., and C. Kingston. 1979. Government policies and secular inflation under flexible exchange rates. *Southern Economic Journal* 47:389–412.

Tversky, A., and Kahneman, D. 1981. The framing of decisions and the psychology of choice. *Science* 211:255–78.

Urich, Thomas J. 1982. The information content of weekly money supply announcements. *Journal of Monetary Economics* 10, 1 (July): 73–88.

Urich, Thomas J., and Paul Wachtel. 1981. Market responses to the weekly money supply announcements in the 1970s. *Journal of Finance* 36, 5 (December): 1063–72.

U.S. Congress. Joint Economic Committee. *Economic Indicators.* Washington, D.C. Various issues.

Vander Kraats, R. H., and L. D. Booth. 1983. Empirical tests of the monetary approach to exchange rate determination. *Journal of International Money and Finance* 2:255–278.

Von Furstenberg, G. 1981. Incentives for international currency diversification by U.S. financial investors. *IMF Staff Papers* 28:77–94.

Weber, Axel. 1992. Time-varying devaluation risk, interest rate differentials and exchange rates in target zones: Empirical evidence from the EMS. Centre for Economic Policy Research Paper no. 611. January.

Westphal, Uwe. 1983. Comments on domestic saving and international capital movements in the long run and the short run. *European Economic Review* 21:157–59.

Whitman, Marina von Neumann. 1975. Global monetarism: The monetary approach to the balance of payments. *Brookings Papers on Economic Activity* 3:491–556.

Williamson, John. 1985. *The Exchange Rate System*. Policy Analyses in International Economics no. 5. Washington, D.C.: Institute for International Economics, September 1983, revised 1985.

Williamson, John. 1992. The rise and fall of the concept of international liquidity. Paper Prepared for conference in memory of Rinaldo Ossola, Banca d'Italia, Perugia, July 9–10.

Williamson, John, and Marcus Miller. 1987. *Targets and indicators: A blueprint for the international coordination of economic policy*. Policy Analyses in International Economics no. 22. Washington, D.C.: Institute for International Economics, September.

Wills, H. 1979. Inferring expectations. London School of Economics. Unpublished paper.

Wilson, Charles. 1979. Anticipated shocks and exchange rate dynamics. *Journal of Political Economy* 87, 3 (June): 639–47.

Wonnacott, Paul. 1982. U.S. intervention in the exchange market for DM, 1977–80, *Studies in International Finance*, no. 51, Princeton: International Finance Section.

Woo, Wing Thye. 1985. The monetary approach to exchange rate determination under rational expectations. *Journal of International Economics* 18 : 1–16.

Wyplosz, Charles. 1986. Capital flows liberalization and the EMS: A French perspective. INSEAD Working Paper no. 86/40. Also in *European Economy*, European Economic Community, June 1988.

Young, Phillip. 1984. Uncertainty, the cost of hedging exchange risk, and international trade. Ph.D. dissertation, University of California at Berkeley.

Index